THE AUTHOR

ALISON ALEXANDER was born and educated in Hobart. She is a well-known Tasmanian historian, having written many histories of Tasmanian institutions as well as several biographies. Her book *The Ambitions of Jane Franklin* won the National Biography Award in 2014.

Of *Corruption and Skullduggery*, Alison writes: 'Government during the early years of settlement in Hobart was scandalously bad, inept at best and corrupt at worst. However, historians have ignored or sanitised this period, or enjoyed its rebellious and exciting aspects.

'Biographers who admired their subjects, historians who believed official documents of the time, and those who wanted to show that the colony started well, glossed over corruption and immorality, presenting it as understandable, even picturesque, in a rough frontier settlement.

'I was among these historians, but I have grown increasingly sceptical. What was really happening? The book's title indicates my conclusion.'

Alison Alexander at Mrs Lord's Springs (Stuart Whitney)

BOOKS BY ALISON ALEXANDER

Upcoming
A companion volume to *Corruption and Skullduggery*, titled *Land of Rogues and Scoundrels: starting from scratch in Van Diemen's Land* is being published in 2025

Biographies and general
Tasmania v. British Empire: the battle to end convict transportation (2022)
A salute to Max Angus, Tasmanian painter (2021)
The waking dream of art: Patricia Giles, painter (2019)
'Duck and green peas!' Finding utopia in Tasmania (2018)
The ambitions of Jane Franklin: Victorian lady adventurer (2014)
Tasmania's convicts: how felons built a free society (2010)
The companion to Tasmanian history (editor) (2005)
A mortal flame: the life of Marie Bjelke-Petersen (1995)
Governors' ladies: the wives and mistresses of Van Diemen's Land's governors (1987)

Commissioned histories
The O'Connors of Connorville: a great Australian story (2017)
Beyond the Mountain: a history of South Hobart (2015)
The Southern Midlands: a history (2012)
Jane Franklin Hall (2010)
From tiny acorns mighty oaks grow: the history of Oak Tasmania (2010)
Yours very truly: Dobson Mitchell & Allport 1834–2009 (2009)
Mary Ogilvy: the evolution of a grand lady, 1946–2006 (2006)
Brighton and surrounds (2006)
Hobart City Council (with Stefan Petrow, 2006)
The Eastern Shore: a history of Clarence (2003)
A wealth of women: the extraordinary experiences of ordinary Australian women from 1788 to today (2001)
Putting people first: Island State Credit Union, 1970–2000 (2000)
Students first! Tasmania University Union 1899–1999 (2000)
Charles Davis: 150 years (1998)
Glenorchy 1964–1998 (1998)
The history of the Clarence District Football Club, 1884–1996 (1996)
Blue, black and white: the history of the Launceston Church Grammar School, 1946–1996 (1996)
The history of the Australian Maritime College (1994)

Journal
Tasmanian Historical Research Association *Papers and Proceedings* (editor since 2014)

CORRUPTION AND SKULLDUGGERY

Edward Lord, Maria Riseley,
and Hobart's tempestuous beginnings

Alison Alexander

EER
Edward Everett Root Publishers 2024

to Lou Smith, formerly Lord
an inspiration

EER
Edward Everett Root Publishers Co. Ltd.
Atlas Chambers, 33 West Street,
Brighton, Sussex, BN1 2RE, UK.
www.eerpublishing.com

CORRUPTION AND SKULLDUGGERY
Edward Lord, Maria Riseley,
and Hobart's tempestuous beginnings

© Alison Alexander 2015, 2024

This edition © Edward Everett Root Publishers
Co. Ltd., 2024

Hardback ISBN 9781915115379
Paperback ISBN 9781915115386

All rights reserved. This book is copyright.
The moral rights of the author have been asserted.

The events in this book took place on land that the
British invaders took from the Aboriginal people.
We acknowledge and pay respect to the Tasmanian
Aboriginal people as the traditional and original owners
of this land and pay respects to their continuing
culture here.

Designed by Julie Hawkins, In Graphic Detail, Hobart.

Cover: Table Mountain, and part of the Harbour and Town
of Hobart 1815, by W.H. Craig
(State Library of New South Wales SV6/1815/1)

Opposite: Map of Van Diemen's Land in 1824, by Thomas Scott,
southeastern portion
(Tasmanian Archive and Heritage Office)

CONTENTS

TIMELINE VIII

INTRODUCTION 2

1   EDWARD LORD GOES TO AUSTRALIA 7

2   FOUNDING HOBART TOWN 19

3   OBSCURE BEGINNINGS 33

4   SETTING UP SHOP 47

5   MARRIAGE 61

6   TROUBLE AT THE DERWENT 75

7   DRAMATIC TIMES FOR THE LORD FAMILY 89

8   INTERLUDE: SCANDAL IN GOVERNMENT HOUSE 109

9   YET ANOTHER INADEQUATE GOVERNOR 121

10   THE LORDS BECOME ESTABLISHED 131

11   THE COMMISSARIAT, EDWARD LORD AND RAMPANT SKULLDUGGERY 149

12   THE LORDS' INVOLVEMENT WITH BUSHRANGERS 167

13   INTERLUDE: APPALLING ACTIVITIES IN THE NAVAL OFFICE 183

14   GOVERNOR SORELL 189

15   EDWARD LORD, ENTREPRENEUR 205

16   MARIA LORD, BUSINESSWOMAN 223

17   LIFE OUTSIDE BUSINESS 243

18   ENTER CHARLES ROWCROFT 261

19   AFTER THE COURT CASE 283

20   THE FINAL DECADES 301

21   AFTERWORD 315

APPENDIX 1: ITEMS MARIA LORD WAS
FOUND GUILTY OF STEALING 328

APPENDIX 2: THE LORDS' MAIN PROPERTIES 329

APPENDIX 3: FAMILY TREE FOR EDWARD LORD
AND MARIA RISELEY 330

ENDNOTES 331

SELECT BIBLIOGRAPHY 240

ACKNOWLEDGEMENTS 342

INDEX 344

TIMELINE

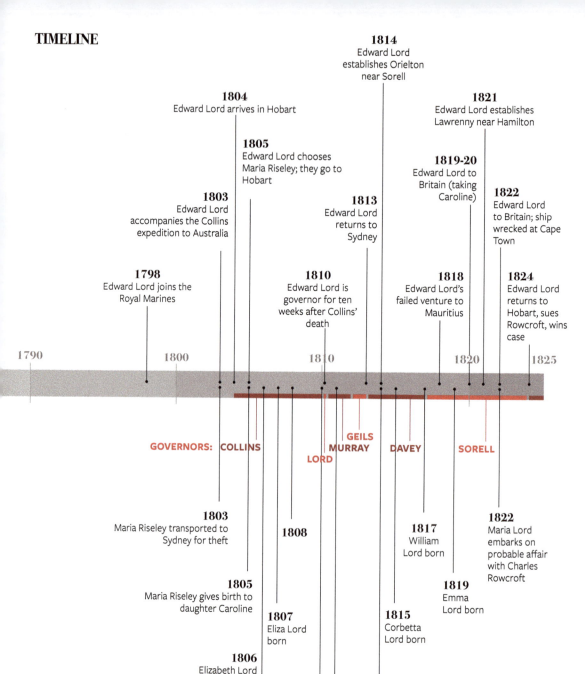

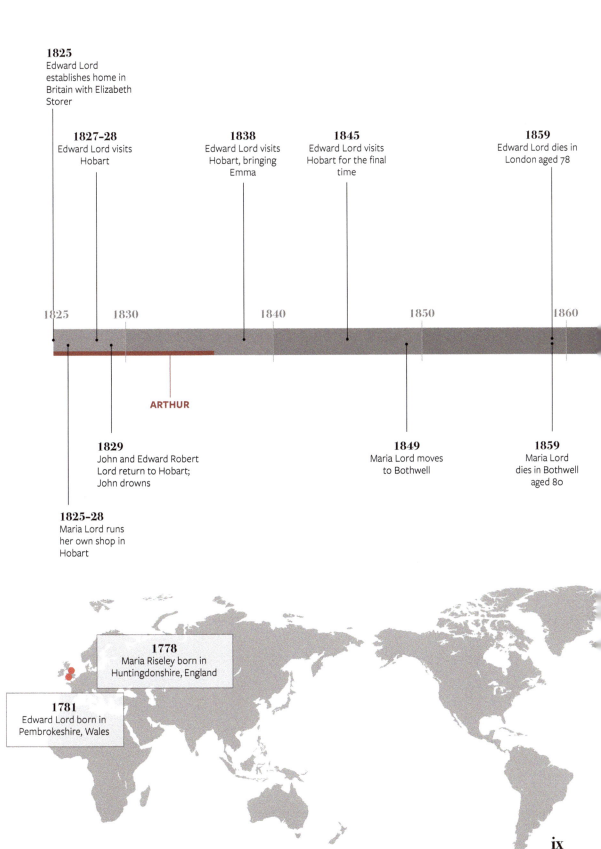

George Frankland's map of Van Diemen's Land, 1839, showing Lawrenny and Orielton
(Tasmanian Archive and Heritage Office)

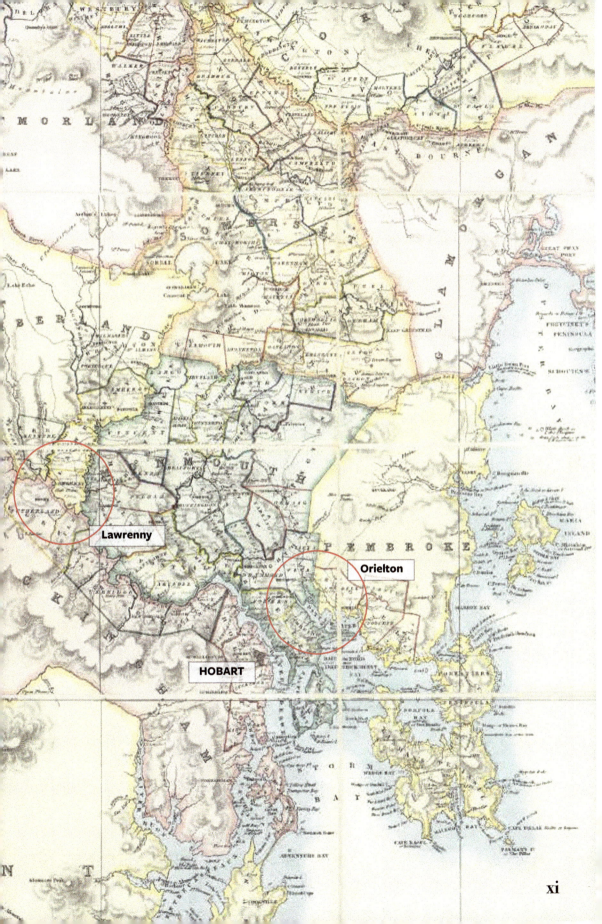

INTRODUCTION

IT'S 1805, AND MARIA RISELEY – single, poor and pregnant – finds herself in the gloomy Female Factory, Parramatta. Female convicts come here to be assigned as domestic servants, to be punished, or, like Maria, to await a baby's birth. She arrived in Sydney a year earlier, aged 25, and like the rest of her boatload of women convicts was assigned to a settler. Often, wrote John Pascoe Fawkner in his memoirs, such servants had 'a dissolute and detestable life' in which sex was part of their duties. That seems to have been the case for Maria, and here she was in mid-1805, at the Female Factory, either heavily pregnant or just having given birth. Her future looked bleak: separation from her baby then back to the round of housework, sex and so on.

Then Edward Lord arrived. Young, aristocratic, imperious, he wanted a woman. A lieutenant in the marines, he had been posted to the tiny new settlement at Hobart Town, where women were scarce. He came to Sydney, a much more promising field. A dashing man of action, Edward wanted quick results. Besides, his taste ran to working-class women rather than the genteel young ladies he might have courted at the dinners and balls of Sydney's elite. He went to the colony's obvious source of women, the Female

Where Edward and Maria met: Parramatta in about 1800, though there is no image of the Female Factory (Caroline Simpson Library & Research Collection, Sydney Living Museums)

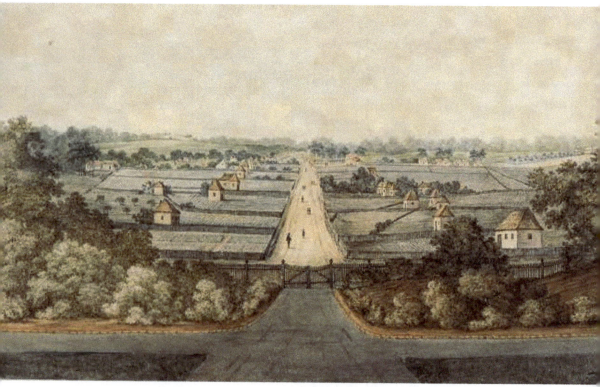

Factory. Convict women would hardly come up to his family's standards of suitability, but at least this method was fast. Edward asked for the women to be paraded before him, 'to select his paramour', wrote Fawkner, in the sole written version of the story. Edward chose Maria Riseley, who was only too glad to escape from the confinement of the Factory. 'She was at once let out, and he took possession of her, as truly for a slave to do his behests, or suffer for neglect or refusal.'[1]

Maria turned out to be even more determined and capable than Edward, and they made a powerful partnership. It was wildly successful: at first. In Hobart, Maria and Edward had just the talents needed to succeed. Over the next two decades they were leaders in developing a fledgling economy in the little colony: owning the most land, grazing the most stock, selling the most meat and wheat to the government, running the largest shop, exporting the most produce to Sydney and further afield and, on Edward's part, leading the community in public affairs. But the Lords also led in less positive aspects: corruption, vicious attacks on opponents, exploitation of small settlers, and taking land from the Aborigines, precipitating the Black War of the 1820s and Aboriginal dispossession.

Was it a dead end, this period of incompetent or even non-existent government, and widespread alcoholism and corruption? A major activity among colonists was milking the British government; and this, though lucrative, was non-productive. These activities formed a shaky basis for a developing economy, and few of the early arrivals made a lasting mark on the colony. Like so many of the original settlers, the Lords ran into problems and faded. It can be argued that their impact was ephemeral, and it was the hard-working, more sober, more competent settlers of the 1820s who really established Tasmania.

'WHO WOULD LOAD THE COLONIAL FAME with details, from which the eyes of mankind turn with natural disgust?' wrote historian John West in 1852, describing Van Diemen's Land's first scandalous years.[2] In the early 1820s upright, god-fearing immigrants and equally upright, god-fearing Governor Arthur did much to clean up what they saw as the appalling corruption and debauchery of the previous two decades. By the time West wrote his history, this early period was a byword for dreadful behaviour.

Later historians either ignored or sanitised this period or, from the mid-twentieth century, enjoyed its rebellious and exciting aspects. In

recent decades, comment has been generally positive. Biographers who admired their subjects, historians who believed official documents of the time, and those who wanted to show that the colony started well, all glossed over corruption and immorality, presenting it as understandable, even picturesque, in a rough frontier settlement.

I was among these historians, but I have grown increasingly sceptical. Was what the Lords represented the way forward? What was really happening? The book's title indicates my conclusion, tinged with John West's summary of the period: 'Kindly, but dissolute' – of which a neat example comes in William Charles Wentworth's description of a visit to Hobart in 1816. The place was even more debauched than he had heard, he wrote, but so friendly that he was swamped with invitations to meals. He rapidly organised a trip inland, just to escape the locals' relentless hospitality.[3]

Edward and Maria Lord were involved in virtually everything in Hobart, and I have used their careers to describe the general picture. Hobart's history was much like Sydney's, fifteen years earlier, with initial

Hobart, the centre of Edward and Maria Lord's activities. Contemporary paintings show a pretty, orderly town, with ships in the river suggesting profitable business activity. No untoward activities, of course. Joseph Lycett, 'Distant view of Hobart Town', 1824 (Tasmanian Archive and Heritage Office)

famine, drunkenness and corruption, and slow growth to modest prosperity. The main difference was that in Hobart few ex-convicts (except Maria) became wealthy, or had much impact. The major actors were some free settlers, and officials appointed from Britain, generally of low calibre.

Three strong influences of the time must be understood to make the story credible. One was social class, which gave Edward Lord his prominence as a baronet's brother, a prominence difficult to comprehend today. The second was the terrible social stigma on convicts and ex-convicts. The third was patronage. Writing *Mansfield Park*, Jane Austen had William Price promoted in the Royal Navy not because of his ability, experience or qualifications, but purely on the recommendation of a friend's uncle. For centuries the British ruling classes assumed that their role was not only to rule, but to enjoy the perks of ruling. When jobs were vacant, people would suggest friends and relations in need of employment. Qualifications did not matter: a British gentleman could turn his hand to anything. Unfortunately for the colony, these men were often the failures, unable to succeed in Britain.

Once safe in their jobs, men helped their own families and friends, and themselves, in any way possible. Such men held power in early Australia. With retribution largely absent, corruption started at the top, and it was scarcely surprising that the rest of the population followed. This can be described as natural, unfettered capitalism, but also as corruption and skullduggery. Whichever it was, it flourished in Hobart: and, like it or not, this was the start of our society today.

Because so little written by Edward and especially Maria Lord survives, I have tried to explain something of what I felt was their characters in the **Flights of Fancy**. They are based on evidence as much as possible, and on the style and opinions of the writers as shown in what evidence is available. My personal conclusion is that Edward was ambitious and good at getting his own way but rash, lacking staying-power, throwing away his fortune; and Maria, much cleverer, more focussed and more capable, used traditional feminine tactics to survive, and to establish herself in modest comfort.

1. EDWARD LORD GOES TO AUSTRALIA

DASHING, GLAMOROUS EDWARD LORD had anything but a dashing and glamorous start in life. Born in 1781, he was the third son of the mayor of a small town in southwest Wales – not quite as obscure at Hobart was to be, but not far off it. However, Edward had one impressive asset: grand relations. His second cousin was a baronet. Baronets might be the lowest level of the nobility, but Jane Austen's *Persuasion* shows how this set them and their families above mere gentry, let alone the middle class, giving them a strong sense of entitlement. Edward Lord and his brother John made all the mileage they could out of their relatives. Since they were also affable and generous, as such people were expected to be, people accepted them as aristocratic gentlemen, a cut above everyone else. This proved extremely useful.

The Lords were a branch of the Owen dynasty, which enthusiasts traced back to a fifth-century Welsh conqueror, Cunedda Wledig. From the sixteenth century the family owned extensive lands in Pembrokeshire, leading the county as sheriffs, lords lieutenant and members of parliament. An oft-told story claimed that in 1701 Sir Arthur Owen galloped all the way from Pembroke to Westminster to give the casting vote as parliament debated whether to accept George of Hanover as England's sovereign. In fact George had a comfortable majority, but the story was part of the Owen myth, showing the family playing a vital role at the heart of the nation. They built up their properties, and the major estate, Orielton, became large and prosperous, with extensive landscaped grounds, a magnificent three-storey mansion boasting an Adam staircase and ceilings, and thousands of acres of farmland.

Orielton in its heyday: imposing mansion, swans gliding on the lake, elegantly dressed ladies, all the accoutrements of the powerful landed gentry (Haverfordwest Library)

In 1786 four-year-old Sir Hugh Owen became the sixth baronet, his estate managed by his strong-minded mother, Lady Owen. He duly became High Sheriff of Pembrokeshire and was elected to parliament. Well down the family in importance, Corbetta Owen, mere niece of the fourth baronet, married Joseph Lord, son of a well-to-do tradesman and himself mayor of Pembroke. While this was creditable enough, it was a far cry from high sheriff and the rest of it, and the Lords were in the difficult position of obscure relations. Joseph and Corbetta did succeed at raising children, producing six sons and five daughters. Edward was born on 15 June 1781, following his brothers John and William.[1]

In 1794 the volunteer Pembroke Company of Gentlemen and Yeomanry was raised to defend the county against threatened invasion by the revolutionary French. Joseph Lord joined immediately. He was possibly involved when the French did invade Wales in 1797, landing not far north of Pembroke. Lady Owen's brother Lieutenant-Colonel John Colby was a central figure, competently rushing troops to encircle the enemy. This – and the action of a local woman who, armed with only a pitchfork, captured twelve French soldiers – secured victory for the Welsh, and would have been a thrilling, perhaps inspiring, story for fifteen-year-old Edward.[2]

Young Edward, the same age as his second cousin Sir Hugh, would have visited the grand estate of Orielton, where Hugh was the centre of attention, the owner of all this magnificence, rich and powerful, his future assured. Edward himself had to return to his much less impressive home in the small town of Pembroke, and the knowledge that he had to make his own fortune. His opinion of his parents can be inferred from his lack of

Aspects of the elegance of Orielton (James Alexander)
Pages 6–7: The lush countryside of the Orielton estate (James Alexander)

enthusiasm at passing on their names. Although he called five of his own sons John, William or Edward after himself and his brothers, he named only his third daughter after his mother, and none of his many sons after his father.

Where the Lord boys went to school is unknown, but since it was never mentioned it was probably somewhere unimpressive, such as a local institution in Pembroke. John, the oldest son, received the best education, attending university in Oxford and becoming a lawyer in London. Always flamboyant, he had a romantic marriage, eloping to Gretna Green with the beautiful daughter of a clergyman (John Lord's life could be the template for the whole genre of regency romances).[3] The younger Lord boys had more mundane futures. William joined the Royal Navy, but money and patronage must have been lacking by the time it was Edward's turn for a career, for he had to start a rung down the prestige ladder. In 1798, aged sixteen or seventeen, he enlisted in the Royal Marines. Soldiers attached to the navy, the marines were inferior to the army and the navy in pay and social status. However, at least Edward was an officer in the armed forces, considered a gentleman. Where he was for the next few years is unknown, but it was a bad time for the family: William died in 1800 and Joseph the following year, leaving Corbetta widowed, with a string of young children to establish.

Edward soon left this sad scene. Adventure beckoned, and in early 1803, aged 21, Second Lieutenant Edward Lord joined Colonel David Collins' expedition to form a settlement on the northern shore of distant Bass Strait. He and several other officers applied for an advance of pay

Pembroke: still a pretty town today, but far from the grandeur of Orielton (James Alexander)

to prepare for the trip, which implies that he did not have much money.⁴ Apart from Collins himself the officers were all young, and Lord was fourth in the chain of command, a heady position for a youth just out of his teens.

THIS EXPEDITION CAME ABOUT because Governor King in Sydney was worried at the interest the French were showing in Van Diemen's Land and just-discovered Bass Strait. The last thing he wanted was the French setting up a rival colony. He urged the British government to send an expedition to claim the shore of Bass Strait, suggesting Port Phillip (modern Melbourne) as the site.

The British government shared King's worry and acted fast. In late 1802 a ship, *Calcutta*, was being prepared to take convicts to Sydney, and it was relatively simple to divert it to Port Phillip, with the addition of stores, administrative staff, marines and a few free settlers. Previously, the governor's military force came from the army, but officers of the New South Wales Corps disgraced themselves in Sydney, vying with governors for power. To avoid this problem, the Bass Strait expedition used marines, under Collins. Twenty-five years older than Lord, Collins was a pleasant, mild-mannered man who, despite having no legal training, had served as judge advocate under Governor Phillip in New South Wales from 1788 to 1797, and on his return to England wrote an excellent two-volume description of the colony. Perhaps because of this, he was appointed to lead the 1803 expedition.

Colonel David Collins
(Allport Library and Museum of Fine Arts, TAHO)

In April 1803 Collins' expedition left England in two ships. Large and imposing, HMS *Calcutta* carried male convicts and some officers, marines and family members. Edward Lord and seven other civil and military officers ('officers' for short) sailed on the much smaller *Ocean*, with some marines and free settlers. In the whole expedition, men far outnumbered women, with 48 women and girls to about 400 men, a ratio of 1:8.⁵

A number of the men who travelled on *Ocean* with Edward Lord became his friends and colleagues, or at least involved in his career. Free settlers John Ingle and William Collins became merchants and good friends of Lord, as did mineralogist Adolarius Humphrey. Less close were surveyor George Harris, from an upright Quaker background, and Leonard Fosbrook the commissary, who was probably older than the rest.

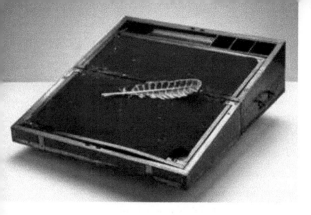

Said by the family to be the travelling writing desk Edward Lord brought with him on the 1803 voyage. Small (18.5 x 26.5 centimetres), made of walnut veneer and gilded brass (light and not too expensive), it is typical of the era. A practical piece of furniture, it had a drawer for pens, pencils, nibs and blotting paper, compartments for ink and other necessities, hinges so it could be folded away neatly, and a lock for privacy (Tasmanian Museum and Art Gallery)

Humphrey and Harris left graphic accounts of the voyage. It started with quite an adventure. At their last landfall in England at Yarmouth, *Ocean*'s officers went ashore for 'an excellent breakfast' – ship's rations were already palling. Not expecting to sail until noon, the men walked into the countryside, but suddenly caught sight of their ship preparing to sail. With great difficulty they managed to reach it, just in time. On board ship Humphrey, Harris, Lord and Fosbrook messed together. They became 'good friends ... which is not always the case in a Mess', wrote Harris. 'We have altogether been as comfortable as a sea life Salt beef one day Salt pork another & Ship biscuit could make us.' They caught some fresh food, such as turtles and sharks: 'I little thought I should ever relish a piece of Shark'.[6]

With nothing much to do on the monotonous voyage – 'almost the same occurrences happening every day' – there was a great deal of drinking. One evening the *Calcutta* officers invited the *Ocean* men to dinner, 'and the wine went around very fast so that at 9 o'clock we were all knocked up'. It sounds a pleasant enough voyage for Edward Lord, with agreeable companions, little work and plenty to drink if not eat. Probably for the first time in his life he had a servant at his beck and call, George Kearley, one of the marines. A sad event was that his handsome little terrier bitch fell overboard and drowned. It was a bad journey for dogs: one belonging to Harris died, he believed poisoned, and Fosbrook's dog went mad and was 'obliged to be thrown overboard'.[7]

There were more cheerful occasions. When they crossed the equator, the ugliest people on the ship acted as Neptune and his assistants, ducking newcomers and shaving them with a rusty hoop and a mixture of tar and grease. Lord, Harris, Humphrey and Fosbrook avoided the shaving by paying a fine in liquor, but ducking was obligatory. They enjoyed it, larking around in the tropical warmth. 'Not one of us had a dry thread', wrote Harris. 'Of course we prepared for the occasion by putting on old Clothes ... [it] afforded a deal of Mirth.' They stopped at Rio de Janeiro where Lord

Fashionable World.

No. DXI.

KING'S LEVEE.

Their Majesties came from Windsor yesterday to Kew Palace, from whence the King proceeded to town, and held a Levee at St. James's; it being the Anniversary of the Coronation, it was observed with the usual demonstrations, and the Noblemen who were Knights of the different orders, appeared in their several insignia; the Court commenced at one o'clock, and was attended by the following Noblemen and Gentlemen of distinction; considering the time of year the Court was rather numerous than otherwise. Among the company present were Mons. Otto, the French Minister, whose successor is hourly expected; the Neapolitan, Prussian, [...] Imperial Chargé des Affaires, the [...]ellor, the Chancellor [...] Portland, Alderman [...]ton.

[...]rosvenor.
[...]topford.
[...]r, Auckland, Pelham, [...]itzgerald, Boston, and
[...] Cottrel, R Chamber [...] J. Douglas, J. Nichol[...]
[...]er, Edmonstone, D[...] Childers.
[...], Collins, Witham. [...]rey.
[...]t, and Dalmahac. [...]Mackintosh, Elliot, S. [...]Jackson, and Aust.
[...]ng were:—
[...]e Prussian Ambassador, having been absent on important business these six months.
Lord Keith, on his arrival from abroad.
Baron Herbert, from Germany, was introduced by Mr. Spencer Smith: he is quite a young man, and attracted the notice of the company by the peculiarity of his dress, being attired in a vest of white satin.
Sir J. Douglas kissed hands on being appointed Equerry to His Royal Highness the Duke of Cumberland.
General Fraser, from the West Indies.
Majors Brown and Cummins, of the 11th Regiment of Light Dragoons.
Mr. Serjeant, Secretary to the new appointed Lords of His Majesty's Treasury.
Captain Grey, Commander of His Majesty's Yacht, during the time the King was at Weymouth.
James Mackintosh, Esq. Barrister at Law.
Lieutenant-Colonel Collins and Captain Hamberton.
John Smith, Esq. kissed His Majesty's hand on being appointed Master of the Mint, and was sworn a Member of His Majesty's Most Hon. Privy Council.
Sir Charles Morgan was also sworn a Privy Councillor, and took his seat at the Board.
A relation to the late General Sloper had audience of the King, and delivered up the red ribbon worn by that worthy Officer as Knight of the [...]

Right: The founder of a new colony is presented to King George III. The royal levée was obviously an impressive affair, though Collins is well down the list of important personages
(Morning Post, 23 September 1802)

Ship News.

PORTSMOUTH, April 12.—Admiral Lord GARDNER has shifted his flag from the *Dreadnought*, of 98 guns, Capt. BRACE, to the *Grampus*, 50 guns, Capt. CAULFIELD. The *Dreadnought* is unmoored, and will sail to-morrow for Cawsand Bay. The *Britannia* was yesterday commissioned by Lieutenant HICKEY. The *Calcutta*, Capt. Woodriffe, and the *Ocean* transport, with convicts and settlers on board, for New South Wales, will sail on Thursday.— Lieutenant-Colonel COLLINS, the Governor, embarks to-morrow. Gangs from the *Russell* and *Aurora* are on shore every night pressing, in which they pick up six or seven hands of a night.

Above: Calcutta and Ocean about to leave England, among warships and press-gangs (Morning Post, 14 April 1803)

and Humphrey, walking along the street, were invited into a large house by a judge. He liked them, and they spent many evenings there. Perhaps, however, they were unimpressed by the meals. Harris certainly was: 'every article of food is *saturated* with *Garlic*'.[8]

After the welcome break in Rio, it was a long three months' sailing across the tempestuous Southern Ocean to Australia. *Ocean*'s trip was unpleasant and tedious, most dreary, wrote Harris:

> We were constantly meeting with squalls of Wind, Rain Lightning & heavy rolling seas, so that many days we could not sit at table, but were obliged to hold fast by Boxes &c on the floor, & had all our Crockery Ware almost broken to pieces, besides shipping many Seas into the Cabin & living in a state of darkness from the Cabin windows being stopped up by the Dead lights – I was never so melancholy in my life before – not a single comfort either for the body or mind – the provisions infamous – the water stinking ... every person with a gloomy Countenance.[9]

Humphrey hated the food: beef so hard he could scarcely get his teeth through it; water stinking and full of bits of wood; bread wet, mouldy and uneatable. For one frightful fortnight he lived on gruel (thin porridge) rather than face the ship's meat – 'beef or horse flesh, or whatever it was, tasted like the smell of a tallow chandler's copper', rancid and nauseating. A grim trip for everyone, and Harris was surely not alone in 'constantly comparing my situation with the comforts I had left behind me in little England'.[10] Did Edward Lord dwell on the difference between his life and that of his cousin Sir Hugh, in the opulence of Orielton? Finally, in October 1803, five months after leaving England, the expedition arrived in Bass Strait.

EVERYONE GREETED PORT PHILLIP with rapture, admiring its beautiful green plains and lofty trees, 'more like pleasure grounds, than a wild savage Continent'. But on closer inspection Governor Collins found the land inhospitable, with little fresh water and poor sandy soil (he did not discover the Yarra until too late). He disembarked at what seemed the most promising site, Sullivan Bay, near modern Sorrento. Everyone was keen to be the first to land, wrote Humphrey. He won, and theatrically drawing his sword exclaimed, 'I take possession of this land in the name of the King of England!'[11] The convicts were put to clearing land and erecting tents, the marines set up a battery and people started to

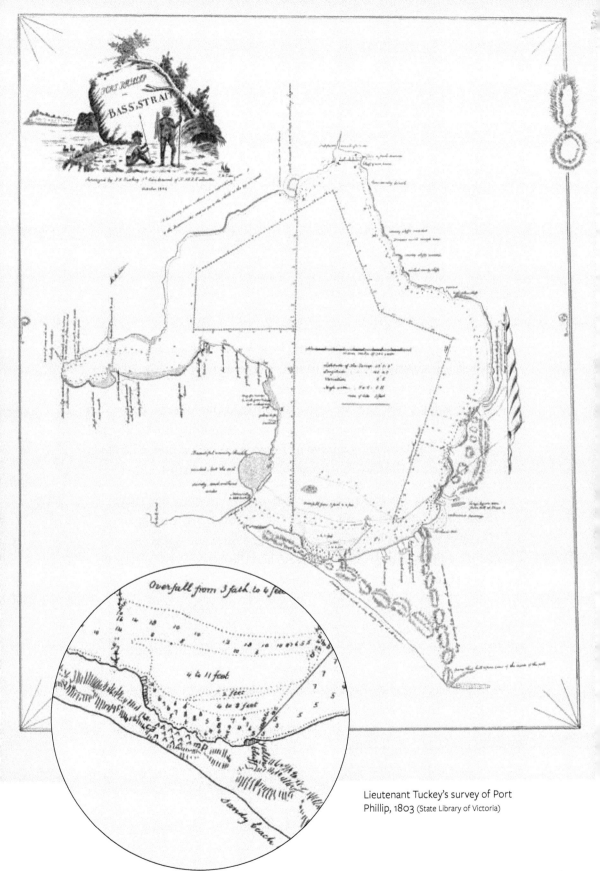

Lieutenant Tuckey's survey of Port Phillip, 1803 (State Library of Victoria)

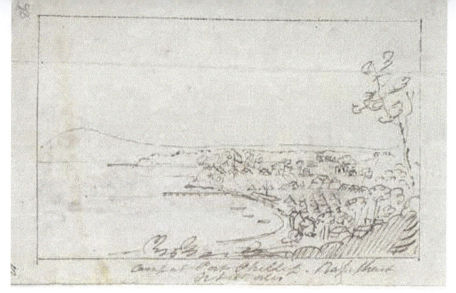

George Harris's sketch of the camp at Port Phillip (British Library, Manuscripts Collection Add. 45156, f. 19)

build huts and plant gardens. But with fresh water and good soil lacking, Collins felt it impossible to stay. He sent a boat to King in Sydney, asking permission to move to Van Diemen's Land.

While waiting for this to arrive, the expedition spent nearly four months at Sullivan Bay, long enough for some community life to develop. Humphrey, Harris, Lord and Lieutenant Johnson of the marines, all friends, messed together, as Harris wrote home. They all had breakfast, and

> We also drink Tea & sup together when we can shoot a few small birds to eat – Breakfast at 8 o'Clock Dine at four – drink tea at six. & sup at 8. – go to bed as you like – and I assure you we live very happy among ourselves never having had the smallest falling out or dispute during the voyage or since.[12]

Writing to his mother, Harris did not mention alcohol, but Humphrey noted that mess rules confined men to a pint of wine a day – a fair amount, four glasses, but they were not getting drunk every night. With few duties for most of the officers, life was pleasant. They enjoyed hunting, adding kangaroo, birds, fish and crayfish to the pot. By summer they were dining on duck with fresh peas and beans from their gardens.[13]

Some members of the expedition relished less innocent activities. No amorous liaisons were mentioned on board *Ocean*, but it was a different story on *Calcutta*, where seventeen non-convict wives accompanied convict husbands. Two naval lieutenants were moved by their plight, thinking that only the most sincere connubial love could have induced them to make the long and dangerous voyage. These innocent young officers were shocked when connubial love was found wanting. 'We had scarcely got into Blue Water before gross immorality in high places broke out', wrote John Pascoe Fawkner, a ten-year-old boy accompanying his mother and convict father. He was horrified when many of the officers started affairs with these convicts' wives. Even before the ship left England, Collins took up with convict Matthew Power's wife Hannah; the chaplain, Robert Knopwood, had a 'thoroughly bad woman' in his cabin; and in Rio George Harris, Edward Lord and their friends were given a box at the opera, but found it already taken by several *Calcutta* officers with 'some convict Wives whom they keep'. These liaisons continued at Port Phillip. On Christmas Day, after everyone attended divine service, the first baby born in the colony was baptised. His godparents were the second-in-command, a respectable married man; and the governor, his mistress and the mistress of another officer.[14] Fine examples of upright living for the unfortunate child!

It must have been an abrupt uprooting for young Lieutenant Lord, growing up in the small town of Pembroke, joining the marines, then finding himself transported across the world to a tiny new settlement. A stark contrast with Pembroke was the weather; as summer set in it grew very hot, up to 132° Fahrenheit (55° Celsius) in the sun – particularly uncomfortable for men wearing hot woollen uniforms. Then Lord's hut burnt down, though if he managed to save his possessions this might not have been too disastrous.[15]

Finally, in January 1804, permission arrived from King for the move to Van Diemen's Land. Governor Collins (technically lieutenant-governor, but always called governor) decided to settle in the south of the island rather than the north, partly because he thought it better sited for commerce, and partly because to forestall the French, King had already formed a small emergency settlement there. So the tents at Port Phillip were dismantled and *Calcutta* returned to England. One officer felt that he was leaving the colonists to curse their hard fate, with their present prospects bad and the future worse; but another imagined the colony transforming itself from 'a coalition of banditti' into a second Rome, giving laws to the world, 'looking down with proud superiority upon the barbarous nations of the northern hemisphere'.[16] Perhaps he had been talking to always-optimistic Edward Lord.

2. FOUNDING HOBART TOWN

EDWARD LORD BEGAN HIS CAREER in Van Diemen's Land in the best British tradition of derring-do. In February 1804 Governor Collins' ship arrived at Storm Bay, the entrance to the River Derwent. Strong squalls, heavy rain and severe lightning drove him east, to seek shelter in Frederick Henry Bay. Collins anchored two miles off present-day Cremorne beach, about fourteen miles (23 km) cross-country from the first British settlement under Lieutenant Bowen, up the Derwent at Risdon.

Collins was keen that Bowen should know of his arrival, so Lord and his friend Humphrey volunteered to walk overland to tell him. Collins pointed out the dangers of a small party trekking through unknown territory inhabited by possibly ferocious people and animals, but the impetuous young men insisted. They would not even wait until the next morning, and at 5 p.m., only an hour after the ship anchored, Lord, Humphrey, two servants and two trusted convicts were rowed to shallow water and struggled ashore through the surf, getting wet through. They carried guns, a map drawn by explorer Matthew Flinders, salt pork and some water. Harris watched them go. 'I am however afraid that, from the country being so mountainous & thickly wooded, they will find it a more troublesome undertaking than they imagined', he wrote pessimistically.[1] He was right.

Previous pages: A painting of early Hobart based on Harris's sketch, attributed to later surveyor George Evans (State Library of New South Wales)

Below: Collins' view from his anchorage in Frederick Henry Bay: Cremorne beach ahead, and behind it the bulk of Mount Wellington (James Alexander)

The party walked to Ralph's Bay, nearly a third of the way, and at nine o'clock camped under a large tree. They lit a fire, had something to eat, and slept. So far, so good. Dawn arrives early in summer, and they started again at 4 a.m., travelling over very high hills, wrote Humphrey – and no doubt these rises which seem modest from a modern car were challenging, in an unknown country before breakfast. When they did stop for refreshment there was no water but, thinking they must find some somewhere, they drank all they had, ate their salt pork (the worst thing when water is short) and moved on. By ten o'clock the sun was powerful and they were extremely thirsty. They found no fresh water; in late summer, creek beds were dry. 'I have never suffered so much for want of drink and was almost unable to walk', wrote Humphrey. After struggling across two hills they could see Mount Direction, at whose foot Risdon lay. It was not far, but they were so exhausted they could not manage the hilly direct route and walked around the shore instead – luckily. On the river was a boat from the Risdon settlement, which rescued them.[2] This venture shows Edward Lord's impetuosity and lack of planning, but also his luck: so often, he managed to struggle through difficult situations successfully.

The rest of the expedition arrived at Risdon three days later, and there was another race to land. Collins wanted his mistress to win the honour

A map of Van Diemen's Land by Harris, 1804, depicting the Sullivan Bay Camp, Risdon Cove Settlement, Mount Direction and Table Mountain, now Mount Wellington
(British Library, Manuscripts Collection)

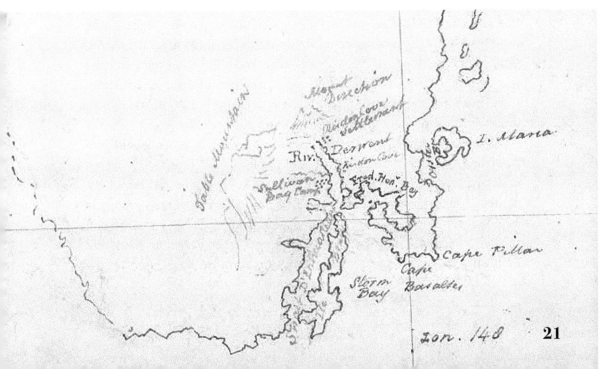

Lord and Humphrey were rowed to Cremorne beach, and struggled ashore through the breakers (James Alexander)

Seals basking in Frederick Henry Bay. Collins' arrival heralded disaster for them (James Alexander)

of being first woman ashore, but some of *Ocean*'s crew grabbed a boat for Mary Kearley, the wife of Edward Lord's servant, and raced her to shore to claim the title (an early example of how nearly every story in early Hobart involved the Lords, one way or another). More seriously, Collins found everything wrong with Risdon: poor access, poor soil, inadequate water and little progress made by a dispirited and quarrelsome bunch of colonists. He chose a much better site on the other side of the river – 'the most beautiful & romantic Country I ever beheld', as Harris wrote rhapsodically.[3] Collins called it Hobart Town, but Hobart soon became common usage.

The settlers must have wondered whatever they were going to find in this new country. The Australian colonies, on the other side of the world, were like the moon as far as people in Britain were concerned: far distant, peculiar, upside-down. Botany Bay was bad enough, but Van Diemen's Land was even more fantastic, its name suggesting frightful demonic activities. It was even mentioned in *Gulliver's Travels*, that novel of weird, impossible places and creatures (not much of a mention, but it was there).

When the British invaded, Van Diemen's Land was probably much as it had been for tens of thousands of years: a hilly island, much of it covered in eucalypt forest. Its inhabitants, the Tasmanian Aborigines, were nomadic hunter-gathers, probably about five thousand of them, living in groups in well-defined territories. They hunted kangaroo, wallaby, possums and smaller marsupials, and gathered berries and other vegetable food, and shellfish around the coast. The main way they made their mark on the island was by using firestick farming to create grassy plains, where wallaby and kangaroo flourished.

In the previous few decades French and British explorers showed great interest in the Aborigines. The French were taken with Rousseau's idea of the Noble Savage, people who showed in their natural way of life virtues lost in decadent civilisation, and the Aborigines were an excellent example of this. However, while nodding to Rousseau, and despite the Aborigines obviously comprising a viable community, Europeans also felt kindly contempt for their lack of complex tools and other artefacts of European life, such as houses and clothes. As usual, scientists ranked them, putting Tasmanian Aborigines on the bottom rung of the Great Chain of Being, the lowest of the low. But though the Aborigines had nothing to trade with whites, their unwarlike nature and grassy plains made settlement inviting.

Relations between the races started badly. In May 1804 whites at Risdon fired on a band of Aborigines, killing at least three and probably more. Settlers claimed this started the enmity between the races, though at the time the Aborigines retreated into the bush and most settlers saw little of them. Over the next twenty years there were some hostilities – Europeans shooting Aborigines and abducting their women, Aborigines spearing Europeans in retaliation – but they mostly occurred on the frontier, inland, away from the main settlements on the coast. Though horrifying, they were not numerous enough to provoke full-scale war, and when in 1824 a governor provided a detailed description of the colony for his successor, he did not even mention the Aborigines.[4]

Van Diemen's Land's other big attraction for Europeans was its temperate climate. The sun-loving scantily clad twentieth century might see the island as chilly, but to people swathed in thick neck-to-ankle-and-wrist clothing it appeared inviting: not too scorching in summer, not much snow in winter. As Edward Lord said in 1812: 'We have neither the extreme heat of England, nor the severity of cold; it is an uncommon fine climate'.[5] (Extreme heat of England? Yet this was what Lord said, or was quoted as saying. He did come from Wales.)

The fact that the island was a convict colony might have seemed a disadvantage but, surprisingly, convicts tended to fade into the background. This was mainly because there was not much visible evidence of them. With the British government busy fighting Napoleon, few convicts were sent to Van Diemen's Land, not enough to need the huge institutions of later years, so there were no convict buildings to catch the eye. When convicts arrived, they were assigned to work for settlers or the government and lived in the community, dressed like everyone else and with no distinguishing marks such as uniforms or fetters. The only obvious convicts were those being punished for serious offences, working on the roads in gangs, sometimes in chains – but their numbers were small. Ex-convicts merged into the general population as labourers, tradesmen or, if women, wives and partners.

There was little discontent among the convicts, and certainly no rebellion. George Harris thought they were well treated, better clothed and fed than the working class in England. Their work was not hard, the sick had medical treatment, and the governor encouraged them, showing 'every possible kindness & attention even to the meanest of the Convicts if his conduct is good'.[6] Presumably most convicts had not wanted to be exiled across the world, but once they arrived they seemed to settle down peaceably enough, in a pragmatic way typical of the colony: we're here, we might as well make the best of it. Van Diemen's Land appeared a small mirror of British society, with a tiny elite and middle class and a large labouring class; it scarcely mattered that these people had mostly been transported. Few convicts rose to prominence, by either wealth or villainy. With so many convicts in the population there was probably more petty theft and drunkenness in Hobart than in Britain, but these offences were common in Britain, too – Hobart was just more of the same.

Harris's sketch of the early settlement at Hobart, with tents on Hunter Island and in the bush along the shore, and a ship anchored alongside (State Library of New South Wales)

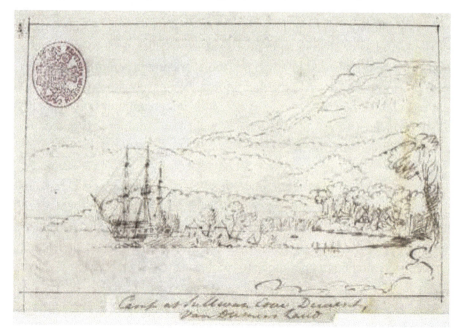

ONCE EVERYONE WAS ON SHORE in Hobart, work started at recreating Britain in the antipodes. Convicts pitched tents under Edward Lord's direction, and cut trees for a bridge over the rivulet. They built a storehouse and a wharf, and for themselves wattle-and-daub huts thatched with reeds. The expedition had brought plenty of food, and people drew their rations: flour, salt beef or pork, tea, sugar, soap and occasionally vinegar and limejuice. After the rest of the expedition arrived from Port Phillip in June, the white population was 433: 39 women, 36 children, and 358 men.[7]

As in most British garrisons, the marines had little actual work, since there were no enemies to need defeating and the colonists themselves were no trouble. Officers enjoyed exploring, hunting kangaroo and socialising, mainly having dinner together. From the first, Edward Lord was an enthusiastic and hospitable diner. Only three days after he set foot in Hobart, he and Humphrey asked Parson Knopwood to dinner, and over the next decades Knopwood recorded in his diary many meals with Lord. After church one Sunday in April 1804, Knopwood invited Lord and Harris home for refreshment. They 'pertook of some Norfolk ham with me, the best we ever eat', wrote Knopwood. 'At 4 p.m. [a surgeon], Mr. Harris and self dind with Lt. Lord and was very merry.' On another occasion Knopwood went hunting with Lord 'and kill a couple of kangarros. At 20 minutes past 7, returnd home to breakfast with Mr. Lord. I dined with Mr. Lord'.[8]

The officers began holding monthly dinners for each other, and the gastronomic climax of the year occurred in October, when Knopwood held a dinner for seven officers, including Lord. They ate fish, kangaroo soup, a saddle of roast kid, a saddle of roast kangaroo, two fowls stuffed with rice and bacon, pork ... Knopwood's diary entry then trails off, but there was certainly no shortage of food.[9] It all sounds very pleasant.

For the next twenty years, Knopwood was a close friend of Edward Lord. Like almost all colonists in Van Diemen's Land at the time, Knopwood had a dubious past, debt forcing him to sell the family property. He was ordained, apparently more as a career move than from a burning desire to spread the gospel, and through patronage became Collins' chaplain. He was far from a strict moralist, and religion sat lightly on the little colony. One convict, one of the few believers, wanted to start a religious society but decided not to because he feared no one would come.[10] Though divine service was meant to be held weekly, it was cancelled if the weather was at all wet, windy, cold, hot or in any way disagreeable, or if Knopwood himself were indisposed – as he tended to be, the morning after the night before. In his diary he showed himself a kindly man, and one woman noted that he was very well liked, though not respected as a parson. This was when Knopwood was elderly, and perhaps mellowed; twenty years earlier, John Pascoe Fawkner lived in Knopwood's house while employed cutting timber, and described the clergyman as a harsh magistrate, overfond of drink and women 'and given to the coarse vulgar propensity of swearing ... a bad man'.[11] Perhaps he exaggerated – Knopwood might not have had much time for sharp-eyed teenagers – but this does suggest that Knopwood was not just the kindly old buffer he depicted in his diary.

Instead of religion, officers were interested in making money: 'Money was the god he worships', as a colonist wrote of one.[12] It was applicable to many more. With relatively small salaries, they aimed to make their fortunes. There were two ways: trading, which was forbidden; or selling meat to the commissariat, by raising stock or hunting kangaroo. Edward Lord, ambitious and energetic, was at the forefront of everything, forbidden or not.

All his life, Edward Lord was quick to seize any opportunity to make money. Initially he worked with Humphrey, and they started by building the first house in the colony. Collins provided materials, convict labour and land, and called the result 'the house in the woods' (today in central Hobart, in Victoria Street). A basic four-roomed hut, it had round windows like the portholes of a ship, but as the settlement's first house it was 'considered as an achievement of civilisation – a trophy gained upon the wilderness', the triumphant description probably coming from Lord himself. He had one of the rooms, Humphrey another, a third was rented to a lieutenant and his wife – an early money-making venture – and the fourth was a sitting-room. The house was finished by June 1804, when Knopwood dined there with Lord. The other officers were still living in tents, uncomfortable in winter; one man reported water ankle-deep under his bed.[13]

The commissariat always needed meat, since it supplied almost the whole community, and bought all available for sixpence a pound. Lord and Humphrey set about supplying it. Dogs were necessary for hunting, and within a few days of landing, Lord and Humphrey bought two. Later they bought three more, and Humphrey estimated that they could kill a thousand pounds of kangaroo a week, which brought in about £23, a handy sum (the commissary earned £91 for the whole year). Raising stock was a much slower way of providing meat, but Lord started buying animals.

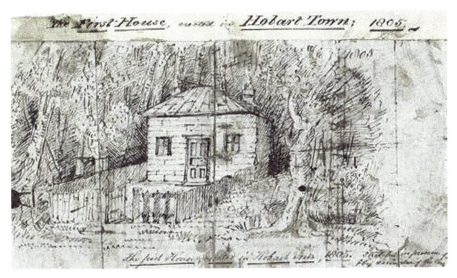

Entitled 'The first House, erected in Hobart Town, 1805', this sketch presumably shows Edward Lord's house, though this was built in 1804 with round windows. However, the sketch gives a good idea of the basic building style of the time (Tasmanian Museum and Art Gallery)

Collins helped Lord and Humphrey purchase a few from a ship's captain (obviously neither young man had much money).[14]

Trading was the most lucrative long-term way of making money. Prices for goods were high, up to three times as much as in England. Few people had cash, so barter was the normal method of payment, as Harris described. 'When you want to make a bargain it is customary to ask the price of the commodity & what the person will be paid in such as Wheat – Flour – Salt Pork or Beef – Kanguroo & & if you think an exorbitant price is put on the article you want, the price pr lb of what you exchange is raised accordingly'.[15] Rum was also used as currency, but Harris omitted this detail in letters home.

Lord's first trading venture involved buying goods from the ship's captain who sold him the animals, and selling them to colonists. He and Humphrey bought some corn, but this was perhaps just for their own use. More lucratively, Collins bought 120 gallons of rum, and passed it on to his officers at the same price. They sold it to colonists for up to six times as much.[16] Collins was indulging his officers, helping them to make money in this illegal way. It had been done in Sydney when he was there, so why not in Hobart? However, even in this permissive climate officers could not break the rules too flagrantly. Edward Lord could not take full of advantage of the need for goods and start a shop himself.

Harris's map of Hobart, June 1804, showing the Rivulet winding through thick bush, tents along the shore of Sullivan Cove and inland, and Edward Lord's new house, out in the bush
(Tasmanian Archive and Heritage Office)

Humphrey felt lucky to work with him. 'Lieutenant Lord is first cousin to Sir Hugh Owen of Wales and has a brother, a counsellor, in Lincoln's Inn', he told his family. 'It was necessary for me to join someone who would look after the stock in my absence in the country [Humphrey was the mineralogist-cum-geologist], and Lieutenant Lord is prudent and steady'. Humphrey was surely the only person who ever called Edward Lord 'prudent and steady', but these were early days and perhaps he was feeling his way (or Humphrey was trying to reassure his family). Collins also approved of Lord. Until the second half of his expedition arrived from Port Phillip, Lord was his second in command, and he reported to Governor King in Sydney that he appreciated Lord's 'attention and vigilance at all times'.[17]

By August 1804 Harris and Humphrey were sending cheerful reports home. Harris had four convicts assigned to him, as well as 'a fine young Ram Cat' named Sir John Harris; three hounds for hunting kangaroo called Lagger, Spanker and Weasel; and three spaniels, Sultan, Van Diemen and Dingo. The names are an intriguing mixture of local words ('Dingo' at this date) and traditional English, typical of the way these transplanted British took on some of the flavour of their environment while also remembering Home. Harris was enjoying himself: 'were it not the great Distance from home & the great expence paid for all the little comforts of life, a single Man might live very contentedly & comfortably at least for a few Years'. Humphrey agreed: 'Everything in the colony has the most favourable appearance. The settlement is in a very flourishing state'.[18] Humphrey and Harris's friend Lord was doubtless just as optimistic.

SO FAR, EDWARD LORD APPEARS IN THIS STORY as a pleasant young man who did his work competently, got on well with his fellow officers and enjoyed social life. All was fine as long as he kept his impulsiveness in check, but sometimes his self-control failed. It did, potentially disastrously, in late 1804.

The adultery of Port Phillip continued at Hobart, with many officers living with the wives of convicts or soldiers. Collins continued his intimacy with Hannah Power, even attending divine service with her. Knopwood disapproved of the intimacy – privately. Soldiers were forbidden to socialise with convicts, and a private caught drinking with one was sentenced to 200 lashes. Noting this in his diary, Knopwood added, 'N.B. The Lieut. Gov. and Lt. Col. of the Royal Marines the same morn breakfasted with a convict and his wife by the name of Mathew Powers – she always lives at the Col. table'.[19] Knopwood said nothing out loud, however. He knew on which side his bread was buttered.

Others were more vocal, disapproving of either the governor's adultery, his consorting with a convict's wife, the favours this convict obtained, or all three. When an East India Company ship visited, there was a grand dinner on board, attended by Governor Collins, the chaplain and the other officers. Collins also took his mistress. The next day a group of officers (not including Lord) dined together and then sent the governor a letter: perhaps they all grumbled over their claret about the governor taking his mistress on this semi-official occasion and, growing brave with their port, decided to object. Two days later the officers withdrew their letter, Collins telling Knopwood the matter was amicably settled. It seems likely that Collins promised to be more discreet, for he stopped taking his mistress to dine on visiting ships, instead taking her to the government farm, out of sight.[20]

This was not enough for Lieutenant Lord. In October, Knopwood described an argument between Lord and Collins over Power (calling

Edward Lord's friend Humphrey, drawn by George Harris
(National Library of Australia nla.pic-an7890477)

him Powers). It occurred at six in the evening and possibly the men had been drinking, since this has the ring of a drunken disagreement. Words arose between Lord and Collins, wrote Knopwood, with Lord claiming that Collins 'kept Powers a pimp for him'. Collins defended Power, and pushed Lord back. Lord said that if Collins were not governor and his superior officer, 'he would knock him down and kick him for falling'. Collins retorted, 'Sir, you may one day see me in a plain coat' – that is, when he was no longer an officer. Lord replied, 'Sir, I believe you will stay here too long' – presumably criticising Collins as governor. They parted, Collins claiming he would never forget this insult. 'Then I hope you will always keep it in memory', said Lord.[21] It sounds petty enough, but Collins did manhandle Lord, and Lord did object to his association with Power.

On 1 January 1805 – perhaps everyone was hungover after New Year's Eve – 'Lt Lord and Powers had another unfortunate dispute', wrote Knopwood. Writing his memoirs sixty years later, John Fawkner described the quarrel as between Lord and Collins. They met as Collins was walking arm-in-arm with Hannah Power. Lord refused to bow, as he should have done to his superior officer. When Collins asked why he would not bow, haughty Lord replied it was because Collins had his 'leman' (unlawful lover) on his arm.[22] Whether Lord quarrelled with Collins or Power, with the governor or his mistress's husband, it had the same result: Collins arrested Lord and imprisoned him indefinitely, without a trial, illegally.

Why did Lord make this rash move? Surely he realised that challenging either Collins or his protégé Power was unwise? Or did he think that, having got away with it once, he could again? Did he have the support of the other officers? Or was it a spur-of-the-moment revolt, the young gentleman unable to bow to Collins with his mistress and/or convict connection on his arm?

Edward Lord was now in an uncomfortable situation, mentally and physically, confined illegally in the summer sun of January. The other officers were on his side, though they did not act at once. However, there must have been obvious unrest, for one Sunday in late January Knopwood, the toady, preached a sermon on Discontent and Censure, for which Collins thanked him before the whole congregation. It did not work; on 30 January all the officers except Knopwood held a meeting. As a result, and probably in protest against Lord's imprisonment, two refused to serve as magistrates. Since there were three magistrates (Knopwood being the third), this made administering justice impossible. Collins gave in, freed Lord after over five weeks in prison and 'made it up with all the officers', promising to ask them to dine. Nothing happened, so someone reminded Collins and he had to invite the officers, including Lord, to dinner.[23] A difficult occasion.

Collins was now in an awkward position of his own making: one subordinate resentful after spending five weeks in prison illegally, and the others (except Knopwood) questioning his acts. He decided to get rid of Lord by giving him leave. However, everything had to look respectable, with no hint of scandal. Lord asked for leave of absence on health grounds and permission to visit Sydney, then England. Two doctors testified that yes, Lord's health meant his immediate return to England was highly necessary. Collins gave Lord eighteen months' leave. With him went Humphrey who, said Collins, wished to extend his mineralogical researches. According to Fawkner, they went to Sydney to find women.[24]

This is the first reference to Edward's poor health, and it could have been now that he began to suffer from asthma. His death certificate in 1859 noted, 'Asthma, 50 years';[25] '50' sounds more general than specific, so he could have suffered his first bout in 1805. There was no successful treatment for asthma, though there were plenty of folk remedies ranging from infusions of herbs, rest or dry air to foods such as the blood of wild horses or millipedes soaked in honey. Sea voyages were often recommended, possibly to escape pollen on land, and these gave Edward relief.[26] It is risky to diagnose at a distance, but perhaps five weeks in prison – the shock, the indignity, the hot and dusty conditions, pollen in the summer air – precipitated his first attack.

By February, Lord was free, and keen to leave. Ships to Sydney were infrequent, but in March Governor King sent a boatload of female convicts to Hobart. The ship sailed back to Sydney with Lord and Humphrey on board. On 18 April they landed. Then, said Fawkner, Lord 'went, and sank himself, if possible, lower than the Governor he had upbraided'.[27] He too took a convict mistress: Maria Riseley.

3. OBSCURE BEGINNINGS

UNLIKE EDWARD LORD, Maria Riseley had no grand relatives, no influential friends, no money and no chance of patronage. She had to rely on herself and her own ability. Fortunately for her, she had plenty: she was an extremely competent, intelligent and determined woman.

Maria's family was more prosperous than the poor working-class which provided most of Australia's convicts, but this was still far distant from the elite Owens. For centuries Riseleys they had lived around the border of Huntingdonshire and Bedfordshire, deep in the English countryside, in occupations such as farmer, yeoman, maltster, miller and clerk, part of the stable, relatively comfortable skilled working class.[1] The name was spelt in many ways – Risley, Risely, Riselay, even Rissley – but Riseley was the usual way in Van Diemen's Land.

Hannah Maria Riseley, known as Maria, was born on 20 December 1778 at Spaldwick, Huntingdonshire, a small rural village in a rolling landscape comprising a patchwork of farms and other small villages. Maria was the second child and eldest daughter of Robert and Mary Riseley, both born locally in the mid-1750s. Mary bore ten children in all, of whom only one is known to have died young. The babies were born at Spaldwick until 1787 – so Maria lived there until she was about nine – then at nearby villages, Molesworth and Catworth.[2]

When Maria's brother John applied for a land grant in Van Diemen's Land he said his father was a farmer, and that he himself had been brought up to farming.[3] He was a competent farmer, which supports his claim, but the family's moves suggest that Robert did not own a farm, for farmers generally stayed put as farms passed down through the generations. Perhaps he was a tenant farmer. He had another string to his bow: between 1777 and 1796 the authorities at Spaldwick paid him for glazing and plumbing work in the church, even after he left the village, which sounds as if he was a good tradesman. Even more promisingly, they called him 'Mr'.[4] Men were

Above: Spaldwick, Maria's birthplace. The photograph was taken long after her time, but it shows the village's deep sense of tranquillity or, alternately, boredom (Mark Heath)

Previous pages: This replica of *Endeavour* is much the same size as Maria Riseley's *Experiment* (*Alwyn Friedersdorff*)

addressed in one of three ways: 'Esquire' for upper-class gentlemen; 'Mr' for respectable men, tradesmen and farmers; and just surnames for the labouring class. Mr Robert Riseley would have had some standing in the community. The family's life sounds settled and relatively comfortable. They were law-abiding, only Maria appearing in a court of law, and Mary's good record of infant mortality, losing only one baby, suggests that she had the resources to look after her children well. But she and Robert were illiterate, so they had not risen far up the social ladder.

As the eldest daughter, Maria was expected to help her mother at home, learning housekeeping in preparation for the day when she herself married. These rural villages had no schools, and with illiterate parents it is unlikely that she received any education. Her next three sisters followed the expected pattern, marrying local men.[5] Maria did not. She left home.

Why? In later life, Maria Riseley proved to be not only intelligent and determined but hot-tempered, not one to put up with boredom. Descriptions of peasant life often depict tediously repetitive existences

The peaceful countryside around Molesworth, cultivated for generations (James Alexander)

Above: Spaldwick: uninspiring for an ambitious young woman (Mark Heath)

Right: St Peter's Church in Molesworth, attended by the Riseley family (James Alexander)

dominated by superstition and ignorance, with women suffering a never-ending routine of housework and childcare – surely stultifying to such a girl. Marriage to a neighbouring yokel would only bring more of the same. Did Maria feel there must be more to life than this? Did the bright lights of the city beckon? Did she run off with an exciting lover? Did she think that since she seemed doomed to housework, she might as well earn a wage from it? Speculation is useless, of course. All we know is that by 1802 Maria had left Catworth. Far to the south, in Camberwell on the outskirts of London, she was charged with stealing goods from William Yapp.

Formerly a London merchant, William Yapp had moved to Camberwell, where Londoners went for rural tranquillity and healing springs.[6] The most likely scenario is that he and his wife Sarah retired there, perhaps still with a shop, and Maria worked for them as a servant – her occupation was not stated at her trial, but this was the most common job for young women. In July 1802 Sarah Yapp charged Maria with feloniously stealing an immense number of items, 68 in total, the property of her husband William:

Clothing
2 gowns
1 petticoat and 1 shift
5 pairs sleeves
1 apron
1 bonnet
2 caps
11 handkerchiefs

1 pair gloves
1 pair stockings
1 pair stays (corsets)
1 pair breeches

Fabric and house linen
26 yards fabric (linen, muslin, calico, quilting, coarse sheeting)
63 yards trimming (lace, ribbon, galloon)
8 linen doyleys
3 tablecloths
5 napkins
1 pair window curtains
2 tassells

Other items
1 knife
1 box
1 lid of a box
1 glass (a mirror or a tumbler)
2 watch strings
3 earrings
3 bottles

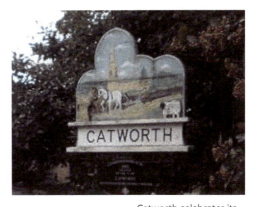

Catworth celebrates its rural past – from which Maria Riseley escaped
(James Alexander)

These 68 items were worth £12/9/6. A servant might earn £10 or £15 a year, and to steal goods worth a year's wage was a major crime. Maria was arrested and imprisoned, probably in the huge stone House of Correction in Guildford, Surrey's county town. She remained in custody for a month, until her case came up at the Surrey Summer Assizes, where she was charged with taking and carrying away from the dwelling house of William Yapp 'with force and arms' this enormous pile of goods.[7]

The list and the charge raise many questions. Did Maria partly clear out the Yapps' house? Surely such a mixed jumble can only have been part of the contents of someone's dwelling, or general shop. However, a 23-year-old woman, however strong, could not take all these goods by herself – 68 items, some bulky and heavy, such as all that fabric. She probably had accomplices; but no one else was tried for the crime. Was this young woman from a relatively sheltered background led astray by a persuasive lover who then escaped, leaving her in the lurch? And what about the 'force and arms' – did she really use weapons, or was this merely the usual formula (which seems to be the case)? The goods must have been found, for so precise a list to have been made – but where did Maria store them? Why did Sarah Yapp rather than William charge her?

Did Maria actually commit the crime? Some factors suggest innocence: she was never in trouble with the law otherwise, before or after; her upbringing sounds law-abiding; and it seems out of character that an intelligent young woman would have committed an offence apparently so easily brought home to her. She never claimed innocence, but since she never seems to have mentioned her convict experience, this question might not have arisen. Only a family story tells of a man who was supposed to come to her trial and prove her innocence, but never turned up.[8] A novelist could have a wonderful time with a scenario where William Yapp was having an affair with Maria and Sarah charged her with theft to get rid of her, or else got rid of her after Maria's hot temper burst out ('I've already scrubbed that damned floor!' – but why not just dismiss her); or where the Yapps were on the fiddle and Maria was set up, made to take the blame. But no evidence supports such enticing theories and, like most convicts, she was probably guilty of the crime for which she was transported.

The public took little interest in Maria's case. A newspaper report of the assizes described how on the opening day, Surrey's county town of Guildford was all bustle and confusion. After the customary formalities the assizes commenced, with 59 prisoners tried. The reporter described one case in which three women were charged with assault and theft, then continued, 'The trials on the Crown Side are for the greater part wholly without interest, embracing only those common-place enormities, which every Old Bailey session teems with, and which to repeat would disgrace your columns'.[9] Maria had joined the ranks of disgraceful criminals who committed enormities, distancing themselves from respectable society, from normal, well-behaved people.

No details of Maria's trial remain, but it must have been alarming. Stealing goods over the value of £2 was a capital crime: death by hanging was a grim possibility. However, the all-male jury was sympathetic, perhaps because she was the only one caught for the crime, or because she looked pathetic or appealing in the dock, or because they did not want the death of another person on their consciences. Juries were often reluctant to condemn women to death, and it was Maria's first offence. Or possibly she

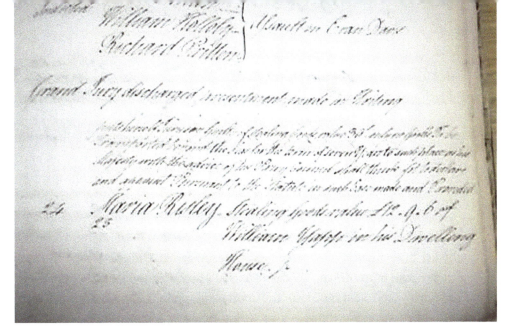

Maria's record at the Surrey Assizes, 1804 (National Archives, Kew)

managed to catch the men's eyes in a certain way: several events in Maria's life are plausibly explained by her exuding sexuality (including, perhaps, Sarah Yapp wanting to be rid of her). As jurors sometimes did, these twelve good men and true found Maria Riseley guilty of stealing goods worth only 39 shillings. There was no apparent discussion as to the worth of the goods, whose value was over six times 39 shillings; the figure was arrived at purely so she would not be put to death. Instead she was sentenced 'To be Transported beyond the Seas for the term of Seven Years'.[10] Her sentence would expire in July 1809.

The experience of being charged, arrested, imprisoned, tried and found guilty with the possibility of execution was probably devastating, especially for a young woman who, as far as we know, had never had anything to do with crime or the law. After being sentenced, Maria was thrust into the convict group, mainly poor women from the labouring class, where necessity meant that theft was commonplace. The main holding place for those awaiting transportation was Surrey's main prison, Horsemonger Lane gaol at Newington. This was new, built in the 1790s as a modern 'model prison', with yards radiating from a central vantage point and wings containing prison wards and night cells, all enclosed within a high wall. Prisoners were separated by gender and offence (debtors, petty criminals and felons): as a felon, Maria was in the most serious class. Horsemonger Lane was a grim place, with executions carried out on the flat roof of the gatehouse – a chilling reminder to Maria of what her fate might have been.[11]

Her fourteen months in prison sound difficult, and perhaps it was here she developed the toughness and knowledge of swearing commented on later. She could hardly avoid them.

Occasionally other women sentenced to transportation joined the group. The most notorious was Mary Mears, alias Molly Morgan, Jones and Hunt. The daughter of a ratcatcher, she was born in 1762 in Shropshire, married a wheelwright and gave birth to a son, but in 1789 was sentenced to transportation for stealing yarn. Her husband joined her in Sydney, but four years later she escaped back to England and worked as a dressmaker in Plymouth, where she bigamously married Thomas Mears. In 1803 their home burnt down. Thomas accused Mary of arson, and she was tried in Surrey and sentenced to transportation again.[12] She could have told the other women a thing or two about a convict's experiences – and she probably did.

BY 1802 TRANSPORTATION TO NEW SOUTH WALES was well established, a well-organised system that aimed to rid Britain of criminals and therefore crime. With far fewer women than men sentenced to transportation, women's ships sailed only occasionally. While awaiting transportation, women were kept in county gaols. When a ship taking female convicts was due to sail, county authorities were told to provide suitable women, those not too old or ill. In late 1803 HMS *Experiment* was in Portsmouth ready to sail, and gaols started to send their contingents.[13]

Surrey sent ten women. It was 73 miles (119 km) from Horsemonger Lane to Portsmouth, and with any luck the women were taken by coach, rather than having to walk. Once on board, to the horror of a bystander these 'abandoned unfortunate wretches' were allowed to parade on the deck, 'dressed in all the finery of their former depredations', their shamefully indecent behaviour and gross conversation shocking the wives and daughters of middle-class passengers, who were used to seeing working-class women as biddable servants.[14] This quotation shows the typical attitude of the respectable towards convicts, including Maria. From now on, whatever she actually did, she was tarred with the brush of a convict, seen by the middle class as uncontrollable, liable to commit all sorts of offences, probably a prostitute.

Experiment carried 136 convict women. It was an average size for a convict transport, a two-decker of 568 tons – by modern standards, a tiny ship in which to cross the world.¹⁵ Hardly any of the women would have been in a ship before; Maria, living inland in Huntingdon, Camberwell and the Surrey gaol, might never have even seen the sea. The unfortunate convicts had a baptism of fire. *Experiment* left Portsmouth on 5 December but ran into a violent gale, and was so badly damaged it had to struggle back to Portsmouth, reaching the harbour a fortnight later. A dreadful experience for the convicts, shut up below, seasick and terrified, as the ship lurched in the huge waves. Back in Portsmouth, doubtless to the women's disappointment, workmen took only a fortnight to repair the ship. HMS *Experiment* finally left England on 2 January 1804.¹⁶

The modern *Endeavour* lying off Hobart. The scene looks idyllic, but conditions were not always so balmy for Maria in her voyage across the world (Alwyn Friedersdorff)

This time there were no disasters, but *Experiment* took 174 days, over six months, to reach Sydney. The ship carried no surgeon-superintendent, so convicts did not have anyone to care for their health, insist on cleanliness, or hold classes in reading and writing. It would have been a long six months for them – those who lived. Six died on the journey, as well as four passengers. Even at the last, an adverse wind kept them outside Sydney Harbour for three days. But finally on 24 June 1804 *Experiment* entered the Heads, and on 1 July the convicts were landed, 21 of them ill, probably with scurvy after such a long period at sea without fresh fruit and vegetables. By this time, convicts who had arrived on the ship in November 1803 had been on board for eight months.¹⁷

On their arrival in the colony, female convicts were issued with a new outfit: a brown serge jacket and skirt – serge was a thick, stout material, usually made of wool, hot and uncomfortable in a Sydney summer – as well as two linen undershifts, a linen cap, stockings, shoes and a neck handkerchief.¹⁸ Most of *Experiment*'s female convicts were assigned to settlers as domestic servants. There are no specific records, but Maria Riseley was almost certainly sent out as a servant – back to the cooking, scrubbing, sweeping, washing and so on of her childhood.

Now, however, there was an extra dimension. Some, perhaps most, of the women's new masters expected their female convicts to provide sexual

Sydney at about the time Maria Riseley arrived (State Library of New South Wales)

services; at an inquiry into transportation in 1812, everyone agreed that most women lived in 'prostitution'. Men often cohabited with their female servants, said Governor Bligh. 'These things could never be prevented.'[19] Not that anyone seemed to try. To the authorities, these women were prostitutes. For the women it was, in effect, institutional rape. Their reaction is unknown, since none of them wrote about it, and no one else tried to see their point of view. Most seem to have accepted what was inevitable, do as they were told and hope for a better opportunity. Some might have detested the sex, some enjoyed it; some masters could have been attractive, some brutal; some of these liaisons ended in long-term, apparently happy relationships – but the women had little choice.

Willingly or unwillingly, Maria Riseley became pregnant, with John Thompson named as the father of her child. A convict John Thompson obtained his freedom in 1803; in 1804 probably the same John Thompson was a wharfinger in Sydney, responsible for loading and unloading goods.[20] If he were the father, Maria was probably working in central Sydney, but once pregnancy hindered her work, she was sent to the Female Factory. She probably arrived there in about April 1805, after nine months as a servant.

The sequence of events after she arrived in the Factory is not clear. The only firm facts are that Edward Lord arrived in Sydney on 21 April;

Maria's baby was born on 25 June; and Edward, Maria and baby Caroline sailed to Hobart in October. The sole version of what happened comes in John Pascoe Fawkner's memoirs, written sixty years later so not necessarily accurate, but the only story we have. As described in the Introduction, in his search for a woman Lord went to the obvious source, the Female Factory, and asked for available females to be paraded before him. He chose Maria Riseley, who was either heavily pregnant or had just given birth to another man's child.[21]

Why? Why would Edward Lord select such a woman? No one ever claimed Maria was beautiful, though the competition was probably not much better, and many of the other women were also pregnant. Perhaps Edward realised Maria's intelligence and saw, in a flash, that here was a woman whose talents would complement his. Perhaps after her respectable upbringing she looked clean and neat, or at least healthy, unlike women raised in poverty, as most convicts were. Perhaps, even if not beautiful she was alluring, had that certain look (as possibly shown to the Guildford jury), the overt sexuality which later attracted a man twenty years her junior. It could even have been love at first sight, Cupid's arrow flying across the grim setting of the Factory into Edward Lord's susceptible heart. For whatever reason, Edward's impetuosity struck again and he chose Maria – not thinking of marriage at this stage, just of obtaining a woman.

The *Sydney Gazette* announces Lord and Humphrey's arrival, April 1805

Edward's choice of Maria, a working-class woman, rather than some young lady from the elite, emphasises an unusual aspect of his makeup: he was no snob. Though, with memories of Orielton, he could doubtless lord it with the best, his intimates were not from this group. In Hobart his friends were not the more obvious 'gentlemen', like David Collins and George Harris, but those of humbler origins, William Collins and John Ingle.

Fawkner's story shows Edward choosing Maria with no hesitation, and Maria accepting as readily. The only question Edward asked was whether she would go to Van Diemen's Land with him. Learning that he was an officer – socially and professionally promising – she agreed immediately, only too glad to escape from the Factory's confinement and scanty food. The move offered her huge advantages. She could keep her baby, instead of giving it up to the orphanage where the death rate was high. An officer was a real catch. Life with him promised at least comfort, and possible wealth. Convict women were almost inevitably taken as mistresses by some man or other, and it was far better to be with an officer than just another struggling settler or ex-convict. Maria was two years older than Edward, but she solved that problem by taking two years off her age from then on.

Fawkner hinted at another problem, harder to solve: 'She was at once let out, and he took possession of her, as truly for a slave to do his behests, or suffer for neglect or refusal'. A slave. Edward was hot-tempered and dealt firmly with anyone who opposed him. As a convict Maria had in practice no power, no rights, still only able to rely on her own capabilities to protect her. But the difficulties this situation might throw up would not have been obvious that day in the Factory. Instead, Edward must have seemed like a knight errant, an unexpected lottery win – appearing out of the blue to rescue Maria from the ranks of scorned convict drudges. Once she was the mistress of an officer, she was assigned to him as a 'servant' and the convict system had no further interest in her (unless she committed an offence, and since she was a sensible woman there was no chance of that). Practically, she was free again.

Maria's baby was born in June, and registered as the daughter of John Thompson and Maria Risley. She was baptised Carolina Maria Risley, though she was known as Caroline.[22] Maria after her mother, of course, but there was no Caroline in the family. Perhaps Maria just liked the name.

Above: Maria Riseley's convict record: empty. She committed no offences to be recorded, but nothing else was put on paper, not her arrival in Hobart in 1805 nor her pardon in 1808 (Tasmanian Archive and Heritage Office)

Fortunately, Caroline was pretty and pleasant, and Edward was fond of her, treating her as his daughter, Miss Caroline Lord. He gave up his plan to visit England, for he could hardly take his convict mistress and her daughter with him. As Governor King explained tactfully to Collins, Lord decided not to proceed to England and told your adjutant the cause; King had had a convict mistress himself and quite understood.[23]

There was another reason for returning to Hobart. At some stage it dawned on Edward Lord that he could circumvent the rules forbidding officers to trade by setting up shop in his mistress's name. Was this in the back of his mind all along, or did he see promise in Maria's intelligence and toughness? Or was it her idea? This was Fawkner's version. Being a worldly wise woman, he wrote, Maria 'set herself to make a house, and to provide means for herself, her children, and her master. She foresaw that much money was to be made, and how: she, by the credit of her master, and her own tact, and shrewdness, obtained a quantity of goods, and proceeded, with these under her control, to Hobart Town'.[24]

Perhaps setting up a shop was Maria's idea, but this seems unlikely, since she had never been to Hobart and knew nothing about it. If George Harris, no businessman, realised the potential of Hobart, Edward Lord, much more business-minded, certainly did. At all events either he, Maria or both decided to open a shop in Hobart in her name. They bought stock to take down, and Edward also took a flock of ewes; Governor King, impressed with this energy, gave him a ram as well. Lord and Humphrey applied to King for more land at Hobart and King agreed, since the two men had a large percentage of the breeding stock there.[25]

With baby Caroline, Edward and Maria left Sydney on 3 October 1805. They went via Norfolk Island, where they bought more stores for the shop. Finally they reached Hobart on 28 November.[26] For Maria, an eight-week trip with a baby would have had its difficulties; but travel as an officer's mistress was still far better than as one of 136 women on a crowded convict transport. She had already risen in the world.

4. SETTING UP SHOP

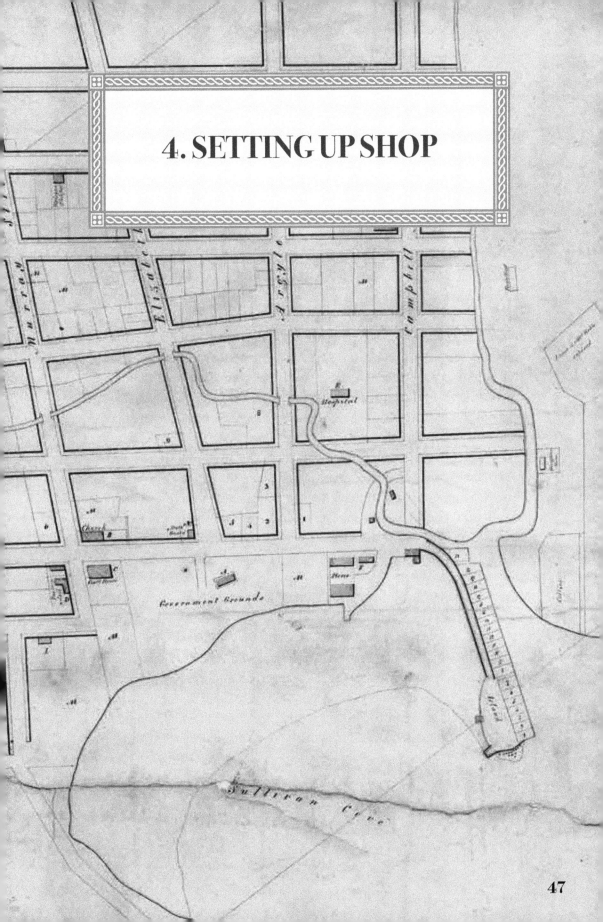

WHEN EDWARD LORD ARRIVED BACK in Hobart in November 1805 after eight months away, he found that no progress had been made. 'The Governor and his chosen associates indulging in vice and idleness, taking no thought of to-morrow; provisions running short', wrote Fawkner in disgust. 'No ploughing, no horses, no bullocks, not even asses – except we may class some of those as asses who should have guided the course of affairs entrusted to their feeble hands in a better manner than they did.'[1]

George Harris agreed: 'Times are very much altered here for the worse'. Life was dull. Hunting, fishing and shooting were the only recreations. There was no 'society'; George and his wife, a respectable lady, could not visit most other officers because they lived with mistresses. Not that there was much to discuss at such events, except last night's robberies. Harris had read and reread the township's few books, and could not even enjoy his favourite occupation, sketching, for want of paper and paints.[2] Not everyone was bored, though. Parson Knopwood enjoyed dining and drinking with friends, gardening, hunting, fishing and, occasionally, his religious duties. His was the happy temperament that can gain satisfaction from life's day-to-day pleasures.

Hunger might have played a part in Harris' grumpiness. The British government provided founding settlements like Collins' with supplies for three years, presumably thinking that by the time they were finished, the colony would be feeding itself. The lords of the British government were not farmers. Nor were the officers who commanded such expeditions, or most of their colonists. Attempts at farming in Hobart were limited and half-hearted, and Fawkner said supplies were squandered, with the governor and his favourites taking all they wanted, and other people using all sorts of tricks to obtain extra.[3]

Once supplies gave out, the colony suffered serious famine. In June 1805 Collins reported that they were running low. London told him to apply to Sydney for anything he needed, but Governor King said he had little to spare. In Hobart, most local sources of food were limited. The little barley grown made such hard rolls that troops threw them at the commissary. Whale flesh tasted good, but few whales were caught. The one fishing net

Previous pages: Hobart after 1811, showing land grants. Lord has grants number 4, on Macquarie Street, opposite the later town hall; and 9, on the corner of Elizabeth and Collins streets (Tasmanian Archive and Heritage Office)

wore out. Colonists collected wild parsley and a sage-like shrub known as Botany Bay greens, but there was not enough to help much. The only abundant local food was kangaroo, which kept starvation at bay but was challenging for people used to a wheat-based diet. 'I may truly say the Colony was in a very dreadful distress and visible in every countenance', wrote Knopwood. 'Had it not have been for the good success in killing Kangarros, the Colony would have been destitute of Everything.'[4]

Alcohol ran out, too: in August Knopwood reported that not a glass of spirits was to be had, a further catastrophe for this hard-drinking society. The colonists were without almost every comfort, wrote Harris. 'We have been 6 or 8 weeks together without a morsel of Bread of any kind – during which we have lived on Coffee made with bran without Sugar[,] & Kanguroo fried in rancid pork in lieu of bread ... We have neither Tea Sugar Coffee

Right: Another reason for George Harris' dissatisfaction was his small house, which he called a two-roomed hovel 'the size of a nutshell'. The man with the herd of animals is well-placed to ward off starvation, however
(National Library of Australia nla.pic-an5380489)

Below: Harris' sketch of a kangaroo outside an early Hobart house – probably eating new shoots in the garden
(State Library of New South Wales)

Soap Candles Oil Wine, Spirits Beer Paper Cheese Butter or *Money*'. People became too weak to work, domestic animals began to die.[5] Even Edward Lord went hungry:

> During the great scarcity, we lived for thirteen months, except at small intervals, upon two pounds [roughly a kilogram] of biscuit a week [and] the wild game of the country; the people certainly suffered very great inconvenience, and very great privations from want of provision; I have often myself been glad to go to bed from want of bread, and have very often been without the little comforts of wine and sugar.[6]

HOBART, SMALL AND HUNGRY, would have appalled most newcomers, but to Maria Riseley it was a land of opportunity. Here she had a chance to use her talents, impossible in England, where she had no money or backing. As with most women at this time, her success came through a man, with Edward Lord providing the finance.

Maria set up her shop soon after she arrived in Hobart in December 1805, for she was well established by the following June. Shopkeeping was a haphazard business: buy any goods anywhere possible, then sell them for as much as the market would bear. Hobart's handful of shopkeepers had to be alert at all times. There were four: settlers William Collins and John Ingle, convict James Lord (no relation) and Maria Riseley. There are reports, mainly later from Bligh, that William Collins and Edward Lord were partners, and perhaps by 1809 they had merged their interests. Maria still seems to have run the shop; Collins had plenty of other activities, such as whaling.

There was no reliable source of goods. Traders could bring goods from Britain, but that was a once-only opportunity. Clearing sales were held when people left the colony or died, but these were rare. Ingle's family sent him goods from Britain, but ships were too few for this to be really helpful.[7] Traders could order goods from Sydney merchants, but their prices were high. The major source of goods was speculative cargoes brought by ships' captains. Merchants kept a sharp eye for ships. William Collins climbed Mount Direction to try to glimpse a rumoured arrival, and Edward Lord sailed down the Derwent to meet another. One such trip was alarming. When he was returning at night from visiting a whaling ship, a whale chased his boat and struck its fins at it. Fortunately, it missed.[8]

Harris's sketch of Hobart, winter 1805 or 1806, with many buildings named. Edward Lord does not rate a mention: perhaps his house was invisible from Harris's viewpoint (National Library of Australia nla.pic-an5576203)

Ship's captains could be tough hagglers, and in 1809 one left Hobart for Sydney with most of his cargo of rice, sugar and tea unsold, his prices too high for local merchants. There was also competition in the colony. At a clearing sale in 1806, Edward bought a pound of tea for the enormous price of six guineas, doubtless against spirited bidding. Not that he would have paid in cash. Money was short and barter more likely. Harris and a ship's captain exchanged kangaroo meat for flour, pound for pound – a real coup for Harris.[9]

Despite the problems, Maria Riseley flourished. She proved a natural businesswoman, skilled and capable, with what Fawkner called 'tact' – an innate skill at negotiation with people, at pleasing her customers.[10] Though probably illiterate, or nearly so, when she arrived in Hobart, she needed to read and write to conduct a business and learnt these skills; she could at least sign her name in 1808. Perhaps Edward or a clerk taught her (in a similar situation, Edward's friend Joseph Foveaux taught his mistress to write).[11]

Maria's convict status did not matter in business. With the vast majority of the population convicts, ex-convicts or convicts' families, people had to work with them and accept them as part of the community.

Hobart never saw the fierce convict-versus-free division of Sydney, partly because fewer ex-convicts became wealthy enough to be resented, and partly because no governor favoured them (as Macquarie did in Sydney), which encouraged dissent. Convict traders like Maria Riseley and James Lord were treated the same as free men like John Ingle and William Collins – and Maria, who was both a convict and a woman, gained just as much respect as anyone else, despite these disabilities. It was definitely looked on as her business from the start: people were in 'my employ', she wrote, and Fawkner was sure she was in charge.[12]

A shop needed to be more central than Lord's original 'house in the woods'. He owned two blocks in central Hobart: one on Macquarie Street between Elizabeth and Argyle streets, and another on the corner of Collins and Elizabeth Streets. The site of the Lords' later house, on the corner of Argyle and Macquarie streets, was granted to John Ingle, but in 1811 surveyor James Meehan described it as Ingle's, 'formerly Lords'.[13] It is not clear on which of these three blocks Lord built his first shop, but they were all excellently positioned for trade, in the centre of the small town and near the harbour.

In this shop Maria started to sell the stock the Lords had brought with them, mainly maize from Norfolk Island for a penny a pint. Flour had run out by now, and everyone had to buy grain. Since the colony had no flourmill, grain was ground through a steel handmill, then sifted through a sieve of kangaroo skin, the holes made by the prongs of a red-hot fork – a triumph of improvisation in this little settlement, so poorly equipped that it did not even have a proper sieve. The flour was gritty and coarse, and the bread heavy and unpleasantly sweet, but it had to be eaten as there was nothing else.[14]

This was bad enough, but in March 1806 the Hawkesbury River in New South Wales flooded. Crops were badly damaged and the harvest was tiny. Hobart people were horrified: 'at once starvation looked us full in the face'. Maria Riseley raised her prices from a penny a pint to half a guinea, 126 pennies, reported Fawkner. There were still plenty of eager purchasers, even though some of the maize was mouldy. Fawkner depicted her as the chief villain in the price racket, charging the outrageous price of six guineas for a pound of tea, for a woman having a baby and desperate for a cup. But this was the price the Lords themselves had to pay at the clearing sale, and if it was the same packet of tea Maria was actually generous, charging only what she had paid for it. Fawkner made no allowances for her, however, scornfully referring to her as 'the marine officer's madam', using the word 'madam' to imply 'mistress'.¹⁵

Other shopkeepers were even more rapacious. Some bought supplies from whalers and sold ship's biscuits at four for £1, perhaps forty times their usual price. 'Such was the hunger that men threw down their pound notes and snatched at the four biscuits, for fear someone would come in and offer more money.' John Ingle made an even better percentage. At Rio de Janeiro on the voyage out, he bought a 60-inch strip of tobacco for three and a half pence. By 1806 he was the only one in the colony with tobacco for sale. 'Such was the madness of smokers' he could ask his own price – five shillings an inch, over a thousand times the price he had paid for it.¹⁶

Harris's exquisite painting of speckled manakins (spotted pardalotes) from 'Hospital Hill', Hobart, 1806. Hunter Island is visible in the river, as is evidence of industry in the stumps of trees (State Library of New South Wales)

All these activities were, if extortionate, at least legal. But Edward Lord, and probably other traders too, went further. The government store provided colonists with their rations and was not meant to operate as a shop, though it did: visiting ships bought goods such as fresh kangaroo meat, and Governor Collins allowed his officers to buy for their own use. In December 1805, just when Maria was starting her shop, Edward bought 50 pounds (23 kg) of sugar, 50 pounds of soap and a pound of pins. In February he bought 50 pounds of flour – a particularly lucky buy, just before news arrived of the Hawkesbury disaster.¹⁷ These are large amounts for one small household (the soap and pins in particular would take years to use); it seems likely that he bought the goods for the shop. However, these large purchases then stopped. Perhaps such illegal activity was too much, even for Hobart in 1806.

The highest profits came from selling spirits, mostly rum. This was essential in the colony, both for drinking and as currency. Prices were high.

Knopwood's bland description of Edward Lord smuggling
(University of Tasmania Library Special & Rare Collections)

Fawkner told how a convict bought a bottle of brandy to celebrate gaining his freedom. Maria charged him £7 – 'seven pounds sterling!'[18] But other merchants would have been unlikely to charge less.

They united to keep prices high. In March 1807, when the famine was at its peak, a rumour that a ship was arriving caused excitement, as surely any ship would carry some food. The governor sent a boat to investigate, but it saw nothing. 'It cast a general damp upon the whole Colony', reported Knopwood. At first light next day, Edward Lord sailed down the Derwent to the ship, which had a cargo of cattle, rice and rum. That evening Knopwood dined with the governor, the ship's captain and Lieutenant Johnson; next day he was 'very unwell'. There was no divine service that Sunday, and Knopwood reported himself 'unwell' for days on end.[19]

He was not alone. According to Fawkner, Maria Riseley and three other merchants united in buying all the rum they could from the ship's captain. They sold it at four times the price they paid, a good profit. Scarcely a sober man could be seen for nearly six weeks. 'The rum was poured into tubs and buckets and bailed out in tin pannicans in front of almost every tent and hut', wrote Fawkner, and the young boy was shocked to see men sitting, lying or rolling about drunk, all over the camp. Officers, marines and all joined in this drunken revelry. He was, however, impressed with the women's behaviour. Some female convicts overindulged, but not one free woman was seen drunk.[20] It sounds as if Maria stayed relatively sober, which was apparently normal for her. No one ever complained that she overindulged in alcohol.

Customs duties, the government's main source of revenue, would have lessened merchants' profits, but they avoided them by smuggling. That upright serving officer in His Majesty's armed forces, Lieutenant Edward Lord, engaged in smuggling. In October 1807, Knopwood noted in his diary, 'Lt Lord landed a Cask of Spirits from HM ship Porpus [*Porpoise*] without any permitt. his man came past my House with it in a Barrow'. Magistrate

Knopwood did nothing about this, merely noting it. Governor Collins tried to crack down on smuggling, and on several occasions the military patrol seized spirits on which duty had not been paid. As a magistrate, Knopwood had to inquire about one such batch. 'I could not fix it that it was going on Board the Ship, therefore ordered it to be returnd', he wrote: no one was going to be punished.[21]

Quite immune from punishment was Matthew Power, husband of the governor's mistress. He bought goods from a leading Sydney merchant, paying with bills of exchange. Someone fraudulently altered a bill from £138 to £538. The merchant accused Power, and the judge advocate in Sydney ordered Hobart magistrates to send Power to Sydney if they found him guilty of fraud. They did find him guilty, but Collins stepped in. Power was never sent to Sydney or punished.[22]

Governor Collins might not have been involved in dirty work himself – he told his brother that following their father's sterling example he had never taken sixpence of government money or made anything through 'disgraceful traffic', though there were plenty of opportunities – but he allowed others to get away with it. Some people complained, but only to themselves or relations. 'They call it the end of the world', wrote James Grove, an educated convict transported for counterfeiting bank notes, 'and for vice it is truly so, as here wickedness flourishes almost unchecked ... words are considered but wind, and strict regard for truth is generally unknown'.[23]

The few merchants in the town had the situation nicely sewn up. They had no fear of punishment, they had cornered the market, and they were making excellent profits. George Harris was disgusted. 'Every prospect at present of making Money seems further off', he wrote; 'all means of doing so being monopolized by one or two individuals' – Edward Lord being one.[24]

Lord did not ignore other ways of making money. He continued to sell kangaroo meat to the government, employing ex-marine Hugh Germain to go hunting for him with two convicts. Each month they would bring in a thousand pounds of meat, Germain recalled, for which Lord received £75, about £900 a year. He would have paid Germain and fed and clothed the convicts, and probably not every month was so profitable, but hunting still brought in an excellent income. Germain's party carried two books, the Bible and *The Arabian Nights*. As they went further afield searching for kangaroo, they named new places from these books.[25] This explains the biblical and middle-eastern names – Bagdad, Jerusalem, Jericho – which dot Tasmania's southern midlands, an unexpected legacy of Edward Lord's entrepreneurial activity. Lord himself saw a good deal of the island. In 1812 he told a parliamentary enquiry in London that apart from the west coast, the island was 'pretty generally known by the inhabitants ... I have myself been a good deal in the interior'.[26]

Perhaps sometimes he himself went hunting. In May 1806 'a gentleman of Van Diemen's Land' wrote an article for London's *Sporting Magazine*. 'Although not much of a huntsman before I left Europe', he found hunting in Van Diemen's Land 'the grandest sport of the field that can be imagined'. Four gentlemen employed huntsmen to obtain kangaroo meat, which they sold in huge quantities to the commissariat. It made a particularly rich and delicious soup, which took the place of bread for settlers. None of Harris' complaints here: the author makes kangaroo sound a perfectly adequate replacement for bread.

Dogs were vital to the hunt, so highly valued that when hard running made their feet sore, their owners made them boots of leather. Kangaroos often attacked them viciously, and garments protected these wounds too. One of the author's dogs had not only the boots, but a leather collar to protect scars at his neck, while his hide was 'so cut and sewed up in all directions' that he looked as if he was from a different species.

There are a few hints as to the author's identity: he employed huntsmen, he owned dogs, he wrote fluently, he was so enthusiastic about the colony he claimed emu fat was equal to the finest butter. He could have been Edward Lord, who fits all four categories, or he could have been Adolarius Humphrey. Whoever wrote it, the article brings to life the fun these young men had, chasing kangaroos and emus across 'the finest tillage and grazing land on this side of the line [Equator]', risking with relish 'difficulties of the extremest nature': 'expence, fatigue and danger'.[27]

Knopwood's diary entry describing churching Maria and dining with Maria, Edward and his friend l'Anson the surgeon (University of Tasmania Library Special & Rare Collections)

MEANWHILE, MARIA RISELEY WAS BUSY, not only with her shop, but at home – organising Edward's household, caring for little Caroline. The Lords employed convicts, probably including a woman to help Maria. A strange situation, since Maria was still a convict herself, as everyone in Hobart knew. Maria's second baby, Elizabeth, was born in August 1806, but died two days later. Maria's third daughter, also called Elizabeth but known as Eliza, was born by 1 January 1808, when Knopwood named the child. Ten days later he churched 'Lt Lords friend'. The churching of women, a religious ceremony for women giving thanks after child-birth, was already going out of fashion.

Neither Edward nor Maria ever showed much interest in religion, and the churching indicates that someone, probably Edward, wanted to be respectable – an unusual desire in a distant convict colony, with two of the participants a convict mistress and an illegitimate baby. But at least Maria was respectably churched. As well as being named, Eliza was baptised, a pleasant occasion at the Lord home.[28] Elizabeth was the name of Edward's grandmother, presumably the reason he chose it, in his family-minded way.

In 1807 the Lords moved outside town. Another officer lived in a comfortable whitewashed lath and plaster house in Sandy Bay, a little south of the main township. It had a shingled roof and five rooms with proper floors (a step up from a thatched roof and dirt floors), and the property included a barn, some cultivated land and a garden. The officer left and Lord rented the house, a pleasant home for Maria and the children.[29] Doubtless, however, they kept their shop in central Hobart.

Maria sounds a capable housekeeper. Edward was a hospitable man who enjoyed good living, in the Owen tradition. On his birthday in 1807 he held a large dinner with seven guests: the other two lieutenants, two doctors, George Harris, Leonard Fosbrook and Knopwood (but not Governor Collins). In the middle of a famine it would have been difficult to provide a celebratory birthday dinner for eight, but Maria managed. Edward's hospitality extended even to unknown unfortunates. When two sailors were killed whaling and had no relatives or friends to offer hospitality after their funerals, Edward did this.[30]

Socially, Maria was not accepted by the respectable ladies, but these were so few they were probably more lonely than convict mistresses. There were enough of these to form quite a coterie – Hannah Power with the governor, Maria Riseley with Edward Lord, and the female companions of

Parson Knopwood and at least three other officers. Of all these illicit couples, Fawkner singled out Edward Lord's activities as the worst – living with his convict woman 'in an outrageously wild manner'.[31] Drinking? Dancing on tabletops? Wild parties? The mind boggles. Writing his memories in middle age, Fawkner did have some documents to guide him, but obviously none relevant to this description, and he probably exaggerated. No other evidence even hints that Maria Riseley lived in anything but a busy, conventional way and, like most of the other mistresses, she stayed with her partner for many years, both apparently faithful to each other. Perhaps Fawkner was so caustic because Maria was a convict, unlike the others who were convicts' wives or daughters, technically free women. He should have thought better of Edward and Maria, who were not actually committing adultery, unlike most others – but no one seemed to worry about that.

In his diary, Knopwood described a fascinating drinking party. One evening he visited his friend convict James Grove, who privately disapproved of immorality but was forced to condone it. They were joined by Matthew and Hannah Power, and Governor Collins and his daughter by a previous relationship, visiting from Sydney: so the group comprised the governor, his present mistress, her husband, his daughter by a former mistress, a convict and the clergyman, all drinking rum together. The next Sunday, Knopwood preached a sermon on Conscience. It seemed to have no effect. There was a flurry in 1807 when David Collins' wife suggested joining him from London. 'I shall welcome her with open Arms', David wrote to his mother, presumably planning on emptying those arms of their current occupant first.[32] However, Mrs Collins decided against the long journey.

IN 1807 NEW COMMERCIAL OPPORTUNITIES beckoned for the Lords. Hobartians were amazed at the arrival of Lieutenant Laycock, who travelled overland from the northern settlement at Port Dalrymple, established in 1804. It too was starving, and Laycock was in search of food. Governor Collins had none to spare, but a route was established between Hobart and the north, much the same as the present highway. Several parties made the journey later that year, 'a march of 10 Days thro the finest Country in the World', as Harris wrote. The Lords used the new route to extend their trading activities. Edward later commented that, so open was the country, the first loaded cart was driven to Port Dalrymple without a tree having to be felled.[33] Perhaps he or Maria travelled with the cart, laden with their goods.

Lord was also keen to acquire more land. Collins organised 100-acre grants for his officers, and gave Humphrey and Lord increased town allotments. The 1807 muster showed Lord owning 200 acres, 43 cattle, 195 sheep and 11 pigs, more than anyone else. Still not satisfied, he asked his brother in England to try and get him a larger grant. Professionally he also prospered, for his superior officers were recalled to England, leaving 26-year-old Lieutenant Lord second in command.34 He and Collins co-operated well, their earlier quarrel forgotten. Now with a convict mistress of his own, Lord could hardly criticise David Collins and Hannah Power.

By late 1807 the whole colony was in a better situation. The threat of famine had eased, with crops promising. Farming was developing as convicts with seven-year sentences gained their freedom, and many were given small land grants. John Pascoe Fawner helped his father on their farm. Wheat was difficult to grow, wrote John, but sheep, goats and cattle increased wonderfully on the plentiful grass. Whaling brought ships to Hobart, reflected in the name of Hobart's first pub, *The Sign of the Whale Fishery* – and among the diners on the opening night were Edward Lord, Knopwood and their friends.35 It looked as if the little settlement had turned the corner after the starvation years. However, new challenges were just around the corner.

Roseneath Ferry, near where the Fawkner family had their farm.
Reality was not quite so idyllic for them (Allport Library and Museum of Fine Arts, TAHO)

married by Banns at Hobart River Derwent, Van Diemens Land this thirteenth day of June in the year of Our Lord One Thousand eight hundred and Eight

By me Robert Knopwood

This marriage was } John Drurance
Solemnised between } Harriet McCarty

In the presence of } Robert Hay
Francis Barnes

This is to Certify that John Duncombe Single man and Elizabeth Hambley Single woman, both of this Town were married by Banns at Hobart Town River Derwent Van Diemens Land, this Twenty Seventh day of June in the year of Our Lord One Thousand Eight hundred and Eight

By me Robert Knopwood

This marriage was } John Duncombe
Solemnised between } Elizabeth X Hambley
mark

In the presence of } William X Slator
mark
Francis Barnes

This is to Certify that Thomas Williams Single man and Frances Readon Single woman, both of this Town were married by Banns at Hobart Town River Derwent Van Diemens Land, this Eighth day of August in the year of Our Lord One Thousand Eight hundred and Eight

By me Robert Knopwood

This marriage was } Thomas X Williams
his mark
Solemnised between } Frances X Readon
her mark

In the presence of } Jos. McCauley Sergt R.M.
Francis Barnes

60

5. MARRIAGE

This is to Certify that _Thomas William Birch_ Single man and _Sarah Guest_, Single woman, both of this Town, were married by Banns at _Hobart Town_, River Derwent Van Diemens Land, this _Twelfth_ day of _September_ in the year of Our Lord One thousand Eight hundred and Eight

By me   Robert Knopwood

This Marriage was Solemnised between } Thomas William Birch
Sarah Guest.

In the presence of } Jonathan Taylor.
Francis Barnes

(A return sent to England 16 Sept 1808.)

This is to certify that _Edward Lord_ Single man and _Maria Risley_, Single woman both of this Town were married by _Licence_ at _Hobart Town_, River Derwent, Van Diemens Land this _Eight_ day of _October_, in the year of Our Lord, One thousand Eight hundred and Eight.

By me   Robert Knopwood.

This Marriage was Solemnised between } Edward Lord
Maria Risley

In the presence of } Wm Collins
Francis Barnes

Married by me
Revd Robert Knopwood. M.A.

EDWARD LORD'S FIRST SURVIVING LETTER dates from 1807. It was largely about Norfolk Islanders, convicts who in the early 1790s were sent from Sydney to fertile Norfolk Island, where they settled down comfortably. But the British government found the colony disappointing and difficult to run, and in 1804 ordered the reluctant population to Van Diemen's Land. Despite delaying actions, they arrived from late 1807. Hobart received 554 newcomers, doubling the population.

From far-off London, the British government bribed Norfolk Islanders to go quietly with promises of land, houses, tools, convict labour, provisions and clothes. This provided Governor Collins with a dilemma, for he had little but land to give them. He did provide some sheep and cattle, but the Norfolk Islanders claimed they were cheated out of them.[1] Collins put the animals in the charge of Edward Lord, 'although he knew nothing of the duties he undertook', said Fawkner. Day-to-day care was in the hands of ex-convict Denis McCarty. These men's own herds increased wonderfully while the government herds dwindled, owing to 'Sleight of Hand Tricks' such as separating newborn calves from their mothers and keeping them.

Previous pages: A copy of Edward and Maria Lord's marriage certificate (Tasmanian Archive and Heritage Office)

Left: Sydney receives news of Norfolk Islanders being taken to Van Diemen's Land, though their reluctance to leave was not of course reported (*Sydney Gazette*, 12 June 1808)

Below: *Lady Nelson*, which brought many Norfolk Islanders to Van Diemen's Land (Tasmaniana Library)

Disgruntled settlers claimed that McCarty, who had been unable to afford a pair of shoes, could 'sport the money in Lt Lords shop by the Hundreds'.[2] Several sources told a similar tale and it was probably at least partly true – the type of corrupt activity a governor should have stopped. There was a division between the new arrivals and the old hands, 'Derwenters' seeing the newcomers as interlopers, Norfolkers viewing Derwenters as a bunch of thieves. 'You cant conceive the extent to which Robberies are carried on here, a great many persons from Norfolk have been robbed', wrote one newcomer to another.[3]

Among the Norfolkers were John Folley and his servant Thomas Keston, whose 'Secret Memoirs' give a frank view of activities. Folley was unhappy with his land grant at Sandy Bay, and Edward Lord persuaded him to exchange it for his own 100-acre grant in what is now South Hobart, which Lord privately regarded as worthless (reported Keston). Folley and Keston felled trees, cleared ground and sowed crops, but little grew and they realised there was no good land on the farm. Folley sold it and took up bricklaying.[4] More sharp practice by Lord.

Keston was not impressed by Governor Collins and 'his so much beloved chandlers' – merchants like Lord. They neglected their duty for their private concerns, did not allow small settlers a fair share of the market, took government goods for their own use, and gave sham trials and severe punishments to anyone who opposed them. As a Norfolk Islander, Keston could ask the governor for land. Petitioners had to catch him in the street and note how he took his snuff, said Keston, 'for if you see him put it up his nostrils by handfuls, it was the best way to leave him for that day'. Keston saw Collins shovelling up snuff and hesitated, but his friends urged him on – 'Go now, he will soon be off, go now you fool you, he will soon be housed and you will not see him to-day any more' – and he asked for a grant. Collins 'look'd on me with all the disdain imaginable', but gave Keston land at Brown's River (Kingston). Now owning land, Keston was put 'off the stores' – given no more rations – though this was not disastrous, as when he was on the stores, often there was nothing but 'stinking kangaroo'. Farming was hard work. He managed to build a hut, clear four acres and sow wheat, as well as start a garden, but at first he had no income and lived on kangaroo rats, bandicoots, native cats and devils, and turnip tops and stinging nettles from his garden.[5] Keston's story shows the contrast between the hard lives of the convict and ex-convict population and the elite who, in the way of elites, tried to keep all the privileges for themselves.

THE NORFOLK ISLANDERS did provide Hobart with one enormous advantage: women. They included many families, whose eldest daughters were in their mid-teens. Old enough, by the standards of the day, for marrying or taking as a mistress. Margaret Eddington, known as Peggy, was born on Norfolk Island in 1793, the daughter of two convicts. Her father died, and it is not clear what happened to Peggy, her mother Elizabeth and her young brother. Rumour said that Peggy caught the eye of the commandant, Captain John Piper, a charming, handsome man twenty years her senior with a taste for young girls. Peggy gave birth to a son, John, and in 1808 the family arrived in Hobart: Elizabeth; Peggy, aged fifteen; her brother John, thirteen; and baby John.

Fawkner was disgusted. Soon after the Eddingtons arrived, he wrote, 52-year-old Governor Collins, 'this bigamist or debauchee', sent away his mistress in favour of 'a good-looking young girl just arrived from Norfolk Island and reported to have been the mistress of Commandant Piper at that island'.[6] All this provides the background to Edward Lord's letter.

Lord had met Piper in 1805, when he stopped at Norfolk Island on the way from Sydney to Hobart. They became friendly, exchanging newsy letters. In December 1807, just after the first boatload of Norfolk Islanders arrived on *Lady Nelson*, Lord wrote to Piper. The letter tells us a good deal about the man. Lord's writing style was fluent, with correct spelling and grammar; his education had been good enough, though the letter needs some full stops added for clarity. He grovelled shamelessly to Piper, a superior officer who might be useful; and showed good wishes to the Norfolk Island settlers, which might have been genuine but also might have been put on for Piper's benefit. Perhaps Lord was offering to help the Eddingtons, which he certainly did in later years. Nothing, of course, was written down about mistresses, illegitimate children and so on. (Captain Kent commanded the *Lady Nelson*.)

Hobart Town River Derwent 5th December 1807

Dear Piper

I received your kind letter of the 8th Ult. by our Friend Kent; and was glad to learn from him that you were in good health[.] I was also glad to find the Norfolk Setters had given preference to this place [rather than Port Dalrymple] tho' the specimens we received p^r Lady Nelson are not of the most eligible description yet as I know there are many respectable and deserving ones

New Norfolk, where many Norfolk Islanders were settled. As usual, the scene looks far more tame and life far easier and prettier than reality (Allport Library and Museum of Fine Arts, TAHO)

> to come[.] I earnestly trust their removal will be attended with benefit to themselves and advantage to our Infant Settlement[.] should you wish some little assistance or attention (that might lay within my power) shewn to any I beg you'll command me as nothing would give me greater pleasure than alleviating in some degree the loss they must sustain by the removal from their revered Commander protector and friend.

Now comes the fulsome flattery, typical of not only Edward Lord but of many junior officers to their superiors:

> My visit to Norfolk Island I look on as one of the most fortunate circumstances that has befallen me since my arrival in this distant and savage clime as it not only introduced me to him I shall ever esteem but convinc'd me at the same time that it does not depend on country or climate whether mankind is to be happy or miserable[.] the former appear'd to reign in its greatest splendour entirely owing to the goodness of One Man whose good offices and friendship I shall always be proud to acknowledge and ever gratefully bear in remembrance[.]

Lord tried to put Piper under an obligation:

> I should be glad to offer something more convincing than words therefore earnestly intreat if I can in any instance whatsoever be of the least service you will not for a moment hesitate commanding my services as I assure you the pleasure and real

> satisfaction will be twofold on my part[.] Kent mentioned your intention of sending some Asses to this place for disposal which he said "in your hurry of business you had omitted mentioning" you may rely on my using every exertion in disposing of them (or anything else you might wish to send) to the greatest advantage

Lord hoped for a letter soon from Piper, and concluded:

> I find I have not time to say anything about myself as the Lady Nelson sails in a few hours but my next shall contain a few repetitions of the nominative singular in the mean time I take my leave and allow me to subscribe myself with sentiments of respect and esteem
>
> My dear Piper
> Your faithful Friend
> and very oblig'd Servant
> Edward Lord
>
> Excuse the Paper as it is very scarce and the best I have got –
>
> [Illegible word, Captain?] Kent just mentioned that Paint Oil is very scarce at Norfolk (and that you have a boat wants painting) I have therefore taken the liberty of troubling him with a small jar for you, which request you'll do me the honor of accepting[7]

Why would Captain Kent mention that paint oil was scarce and Piper had a boat needing painting – especially when his ship was about to sail, with all a departure's last-minute flurry and bustle? It seems likely that Lord was urging him: what can I give Piper that will put him under an obligation to me? What does he need? Come on, there must be *something* Maria has in the shop that he wants. Ah, paint oil, just the thing. A small jar will do.

ABOUT THE TIME PIPER RECEIVED THIS LETTER, Collins was facing a worse problem than complaining Norfolk Islanders. It centred on his superior officer, Governor William Bligh: an outstanding sailor, an efficient organiser, but a horrific boss, whose subordinates dreaded his violent temper, bullying and nagging. This was a time when leaders were leaders, with no sentimental nonsense about consultation, but Bligh's history of three mutinies and a long series of problems, even court cases, involving subordinate officers suggests he took his position to extremes. However, his superiors admired him, particularly his brilliant navigation of 3618 miles in an open boat to safety after the *Bounty* mutiny. In 1806 he arrived in Sydney as governor, sent to stop corruption, specifically rum trafficking.

Sydney's officers and traders had no intention of taking this lying down. They had tamed previous governors and intended to continue. Bligh gave firm orders – no illicit stills, no bartering in spirits, tighter government control – but played into his opponents' hands by his own corrupt activities, organising large land grants and plentiful convict labour for himself, putting himself above the law, declaring, 'The law, Sir! Damn the law: my will is the law'. He interfered with the New South Wales Corps and tried to curb powerful settlers, but here too gave his opponents ammunition by his misuse of authority. However, there were two sides to the conflict, and it can be convincingly argued that Bligh's actions either did or did not justify rebellion.[8]

In January 1808, matters came to a climax when Bligh threatened to imprison six officers for treason. Major George Johnston, commander of the New South Wales Corps, deposed him and took over as acting governor. The news reached Hobart on 1 March, at the same time as three local men who had captured one bushranger and killed another. They brought in their prisoner, whom they forced to carry his mate's head in a bag – a day of unusual excitement for Hobart.[9]

A cartoon of Bligh's arrest by the rebels, making him look undignified, trying to hide under the bed. They actually found him behind his bed, not much of an improvement
(State Library of New South Wales)

The dramatic news of Bligh's overthrow created a dilemma for his subordinate officials. Their clear duty was to support Bligh. Otherwise they risked serious career damage, since the British government must surely punish rebellion. But now they depended on the rebels for vital supplies, while the British government was slow to react (a replacement governor did not arrive for two years): obviously not too worried, almost giving tacit acceptance to the rebels. To complicate matters for Collins, no one in Hobart knew what had really happened – 'what the particular acts are I do not know, as I have heard so many & various different reports', Harris wrote – or how securely the rebels held power.[10] It would be disastrous to support them but see Bligh seize control again, breathing vengeance.

However, at least Collins had distance in his favour. In obscure Hobart he was able to sit on the fence. When Johnston sent a friendly letter offering supplies – a pleasant change, after meagre help from King and Bligh – Collins responded positively. He also sent Bligh a private letter of support. And, as a third action, Edward Lord went to Sydney, presumably sent by Collins to find out what was going on. He arrived in May 1808.[11] Whatever his instructions from Collins, he sided with the rebels. He did not seem to consider his career; possibly he was already planning to resign from the marines and concentrate on making money in Australia.

Lord had a stroke of luck when Major Joseph Foveaux returned to Sydney from leave in England. Senior to Johnston, Foveaux took over and proved a competent administrator. He and Lord, similar men, became friends. As Foveaux's biographer put it, he 'could convince himself that his duty was always consistent with personal advantage', and the same went for Lord (and many other officials). Both men were ambitious; both viewed Collins with contempt, with Foveaux at least scheming to replace him; and both suffered from asthma, a rare enough disease for a sympathetic swapping of remedies with a fellow-sufferer to be welcome. Lord was quick to capitalise on this opportunity. Either Johnston or, more probably, Foveaux gave him a grant of 500 acres, and Foveaux provided a pardon for Maria Riseley and made Lord a magistrate.[12] Lord had six weeks to discuss

Lieutenant Lord arrives in Sydney, May 1808
(*Sydney Gazette*, 22 May 1808)

colonial matters with Foveaux – after which Foveaux wrote to a friend that at Hobart under Collins 'a System of the most unexampled profusion, waste, and fraud, with respect to both Money and Stores, have been carried on, almost without the affectation of concealment of sense of shame'. Despite drawing scarcely credible sums of money, Collins had not even built a shed to secure his stores from theft or weather.[13] This information surely came from Lord.

Lord had a long wait for a ship to Hobart, but he finally sailed south on 18 September. He arrived in early October. Straight away, on 8 October, with Maria a free woman, he married her.[14]

This was extremely unusual. Many officers and gentlemen had convict mistresses, but hardly any married them. Gentlemen were expected to marry ladies. Socially, Maria was disqualified on many counts from marrying a gentleman, let alone one related to an baronet: she was a convict, a criminal; she was from a much lower social class; she had no money. In England this marriage would have been disastrous for Edward and if he returned there, as most people planned to do, he would suffer. Yet he married Maria as soon as he possibly could. She signed the marriage register, able to write by now, and the witnesses were Lord's friend William Collins and an ex-convict clerk who often performed this role. Not Lord's officer friends; perhaps they refused to support such a marriage, or perhaps he did not like to ask them.

Why did Edward enter this socially suicidal marriage? Perhaps he loved Maria overwhelmingly, so much that nothing else mattered. If

> Lieutenant Governor Foveaux has been pleased to appoint Lieutenant E. Lord, of the Royal Marines, to be a Magistrate in the County of Buckinghamshire, in the Settlement under the Command of Lieutenant Governor Collins, at Van Diemen's Land.
> Head-quarters, Sept. 13, 1808.

Foveaux appoints Lord a magistrate, in the most impeccable official language. No casual reader would take this for a rebel appointment (*Sydney Gazette*, 25 September 1808)

so, his love must have been really overpowering, for this ambitious man to take such a lowering step. Perhaps the impetus came from Maria, with her strong character. Or perhaps Edward soberly worked out the advantages. She was a wonderful merchant, bringing in money. She was an excellent housekeeper, producing a birthday dinner in a famine, keeping him comfortable, running an immaculate home – servants would have done their work thoroughly with Maria in charge. Was Edward seeing an opportunity for financial advancement and seizing it, in his usual way?

As well, Maria was fertile, and perhaps he wanted his children legitimate. Perhaps she was fantastic in bed: the suggestion of strong sex appeal recurs throughout her story. For whatever reason, ambitious young Edward Lord, aged 27, married ex-convict Maria Riseley, just two months off thirty. This is another indication that he saw his future in Australia, where an ex-convict wife, though undesirable, was not disastrous, rather than in conservative Britain where she was.

For Maria herself the wedding was a wonderful triumph. The number of convicts who married gentlemen was tiny, in single figures among Van Diemen's Land's 13,000 female convicts. At one jump she changed from being Maria Riseley, convict mistress with two illegitimate children, socially and morally disreputable, to Mrs Edward Lord, wife of an officer and gentlemen, theoretically with the prized status of lady. An interesting point is the hurry to marry: convicted in July 1802 to serve seven years, Maria was only nine months from freedom, but Edward obtained the pardon and they were married as soon as possible. It was not as if she were pregnant. Perhaps Maria, Edward or both could not bear her convict status a moment longer. The wedding matches the desire to have Maria churched after childbirth: respectability at all costs.

His aims achieved, Edward Lord leaves Sydney, September 1808
(*Sydney Gazette*, 18 September 1808)

However, Maria could not leave her convict past behind. Everyone in the colony knew, was to know for decades to come, and often knows even now, that she had been a convict. Ex-convicts remained tainted with the stigma of their criminal past forever, if people knew about it. Many managed to hide it, by changing their names, moving elsewhere to start afresh, claiming to be free immigrants; but for a notorious convict like Maria Riseley, the mistress then wife of a well-known officer, this was not possible. She was tolerated, because there were so many ex-convicts in Van Diemen's Land in all walks of life that they had to be accepted as part of the community; but she was still seen as tainted.

Flight of Fancy: who made the big decision?

POSSIBLE SCENARIO 1

Scene: *The Lords' drawing-room. Maria is working on her accounts. Edward bursts in.*

Edward: Maria! Wonderful news!

Maria (*looks up, after carefully marking her place*): What, dear?

Edward: Collins is sending me to Sydney to find out what's going on!

Maria (*cautiously*): That long trip, Edward?

Edward: It's my opportunity! I can side with the rebels, they'll be glad to have me, and they'll reward me well!

Maria: But that's mutiny – your career …

Edward: I've decided to leave the marines. Far more opportunities here, in business. So that doesn't matter. The rebels have power now – I can get a land grant, a big one, and a pardon for you, Maria!

Maria: Oh Edward, a pardon! How wonderful! To stop being a convict!

Edward: Yes, and we can get married!

Maria (*stunned*): Married?

Edward: Yes, married, Maria, don't you want that? We'd be much better married – more respectable, the children legitimate, you'd be a proper wife.

Maria (*still dazed*): You wouldn't mind, Edward, with me … you know …

Edward: Once you're free, that's all in the past! I'll marry a free woman, and that's the end of it. Well, Maria, will you marry me?

Maria: Yes, Edward, yes! How wonderful! Quick, when can you go to Sydney? What do you need packed?

Edward (*laughing*): Not so fast, not so fast! The ship won't leave tonight! How about showing me a little appreciation, my girl? (*seizes her and they dance round the room and into the bedroom …*)

POSSIBLE SCENARIO 2

Scene: *The Lords' drawing-room. Maria is working on her accounts. Edward enters.*

Edward: Well, Maria, interesting developments.

Maria (*looks up, after carefully marking her place*): What, dear?

Edward: Collins is sending me to Sydney, to find out what's going on. He's at a loss as to what to do (*snorts derisively*).

Maria: What's new? (*They exchange knowing glances.*) Will this help us, Edward?

Edward: I'm thinking, Maria, the rebels will be glad to have supporters. They might be persuaded to, er, give substance to their thanks. A land grant, you know.

Maria: Yes, and if you resign from the marines, as we've discussed, siding with the rebels won't matter. Promotion is so slow, Edward, it's not worth it, compared with the opportunities in business here.

Edward: I suppose so. Yes, I suppose you're right. A big land grant would set me up well.

Maria: And a pardon for me, Edward.

Edward: What? You'll be free next year, Maria, why the rush?

Maria: Well, dear, we could get married.

Edward: Married!!! But ...

Maria: If I were free, you could marry me. A free woman. As good as anyone.

Edward: But ... !!! ??? *** !!!

Maria (*muses*): Or I could set up a business on my own, once I'm free. I've got a good head for it. The profits this last year ...

Edward: Yes, yes, they're very high, I know that, well done. But marriage! I mean to say ... my family ...

Maria: On the other side of the world. I'd like some security, Edward.

Edward (*grasping at straws*): Aren't you secure now? The house, the children, the shop, me – what more do you want?

Maria: It all belongs to you, Edward. I have nothing myself. I'd be much happier married to you. Just think what we could do, working together, making money, getting land, growing rich!

Edward: But we don't need to get married!

Maria: I think we do. We'd have many more opportunities for making money if we were married.

Edward (*unable to follow this reasoning but not liking to admit it*): I suppose so.

Maria (*quickly*): Good! That's agreed. Off you go to Sydney, get that land grant and my pardon, and off we go!

Nineteenth-century sources never mention sex, but of course it was there, often a major motive for people's behaviour. The scene could even have gone like this ...

POSSIBLE SCENARIO 3

Scene: *The Lords' drawing-room. Maria is working on her accounts. Edward rushes in impetuously.*

Edward: Maria, Maria darling! Wonderful news!

Maria (*leaps up and runs to him*): What, dearest?

Edward (*seizes her and gives her a smacking kiss*): Collins is sending me to Sydney to see what's going on there! My opportunity!

Maria: Opportunity? How, Edward?

Edward: I'll side with the rebels, they'll be grateful, they'll reward me! Land, a magistracy – and a pardon for you, sweetheart!

Maria: Oh, Edward! Wonderful! (*throws her arms round his neck*)

Edward (*laughing*): You're strangling me, Maria! Let me go!

Maria (*laughing and crying at once*): A pardon! Edward, my hero!

Edward: And we can get married! We said we would, as soon as you were free, and now we can! My honeypot, my wonderful girl!
(*They start tearing at each other's clothes and enjoy rampant sex then and there on the floor, not even able to get to the bedroom. Convict servants snigger in the kitchen. This is nothing new.*)

Proclamation.

WILLIAM PATERSON.

Whereas an Agreement was concluded between me and WILLIAM BLIGH, Esquire, late Governor of this Territory, of which the following is a true Copy, viz.

"*Sydney, New South Wales, February 4, 1809.*

"It being deemed by Lieutenant Governor PATERSON absolutely essential to His Majesty's Service, and the Interests of this Colony, to send Governor BLIGH immediately to England, and it being the intention of Lieutenant Governor PATERSON to take up the Ship Admiral Gambier for his Conveyance, Governor BLIGH has represented that it would on many accounts be much more desirable to him to be allowed to return home in His Majesty's Ship Porpoise.

"Lieutenant Governor PATERSON, anxious to contribute as much as possible to the convenience of Governor BLIGH, consents to his proceeding to Europe in the Porpoise, on the following Conditions; to the STRICT OBSERVANCE OF WHICH GOVERNOR BLIGH HEREBY SOLEMNLY PLEDGES his HONOR, as an OFFICER and a GENTLEMAN.

"That he will Embark with his Family on board the Porpoise, on the 20th instant, and will put to Sea as soon after as the Wind and Weather will admit.

"That he will PROCEED TO ENGLAND WITH THE UTMOST DISPATCH; and that HE WILL NEITHER TOUCH AT NOR RETURN TO ANY PART OF THIS TERRITORY, UNTIL HE SHALL HAVE RECEIVED HIS MAJESTY's INSTRUCTIONS, OR THOSE OF HIS MINISTERS.

"That he will not in pretence whatever Colony, interfere in thereof; and

"That he will not thr way of the Porpoise ceeding with him pulated time".

"In consequence nant Governor PATE the additional restraint Governor BLIGH since and to permit him House, and to comm in the same manner to make such arrang necessary for his Voya sons to accompany him to name, agreeable to in the Lieutenant Go 28th ultimo.

(Signed)
(Signed)

And whereas the s in *direct violation of his cer and a Gentleman* in, has not *departed fr lated time;* and in fu caused to be distribute wicked and evil-dispo the high Crimes and M stands charged) certain Papers, intended to t this Colony, to disturb subvert good Order a the security of public personal Liberty.

6. TROUBLE AT THE DERWENT

quences meant to result from the designs of the said WILLIAM BLIGH, Esq. and his Accomplices, I do hereby positively charge and command all His Majesty's Subjects within this Territory not to hold, countenance, or be privy to any communication or correspondence, by personal Interview, Letter, Message, Signal, or otherwise, with the said WILLIAM BLIGH, Esq. or with any person belonging to his Family, Establishment, or Retinue, at present embarked on board His Majesty's ship Porpoise, or with any person known to be in his or their Employment, Service, Confidence or Intimacy, now on board said Vessel. And all Officers Civil and Military, and all other His Majesty's faithful Subjects within this Territory are hereby required and commanded to Aid, Assist, and Promote, by all the means in their power, a strict obedience to this Proclamation: and to give immediate Information to me, or to some other of His Majesty's Officers, Civil or Military, of any person or persons who shall attempt to act in Defiance, Opposition, Neglect, or Evasion thereof, in order that such Offender or Offenders may be dealt with as abettors of Sedition, and Enemies to the Peace and Prosperity of the Colony.

Given at Head Quarters at Sydney, New South Wales, this 19th day of March, 1809.

GOD SAVE THE KING!

By Command of His Honor the Lieutenant Governer,
JAMES FINUCANE, Secretary.

75

MARRIED LIFE LOOKED PROMISING for Lieutenant and Mrs Edward Lord. They had their two little daughters; they ran a successful shop; and Lord's grant of 500 acres made him by far the largest landowner in the colony – the next had only 114 acres. He was moving into other ventures too, as he and William Collins built Hobart's first mill, so the colony could grind its own flour (though there is no further mention of their involvement). As an official, Lieutenant Lord was also successful. His superior, Governor Collins, always supported him, even giving him two well-paid sinecures: naval officer, a position later abolished because there was so little to do, and inspector of public works, such works being almost non-existent. The combined wages came to over half the governor's annual salary.[1] A handy sum for virtually no work.

It was not that Collins and Lord were natural friends. Collins was a quarter of a century older than Lord, liking a quiet life, not really interested in money and go-getting. He even thought he would have made a good parson – 'Nature intended and fashioned me to ascend the pulpit' – despite his string of mistresses.[2] (So much for religious ideals in Hobart.) Nature had certainly not intended Edward Lord to preach religion.

What was his power over Collins? He probably lent Collins money. Collins was not good with finance and died deeply in debt. Lord often used the ploy of giving people loans to get them in his power. With Collins his debtor, Lord could do what he liked, under threat of calling in his debts.[3] As well, with his stronger character Lord seems to have dominated Collins. The governor was no leader, lacking Lord's force and push, and he disliked conflict. Then there was Lord's superior social position. Collins had no powerful relations, and must have been only too well aware of the existence of Edward's cousin Sir Hugh Owen, Bart, M.P. and the rest of it – who could all too easily have a word in someone's ear in the corridors of power in London. Collins himself was vulnerable, with no patron to defend him. For all these reasons, in the saga that follows Collins seems to have obeyed Lord automatically.

Lord showed his power, and his character, in an incident on 2 December 1808. Collins was visiting New Norfolk, so Lord as second in command was in charge in Hobart. Suspecting that Mary Granger, a convict

Previous pages: Governor Paterson makes public, in capital letters, Bligh's promise to go straight to England and not to interfere in the colony – probably well aware that Bligh was not going to go quietly (*Sydney Gazette*, 26 March 1809)

working in his house, had stolen a glass tumbler, he ordered her confined in the stocks for an hour. This was illegal, for a punishment could be ordered only by a magistrate. Some convict women, including Martha Hudson who had come to Sydney in *Experiment* with Maria Lord, went to Maria 'and putting her in mind of her former situation, interceded for Mary Grangers being released'.[4] 'Her former situation' – as a convict. Edward or Maria, or probably both, were furious. Maria had been a convict two months earlier: but that was then. This was now, and no one was going to bring up Mrs Edward Lord's former convict status and get away with it.

Even worse, standing near the stocks Martha 'made use of language reflecting on Mrs. Lords former Character', referring to Maria's convict past in public. Edward Lord ordered Martha tied to the back of a cart and flogged up and down the parade. This spectacle was unusual – and indecent, because to have a bare back for flogging the woman would be naked from the waist, baring her breasts. Collins had sentenced a woman to 25 lashes in 1806, so there was a precedent, but these were the only two instances in Van Diemen's Land.[5] Again, there was no trial. Edward Lord was taking the law into his own hands (just as Collins had done with him in 1805). This sentence was not only unnecessarily severe but brutal, even sadistic: why else make such a public spectacle of a flogging?

George Harris had been brought up a Quaker, with a dislike of corruption, brutality and misuse of power. He was a magistrate and took his role seriously, upholding the rule of law. Seeing a woman flogged, hanging at the cart apparently fainting, without a doctor attending – another legal requisite Lord ignored – Harris asked him whether this was a civil or military punishment. Lord answered that he was the commanding officer, and Harris had no right to enquire. Harris claimed he did. 'Do you know who I am?' Lord asked him. 'I am now Governor & Commanding Officer and will do as I like without your interfering.' He ordered Harris off the parade ground, but Harris said he would go where he chose, for he (Lord) was only Lieutenant Lord. However, in the end Harris did go home, not wanting his heavily pregnant wife upset. As he left, he heard Lord say that this was mutiny and order a drum beat to arms (calling all marines on duty, armed) – a gross overreaction.[6]

Once Lord was backed by military power, he held all the cards. He sent marines to bring Harris to the parade ground, one enforcing this with a pistol held to Harris's back. Lord asked what Harris meant by such insolent behaviour. Harris questioned the legality of his proceedings. Lord put him under house arrest – without a trial, which almost goes without saying by now. Meanwhile, Martha Hudson had received two dozen lashes. Lord asked a doctor, his friend I'Anson, if she could bear two dozen more. I'Anson agreed.[7] These were tough times.

Three days later Governor Collins returned. Although he and Harris were friends – both came from Exeter, and in happier times Harris called Collins 'as pleasant a man as can be' – he backed Lord. Harris, he said, lacked respect to the officer in charge, denying his authority to inflict punishment on a wretch that justly deserved it, and 'Lieut. Lord was acting during my late temporary absence in strict conformity with His Majesty's Instructions'. Collins, former judge advocate, must have known that this was incorrect, that Lord had ignored many legal requirements, but Lord persuaded, or forced, him to support him, perhaps arguing that authority must be maintained. Harris remained under house arrest. Collins sent friends to mediate, but though Harris was willing to apologise, Lord refused. Ridiculously, he claimed Harris had been drunk and other people persuaded him to create a disturbance.[8]

Harris wanted a public investigation in Sydney, though fearing that while Lord 'possesses that influence in the Colony, he at present enjoys', he would try to prevent this. He did. 'Every obstacle has been thrown in my way to prevent my obtaining redress.' Colonel Paterson, Foveaux's superior officer, had taken over in Sydney, but he was ill and Foveaux, Lord's friend, remained de facto ruler. When Collins asked about Harris' investigation, Sydney replied that the dispute between Harris and Lord should be settled in Hobart, as 'a public trial here would lead to much unpleasant recrimination' – details of Lord's illegal actions might come out.[9] Foveaux was not going to let that happen.

For months Harris remained immured at home, unable to gain justice despite complaints to London and support from other officers. In May 1809 two of these deposed that on 2 December Harris was perfectly sober, and 'the only violator of public tranquillity was the said Lieutenant Edward Lord'. All the officers signed a second deposition saying they could not for a moment believe Harris was guilty of abetting

George Harris's depiction of the Tasmanian tiger (actually a painting made later from an engraving done by Harris). Perhaps his house arrest at least gave him time to paint
(Allport Library and Museum of Fine Arts, TAHO)

mutiny. However, Harris was released only in August, when Collins had no choice: he had to appoint an acting commissary and no one else was available.[10]

Maria Lord was not mentioned in the story, after the initial business of her convict past being recalled. However, settler James Belbin told his family a different version. It was written down only in 1880 and seems to combine two events, but does show how the family remembered Maria Lord.

The Belbins said the incident began with a quarrel between Mrs Roberts (Martha Hudson's married name) and 'a siren' under the protection of Lieutenant Lord, whose many talents included a capacity for business and aptitude for driving hard bargains. She was the manager of Lord's huckstering establishment, all it was at this time. There a row took place between her and Martha Hudson. Both were eloquent, but Martha kept up such a fusillade that Maria was forced to flee for cover 'into a distant recess of the residence, into which, even Mrs Robert's vociferations could not penetrate'. This is the one description which shows Maria as vulnerable.

When Edward Lord came home, the Belbin account continued, he was furious, arrested Martha, gave her a mockery of a trial and sentenced her to the shameful indignity of a flogging. James Belbin, as impulsive and outspoken as Lord himself, was shocked to see a half-naked woman tied to a bullock-cart, being flogged. He shouted, 'Shame! Shame!' and added, 'Can this be a land of Christians, or one of savages only, where such an exhibition is permitted?'[11]

The Belbins depicted both Collins and Lord as cruel and vindictive, and certainly Edward Lord's personality as shown in this saga – hasty temper, tendency to violence and dislike of any challenge to his autocratic rule – suggests that he was a difficult husband, perhaps even abusive. Fawkner hinted at this, saying that Edward took possession of Maria 'as truly for a slave to do his behests, or suffer for neglect or refusal' – note the word 'suffer'. Maria had no family in the colony, no one to defend her, or give advice or refuge. Perhaps that had been another attraction for Edward? However, she was a strong, determined and clever woman, and emerged unbroken from the experience of being married to him. Presumably she

Above: Martha Hudson's convict record. Like Maria Riseley's, it is blank. No illegal acts of an acting governor were going to be recorded (Tasmanian Archive and Heritage Office, CON 40/1/5)

worked out how to co-exist with him to her best advantage. Just possibly, with her own strong character, she dominated even tough Edward within the family circle. But perhaps at home, too, she sometimes needed to take cover in a distant recess from Edward's violence.

While the Lord–Harris saga was being played out, life in Hobart continued. According to James Belbin, who as well as telling stories to his descendants kept a contemporary diary, as far as the officers were concerned it was corruption all the way. They received extra wheat when provisions were short, and drew other goods from the stores illegally; 'L and C' (Lord and William Collins?) smuggled spirits; and so it continued.[12] Thomas Keston, another small settler, said corruption was a result of the low calibre of men sent to rule the colonies. Honest gentlemen who could live comfortably in Britain did not come out 'to make a large fortune in the depraved & scandalous manner as our selfcreated Gent[leme]^n have done'. It was all very well for people to condemn the Bey of Algiers and similar foreign rulers as contemptible savages, wrote Keston sternly, but English officers with authority over their fellow creatures had committed far worse crimes: 'the Life of a poor Man is no more in their Hands than a Fly for they will be lashing them by candlelight there not being day light enough for their savage Practices'. Men were set over the colonists who were more fit to be in a lunatic asylum than to hold office under our gracious sovereign.[13]

Despite this misrule and corruption, according to John Fawkner conditions were improving for the general population. Mainly by their own efforts, they were enjoying good harvests, increasing numbers of sheep and cattle, and plenty of employment at good wages.[14] The easing of the famine must have been a huge relief to Governor Collins. However, 1809 also presented him with a frightful challenge. It led to the only time in Tasmania's history that its European inhabitants were fired on by a hostile power. He happened to be the governor of New South Wales.

AFTER THE NEW SOUTH WALES CORPS overthrew Bligh in January 1808, they offered to let him return to England on the condition that he did not stop on the way, and possibly gain support. He finally agreed, and in March 1809 boarded HMS *Porpoise*, promising to go direct to England. After ordering the captain to fire on Sydney (the captain refused), Bligh broke his word by sailing to his strongest supporter in Australia: Governor Collins. His aim is not clear: to establish a power base? or merely wait out the time until the replacement governor arrived

Sydney in 1810. Despite rebellion and strife, it is becoming a bustling little port
(Allport Library and Museum of Fine Arts, TAHO)

from Britain to punish the rebels? It was well over a year since the rebellion; surely the new man would arrive soon.

As Bligh sailed up the Derwent, Collins had to choose a side. Which? Support Bligh and alienate Sydney and its supplies? Or support Sydney and risk retribution and possible dismissal from London, not to mention a nasty predicament with Bligh on his doorstep? Nearly forty years in the marines had imbued Collins with loyalty and obedience. When Bligh arrived, Collins boarded *Porpoise* to greet him courteously and offer support. Bligh promised not to interfere with Collins' government, but then proceeded to alienate Collins, his one powerful friend in Australia, by his usual antagonistic behaviour. Next day he landed, and Collins laid on the maximum ceremony: gun salutes from all available ships and the shore battery (a grand total of 106 salvos), marines drawn up under arms, chief officers lined up to do the honours – but at their head was Edward Lord who, Bligh knew, was hand-in-glove with his enemies. As well, wrote Bligh, a 'few poor Inhabitants' raised a cheer. He was so unimpressed that he did not remain on shore to dine with Collins.[15]

Bligh approved of nothing at the five-year-old settlement, and doubtless told Collins so. Government house was only 'a poor miserable shell, with three rooms, the Walls a brick thick, and neither wind nor water proof'. The rest of the settlement comprised a dilapidated building used as a shelter; the new commissariat store, half-built; the old store that could only house part of the goods, the rest left lying in the open; 'a deplorable house in the Lumber Yard, under the shed of which Divine Service is performed'; and the inhabitants' small huts.[16] (And Lord's larger house at Sandy Bay, but that was out of town and perhaps Bligh did not see it. Besides, it spoilt his story.)

Even worse, the place was corrupt. It was Sydney in miniature, wrote Bligh: a few men holding all the 'indulgencies' and accumulating wealth, while the poor suffered. He mentioned Edward Lord specifically: he and William Collins kept a shop that 'engrosses the advantages of trade, to the great injury of the settlement'. And Governor Collins lacked decorum, 'walking with his kept Woman (a poor, low creature) arm-in-arm about the Town, and bringing her almost daily to his Office adjoining the House' – not just a social and moral offence but a military one, allowing an outsider in the office with its confidential government papers. Lord was as bad as Collins, wrote Bligh: a friend of the rebels, married to a convict woman 'of infamous character'; Lord might say she was free, but to Bligh she was still a convict, since he did not recognise pardons issued by rebels. Lord, he added, was an early subject of conversation between Collins and himself, and one can imagine what Bligh said. Despite this, when Bligh asked for a guide to the settlement, Collins sent Lord, his enemy! 'With this officer I made only one visit', Bligh wrote curtly.[17] Why would Collins have chosen Lord? It seems unnecessarily antagonistic, but perhaps Collins thought it right for his second in command. Or else Lord forced him, for the chance of either toadying to or infuriating Bligh. If he tried toadying, explaining away his friendship with Foveaux, for once his silver tongue was unsuccessful.

What were Lord's motives in opposing Bligh? Perhaps by now he had decided to resign from the marines, so future career damage would not matter. His main aim was probably to support his new friends in Sydney (and put them in his debt) by stopping Collins from providing a base for Bligh, a loyal bastion showing up the Sydney delinquents. It seems that Lord persuaded Collins to defy Bligh, greatly helped by Bligh's own actions. Left to his own inclinations, wrote Collins, he would have supported Bligh, but unnamed influences (Lord being the most likely) and Bligh's 'unhandsome' behaviour meant he could not.[18]

'Unhandsome' seems a mild way to describe Bligh's activities. Despite his promise not to interfere, he encouraged the inhabitants to see him as the governor-in-chief, Collins' superior, by putting up placards announcing he would redress grievances – aimed at the discontented Norfolk Islanders, half the population. Then, when Collins asked him to agree to his importation of cattle, Bligh refused.[19] These were cattle Foveaux had criticised Collins for buying, accusing him of extravagance. Bligh's support would have helped Collins avoid severe reprimand, even dismissal.

James Belbin complains about Lord in his private diary
(University of Tasmania Library Special & Rare Collections)

On 23 April a proclamation arrived from Colonel Paterson in Sydney forbidding contact with Bligh, with instructions to Collins to display it. Still ambivalent, Collins did nothing. Lord was not so hesitant. Some Norfolk Islanders were going to present an address of loyalty to Bligh, but Lord tore it up and arrested the ringleader, James Belbin, who 'was forcibly dragged from my Children and my Dwelling by Mr Lord'. He complained that Lord kicked him, threw him in the mud and threatened to hang him as a mutineer. Thomas Keston was appalled:

> Lt Govr & Lt Edwd Lord broke into his house & broke open his Chest & took all his writings fm him, their actions were so dirty in those days that it was a Crime for any poor man to keep any accounts of the Villainy that was going on ... I cannot see what right a L^t of Marines has to break into a free Inhabitants house & rob the man of his Papers with impunity.[20]

Belbin's case was heard by magistrates: Knopwood, who acted as a gentleman (said Belbin), and Lord who 'turbulent and prejudiced against me upbraid me with once being a Convict which Sarcasm rebounded on himself' – Lord and his convict wife! Meanwhile, Collins gave in. He ordered the colonists not to contact Bligh.[21]

Furious, Bligh moved back on *Porpoise*, whose midshipmen included fifteen-year-old George Collins, Governor Collins' illegitimate son. Bligh had the unfortunate boy flogged for drunkenness and neglect of duty, a trumped-up charge. Next, Bligh drew up his own proclamation naming Paterson as a rebel, and ordered Collins to print it. Collins agreed, but strangely enough there was no ink for the printer, though the mark where it had recently stood was plain. Undaunted, Bligh asked Collins to read it to the inhabitants. Collins refused.[22]

Bligh sailed out on the River Derwent and hailed passing boats, ordering them alongside under threat of being fired on. One refused until Bligh fired two musket shots over it, this being the occasion when a hostile power fired on a government vessel. However, Bligh did not go so far as to fire on Lord when Collins sent him to intercept a ship from Sydney in case Bligh tried to seize its despatches. These included one from Paterson, ordering Collins to read his proclamation to the colonists.

This time Collins obeyed. He told Bligh he could have no more communication with him, and would fire on any boat of his that tried to land. *Porpoise*'s captain stated his right to send watering parties ashore, but Collins stopped the men landing.[23]

Keston has a story whose date and context are not clear, but shows Edward Lord acting in his usual impulsive, dashing manner. One day while *Porpoise* lay off Hobart, wrote Keston, Collins

> sent Lt Ed^d Lord with a Boat & party of Marines on Board the Porpose but when the Boat came close to the Ship, the Commander in Chief [Bligh] hail'd her & asked the Officer what he wanted on board of his Majesty's Ship & I do not know what answer [Lord] gave his Excellency but he martialled up in terrible array & ordered his Party to fix their Bayonets against a 20 Gun Ship

A wonderful sight, a group of men standing in a small boat with fixed bayonets, challenging a large warship bristling with twenty cannon! Fortunately for Lord, continued Keston, the ship's guns were not loaded. After this display of force, such as it was, Lord retreated.[24]

Seeing no profit in staying near Hobart, Blight sailed to the mouth of the Derwent at Storm Bay, waiting for the new governor of New South Wales to arrive. For supplies, he bought or seized food from passing ships, and received food from Norfolk Islanders. Collins threw two of these in gaol. However, when merchant John Ingle supplied Bligh with food he was not punished. He was Lord's friend.[25]

Bligh remained at the mouth of the Derwent for months. Doubtless he was even less impressed with Collins when his young mistress provided him with a daughter. However, on 22 December Bligh heard that the new governor was arriving in Sydney, and hastily sailed there.[26] Collins wrote to his brother:

> God knows, I never had any malice in my heart until I came in contact with this detestable brute ... He is a tyrant, and possessed of every bad quality that can enter into the composition of the worst of tyrants. He has been skulking here for nine months in a corner of Van Diemen's Land, endeavouring to do me all the mischief in his power by exciting my settlers, and declaring he would ruin me.[27]

This enemy was now back in power, or at least with influence. The British government was taking control again. Rebels could be punished. Collins and Lord were in the firing line. What would happen?

Right: Everything must look innocuous and normal. This bland report concealed the fact that Her Majesty's ship *Porpoise* was not merely waiting in the Derwent, but was in armed opposition to its government (*Sydney Gazette*, 20 August 1809)

Below: 'Entrance to Storm Bay' by Mary Morton Allport: where Bligh waited out the time till the new governor arrived
(Allport Library and Museum of Fine Arts, TAHO)

Flight of Fancy:
Edward Lord guides Governor Bligh around Hobart, April 1808

SCENE: *Inside government house. Collins and Bligh are standing in the drawing room, in a rather sticky silence. A servant enters with a message for Collins. Obviously relieved, he addresses Bligh.*

Collins: All is ready for your tour of Hobart Town, Your Excellency. Lieutenant Lord will be your guide.

Bligh: Lord! That mutineer! Hand-in-glove with Johnston and Foveaux! Married to that dreadful convict female! I'll go nowhere with him!

Collins: Your Excellency, Lieutenant Lord is my second in command. It is right and proper that he should guide you. To assign any lesser ranking officer to the duty would be to demean your status.

There is no answer to this. Bligh glares at Collins, and strides from the room.

At the steps of government house, Lord is waiting with two horses.

Lord: Good morning, Your Excellency, and what a fine morning we have for our ride! I've brought you my best horse, Star – I think you'll find him suitable.

Bligh grunts, which could be translated as thanks. Mounts horse.

Lord: And where would you like to start, Your Excellency?

Bligh (*coldly*): You are the guide.

Lord: Well, here we are at government house. Not much, but... (*shrugs shoulders*) ... Governor Collins, you know ... (*shrugs shoulders again*). Sad of course that there's no respectable lady as hostess. We married people feel this very much, but ... Now this is William Collins' shop.

Bligh: Aren't you his partner?

Lord: No, no, not really. My wife gives him a hand occasionally. She has an excellent business head, for a woman. Now we're coming to the commissariat store, not finished, but … what can you do … and there is your ship, *Porpoise*, at anchor. A fine vessel. As we turn north …

They tour the rest of the little town. It takes about fifteen minutes.

Lord: Not as fine as Sydney, of course. The progress made there under your governorship has been remarkable.

Bligh (*goaded into a reply*): Fine speech from a friend of the rebels!

Lord: Hardly a friend, Your Excellency! Governor Collins sent me to see what was happening in Sydney, which I did, and if they pressed a small grant on me, I felt I could do no other than take it. I returned as soon as I could to make my report, which of course detailed the appalling and illegal activities of the rebels.

Now we turn towards Sandy Bay, and we can see the progress the farmers have made. My wife will have a spot of morning tea waiting. I expect you'll be glad of a rest among home comforts.

Bligh: I have another engagement, sir! (*dismounts and stomps off towards government house*)

7. DRAMATIC TIMES FOR THE LORD FAMILY

T||HE YEAR 1810 WAS MOMENTOUS for Edward and Maria Lord. It brought one expected and welcome event, and two entirely unexpected changes which revolutionised their lives. The first bombshell came from Wales.

When Edward last visited Wales around 1802, his second cousin Sir Hugh Owen was Baronet Owen of Orielton, MP, Lord Lieutenant, wealthy and successful. Edward's older brother John was a lawyer in London. Edward himself lacked a patron, so essential to advancing a career. He might boast of his grand relatives, but obviously Sir Hugh did nothing to support him, for Edward remained a lowly lieutenant.

On 8 August 1809 all this changed. Sir Hugh died suddenly, aged only 26. Even his strong-minded mother could not stop the legal heir, an Owen second cousin, from inheriting the baronetcy, but she could do something about the property. Presumably the Lords had been courting these rich relations, and it bore fruit. There was drama when Sir Hugh's will was read, for he left all his estates, worth the massive sum of £10,000 a year (the same income as wealthy Mr Darcy's in Jane Austen's *Pride and Prejudice*), not to the new baronet but to another second cousin, John Lord. The Owens claimed the will was forged – there was a rumour that Sir Hugh's mother had put a spider in the corpse's mouth to simulate movement when the will was signed – but it stood. The only condition was that John Lord change his name to Owen, which he naturally did at once.[1] Suddenly he had plenty of money. It became vital for Edward to visit Britain.

He was already expecting a happy event. In March 1810, Maria gave birth to a son. Edward, so proud of his family, sounds the sort of man desperate for a son, and at last, after two daughters, the heir arrived. He was even legitimate. Edward named him John Owen Lord – not so much as a nod towards Maria's family.[2]

Then a second unexpected death occurred. David Collins was right to be worried about the British government's attitude towards him. Because of his own actions, and criticism from Foveaux, London thought he was extravagant – a terrible flaw in a colonial administrator, wasting government money. He also supported the rebels, opposed Bligh and denied supplies to a Royal Navy vessel, all serious charges. The new governor in Sydney, upright and competent Lachlan Macquarie, took it for granted that Collins

Previous pages: The problems of travel. This painting of the sea about Cape Pillar on Van Diemen's Land's east coast gives an indication of the small size of ships and the large size of waves
(Allport Library and Museum of Fine Arts, TAHO)

would be dismissed.³ Even his new mistress could not cheer him. It would have been hard for anyone, let alone a sixteen-year-old girl. Perhaps, indeed, the exertion of keeping up with a young mistress added to his woes.

In January, a chilly despatch from Macquarie made Collins very sad and thoughtful, wrote Fawkner. On 3 March he celebrated his fifty-fourth birthday, and doubtless enjoyed dandling his three-month-old daughter on his knee. The baby was just old enough to smile at him, to gurgle entrancingly. But on 11 March her father received an even colder letter from Macquarie (Bligh had reached Sydney). Macquarie expressed regret that Collins had 'denied the legal authority of Governor Bligh ... you will of course explain your motives for doing so to His Majesty's Ministers'.⁴

Then Collins caught a cold. He seemed to recover, but suddenly collapsed and died.⁵ Many contemporaries thought poorly of his administration, but though he blinked at corruption and saw himself above the law, many administrators did this, and he did establish the colony.⁶ Perhaps 'fair; could have done better,' is a reasonable judgement. The *Derwent Star* – a newspaper Collins had just started – was effusive: grief and consternation were shown on all faces. Not everyone's. Thomas Keston despised Collins, 'a servile Creature to his superiors, affable courteous & liberal to his equals & the fair Sex & a great Tyrant to his inferiors'. Knopwood preached a sermon telling settlers they should lament the loss of their well-beloved governor, continued Keston, 'but there was but little attention paid to what he said'.⁷

On Collins' death, Lieutenant Lord took over as second in command. Maria Lord became the governor's lady, the only time in all Australian history an ex-convict filled this role. No one commented on this, probably because nothing much happened. The appointment was temporary and brief (ten weeks, as it turned out), and Maria had

Collins' short-lived newspaper, *Derwent Star*, describes his death. George Harris was apparently the journalist (Tasmanian Archive and Heritage Office)

> The event alluded to is fo recent in the memory of every one, and the death of LIEUT. GOVERNOR COLLINS is fo fincerely felt and deplored by all the refpectable, the induftrious and honeft inhabitants of this Colony, to whom he was truly a father and a friend ; that no apology is neceffary for appropriating this Number folely to record the mournful occurrence.
>
> The LIEUT. GOVERNOR, had for fome days been indifpofed by a Cold, and had partially confined himfelf to the houfe but on the day of his demise (Saturday the 24th of March laft) he found himfelf confiderably better, and transacted bufinefs with S. Warriner his Clerk at 4 o'Clock in the afternoon. When Mr. Bowden the Medical Gentleman who attended him called, he exprefsed his hope that he fhould very foon be about again—He was then taking a cup of tea, and fhortly after defiring Mr. Bowden to make ufe of fome refrefhment, he was obferved to ftretch out his hands and fuddenly fall back in his Chair apparently in a fit. Mr. Bowden immediately gave the alarm procured afiftance and got fome cordial down the GOVERNOR's throat without effect he never fpoke more !—And only when removed to a Couch gave one deep figh and expired—All Medical aid was in vain for alas ! the tide of life had ebbed never to flow again "—He died exactly at half-paft 7 o'Clock P.M.

> the Principal Officers, Civil, Military, and Naval, with their Ladies.
>
> By the Cyclops from Hobart, we receive the lamentable intelligence of the Death of Lieutenant-Governor COLLINS, who departed this life suddenly on the evening of the 24th of March last, while sitting on his chair, conversing with his surgeon, who had attended him during a short illness of six days.
>
> The most marked respect was paid to the remains of the above Officer by every description of persons in the Settlement. The funeral service was performed by the Rev. Mr. Knopwood, who delivered a pathetic and truly appropriate sermon on the occasion. The funeral was attended by all the Officers of the Settlement, Lieutenant Lord of the Marines following the bier as chief mourner, succeeded by a numerous train of mourners; upwards of 600 persons having assembled to pay the last duties of respect to their revered Commander.
>
> The Command of the Settlement of Hobart devolves on Lieutenant Lord, until His Excellency the Governor in Chief's Instructions shall be received.

The *Sydney Gazette* reports Collins' death and funeral – after its social update (*Sydney Gazette*, 21 April 1810)

just given birth, which would discourage social activity. She probably did not even move from her comfortable house in Sandy Bay to small, dilapidated government house, and she held no functions. Perhaps this was prudent, for Hobart's few respectable ladies might have boycotted a reception hosted by an ex-convict.

Edward was much more energetic. After his past activities, the reader might be prepared for anything. He knew his power was temporary: it was up to Macquarie to appoint an acting governor, who would only hold office until London sent a permanent governor. After Bligh's complaints it was unlikely that Macquarie would appoint Lord, and Lord wanted to go to England to capitalise on his brother's luck. In April he applied to Macquarie for leave on health grounds, certified by Hobart's doctors (his friends).[8] However, for a brief period Edward Lord did have power. What use did he make of it?

When Collins died, his doctor Matthew Bowden sent for Knopwood, as chaplain, and Lord, now in charge. The three went through Collins' papers, destroying some. This is not as culpable as it sounds. Few if any official papers are missing, and Collins' friends were probably removing indiscreet personal papers, as was customary. When Collins' brother died in 1796 a fellow officer 'look'd over his papers and burnt a great number which he thought would not be proper to be sent home', and Collins himself had scope for plenty of these.[9] Lord and Bowden were merely looking after their friend's interests in the usual way.

The next activity was Collins' funeral, which Lord organised. He continued to look after the interests of himself and his friends, justifying his actions to Macquarie in a bland report. He thought it absolutely necessary that every mark of attention should be paid to the remains of the governor. It all sounded very proper: over six hundred people at the funeral, a solemn military parade, everyone in deep mourning. Then came the crunch:

> In a Settlement like this, where every Article is enhanced to a very Considerable Amount, I trust Your Excellency will see that those marks due to the rank of the deceased could not have been paid him in a manner different from the present, or at a smaller expence.

Lord had no doubt, he wrote, that Macquarie would approve the attached bills in favour of John Ingle, Hobart merchant (and Lord's friend). Notes were attached, Ingle swearing he sold only at regular prices, and magistrates Harris and Knopwood assenting.[10] (All in it together?)

The list of items is mind-boggling. Black armbands and hatbands would have been understandable, but Lord spent wildly. Fourteen women – eleven marines' wives and three servants at government house – received entire new outfits: shoes, stockings, gloves, a black gown, a petticoat, a bonnet, two handkerchiefs. Surely they could have worn their old petticoats and stockings, which were not even visible? The men, a far larger number, received waistcoats, fine hats, breeches and other garments, and then there was silk for the pall, satin ribbon, sewing silk … It all came to the outrageous total of £507, more than the governor's annual salary. Macquarie was horrified. Lord sent him the accounts for approval, 'but the Amount appeared to me so very great that I declined giving them my Sanction', he wrote to London. He told Lord that he, Lord, was responsible for the accounts, but out of respect for Collins' memory Macquarie would recommend they be paid.[11]

Some of the money probably went to Lord himself. It is unlikely that one shop in Hobart in 1810 stocked the hundreds of metres of material, tens of dozens of handkerchiefs, shoes, shirts and so on. Probably all merchants, including Maria Lord, pooled their resources in the name of John Ingle, a respectable merchant and free settler, never an officer or convict: an acceptable figurehead. In stark contrast, Collins himself made no profit from the colony. He died owning two shillings and eightpence in cash, and owing large debts.[12]

As a memorial to Collins, Lord began building a small wooden church over his grave, but it blew down in a gale. Fawkner was caustic:

> Those who did not like the loose unchristian behaviour of the Governor gave it out that His Satanic Majesty had taken both the church and the Governor, and some said it was a pity that he did not take the Parson too, for they were much alike in deliberate wickedness, and indulged equally in deeds of licentiousness, giving a most villainous example.[13]

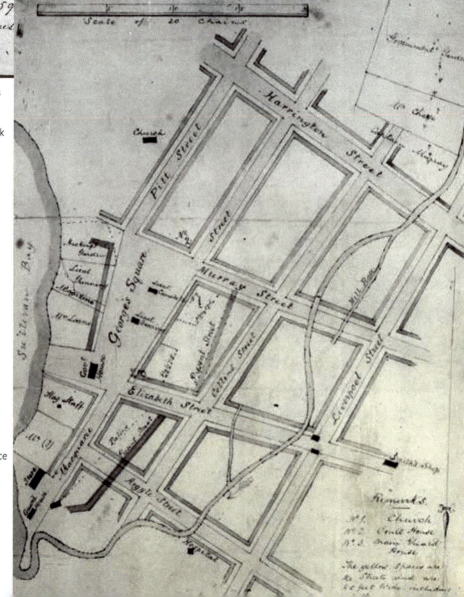

Above: In his notes for his 1811 survey, James Meehan described the block on the corner of Macquarie and Argyle streets as 'Ingles front (formerly Lords)'
(Tasmanian Archive and Heritage Office)

Right: James Meehan's map of Hobart in 1811, showing existing ('present') streets, and the new streets Macquarie organised. Few buildings are indicated, so there is no information about any building on the Ingle Hall site. This merely shows a paling fence crossing the block
(Tasmanian Archive and Heritage Office)

Once Collins was buried, Lord set about running the settlement. He was extremely energetic, sending Macquarie no fewer than nine despatches in his first few days in office. He asked for more soldiers to guard the colony, detaining a visiting military party to increase security: Macquarie approved. Lord forwarded an address from the settlers complaining at being paid less for meat and wheat; and requests for pardons for several convicts, and grants of land for Knopwood and Lord himself (the 500 acres from Foveaux had been nullified). He reported that officers had too many convict servants at the expense of settlers, and that he had seized 400 gallons of smuggled spirits – Lord, himself an officer and former smuggler![14]

These despatches show him trying to rule efficiently and fairly, which agrees with the only description of his administration, by Thomas Keston. He praised Lord, who 'changed the face of things for a short time'. For the first time the government listened to settlers' complaints. Anything Collins had withheld that Lord found was their just due, he gave them. Settlers felt they had security, and began to improve their premises. Lord helped Norfolk Islanders, giving them convict labour and all the clothes and bedding in the store. He stopped marines patrolling the streets with loaded pistols. No one could be put in prison without a trial. 'It was not in the Power of every busy ill disposed Person to Confine People to the Guard House, as they used to do', wrote Keston. Instead, they were brought before magistrates and had a chance of obtaining justice. Overall, 'Hobart Town began to have the appearance of a civil Gov^t. instead of a martial one'. The Reardons, a Norfolk Island family, showed their gratitude by naming their son Edward Lord. A century later, Edward Lord Reardon's obituary stated that his father had gained a land grant through the good office of Lieutenant-Governor Edward Lord.[15]

How can this be reconciled with Lord's earlier arbitrary actions? It was probably because no one challenged him. Everyone was happy with his rule: the Norfolk Islanders with their handouts, the general population with the rule of law, the marines with their new clothes. Even George Harris was reconciled. In assisting settlers, gaining nothing for himself, perhaps Lord was behaving in the noble Owen tradition, as if he were the baronet exercising paternal benevolence over his dependants.

However, if Lord or his supporters were challenged, he reacted in his traditional way. It might be the rule of law for everyone else, but not for Edward Lord himself. So, said Keston, he perpetrated 'one of the most shocking, cruel & unfair acts of any I ever knew under British government'.

A New Norfolk settler accused Denis McCarty, Lord's overseer in the government herds racket, of defrauding the Norfolk Islanders of their government provisions. He was probably right but, like Collins, Lord defended his friends. The settler, said Keston, had a sham trial and was sentenced to 500 lashes and two years on the public works.[16] Since few records remain from this period, the accuracy of this claim is not known.

Another complaint came from Roland Loane, a merchant who arrived in Hobart in 1809 with goods he claimed were worth £20,000. His business was, he wrote, 'a powerful check upon that Systematic mode of extortion then prevalent, and materially restricting Lieutenant Edward Lord in his pursuits of Trade'. Collins appointed Loane a magistrate, but on becoming governor Lord dismissed him. This is only Loane's version of the story, and a competent judge described his account as full of atrocious falsehoods. However, there were other, vaguer assertions that Lord exceeded his authority in trying to obtain land for himself or his friends.[17]

Lord had little time for any formal functions, but did give the usual vice-regal dinner on 4 June 1810 to celebrate the king's birthday. His friend Matthew Bowden greatly enjoyed the evening 'at your splendid and truly hospitable board'.[18] One can imagine how Lord too relished it. He was in one of his favourite situations, the generous host entertaining lavishly: welcoming his guests, warming his posterior before the fire, insisting that glasses were filled, that plates overflowed, and having the honour of proposing the Loyal Toast: 'His Majesty, the King!'

Lord sounds competent as acting governor, his actions a mixture of ruling efficiently and assisting his friends and himself. Since many governors in Hobart's first twenty years were only interested in the latter aim, he was something of a relief, especially in comparison with his three immediate successors.

TEN WEEKS AFTER COLLINS' DEATH, the next governor arrived from Sydney. Macquarie approved Lord's actions, but appointed as governor a man from his own 73rd regiment: Captain John Murray.[19] Murray brought approval for Lord's leave of absence, for twelve months from embarkation. Macquarie also instructed Lord to settle his government's accounts by drawing bills on the London treasury, as Macquarie refused to be responsible for the accounts of his subordinate commanders. However, Murray would not allow Lord to draw the bills. Furious, Lord went to Sydney. He cleared up the problem (Macquarie reprimanded Murray) and thanked Macquarie and his wife with 'profound respect' for their very polite attention, though this was probably his usual sycophancy rather than an accurate description of their relationship.[20] Macquarie continued to be horrified by Lord, not just over the funeral expenses, but by the huge sums Collins and Lord spent in Hobart as governors, far more than other subordinate commanders. He told Lord that he, Lord, would have to explain the bill to London, and also told London everything: 'I trust [Lord] will be enabled to explain satisfactorily to [Treasury] and Your Lordship the Cause or Necessity for the Expenses of that Small Settlement [Hobart] amounting to so very high a Sum in so short a Period'. Presumably this was more than the funeral expenses, but no list of these bills remains.

It sounds like an extension of the funeral racket: Lord assisting himself and his friends with large government orders. He eventually managed to finalise the accounts, and in February 1811 Macquarie praised him, adding, 'I hope you will soon have a good opportunity of proceeding to England *direct* from the Derwent' – that is, not via Sydney.[21] He had had enough of Edward Lord.

Macquarie's expression can be imagined when, a few weeks later, Lord arrived in Sydney. 'Your old friend Mr. Lord and family is coming', Lord's colleague Thomas Birch told an acquaintance there. 'I hope you will have the pleasure to see him' – to ask him to pay a debt Lord owed Birch.[22] However, it does not seem that Lord intended taking his family to England: the trip would involve six months in a confined ship with a baby, a toddler and a six-year-old, then introducing to his elite relatives an illegitimate stepdaughter, his own illegitimate daughter, and his ex-convict working-class wife. Why not leave them in Hobart? One possible reason is that ships were banned from selling cargoes there. They had to go through Port Jackson. Trade became much less profitable, with the price of goods doubled, according to Lord. 'God knows what will become of us', Bowden told him.[23] Perhaps the Lords planned to move their trading activities to New South Wales, or perhaps Maria refused to stay in Hobart without Edward's respectability as a buffer against her convict past.

Ships to England were infrequent, and Edward had a long wait. In June he set sail, but terrible weather forced his ship back after only four days. It left again without him.[24] Perhaps he felt too wretched after the horrors of the storm. Instead, he enjoyed marital life, for Maria conceived that month. Meanwhile, Lord's friend Dr Bowden was his agent in Hobart. He sounds honest, but not particularly competent: 'I do not know whether I have done right in receiving [three notes for money]'. He sent his best wishes to Lord, Mrs Lord and 'your dear little ones', a rare mention of the children.²⁵

Lord's delay in Sydney allowed another spat with Macquarie. From Hobart, Governor Murray sent Macquarie a bill for £145 that Lord had run up with the commissary since 1803, mainly for alcohol. Macquarie presented it to Lord, who replied that he was at a loss to make out what was wanted. He had received the articles, but

> as Your Excellency declined interfering or taking any responsibility for the Acts of the late Lieut.-Governor Collins and my Administration over the Settlement at Hobart Town, and in the most pointed manner in which Your Excellency particularly expressed that you left it wholly for me to account to His Majesty's Ministers for the Acts of the late Lieut.-Governor and myself

Lord continued, utterly losing himself in syntax, that he would include the present bill with the others in London.

Curtly, Macquarie told Lord to pay now. Lord replied that as the government owed him money for his salary as acting governor, he would be happy to receive the balance. He excelled at twisting facts and putting people in the wrong (Macquarie had 'declined interfering' on quite another matter, while in ten weeks Lord had earned only £90 as governor, less than the bill), and Macquarie was infuriated. He told his superior in England about it, adding that Lord 'wrote some very petulant and impertinent Letters … I did not, however, resort to any harsh Measure in Consequence of his very improper Conduct, lest my doing so should have prevented his Return to England'.²⁶ Why was Lord so unnecessarily rude to Macquarie? It seems unwise, to a governor with so much power, and there was no question but that he owed the government the money. Perhaps it was his fiery, arrogant nature overcoming common sense, a feature throughout his life.

Lord was also involved in a court case. Merchant Roland Loane, furious that Lord had dismissed him as a magistrate, sued him for £98. Macquarie's secretary summed up the case as originating when Lord, as governor, certified a receipt to Loane without comparing it with the original voucher from the commissary (presumably for, say, £100, which someone had changed to £198): skullduggery on someone's part, but also laxity on Lord's. Loane won the case, and won again when Lord appealed.²⁷ This is a rare example of Edward Lord coming off second best.

There were more light-hearted activities. During the Sydney races that August, Lieutenant Lord's black mare Star raced James Cox's Fidget two miles for fifty guineas. Star won, a handy sum. A document dated 'August', with no year, probably refers to this time. It shows Edward making a wager with D'Arcy Wentworth, a leading Sydney colonist: a hundred guineas, a large sum, that his horse could run round the Sydney racecourse in two minutes. Then a ship for England turned up and Lord had to leave before the race could be held. He ordered that 'the only two horses capable of Galloping well belonging to him' – so he must have owned a number of horses – be trained for the race, but one broke loose in the stable and both kicked each other so savagely that both died. Lord left the race club to decide who won the bet.[28] Fawkner said Lord lost his money gambling,

Edward Lord bets D'Arcy Wentworth that a horse of his could run round Sydney race course in two minutes (State Library of New South Wales)

and these stories are the only concrete evidence, showing him betting large sums on what to the non-gambler (and perhaps to Maria) seem pointless challenges. They also show him losing valuable horses through the carelessness of employees; he does not sound like a thorough supervisor.

Finally, in September, Macquarie surely heaved a heartfelt sigh of relief: the whaler *New Zealander* left Sydney with Edward Lord on board. Macquarie had relented sufficiently to give him despatches for London – not urgent, with any luck, for the voyage was frustratingly long. It did show Lord opportunities for profit in the southern hemisphere, by whaling and also pearling, as a fellow passenger was taking a large quantity of pearls to England. Lord had plenty of time to admire them. It was not until May 1812 that *New Zealander* arrived in England – with news that Lord, presumably wanting a faster passage, had transferred at St Helena to a frigate, HMS *Psyche*. In the Bay of Biscay *Psyche* sprang a leak and put back to Corunna in Spain. Lord cannot have arrived in England until late May at the earliest, eight months after leaving Sydney.[29]

He spent a bare five months in England, much of it in London. The capital was the source of power, patronage and wealth. Colonial governors had limited powers: London took good care that it kept control in its own hands, especially of appointments, promotions and large land grants. Lord's friend Joseph Foveaux believed that it was not possible to make any impression on London unless you were on the spot.[30] Lord would have been well aware of this.

His main weapon was his brother John, who was well situated to help. He had been elected to parliament and presented to the King, and he had requested and received a baronetcy: by the time Edward arrived, his brother was Sir John Owen of Orielton, M.P.[31] Sir John lent Edward the huge sum of £20,000 and helped him obtain a large grant of 3000 acres in New South Wales from the secretary of state for the colonies, Lord Bathurst. Bathurst explained to Macquarie that this was far beyond what he considered any individual capable of cultivating properly, but Lord produced a promise of 1805 by his predecessor, Lord Castlereagh, to grant the land to him – 1805, when Lord was in distant Van Diemen's Land, his brother John was still an unremarkable London lawyer, and they had little if any influence.[32] The chance of that particular document being genuine seems slight. However, in 1812 Sir John was in parliament, supporting Castlereagh's party. Castlereagh was foreign secretary, trying to defeat Napoleon, and a land grant in distant Australia must have seemed trivial. One can imagine the cosy after-dinner chat that produced that particular promise. But Lord's application to become governor in Hobart was rejected: not even Sir John Owen's influence could overcome harsh criticism from Bligh and Macquarie.[33]

Lord was active in other ways. Perhaps he enjoyed social life, drinking, horseracing and gambling with his brother: nothing was written down, but the man who made the bet in Sydney with D'Arcy Wentworth would have surely taken part in similar entertainments in England. More respectably, he gave evidence to a parliamentary inquiry into convict transportation. The only witness from Van Diemen's Land, he described the island in glowing terms. It was much superior to Sydney in health, climate and soil, 'in every respect far more productive', 'as fine, beautiful picturesque country as can be'. The island was large enough to deserve the name of a continent, he said optimistically. It had excellent iron ore and coal, and its pasture was so rich that cattle grew four times as heavy as their imported parents (surely an impossibility – but Lord never minded exaggeration). Settlers produced two-thirds of their food and with proper encouragement could provide it all, and the people were well behaved. He did agree that the lower orders, 'and in some instances in the higher', looked for spirits with avidity, as his questioner phrased it, but they were hardly alone in this in 1812, and overall it was an extremely positive picture of a promising colony. Oddly, Lord was not questioned about transportation.[34]

Lord was also a witness in the trial of Francis Shipman, a convict clerk in the Hobart commissariat, accused of forging a bill of exchange. Lord and another officer gave evidence that the bill was written in Shipman's handwriting, not the purported author's; Shipman was found guilty.[35] As well, Lord arranged to take his wife Maria's sister Catherine to Australia; resigned from the marines; and either bought or more likely chartered a ship, *James Hay*, stocking it with 'a valuable and extensive investment of British goods' he said was worth the immense total of £30,000: £20,000 from his brother John, and £10,000 he and Maria had made in Van Diemen's Land.[36] With his usual eye for an opportunity, he decided to sell the goods in Hobart, where ships had been banned from selling cargoes for the last few years. Lord persuaded Bathurst to reverse this, and write a letter telling Macquarie so. He must have felt satisfied as he stood on the deck, bound for Australia. First killing in a port closed to trade for years! Hobartians would be clamouring for his goods. This voyage took only half as long as his recent Sydney–England trudge: he left England in November 1812 and arrived in Hobart in February 1813.[37]

Parramatta in 1811 when Maria Lord lived there: a small, rural settlement, with Aborigines on its outskirts (Caroline Simpson Library & Research Collection, Sydney Living Museums)

There a rude shock awaited him: he was not allowed to trade. He claimed it was Macquarie's fault, that Macquarie ignored Bathurst's letter, telling the new governor, Thomas Davey, not to let any vessels trade in Hobart, and not to let Lord land. Only after Lord had been forced on to Sydney did Macquarie open Hobart to trade. This sounds like Lord twisting facts again. Law-abiding Macquarie was unlikely to ignore government orders, and the timing seems too tight for the one ship that arrived from England in the period to have brought Bathurst's letter.[38] A more likely explanation is that Macquarie did not receive the instruction until later.

A letter to Lord from his friend Anthony Fenn Kemp gives another side of the story. Kemp wrote from London just after Lord left, to tell him that shells a friend of his, Garnham Blaxcell, sold to Captain Barclay in Sydney for £1250 brought next to nothing in England. Barclay was, naturally, 'quite violent & very warm in his language about being taken in as he calls it ... indeed the whole of the Jerusalem Coffee House [a centre of commercial gossip] rings with the notoriety of the Colony'. Leading merchants 'have begun to express their alarm'. Kemp advised Lord to alter his own speculation to whale oil.

'I am sure you will do all in your power to release your worthy Brother from the responsibility he has incurred for the James Hay & cargo as soon as possible', continued Kemp. 'What a dreadful disappointment in the Return cargo will be to you ... I will not mention to your Brother any thing to alarm him respecting the Speculation'.[39] It is not clear exactly what havey-cavey business was going on, but this does suggest that Lord's version of the *James Hay* fiasco, blaming Macquarie for his loss, could have glossed over his own share of blame.

WHILE EDWARD WAS AWAY, Maria lived quietly in Parramatta with her four children: Caroline, Eliza, John and the new baby, Edward Robert, born in 1812: with her husband away, Maria could give the boy her father's name, Robert. She extended her usual competence to child-raising, for of eight births only one infant died, a good record (at the same time, her in-laws Sir John and Lady Owen were losing baby after baby). By now the Lords were well-to-do, and Maria could afford servants and a comfortable life. Seven-year-old Caroline would be starting her education, becoming a companion to her mother. Family life sounds pleasant enough, if a little humdrum for Maria, with no shop to manage. She thought of returning to Hobart but decided against it. Matthew Bowden continued as the Lords' agent, assuring Maria that he was acting as best he could in their interests – so he reported to her as well as Edward, showing they were partners in the enterprise.[40]

Maria had some business activities at Parramatta. Before he left, Edward bought 150 cattle. Maria was in charge of them, adroitly sending them to graze on crown land without permission – 'extremely improper and daring', said Macquarie. In February 1812 she offered for lease a farm on the banks of the George's River. Had the family been living there, or was she dabbling in real estate? Maria also gave donations to help establish a burial ground, school and road.[41]

Edward Lord arrived back in Sydney on 30 March 1813, after eighteen months away, five in England and thirteen at sea. Maria and the children welcomed him, and he could exclaim on how the older ones had grown and see his year-old son and namesake for the first time. Maria had the pleasure of meeting her younger sister Catherine, the first member of her own family she had seen for a decade. She did not have her company for long, as in August Catherine married Lieutenant James Taylor of the 73rd regiment.[42] Marriage to an officer and gentleman: this was social success for a girl from a fairly humble background.

Ship News.

On Tuesday arrived the brig *James Hay*, of 185 tons, Capt. WILLIAM CAMPBELL, accompanied by EDWARD LORD, Esq. late of the Royal Marines, with a valuable and extensive investment of British goods.—Passengers, G. JOHNSTON, Esq. and Daughter.—The above vessel sailed from Yarmouth with convoy the 10th of November last, with the armed brig *Emme*, of 10 guns, commanded by Lieut. BISSETT, with which vessel she parted off Lisbon: She called at St. Jago's to refresh, and after a stay of 6 days resumed her voyage; touched also at the Derwent last Monday se'nnight, and only delayed one day, thence completing her passage from England in four months and 14 days.—Also a passenger by the James Hay, Miss Reisley.

Edward Lord arrives back in Sydney 1813, his disappointment at Hobart glossed over. The *Sydney Gazette* has thought up yet another spelling of 'Riseley' (*Sydney Gazette*, 3 April 1813)

Edward Lord, always quick to act, did not waste time in Sydney. Within ten days of his arrival his cargo was advertised for sale at Garnham Blaxcell's warehouse. It comprised mainly clothing and fabric, everything from 'a choice selection of the most fashionable millinery' to materials with the most exotic names: sarsnets, bombazetts, shaloons and calimancoes, corded dimities, jaconet and regency cord muslins, as well as buckabuck, damask table linen and 'printed cambricks and calicoes of the newest patterns'. Other goods ranged from jewellery and sewing silks to more mundane porter and pickled herrings.[43]

Lord also remembered the pearls he saw on his voyage to England, advertising for 25 seamen to crew *James Hay* on a voyage eastward. Apparently he tried to recruit Tahitians, for a few weeks later, Macquarie told him that three natives of Tahiti lately in his employment had complained that they had not received the wages, clothes and provisions he promised. Macquarie instructed Lord to redress these claims. The outcome is unknown, but *James Hay* did sail to Tahiti, where the captain employed 35 pearl divers. On his return to Sydney in early 1814 he reported on a rebellion among the Tahitians, but said nothing about the success or otherwise of the pearling.[44] Edward Lord did not repeat the venture.

IT IS NOT CLEAR WHETHER EDWARD LORD returned to Australia intending to stay in New South Wales or return to Van Diemen's Land. Asking for his land grant in New South Wales suggests the former, but once more he and Macquarie clashed. Lord asked for his 3000 acres at Emu Plains. Macquarie told him this land was set apart for government cattle, and in any case Lord could not have his grant yet, as the chief surveyor was away and his subordinate was not experienced enough to measure such a large grant (surely Macquarie dictated these last words with dark pleasure).

He did put the Lord family on government rations and assigned Edward six convict labourers, but 'this Gentleman is still very much dissatisfied at not receiving greater Indulgences' and at losing Emu Plains, Macquarie told Bathurst:

> Mr. Lord thinks, because he happens to have a Wealthy Brother, who is a Member of Parliament, he ought to receive whatever he asks for. I believe he intends applying through his Brother for a larger Grant of land, and Still greater Indulgences.

Macquarie advised Bathurst not to give Lord more land: 3000 acres was quite enough for 'any Person coming out to this Colony in Mr. Lord's Rank in Life' – or, as Macquarie put it in another letter, Lord had already received much more land 'than any Merits which he possessed, seem to entitle him to, when considered in the same Light with other Free Settlers'. Why so disparaging? A mere ex-lieutenant? The ex-convict wife? One would have thought a baronet's brother had quite a high rank in life, while most of the other free settlers were nothing much to write home about. By now, however, Macquarie detested Lord. Bathurst agreed with Macquarie about the land, replying that he would grant Lord no more. He realised now that Lord had only obtained the first grant through chicanery.⁴⁵

The first mention of Elizabeth Storer, a servant of the Lords as they leave Sydney for Hobart in 1813
(*Sydney Gazette*, 28 August 1813)

In the end Lord took up only half his land grant in New South Wales, a 1600-acre farm near Narellan that he called Orielton. By July 1813 he also owned, or leased, Herbert Banks Farm near Liverpool. But something persuaded him not to stay in New South Wales: perhaps Macquarie's dislike, or perhaps the advantages of Van Diemen's Land that he had so enthusiastically extolled in London, especially now it was open for trade. In September 1813 Edward, Maria and young Edward Robert, with two servants including Elizabeth Storer (of whom much more later) sailed to Hobart. Perhaps Edward took Maria to start organising their concerns in Hobart, leaving the older children in the charge of their aunt Catherine. In January 1814 he returned to Sydney, a difficult trip as the ship was blown well south of Van Diemen's Land before being able to sail north. However, he made it, and in Sydney checked on the *James Hay* pearling venture; organised the transfer of the rest of his land grant to Van Diemen's Land; bought a trading ship, *Spring*; and on it brought the rest of his family back to Van Diemen's Land: Caroline, Eliza and John, with five servants. To Macquarie's horror, he also applied for 2000 more acres in Van Diemen's Land. Certainly not! was the answer.⁴⁶

The Lords returned to Hobart after three years away to find that much had happened. Local people had little to praise in their rulers, but plentiful material for gossip.

105

Flight of Fancy:
Edward Lord's mother tries to probe

SCENE: *The Lord dinner table in Pembroke, early June 1812.*

Edward has been welcomed home, enquiries made after his asthma, his trip. Now ...

Mrs Lord: Edward, dear, do tell me about your family. So many letters seem to get lost on the voyage, and I've never learned the details.

Edward: You'd love the children, Mother, your dear little grandchildren. Caroline is a sweet girl, so pretty, and Eliza toddles about in such a fetching way. As for John Owen! He's so promising. He must be two now, and when I left he was already starting to talk. He has a definite look of you, he's a real Owen, while Eliza has Father's beautiful blue eyes.

Mrs Lord: How old are the girls now, Edward?

Edward: Let me see, Eliza is, er – I'm a typical father, I never know – she'll be four later in the year, and it's a few days from Caroline's sixth birthday. By the way, Mother, I hope you've remembered it's my birthday next week. Your wonderful Welsh cakes, I wonder if we could have them? I've been so looking forward to your superb dinners!

Mrs Lord: How do you cope with all those dreadful convicts?

Edward: We have nothing to do with them socially, of course, though some make good enough servants. Maria is excellent at training them.

Mrs Lord: How is your wife, Edward dear?

Edward: Maria is a marvellous wife! She's nearly as capable at running the household as you are, Mother. We were short of food in the early years, but she provided the most wonderful dinner party for my birthday! Almost as good as this delicious lamb we're eating tonight.

Mrs Lord: Where do her people come from, Edward?

Edward: They're on the land in Huntingdonshire. A pity it's so far away, too far for you to visit. Maria has a number of brothers and sisters. I'll ask one of the girls if she'd like to come to Van Diemen's Land – Maria would love to see someone from her family …

Mrs Lord: And what took Maria to the colonies?

Edward: There are such good opportunities for young ladies! And Maria is so courageous, with such a taste for adventure.

Mrs Lord: Did she go by herself?

Edward: Certainly not! She had respectable companions.

Mrs Lord: Where did you meet her?

Edward: On a visit to Sydney. We were introduced at a gathering, and I knew at once she was the one for me. She reminded me so much of you.

Mrs Lord: And when did you marry?

Edward: Straight away, in October 1805. The eighth of October is our wedding anniversary. We'll have a party next year – and speaking of parties, have you heard of this new dance, Mother, the waltz? It sounds very dashing …

Mrs Lord: But you didn't mention your wedding in the letter I received in 1807.

Edward: Letters do get delayed – and goodness, I've forgotten the presents! Such lovely pearls, I know they'll suit you! Just a minute, I'll fetch them …

Mrs Lord gives up, remembering that Edward always was very good at explaining.

8. INTERLUDE: SCANDAL IN GOVERNMENT HOUSE

'WE HAVE HAD STRANGE DOINGS HERE. Indeed the place gets worse & worse', Matthew Bowden wrote from Hobart to his friend Edward Lord in 1811.[1] These doings make the Collins period look like a mere kindergarten of immorality and corruption, the Lord period a brief ray of sunlight. Though tangential to the Lords' careers, this chapter is included to show extremes of behaviour in Van Diemen's Land. Edward and Maria Lord might have had some failings, but others had more.

If Macquarie had disapproved of Lord as acting governor, he faced worse shocks in the future. He arrived in Sydney full of zeal to fulfill his orders: stop graft and corruption, establish morality and the rule of law. Macquarie was a competent and upright man with power to enforce his rulings, the first in the Australian colonies since Governor Phillip twenty years earlier. His physical power came from his soldiers, his own 73rd Regiment, which like Macquarie himself hailed from Scotland. The dissolute Rum Corps, scourge of so many former governors, was disbanded.

After an exciting trip out – catching a Portuguese slave ship with 540 females on board, and stunning the inhabitants of Rio de Janeiro with their kilts[2] – Macquarie and the 73rd arrived in Sydney in December 1809. Determined to establish efficient, honest government in his subordinate settlements, Macquarie chose as lieutenant-governor at the Derwent a member of his regiment, Captain John Murray, 'in whose Honor and Integrity I can place unlimited Confidence'. Murray was in charge of troops at Parramatta, earning £91 a year, so the governor's £450 was a pleasant rise. Macquarie instructed him to settle the Norfolk Islanders' claims, stop smuggling, encourage agriculture, observe strict economy, build a barracks, establish a police force, enforce religious observance 'and exert yourself to the utmost in exciting the Inhabitants to Sobriety and industry, religion, and Morality'.[3] Murray ignored such boring tasks.

He arrived in Hobart in July 1810 with his wife Lucy and their young son Charles. Surveyor George Harris was thrilled. At last there was a respectable governor's wife, and ladies could attend entertainments at government house. 'Several splendid ones have been given by the new Commandant – He is a very pleasant Gentlemanlike Man and Mrs. M. a most accomplish'd

Previous pages: Hobart remains a small township in the middle of vast areas of bush – though the artist depicts an encouraging amount of shipping in the harbour (Allport Library and Museum of Fine Arts, TAHO)

Opposite: Lord's friend Matthew Bowden sends him news of Hobart and its scandals
(State Library of New South Wales)

a much dearer rate than we have ever been accustomed to pay here. The Captn. landed great part of his Wheat and was to have left it with me, but he suddenly changed his mind and reshipped it — and I was obliged to detain a part of it until I was paid the expences I had incurred in consequence. He is certainly one of the meanest men we have had from that quarter. — As you surmised, Forbrook comes up in this despot respecting the business of the Store Receipts. Murray utterly denies any knowledge of the transaction, and it is avowed and I believe sworn to by D. Mc Carty that the Wheat was turned into the Stores by him previous to the issue of the receipt. Boothman and Macum accompany Forbrook to Sydney, and he does not scruple to say that he is going up to prosecute you for defamation of Character!!! —

Murray and Mrs M. have separated and Wright is sent up with "Mr Despatches." — They went out a few days ago. M— fired and M— fired and M— fired in the air — A day or two after Wright was ordered to hold himself in readiness to carry the Despatches, and the business will be I fancy fully discussed at P.S. So you see we are not without our troubles at the moment. — A small party dined with the Commandant yesterday — of which I formed one. I could not help contrasting the day with the last anniversary when we were all so happy at yours splendid & truly hospitable board. — However I still hope for better days.

Murray will certainly be removed whatever may be the result of Forbrook's business — Gunning is appointed

Woman – they are indeed an acquisition in these remote parts.' One reason for this enthusiasm was that Murray suspended the judge advocate, Samuel Bate, for 'Contempt and total ignorance of the most common Laws of his Country', and appointed Harris in his place, Harris having been trained as a lawyer – an unusual background for a judge in Australia at this time.[4]

Macquarie's confidence in Murray soon waned. First he was disappointed with the way he argued with Bate and then Edward Lord (as described earlier, over Lord drawing bills to complete his accounts).[5] Worse was to come. The ship *Union* left Cape Town with a cargo of spirits, cleared for Penang. Instead it sailed to Hobart, where Murray should have checked its papers, refused to let it contact land and ordered it to Penang. Instead he allowed it to land spirits, 'sanctioning an illicit and contraband trade', and gave it clearance for Sydney where its owners, Edward Lord's friends William Collins and Garnham Blaxcell (a Sydney merchant, of whom more later, all of it extremely dubious) tried to land the rest of the spirits illegally, using every trick in the book. Macquarie had a great deal of trouble preventing this. Edward Lord was involved, peripherally – his friend Matthew Bowden commiserated with him over his 'trouble' in the affair, and he travelled to Sydney in *Union* – but Macquarie saw William Collins, Blaxcell and Murray as the villains. He told Murray that his conduct was most reprehensible, and hoped this reproof would have its effect.[6]

Governor Macquarie: upright and honest (Tasmanian Archive and Heritage Office)

It did not. Murray gave his inspector of public works, Lieutenant Wright, the contract to build the barracks: allowing a man to be both builder and inspector. Wright did a terrible job. In 1811 Macquarie found the unfinished building 'wretchedly bad in every respect', with such defective workmanship he ordered it demolished. And Wright had the gall to ask for a refund of his expenses![7]

The next opinion of Murray's regime comes as no surprise. Settler Thomas Keston's 'Secret Memoirs' cannot be entirely believed – he could not have been an eye-witness to at least some of the scenes he described

– but they reflect Hobart gossip, while other sources prove him at least broadly accurate:

> I am now entering into one of the most scandalous Gov^ts. that ever poor mortals were condemned to serve under ... the man I am speaking of [Murray] has long been launched into the Vortex of Dissipation & a contemptable ambition of excelling his Companions in ostentatious & licentious Practices & he brought a kept Miss [his wife] with him whose taste was congenial to his own for every fashionable folly & the most profuse extravagances

Once more a junior officer set free from immediate supervision cast aside prudent behaviour for the sake of present enjoyment. Why throw away that £450 a year, not to mention future promotion, for the sake of a few drunken revelries? Macquarie was sure to hear about them, retribution was sure to follow. Perhaps at this remote little settlement Murray, and others, suffered under the happy illusion that they were in a secret pleasure-ground, some sort of Valhalla, where they could do anything they liked without censure from boring, prudish superior officers.

The power of being in command went to Murray's head, Keston claimed:

> the high Spirits of this Pair so began to shew itself, no longer content with the plain way they were obliged to follow before under a strict & well disciplined Commander at Sydney & when he found himself from under the immediate Command of him and no Controul, he began to live in the most fashionable Style our little Colony would allow of[8]

Since government house was in bad repair, Murray bought a pretty cottage with government money. Matthew Bowden was unimpressed with the hospitality there, even on the important occasion of the anniversary of the King's birthday. 'A small party dined with the Commandant yesterday – of which I formed one', he wrote to Edward Lord. 'I could not help contrasting the day with the last anniversary when we were all so happy at your splendid & truly hospitable board.'[9] Lucy Murray does not sound much of a housekeeper. It transpired that she had other interests.

As far as actual governing went, Murray did little. Keston thought his governance slack and corrupt. No accounts were kept; the treasurer's clerk told Keston he had nothing to do but make out a few bills, draw out the money, give some to his master and keep the rest for himself. 'I have got a fine sporting master', said the clerk. 'He is the Gentleman for Boatracing & Cock fighting, he sports the money, he thinks nothing of 50 or 100 £ at a Bet' – but these sporting gentlemen, 'lazy, proud ignorant & saucy', left many debts unpaid.[10]

Rather than governing, Murray enjoyed carousing, paying with regimental money. In return, 'he allowed the Soldiers to commit all kinds of Depredations on the peacable Inhabitants with Impunity … & when any of the Inhabitants made a Complaint to him, he would tell them they must keep clear of his Soldiers' – just like Collins and Lord, favouring their soldiers at the expense of settlers. One settler, Roland Loane, complained to Macquarie that some soldiers attacked his house one night. They were arrested, but Murray released them without inquiry. As well, Loane was not paid for meat he sold to the government. 'Highly reprehensible', wrote Macquarie.[11]

Murray ruled autocratically. Hobart people thought a shopkeeper was dishonest. As it was useless to apply to Murray for justice, a free settler pasted a placard telling the story on a large tree stump, the usual way of publicising complaints. Along came Murray, the shopkeeper complained to him, 'a kind of Court Martial sat there and then', and the settler was sentenced to 300 lashes – though, legally, free settlers could not be flogged.[12]

> Our Commandant is now seen in his true Character, he is continually in a State of Inebriation & Stupidity & allowing all manner of Vice to be carried on, Cock fighting Horse Racing, roasting Sheep & Bullocks whole on the Parade & allowg. the Soldiers to commit all sorts of Insults & Outrage on the Inhabitants breaking down their Garden fences & beating People with the Palings

wrote Keston. This is when Bowden told Edward Lord that Hobart was getting worse and worse. The juiciest piece of gossip was that 'Murray and Mrs. M. have seperated'. Lieutenant Wright was the cause.[13] Keston has the details, written in long, breathless sentences:

> Now our Commandant becomes so nasty & filthy in his Bed that his darling Angel cannot bare to lay in the same Bed with him or be in the same Room with him & she takes every opportunity to go to Lt Wright a fine young Man, Inspector of public works out

> of his disgusting Company. The Commandant would get drunk every night & Miss would put him to bed & when he was asleep, she would go off to his Lieu^t & they had been carrying on this Sport a long time before our drowsy Gent^n. found it out

Perhaps by one of those anonymous notes tacked to a tree?

> one night he came home & pretended to be very drunk & Miss put him to Bed as usual & when she thought him asleep, she went off to this amorous young man but he was watching her manuvers & he heard her go out & sent one of his Servants after her, to see where she went to & the man came back & told him she went to L^t. Wrights & he stopt about a Quarter on an Hour & then started off & catched them both in Bed together

The uniform of the 73rd regiment, modelled by Hamish Maxwell-Stewart (James Alexander)

Murray 'put Miss away' and challenged Wright to a duel. Murray fired to kill, but missed; guilty Wright fired in the air. Murray sent him to Sydney, where he leaped into regimental life, winning a horse race.[14] (The following year he was cashiered for neglect of duty and conduct unbecoming to an officer and gentleman: abandoning his post to drink and play cards with his social inferiors.[15]) Meanwhile, Lucy Murray went to live with Samuel Bate, the judge advocate dismissed by her husband, whose wife had returned to England. The general opinion, Bowden told Lord, was that Murray would be removed from his command. The atmosphere in Hobart was terrible: 'we are all extremely dull and very uncomfortable'.[16]

Then a bombshell fell on Murray. In November 1811 Macquarie, understandably curious, arrived to inspect the southern settlement. In his diary he praised sparingly and criticised rarely, but was often ominously silent. He barely mentioned Murray. The Macquaries held nightly dinners for Hobart's gentlemen, including malcontent Roland Loane, gossipy Knopwood, and a relative of theirs, an officer stationed in Hobart. As the port circulated, surely Macquarie found out everything. He told Murray that he would be replaced as governor, though he would make this fellow officer a magistrate and give his son a grant of land, with a trustee to ensure Murray did not sell it.[17]

The new governor, Major Andrew Geils, arrived in February 1812. Murray now utterly disgraced himself by taking back his immoral wife – condoning her behaviour. Macquarie wrote him a stinging reproof:

> I am sorry it is not in my power any longer to address you, Sir, in a familiar or friendly Manner.
>
> The late very extraordinary and highly unjustifiable Step you have adopted, of taking back and living with your wife, after being yourself the Publisher to the World of her shameful and abandoned conduct justly forfeits the good opinion, respect, and friendship of not only myself, but also of all your Brother Officers.[18]

They could not be expected to serve with Murray, who should resign. Murray refused, and it seems unlikely that Macquarie thought any better of him when he and Lucy parted again. In 1814 part of the 73rd was ordered to Ceylon (Sri Lanka), so off Murray sailed, taking his son and leaving enormous debts. He had also sold the pretty cottage and his son's land

The king's palace at Kandy in 1819, painted by Murray's fellow-officer Lieutenant William Lyttleton. Kandy's capture provided each British soldier involved with a small fortune
(Allport Library and Museum of Fine Arts, TAHO)

grant, both illegally. But change came, as Edward Lord reported to a friend in 1815. 'Murray has quite reformed (never drinks) and ... his prize money exceeds Ten Thousand Pounds'. This was gained as booty in an expedition in Ceylon against the Kingdom of Kandy.[19] How irritating it must have been for Murray's debtors in Hobart. Naturally, none of the booty went to repaying them.

Meanwhile Lucy Murray found true love, or at least a long-term partner. Thomas Kent was an adventurer, who failed at producing hemp, growing flax in New Zealand, mining coal on Bruny Island, burning seaweed for alkali and producing tannin from wattle bark. One of his few successes was buying from Murray his son's land grant and selling it to Edward Lord at a profit. Lucy Murray was living with him by 1814.[20]

Sued for debt, in 1822 Thomas Kent skipped the colony. Lucy followed him, and in London Kent obtained a land grant to produce tannin in Australia (showing how gullible some officials were, and how easily they gave land grants). John Murray died, and Lucy and Thomas married. In 1829 they sailed to Sydney; the ship stopped at Hobart, where the *Colonial Times* printed a fascinating paragraph. Did its readers realise that Mrs Thomas Kent, who had just arrived in the colony, was formerly Mrs Murray, a resident in the colony?[21] One imagines the reaction. *That* woman! Do you remember ...?

SHIP NEWS. Yesterday arrived the brig *Active* from the Derwent.—Passengers, Lieutenant Colonel Geils, Mrs. Geils, and Miss Geils; and Mr. Edward Lord.—She left the River Derwent the 14th instant; but was by strong northerly winds blown considerably to the southward of the South Cape of Van Diemen's Land.

The Geils family and Edward Lord arrive in Sydney, 1814 after a rough voyage from Hobart (*Sydney Gazette*, 29 January 1814)

In Sydney, Thomas was arrested for debt and the land grant vanished in repayments. In 1830 Lucy died, 'to the unspeakable grief of her attached husband', who himself died two years later.[22]

THE NEXT GOVERNOR, MAJOR ANDREW GEILS, arrived in Sydney with his family in 1811. The voyage from England must have been appalling for his wife Mary, with six young children, a rough trip, seasickness and a martinet husband. If Andrew Geils was anything like his son (see below) Mary might have had to cope with domestic violence. The Geils were not long in Sydney, for Macquarie ordered them to Hobart to replace Murray, having formed a high opinion of Geils' honour and integrity.[23] It did not last.

> **SYDNEY.**
>
> Sitting Magistrate for the ensuing Week — S. Lord, Esq.
>
> Assize of Bread for the ensuing Week.—Fivepence for a loaf weighing 2lbs. when cold.
>
> On Tuesday the Ruby, commanded by Captn. Ambrose, sailed for Calcutta via Hobart Town, whither she conveys the Detachment of the 73d Regiment, and 80 male prisoners, announced in General Orders for that Settlement.
>
> Major GEILS and FAMILY also embarked in the Ruby for Hobart Town at nine in the morning, on which occasion a Lieutenant Colonel's Salute of nine guns was fired from Dawes's Battery;—His EXCELLENCY the GOVERNOR and Mrs. MACQUARIE accompanied Major GEILS and FAMILY down the Harbour, and returned about mid-day.
>
> Thursday evening returned the schooner Boyd, from Norfolk Island, from hence 16 weeks, 8 of which she was beating off the Island, from whence she took her departure a month since, leaving the

The Geils family leaves for Hobart in 1812, with a respectful salute – though the *Sydney Gazette* reported this after its news of convicts embarking (*Sydney Gazette*, 15 February 1812)

Geils ruled with a firm hand. The troops were thoroughly drilled, church was compulsory, prisoners were not allowed to leave town without a pass, and female convicts living 'in a state of profligacy and infamy' were not to be victualled. These decisions pleased Macquarie.[24] They were about the only actions of Geils' that did.

After this promising start, Geils lapsed. Once more, a governor who had been given what amounted to complete authority, at least in the short term – Macquarie could write fulminating letters, but there was little he could actually do – used his power to promote his own interests. Geils seized the opportunity, not to carouse like Murray, but to accumulate land and money. He asked for a 3000-acre grant. Outraged, Macquarie granted 1200 acres to Mary Geils only, for it was illegal to grant land to a governor. Geils bought four farms and spent much time and government equipment developing them, instead of governing. Nothing much was happening in Hobart, Matthew Bowden wrote to Maria Lord; there were few ships, and the place was never more dull and uncomfortable (the same adjectives he had used to describe the town under Murray).[25]

Soon Macquarie realised that Geils was appropriating government property, taking large quantities of spirits, grain, sugar and hardware from the stores; putting no fewer than 29 convicts on his own private work; and making no progress in public works. He was, said Macquarie, 'a Man of weak judgment, extremely venal and rapacious, and always inclined to sacrifice the interests of the Public to his own sordid and selfish views'. He thought Geils should be cashiered.[26]

Fortunately for Geils, the new governor arrived before Macquarie was able to take action against Geils. Like Murray, Geils returned to being a soldier, but he clashed with Leonard Fosbrook, the commissary, both accusing each other of peculation and embezzlement. At a military inquiry in Sydney, Fosbrook accused Geils of ill-treating him, taking huge amounts of government spirits, provisions and equipment illegally, using government men on his own work and selling pardons. Geils' defence was masterly, a mixture of bombast, sentiment, declamation and stout denial. The charges were purely Fosbrook's malice; they were absurd; Geils as a gentleman could not possibly act like this. The inquiry, conducted by his brother officers, found a court martial unnecessary. Macquarie believed otherwise, but was powerless to act.[27] Perhaps he did not wish to: regimental loyalty meant he treated both Murray and Geils leniently.

Back in Hobart, the Geils family attended a ball at government house. The shortage of ladies meant Hannah and Mary Geils, aged sixteen and seventeen, comprised two-fifths of the single women. The family's fortunes then went downhill. Like Murray, they went to Ceylon, and suffered a terrible voyage: severe illness, everyone ill, the baby dying. The parents sent their four eldest boys back to Britain for their education. Rounding southern Africa in bad weather, the ship's captain thought he was further west than he really was, turned north at night and ran into the coast. The ship was wrecked and most passengers, including all four Geils boys, drowned.[28]

Mary and Andrew were devastated by 'this most dreadful and unparalleled misfortune'. However, Andrew inherited the family's Scottish estate, where Mary bore two more children: a total of ten, of whom five died young. Andrew tried to become the next governor of Van Diemen's Land, but not surprisingly he was not appointed.[29]

Andrew and Mary's son John married an heiress, but she left him and took the rare step (especially for a woman) of applying for a divorce, accusing him of cruelty to her and adultery with two female servants. John fought the case all the way to the House of Lords, but his wife gained her divorce.[30] That ball in Hobart in 1814 must have seemed the high point of the Geils family's fortunes.

The stories of Murray and Geils show what was happening in Van Diemen's Land while the Lords were away: the next governor was to have a much stronger influence on their fortunes. Under Thomas Davey, Edward and Maria Lord found opportunities to expand, to lay the foundations of their fortune.

le Mountain, and part of the Harbour and TOWN of
Governor DAVEY, AND THE OFFIC

9. YET ANOTHER INADEQUATE GOVERNOR

'PENAL COLONIES ARE STRANGE PLACES and strange creatures are these rulers over the people in such colonies', wrote John Pascoe Fawkner; and none was much stranger than Van Diemen's Land's next governor, Thomas Davey. Giving men jobs on the basis of recommendation by their patrons rather than their ability or training resulted in some terrible decisions, but few worse than this. Better options were available, for more capable men applied, notably Edward Lord and Joseph Foveaux; but Davey had the most powerful patron. Macquarie told London that no man was more unfit for the position, and it is hard to argue with him.[1]

Like almost everyone else who claimed to be gentry in Van Diemen's Land, Thomas Davey's social position was marginal. His father owned a woollen mill in the town of Tiverton in Devon. Thomas, baptised in 1758, was his only child. Thomas' mother died when the boy was seven. By one of those unbelievable quirks of fate, her name was Temperance.[2]

In an age when patronage was all-important in getting ahead, the Davey family relied on the local lords, the Ryders. Dudley Ryder was a member of parliament. At first his, and therefore the Daveys', success was only moderate, and Davey senior needed 'sturdy begging' to obtain a commission in the marines for his son. What had Thomas already done, that such begging was needed? After a decade of undistinguished service, Davey volunteered to join the First Fleet to Australia. He claimed to be the first to land there, but histories do not mention him in any context, so his contribution to the founding of Australia seems negligible. He gained no promotion, despite requests to Ryder. In 1794 he returned to England and married. His wife, Margaret, was described as meek, uncomplaining, highly respectable and 'very kindly spoken of by all'. The Daveys' only child, Lucy, was born in 1796.[3]

Davey claimed he played a leading role in suppressing the naval mutiny at the Nore in 1797 and fought at Trafalgar but, again, histories do not mention him. However, better days arrived. In 1804 Ryder's close friend William Pitt became prime minister. Ryder held high office, was created Earl of Harrowby, and as such had huge clout in disseminating patronage,

Previous pages: Hobart in 1815 by W.H. Craig. A London society artist, Craig was transported for theft. In Sydney he was punished again for forgery, escaped and was caught, sent to Van Diemen's Land and liberated by bushrangers, whom he dobbed in to the authorities – yet another astounding story from the early days. To please Governor Davey, he painted this view of Hobart (State Library of New South Wales) saving Davey from being cashiered as a bankrupt, and gaining him promotion. Then Davey asked Harrowby for the position of Van Diemen's Land governor.[4]

The man in charge was Lord Liverpool. Harrowby sent him Davey's hugely exaggerated CV, adding, 'I understand that the situation which he sollicits, is one in many respects so disagreeable, that he is not likely to have many competitors'. If Liverpool thought Davey 'not unfit', Harrowby would appreciate his being given 'an honourable and what he considers a comfortable retreat'. The application looked acceptable, and in December 1811 Liverpool appointed Davey lieutenant-governor at almost double the previous salary, £800 instead of £450.[5] Harrowby again, presumably.

Thomas Davey as a handsome, respectable-looking young man
(Allport Library and Museum of Fine Arts, TAHO)

Liverpool cannot have bothered with background checks. When Davey was appointed he was in prison for debt, after borrowing regimental funds and not repaying them. Senior public servants were so appalled that they withheld Davey's salary until this debt was repaid. The under-secretary of state even took the extraordinary step of warning Macquarie about him. (Conversation in the public service tea-room can be imagined: these damned politicians and their dreadful sycophants and hangers-on!) As soon as Davey was appointed he started bombarding the Colonial Office with requests for advances in pay, a secretary, free stationery … He needed the advance, for he had other debts, and could not leave prison to take up his appointment until they were paid. Finally in June 1812 he sailed for Sydney, though his baggage went on a different ship. He did his best to leave without Margaret and Lucy, who heard of the appointment by chance, and only just managed to reach the ship in time. Davey was probably grateful in the end. A heavy drinker, he was prone to accidents and nearly died after falling from the ship's transom.[6] It was a wife's duty to nurse a husband, and uncomplaining Margaret doubtless did so.

In October 1812 the Daveys arrived in Sydney, where they waited three months for a ship to Hobart: time enough for upright Macquarie to observe that, though Davey appeared honest and well-meaning, he exhibited 'an extraordinary degree of frivolity and low buffoonery'. Macquarie feared that without a superior to control him, Davey would 'altogether lose sight of that Manly and dignified deportment' which his rank and advanced age (55!) should have brought about. What can Davey have done? Perhaps John West has the answer. Davey, he wrote, 'took pleasure in practical jokes and rough humour: his countenance was strongly marked, and, by a peculiar motion of the scalp, he delighted to throw his forehead into comical contortions'. Macquarie's expression on seeing this can be imagined. Davey had a saving grace, however: his wife and daughter were 'both very amiable and highly respectable'.[7]

Macquarie limited Davey's powers as much as possible, and warned him against designing characters who would try to impose on him with artful insinuations and plausible projects: Knopwood the clergyman ('a man of very loose morals'), Fosbrook the commissary ('corrupt'), Adolarius Humphrey, Thomas Kent, Dr Matthew Bowden and others, often friends of Edward Lord.[8] Most became Davey's friends as well. Lord himself, being away, was not on the list.

The Daveys arrived in Hobart in February 1813. Hobartians had had plenty to surprise them already in their governors, but Davey was something else. Before the Daveys landed (so the story went) Margaret, wishing to impress the colonists, was preparing her best bonnet. Thomas poured a bottle of port wine over it. This eccentricity was private: the next was public. All Hobart was there to welcome the new governor, and Davey landed to a salute of guns. Remarking that the summer day was as hot as hell and a little hotter, he pulled off his coat and walked up Macquarie Street in his shirt sleeves. Then he announced himself at the house where he was to stay.[9] This was not done. Gentlemen appeared in public properly dressed, and they waited for servants to announce them. Though amusing, this was not what colonists expected from the governor.

Shortly after he arrived Davey suffered a bad fall in riding, which led to a severe indisposition. This was the *Sydney Gazette*'s respectable version.[10] In Hobart, Thomas Keston had details:

> this amphibious Soldier after he had landed a week or two must mount a Horse to take a ride to New Town, two Miles from Hobart Town & his Honor having a midling Cargo of his well beloved Grog on Board & the young Steed not being used to have such a Composition at the Helm rolling on his Back, thought proper to spill him off without any respect to his Rank

Sydney hears the respectable version of Davey's fall from his horse
(*Sydney Gazette*, 10 April 1813)

> From Captain REID, of the Minstrel, we are concerned to learn that Lieutenant Governor DAVY had suffered a severe indisposition, originating in a fall when riding; but from which we have the consolation to add, he was fast recovering, and was expected to make an over-land excursion from Hobart Town to Port Dalrymple.

Keston detested the way Davey did not keep his word:

> his Honor had aplenty to attend on him every day for some weeks to ask some favor or other[,] & he never sent any one away with bad Hopes for he told all that asked him for any thing that they should have it but he did not tell them when[, but] he seldom performed any promise, he was a Giant in Promises but a Pigmy in performances

Like Murray and Geils, Davey had little enthusiasm for governing, having another, overriding interest, in his case drinking: 'he did not mind who the Devil governed as long as he got his Bottle & Glass'. Even in this colony of hard drinkers, Davey made his mark. Some drinking was officially encouraged. On royal birthdays and imperial occasions such as news of the victory at Waterloo it was a glass of rum all round, but Davey went too far even then, for he would stand at the gate of government house with a cask of rum, giving passers-by drinks from a tin pannican. Friendly, affable, popular, but hardly showing the manly dignity Macquarie hoped for. No wonder colonists called him 'Mad Tom, the Governor'.[11]

Best of all, Davey loved a convivial evening, with his celebrated concoction, 'Blow-my-skull'. As a contemporary noted:

> This was a colonial beverage in use in the earlier days of Tasmania, and was named and drunk by an eccentric governor, who had a stronger head than most of his subordinates. A wattle hut used to be improvised within a few miles of the capital, and temporary chairs and a strong table being fixed, the governor would take the seat of honour, having in front of him a barbecued pig, and on his honour's right hand, a cask of "blow my skull" – sufficient for all comers – no special invitation being necessary.

This was bad enough – governors were meant to entertain only respectable people – but worse followed:

> A challenge to liquor from the representative of majesty in a roomy pannikin, could not well be declined, although the ceremonial observed in the bush was not over strict. "No heeltaps!" called out the governor in a voice of authority, and the unfortunate stranger was at once *hors de combat*; while the governor having an impenetrable cranium, and an iron frame,

could take several goblets of the alcoholic fluid, and walk away as lithe and happy as possible, attended by an orderly who could scarcely preserve his equilibrium.[12]

The ingredients for this 'remarkably powerful drink' are: two pints of boiling water, one pint of rum, one pint of ale or porter, half a pint of brandy, enough sugar, and lime or lemon juice to taste. 'Heeltaps' are the small amounts of liquor remaining in drinking vessels (literally, one of the thicknesses of a shoe's heel): guests were to scull their drinks – a good idea, given the mixture of flavours. Macquarie's horror can be imagined: a governor out in the bush, encouraging excessive alcohol, hobnobbing with

Major Abbott tells Hobart scandals to his friend John Piper in Sydney: The Police Fund was empty, and 'Davey it is said owes it 500£ himself. – He allowed Gordon & Lascelles to land 2200 Galls of spirits duty free per the Eliza, Capt Murray, so that Governt is a loser of near 800£ by this'
(State Library of New South Wales)

everyone, convicts and all, using his 'voice of authority' not to encourage sobriety but in opposition, to order people to drink. Appalling! Macquarie knew all about it: every ship from Van Diemen's Land 'brings fresh reports of Col. Davey's dissipation and profligacy'.[13]

John West agreed. Under Davey, he wrote, the Union Jack flew over a state of society such as never before a government allowed. He described the carouses in the bush, adding that sometimes the gaol gang (the worst-behaved convicts) attended, and they followed 'the jovial ruler; and when the moon arose, the Governor and his attendants, of various grades, might be seen winding home together ... Such was this trustee of national justice!'[14]

Though amusing, providing excellent entertainment for the colonists, such behaviour by a governor was not just improper, but a dreadful example. Davey himself might feel secure with his position and patron, but he encouraged others, less secure, to play havoc with their futures. Rum ruined lives, and drunkenness prevented many people's prosperity, wrote colonist John Hayes. People would buy rum even if they had not a morsel of food. To place an alcoholic as governor of these people legitimised and encouraged alcoholism. Even Davey did not escape scot-free, for he kept having accidents, overturning his carriage and becoming bruised for example.[15]

Macquarie rapidly lost whatever faith he had in Davey. Davey's luggage was lost on the way to Australia. Since he had been in a debtors' prison it seems unlikely that it was valuable, but as compensation he asked for an enormous land grant of 5000 acres, and managed to gain 3000. Macquarie was shocked, and also feared that Davey was corrupt, drawing bills on treasury that he knew would not be honoured.[16] Macquarie was also horrified at the way Davey allowed corruption among his subordinates. It was frequent and deep-seated; anyone could do anything if palms were greased. Fruitlessly, Macquarie ordered these practices to cease. He suspected that Davey himself was involved, at least in allowing clandestine trade and the smuggling of spirits. He had no proof or he would have acted, he said, but rumours were persistent and widespread. As well, Davey was despotic, power going to his head as it did with so many others. The law said free men could not be flogged, but a farmer who complained that Davey's groom had stolen a halter received 25 lashes for bothering Davey. Another man 'ordered to the triangles' reminded Davey that he could not flog free men. 'Davey jestingly replied that "he would try", and the flagellator very soon decided the point in the Governor's favour.'[17]

The list of Davey's failings continues, but perhaps the worst to Macquarie was that he put little effort into governing – not surprising in an alcoholic. Fawkner commented that, completely led by his 'toadies', he spent more time planning drinking bouts. Public works should have been a major area, but in four years he merely completed the barracks and built a gaol. He also made a few changes to the police and tried to crack down on bushranging: a meagre total. Some progress was made – in exploration, agriculture and whaling – but it was due to private individuals, not the governor.[18]

Davey did have some positive qualities. Old hands described him as 'kind and warm-hearted in a high degree, even though somewhat rough in his manner'. He also provided entertainment, as people related the latest exploit. For example, one day a half-drunk man unbuttoned his clothes and turned his bare flesh towards the government house. Davey called for his rifle – he was a good shot – and fired at 'the naked part of the man'. He hit his target, and it was six months before the man could work again. Making the best of things, perhaps with information from Davey's friend Edward Lord, John West commented that since Hobart was a mere camp, 'the etiquette of office' was unnecessary.[19] However, a little governing would have been beneficial.

Parson Knopwood, skilled at omitting from his diary anything negative, gave a glowing picture of his crony the governor, depicting the Daveys attending church, visiting Knopwood's garden, holding balls and going to their farm. Davey gives an 'elegant entertainment' to the colony's gentlemen on a royal anniversary, lays a foundation stone and so on: the very model of a governor.[20] But even Knopwood's diary reveals that Thomas was often apart from his womenfolk,

HOBART.

SITTING MAGISTRATE.—A. W. H. HUMPHREY, Esq.

Yesterday evening an elegant Ball and Supper was given by His Honor Lieutenant Governor Davey; at which were present the principal Military, Naval, and Civil Officers, and Ladies and Gentlemen of the Colony; and the Evening was spent in the greatest conviviality.

The present state of fine weather, with the late favourable and seasonable rains, have proved highly advantageous to the Agriculturist, enabling him to get his land into good tilth for the present seed Season; and it is to be hoped that our next Harvest, under Providence, will prove equally as abundant as the last, amply rewarding the toil of the Farmer.

Yesterday se'nnight a heavy gale from the S. W. occasioned a fall of Snow on the Table Mountain, the first fall this Autumn.

On Tuesday a splendid and most hospitable entertainment of a Dinner, Ball and Supper, was given by Edward Lord, Esq. in the characteristic spirit of his Country, to all the Ladies and Gentlemen, and Officers Civil, Naval and Military of Hobart.

By His Majesty's armed brig *Kangaroo*, the Colony received an increase of Inhabitants by 40 Male and 60 Female Convicts; but as the male Convicts were the very worst of Characters selected from the Gaol Gang of Syd-

For once, Davey's 'greatest conviviality' has a respectable sound, but though his ball was described as elegant, the Lords' affair received higher praise, as 'splendid and most hospitable' – it included dinner
(*Hobart Town Gazette*, 11 May 1816)

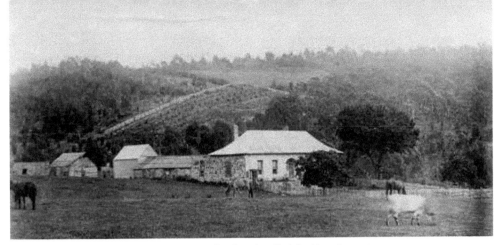
Roseway, the house Davey built at Kangaroo Valley (Lenah Valley) for his retirement. The architecture, especially the roof, is typical of the period (Allport Library and Museum of Fine Arts, TAHO)

and no one commented on how Margaret Davey coped with such a husband. He must have seen her as unimportant, for otherwise this easily led man would have come at least a little under her respectable influence.

Another person who lacked power to influence Davey was Macquarie, who tried endlessly to pull him into line. He must make progress in public works; he must not make land grants without permission; why were there only 88 gallons of spirits left in the store from 2000 received? And so on. Davey took no notice. Macquarie told an official he had written to Davey on some matter, 'but most likely he will pay as little regard to these orders as he has to all my former ones'.[21]

Naturally, Macquarie told London his opinion. Davey 'is so dissipated in his Manners and Morals, so expensive in his habits, so very thoughtless and volatile, and so very easily imposed upon by designing plausible Characters, that I cannot but think him a very unfit man for so very important a Situation', he wrote as early as 1814. It became worse. Davey was incapable of governing, venal and corrupt. Macquarie wanted him replaced. Davey retaliated by telling London everything discreditable about Macquarie he could find, while claiming that under Davey himself, 'Religion, Virtue, Morality and Example was the order of every Succeeding day'.[22] Harrowby or no Harrowby, London was not convinced – but took time to act. Davey stayed four years as governor in Hobart.

Macquarie might have been bitterly disappointed in Davey; but Davey was the ideal governor for Edward Lord, a skilled 'designing and plausible character' if ever there was one. Davey could be flattered, bribed and led astray, he loved generous hospitality, he did not mind people's convict pasts. He sounded just the man for Edward and Maria Lord.

10. THE LORDS BECOME ESTABLISHED

IN EARLY 1814 THE LORD FAMILY was reunited in Hobart: Edward (32) and Maria (35), both in the prime of life and full of energy, and their children Caroline (8), Eliza (6), John (4) and Edward Robert (2). When they left the colony in 1811 they had made £10,000 profit, according to Edward: a good total worth about $1,250,000 (AUD) in 2015.[1] But though satisfactory, it was only half the fortune made by their friend Ingle. In the next few years, however, Ingle returned to England with his takings, and under Davey the Lords became the most prominent couple in the colony, building on their earlier enterprises, finding new ways to profit.

How did they do it? It was a mixture of Sir John Owen's money, Maria's business ability, Edward's public relations, assistance from Davey, corruption and luck: no accidents, no deaths, no natural disasters – yet. Van Diemen's Land was also a better place for money-making. Though recent governors had done little and the population had not increased much, the inhabitants themselves had initiated some progress. Settlement expanded, running from New Norfolk northwest of Hobart, to Bagdad in the northeast, and down to the Coal River Valley in the east, where wheat grew well. Good crops were also being grown in the north. From 1813 Van Diemen's Land exported wheat to Sydney, as well as 'Derwent potatoes ... so highly esteemed for flavour and goodness', 'Derwent onions', seal, kangaroo and wallaby skins, salted beef, skinless barley and an excellent wood, Huon pine, discovered in the south and west. Here was another commercial opportunity, shipping these goods to Sydney.[2] Whaling and sealing were developing around the coasts, with Hobart a commercial and recreation centre for the industry; Knopwood proudly reported five ships in harbour at the same time, including two whalers. Shops and pubs increased, and Hobart became a mixture of government township and raucous port.[3] All very promising for an entrepreneur.

Sydneysiders can buy fine Derwent potatoes, already with a good enough reputation to be specifically named (*Sydney Gazette*, 7 May 1814)

Socially, the colony remained a rough masculine outpost, where men outnumbered women five to one. All Europeans were trying to establish themselves in a challenging environment, most using any means to hand, legal and ethical or not. Drinking, theft, fights, murder, arson, bushranging, corruption: life was typical of new communities such as America's wild west, away from the standards and manners of Jane Austen's Britain. The *Hobart Town Gazette*, established in 1816, presented a more or less respectable picture of the colony but, even so, described events that would have made Austen shudder. This gem appeared beside a report of a man voiding a 15-yard tapeworm – news was scarce in Hobart:[4]

> AUCTION of a WIFE! – A Hibernian whose finances were rather low, brought his wife to the hammer this morning, and although no way prepossessing in appearance, to the amazment of all present, she was sold and delivered to a settler for one gallon of rum and 20 ewes. From the variety of bidders, had there been any more in the market, the sale would have been very brisk

A rough and ready society, but cheerful and tolerant. It just suited the Lords: everyone free to make money as he or she wished, and providing an outstanding market for alcohol.

Hobart was a rough outpost in 1816 *(Hobart Town Gazette,* 1 March 1817)

Edward Lord had two advantages over other traders. He had plenty of money: he claimed his *James Hay* cargo brought less in Sydney than Hobart, but a £30,000 investment was still going to be rewarding. As well, Lord quickly became the best friend and supporter of the all-powerful governor. As with Collins, he probably put Davey in his power by lending him money: Davey was chronically short of cash, just the sort to need constant loans. As well there was Davey's guilt at the *James Hay* fiasco, which Lord milked for all it was worth. By a mixture of charm, money, friendship and support, Lord soon had Davey in the palm of his hand. There was one flaw: Davey was unreliable, tending to agree with whoever saw him last. But astute Edward Lord would have made sure he was in that role. In this excellent position, Edward and Maria Lord set about making money.

They greatly increased their landholdings. Edward had 1500 acres of land owing from the London grant. The most promising area was the Coal River Valley with its luxuriant crops of wheat, and Edward took up his grant just north of modern Sorell, an attractive valley of gently rolling pasture.

Naturally he called the property Orielton Park (or just Orielton), after the Owen property in Wales. He also leased crown land, and rapidly expanded his stock. By August 1814 he had cattle and stockmen as far away as the Tin Dish Holes in the centre of the island, north of Oatlands, and he sold large amounts of meat to the commissariat. These sheep and cattle were expensive. In 1816, for example, Edward Lord bought 1121 sheep and lambs at 40 shillings each for £2242 – more money than most people could ever dream of owning.[5]

The Lords did not live at Orielton, which was too far from their business in Hobart, and their house there was described as 'indifferent'. However, the estate impressed people. In 1816 Orielton Park, 'the Seat of EDWARD LORD, Esq.' as the *Hobart Town Gazette* put it, hosted horse races for gentlemen and settlers (note the social difference). They were delighted with the beautiful and picturesque scene. The races had large prizes, more money was spent in bets, hospitable Edward doubtless provided food and drink, and the day was much enjoyed by all.[6] But Edward did not own any of the horses and no more races were reported at Orielton, so perhaps his interest in racing was waning.

In 1817 a snippet of news from Orielton was published in the *Hobart Town Gazette* under the heading 'NON-DESCRIPT ANIMAL'. A male 'of the tyger species', long a terror to sheep, had been finally cornered by a stockkeeper and two dogs. Though it fought valiantly, they managed to kill it.

The landscape of Orielton, with the sea in the far distance. The modern house stands left (James Alexander)

The body was measured – 6 feet 4 inches (1.6 metres) from nose to tail – then stuffed. It was put on display 'and has been viewed by the curious from the adjacent districts'.[7]

Lord probably grew wheat at Orielton, but provided much more to the commissariat, as described in the next chapter. The Lords also shipped wheat and other exports to Sydney, from Hobart and Port Dalrymple. In February 1814 the brig *Spring* arrived in Sydney from England. It had visited Hobart on the way and Edward Lord bought it, probably in Sydney where he had gone to collect his children. Macquarie gave him permission to take a cargo of sundries to the Derwent in *Spring*, then collect grain at Port Dalrymple to bring to Sydney – Lord already had the ship's duties planned.[8]

Back in Hobart, in June 1814 he went to Port Dalrymple to organise a cargo, and in July *Spring* took potatoes and wheat to Sydney. Over the next few years it took wheat and other cargo to Sydney, and went sealing to Kangaroo Island, in 1815 returning with 6000 seal and kangaroo skins, as well as 40 tons of salt. These were all good sources of income. The ship

Below: Everyone in Hobart knew about Edward Lord's exasperating travel problems *(Hobart Town Gazette, 20 July 1816)*

Below: The lake country in central Van Diemen's Land, excellent for grazing cattle. The man on horseback in the foreground could well have been Edward Lord
(Allport Library and Museum of Fine Arts, TAHO)

SHIP NEWS,—On Thursday se'nnight the brigs *Ontario*, and *Spring*, which both sailed from this Port on the 9th Instant, were obliged by contrary winds to take refuge in Storm Bay Passage; and on Sunday last, wind not permitting the Vessels to proceed on their Voyage, EDWARD LORD and G. W. GUNNING, Esqrs. who went Passengers in the latter Vessel returned overland to Hobart Town.

was useful for transport, Edward travelling in it to and from Sydney.[9] There he would have checked on the export business, as well as his other Orielton Park property.

To organise cargoes in the north, the Lords employed an agent at Port Dalrymple. They often visited themselves, though these journeys could be difficult. There was only a rough track, and the trip involved a ride of several days, camping on the way, in danger of attacks from bushrangers and Aborigines. (Roads were so rough that even in Hobart, when Knopwood and Lord were dining with their friends the Ingles, 'Mr Lord and self came away as soon as the cloth was off the table, the road so bad'.) Travelling by sea was not always an improvement. In July 1816 Edward sailed in *Spring* for Port Dalrymple, but a severe gale forced the ship back to Hobart five days later. He went overland instead, taking a fortnight for the return trip.[10]

The Lords seem to have had a shop in Port Dalrymple. In March 1814 Knopwood met a party going to Port Dalrymple with a quantity of Mrs Lord's goods, which suggests she had a shop there, and the next month she went there herself. In November she and Edward took two of the children north, an exciting trip for the youngsters.[11] However, her Hobart shop was her main centre of business.

Edward was involved, mainly in buying goods; in 1815, for example, a colonist noted that a ship had arrived from India with spirits, tea and so on, and Edward Lord bought it all.[12] It was Maria's job to manage the business day-to-day. Alexander Laing was one customer, and recalled bringing a bottle of rum from Sydney. In Hobart he sold it to James Belbin for currency bills worth £1, which Mrs Lord, 'who kept a very large general store', swapped for a pair of yellow nankeen trousers.[13]

Many customers were small farmers, Norfolk Islanders or ex-convicts, living in the country. They sent servants to the store with notes, often scrawled and blotchy. For example:

Feb[y] 18th 1816

M[rs] Lord

Please let the Bearer Guidon have One hundred Weight of Salt on my account

Dan[l] Stanfield Jnr

Colonists often ordered in large amounts: Governor Davey wanted a pound of pepper, 440 grams. He must have liked his food fiery: perhaps all that alcohol had dulled his palate. In other notes, Miss Davey from government house wanted some white bugles (glass beads used in trimming dresses) and Davey ordered green paint, but most people wanted alcohol:

Mrs Lord

Please to send by the Bearer Slambo 1/2 Gallon of Spirits on my Acc^t.

R^d Coleman

Feby 4 Monday morning 1816

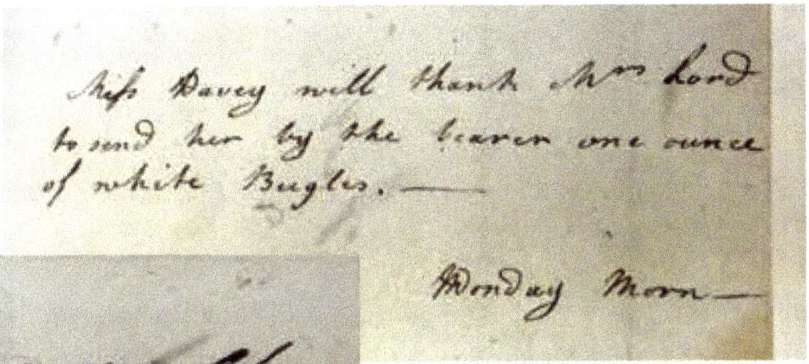

Above: Lucy Davey asks Mrs Lord for white bugles for trimming a gown (State Library of Victoria)

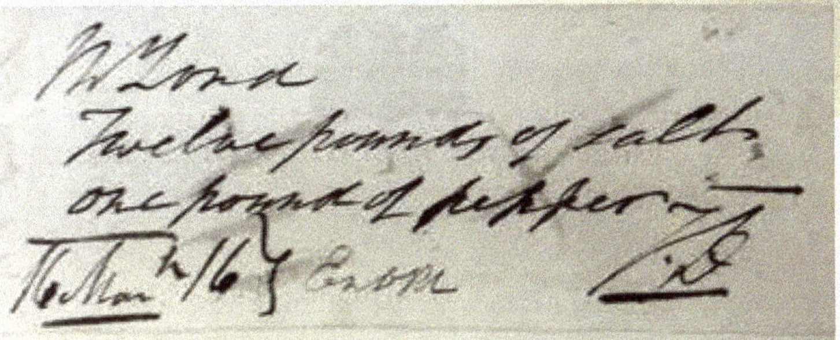

Above: Governor Davey signs his order to the Lords for salt and pepper merely with 'T.D'. The request is also signed by the Lords' clerk Richard Lewis (State Library of Victoria)

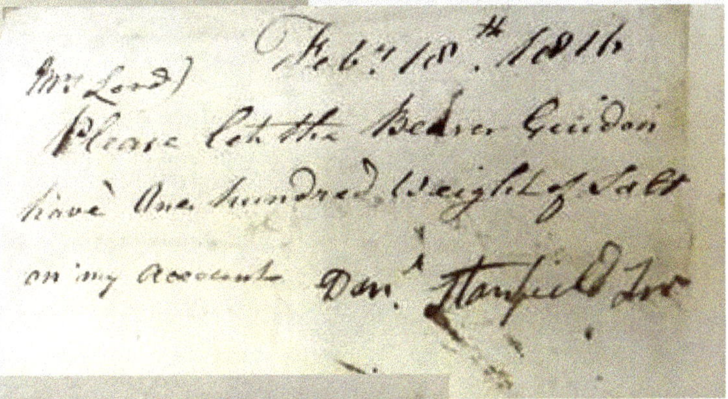

Below: Richard Coleman orders half a gall of spirits from Edward Lord, 1816 (State Library of Victoria)

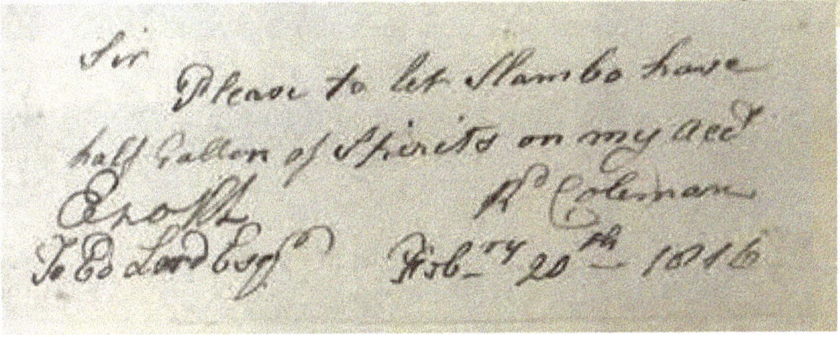

Above: Daniel Stanfield asks Mrs Lord for salt, 1816 (State Library of Victoria)

Or a more complicated order:

> June 22. 1816
> Mrs Lord
>
> Please to deliver to the Bearer Cowar's Greenwood the three Gallons of Brandy I Left the order for from <u>Lowe</u> and if Convenient Please fill the Keg and I will Settle for it when I come to town
>
> your Obedient Servant
> Joseph Whitfield

One note suggests an intriguing scenario:

> 1814 December the 25 Hollow Tree
> Mrs Lord please to let the Blackman Cazzar Have two Gallons of Rum for me and place the Same to my Account yours William Morgan[14]

This could be the scene. Site: the Morgan household at Hollow Tree, now Cambridge. William Morgan, the son of convicts, is well known, more for sheep stealing than honest farming. Later he will be imprisoned, but for the present he is free and flourishing. On Christmas morning, he discovers that he is out of rum. Disaster! Cazzar – probably his spelling of Caesar – must go to town for more. Cazzar might have been a sailor, a runaway slave from America, who deserted his ship in Hobart and took a job with the Morgans.

While Morgan writes the note to Mrs Lord, Cazzar saddles the horse (surely he would be allowed to take the horse, for speed if no other reason). He rides to Kangaroo Point, at least an hour away, stables the horse, drags the boatman from the bar, and is rowed across the river to Hobart. He walks to the Lord house where Maria, having attended church, is supervising the preparations for Christmas dinner ('You're peeling those potatoes too thickly, Mary Ann. Come on, the sooner you finish, the sooner we can eat them'). Maria opens the shop – she's used to people wanting items at all hours of every day – and provides the rum, then surely gives Cazzar a bite to eat. Then it's back across the river with his keg – a zigzag row by this time on Christmas Day – and the return ride to Hollow Tree, where the parched Morgan family welcomes him with cries of joy. With any luck he's in time for dinner, eaten at about three o'clock.

Though Maria and Lord had their own special areas, both were involved in the success of the whole enterprise. Maria, almost always in Hobart, undertook day-to-day management. Alexander Laing had a job at Orielton, but was offered another position. To take it up, 'I had first to call upon Mrs. Edward Lord to ask her permission to leave, provided I obtained the situation, to which she consented'.[15] Nothing about asking Edward. His main involvement seemed to be making deals involving the government, using his friendship with Davey to claim favours. In 1815 Macquarie rebuked Davey: the highest price of wheat in Sydney was ten shillings a bushel, but Davey was paying Lord twelve shillings, 20 per cent more. Davey was to cancel the contract at once. Even worse, Macquarie found that Davey was paying freight for Lord's wheat. This was most unwarrantable, thundered Macquarie. Lord must refund the money or Macquarie would inform London, for he strongly disapproved of 'such lavish and prodigal expenditure' of public money. But Davey continued to pay Lord high prices. A rival Hobart merchant noted that Davey paid Lord a high price for soap that the merchant would gladly have sold more cheaply.[16] Lord made an extra £300 on the deal.

Davey also helped Lord avoid high customs duties on spirits, admitting that he let Lord import spirits to make up for his disappointment when he, Davey, did not let Lord land goods from *James Hay* in 1813. All sorts of shifty deals appear. The merchant disappointed about the soap noted that Davey bought from Lord 2000 gallons of poor-quality Mauritian rum at a generous price. In 1816 Lord and Davey hatched a scheme whereby Lord's duties on 5000 gallons of rum were waived in exchange for a site for a new government house. This was an excellent bargain for Lord, but Macquarie refused to allow it, or to allow Lord to sell the site to the government for an exorbitant sum.[17] Lord did get away with paying reduced duties on one cargo of spirits – but this must not happen again, ordered Macquarie. These were the payments Macquarie discovered; who knows what else went on between Davey and Lord that was not recorded. As one settler wrote to another in 1816, 'it is not prudent for me to commit to paper all I know respecting Lord'.[18]

The other way to avoid paying duties was by smuggling. Macquarie was appalled by its extent in Van Diemen's Land. It had been bad enough in Murray's time, from Murray's own confession, but under Davey 'the series of notorious, disgraceful, and daring instances of Smuggling, which have recently taken place at the Derwent far exceed anything that has ever

The nooks and crannies at the entrance to the River Derwent, ideal for smuggling
(Allport Library and Museum of Fine Arts, TAHO)

yet occurred there or at any of the other Dependencies of this Territory'. Macquarie ordered Davey to restrain 'that extraordinary propensity to smuggling, which appears to pervade all ranks and descriptions of People' in Van Diemen's Land. Macquarie heard that Davey let various men land 15,000 gallons of spirits in the past twelve months; he did not entirely believe it, but even the 5000 gallons Davey acknowledged was too much. Macquarie believed that Davey condoned smuggling.[19] Others certainly thought so: Judge Abbott informed a Sydney friend that Davey allowed two men to land 2200 gallons of spirits duty free, and that Davey owed the government £500 – a shocking state of affairs.[20]

There is no evidence that Edward Lord was involved in the smuggling racket, but he would take good care there would not be. Probably he was in it with the rest; he certainly was in earlier and later years. Many smugglers escaped detection (or bribed their way clear) and were never brought to justice, so the full story is not known. What machinations must have been going on, unrecorded and lost to history!

Fifteen years later, a story was told of how Edward Lord acted first and asked permission later, in true buccaneering style. There is no other evidence for it, but it shows what local people thought of Lord: always alert for an opportunity. Apparently Governor Collins gave a piece of prime waterfront land beside government house to the East India firm of Palmer & Co., who had little interest in a vacant block in a tiny, remote settlement and did nothing with it. Lord had his eye on this excellent site. After Collins' death he built a cottage there, to establish a claim, and later asked Macquarie for the block. Macquarie decreed it belonged to Palmer. In 1821 the government bought the block for £600, which must have infuriated Lord.[21]

BESIDES DOMINATING BUSINESS in Hobart, the Lords made a splash socially. It is not clear where they were living at first, but they planned a grand dwelling. While they were in England, John Ingle occupied the block on the corner of Macquarie and Argyle streets, but on their return Edward seems to have bought or claimed it back from him. There someone, most likely Lord, built a house, a charming two-storey brick dwelling – four floors, counting the large cellars and attics. (There have been claims that John Ingle built the house, but I believe Lord did: see Appendix 2.) Lord would have probably designed it himself, since there were no architects in the colony. Memories of Orielton encouraged gracious proportions, lofty ceilings, beautiful window shutters made of Huon pine and a blackwood staircase. It was a showpiece, the largest house in Hobart, a great achievement in the small township. It was only called 'Ingle Hall' from the 1870s; when Edward and Maria lived there it was probably just called 'the Lords' house'. They moved there in 1816.[22]

With a respectable wife in government house to lead society, entertainment developed. The Daveys held six balls in their four years in the colony. Others followed, especially when visiting ships provided more guests. October 1814 was busy. On 5 October Knopwood and two ladies

Edward Lord's friend Charles Jeffreys' sketch of Hobart in 1817, with his ship *Kangaroo* in port. The Lords' house, where Jeffreys so often enjoyed dinner, is to the east of government house: two storeys, five windows across the front (Allport Library and Museum of Fine Arts, TAHO)

Scenes from the Lords' new house: when built in 1816, it was the largest house in the colony
(Paul Yonna)

hosted a large dinner for 22 people, including the Daveys and the Lords; the next evening saw a ball on a ship; two days later William Collins and his wife held a dinner, ball and supper for 33 people in a grand tent; on 10 October the governor gave a tea, ball and supper. The next day, Knopwood cut 92 heads of asparagus from his garden and sent them to the Lords. That evening they gave a great dinner, ball and supper to all the ladies and gentlemen, 'the greatest dinner given in the colony', according to Knopwood. He left early at 9 o'clock, but everyone else stayed very late.[23] Four balls and a large dinner in a week, with the Lords' entertainment eclipsing everyone else's: this was social success.

Such giddy weeks were rare, and it was two years before the Lords held their next ball. On 7 May 1816, recorded Knopwood, 'At 5 there was the grandest dinner, ball and supper given by Mr. & Mrs. Lord to all the ladies and gents in the colony. We sat down 50 in company. The dinner and every things was very great.' The *Hobart Town Gazette* agreed: Edward Lord Esq. gave a splendid and most hospitable entertainment 'in the characteristic spirit of his Country' – Wales? The next afternoon, a friend visited Knopwood and 'we went and calld on Mr. Lord. There was the Lt. Govnr and the gents at lunch. They all stayd till the eve'. So Maria Lord had to organise not only the dinner and supper for fifty people, but a large lunch the next day. Her entertainments were described as 'grand' despite her fondness for frugality; doubtless the lunch guests sat down to a beautifully presented meal of leftovers. A few days later, Knopwood wrote of an entertainment at government house merely as 'a ball and supper'. Clearly the Lords' ball outdid the governor's.[24] Where the Lords held the ball is not clear; they were not in their new house yet.

Although she hosted balls that the gentry appear to have attended, Maria Lord's social position is not clear either. It was during this period that convicts had the greatest chance of being accepted socially. In Sydney, Macquarie believed that once convicts had served their sentences, they should be regarded on the same footing as people who had not committed crimes – that is, their convict past should be ignored. He encouraged successful emancipists, even inviting them to dinner at government house, the colony's highest social honour.

Many of Sydney's gentry hated this attitude, but most Hobart people were more tolerant, especially with Governor Davey leading the way, drinking with convicts. In 1814 Knopwood drew up a list of gentry living in Hobart: 24 gentlemen, 17 ladies and 25 children – a total of 77, a reminder of just how small the elite was, only 6 per cent of the total population of about 1200. The Lords were included, as were another ex-convict and an ex-mistress; but Knopwood excluded Lucy Murray, a born lady who had disgraced herself socially.[25] An odd list, but perhaps Knopwood's easy-going ways, and his background as the son of a mere farmer, meant he was not much of a judge of social position. Still, Maria Lord made his list of gentry.

It is doubtful, however, if she entered government house, the real test of gentility. Knopwood listed those present at many functions he attended. Though Thomas Davey dined with the Lords at their house – so Maria was acceptable as his hostess – Margaret Davey never did, and though Edward Lord was often at government house, Maria never was. The Lords did not attend the two balls at government house for which Knopwood provided guest lists, and at other times he recorded events such as 'E. Lord Esq. and self dind with the Lt. Govnr. and Mrs. Davey'; 'Mr. & Mrs. Hogan, Miss Barrey, Mr. Lord, Mr. Broughton, Mr. Archer and self dind at Government House'. If Mrs Hogan and Miss Barry were at these dinners, surely other acceptable women would have been invited: it looks as if the ex-convict was excluded.[26] But there could have been other explanations.

Maria might not have wanted to waste her time at social functions, for she was very busy, not just with business but with her family. In May 1815 she gave birth to her sixth child, a daughter called Corbetta after Edward's mother. Knopwood called on Maria several times, and christened the baby in June. It was the usual convivial gathering: dinner and the christening in the Lords' home.[27] There was no churching any more. The Lords' position was secure, so there was no point to be proved by such ceremonies.

The older children needed education, but there were no schools in Hobart worthy of the Lord family. The girls, Caroline and Eliza, were educated at home by a governess, but John, the son and heir, was sent to England for his education – at six. A friend of Edward's sailed on the same ship and perhaps agreed to care for the little boy; but six is a young age to send a child away.[28] Surely someone in Hobart could have taught him his three Rs? But it was not just about education. John Owen Lord was sent to England to become a proper gentleman, away from the raff and scaff of Van Diemen's Land (and his ex-convict mother?). This was usual for those few colonists who wanted their children brought up as gentry: army officer Edward Abbott sent seven- and eight-year-old children to England as did, in Sydney, D'Arcy Wentworth and army officer George Johnston – whose mistress, the mother of his children, was also a convict.[29]

Knopwood's diary gives glimpses of the Lords' family life. He was fond of children, and noted that Caroline brought 'two little ones' to his garden in summer to eat fruit. He often sent Maria Lord fruit, such as dishes of raspberries – she made one batch into raspberry jelly for him – and he frequently dined with the Lords, or with Maria alone if Edward were away. Sometimes he took his adopted daughter Betsy Mack, aged about eight, a friend for the Lord girls. Maria often had guests to dinner, and Knopwood himself would drop in and be pressed to stay: 'I rode to Mr. Lords; they wanted me to dine but being unwell I dare not be out at night'. Edward often visited him, once handing on the latest English newspapers, only seven months old. Maria saw one family member, her sister Catherine, when the Taylors visited in 1814 for six weeks on their way to Ceylon with the rest of the 73rd regiment.[30] What with her activity in the family business, running the house, caring for the children, and frequent entertainments including the occasional grand ball, Maria had her hands full.

The Lords employed a number of servants who had to be managed, and sometimes there were problems. In 1815 their servant John Lawrence had a fight with Knopwood's man, John Marsden, who broke three of

Lawrence's ribs. Lawrence died, and a verdict of manslaughter was brought against Marsden. Edward Lord paid for Lawrence's funeral, which both Edward and Maria attended. There was another disaster when their servant James Waters was riding back from Port Dalrymple to Hobart. Trying to cross the River Derwent

at Herdsman's Cove he vanished, presumed drowned, though his horse survived. This was additionally melancholy, ran the report in the *Hobart Town Gazette*, because Waters was honest and faithful, 'a character rarely to be met with, in his situation, in this part of the world'.[31] ('In his situation' implied that he was a convict; even in this rough-and-ready community, it was not polite to refer openly to people's shameful convict status.)

There were a few other problems. Surveyor Evans hinted at a financial difficulty in a letter to Lord in October 1816, asking for an account to be paid since he, Evans, was being asked to settle someone's concerns. 'Nothing but the above reason could urge me to ask you for it at this time.'[32] The Lords had just moved into their new house and given a huge ball, so perhaps their finances were stretched. However, any such problem seemed soon overcome.

Then there was Edward's health. Though Maria was seldom reported as ill, Edward Lord suffered sporadically from what he described as 'severe and alarming attacks of Asthma'. In the summer of 1816, perhaps because of pollen in the air, he was so unwell that he went on a four-day sea cruise. He returned better but weak, planning another recuperative trip. 'Everyone happy to see him', wrote Knopwood. 'I calld upon him and dind with him' – as he frequently did, at the hospitable Lord table.[33]

In 1816 news arrived of the defeat of Napoleon at Waterloo, and in honour of the great victory Governor Davey instituted the Waterloo Club, also known as the Royal Forest Club. It consisted of eleven men: Davey, Lord, his friends Humphrey, Lascelles, Knopwood and William Collins, and five others, government officers, surgeons and influential settlers, several of them the designing characters against whom Macquarie had warned Davey (and several with notable roles in the remainder of this book, such as John Drummond and Samuel Hood). Members met every Saturday at the Thatched House on Mount Waterloo (now Battery Point), bringing their own plates, knives, forks and liquor. They took it in turns to provide 'a good and wholesome Dinner', which had to be on the table at three o'clock precisely. Edward Lord provided the second dinner, which must have been something, outdoors on a September day with rain, sleet, and snow on the surrounding hills.[34] No doubt the diners were well warmed by alcohol. These dinners petered out, but there were many similar carouses, such as gentlemen's dinners at government house, and Davey's functions in the bush with his famous Blow-my-Skull. Edward Lord was often present.

More socially acceptable was his sole public activity. In 1815 he and most of his friends formed a committee that requested a criminal court in Hobart. Having to go to Sydney for trials was a terrible nuisance for local people, and the committee gained signatures from almost all the free adult males of Van Diemen's Land.[35] They achieved something: a judge and a limited court system.

All in all, the Lords were busy and successful, with their economic activities – farming, trading, shipping – and an active social and family life. How Edward in particular did this can be gauged by a study of his dealings with the commissariat department, the main purchaser of goods in Van Diemen's Land.

In 1850 the story of the Royal Forest Club was told as an entertaining oddity from the past
(*Courier*, 20 February 1850)

Although Van Diemen's Land affords no field for the zealous researches of the antiquary, and we can discover few shrines by which the memory of men worthy in their day can be rendered venerable in our eyes, yet by the publication of the following document we may call up some time-gone reminiscence without presuming to the style and dignity of ancient chroniclers. As a memorial of the early days of Van Diemen's Land the document is not without interest, and to the only survivor of the Royal Forest Club it will appear

"Like a dim picture of the drowned past." — HOOD.

THE ROYAL FOREST CLUB,

Held at the Thatched House, on Mount Waterloo, every Saturday during the summer months, commencing on Saturday next, the 7th of September, 1816.

N.B.—The conditions of this club are such, that every member provides himself with a plate, knife and fork, and also with his own LIQUORS—and further, in his turn, to furnish the Royal Forest Club with a good and wholesome Dinner, which must be on the table at three o'clock precisely, every Saturday.

"GOD SAVE THE KING."

Names of the Members of the Royal Forest Club.

T. DAVEY, Lieutenant-Governor.
EDWARD LORD.
A. W. H. HUMPHREY, J.P.
JOHN DRUMMOND, Naval Officer.
THOMAS LASCELLES, Secretary.
WM. BLYTH.
SAML. HOOD.
EDWARD LUTTRELL.
REV. R. KNOPWOOD.
JAMES GORDON, J.P.
WM. COLLINS.

The club was instituted by Colonel Davey, in commemoration of the great victory of Waterloo. Mount Waterloo was where Mulgrave Battery now stands, and received that designation at the time its gigantic compeer, Mount Wellington, received its present name. The latter was previously called by the English, Table Mountain, and by the French Mont Plateau. The only member who has not "shuffled off the mortal coil" is Mr. Lascelles, who was then Secretary. Mr. Lord was a Lieutenant in the Royal Marines, and, previous to the arrival of Colonel Davey as Lieutenant-Governor, was one of the Commandants of Van Diemen's Land. Colonel Davey died on the 2nd May, 1823. Mr. Drummond was the Port Officer, and Mr. Hood was Assistant Surgeon of the 46th Regiment. Adelarius William Henry Humphrey, Esq., was the Police Magistrate of Hobart Town, a situation which was afterwards held by Mr. Lascelles. The signature Edward Luttrell was that of Dr. Luttrell, the principal Colonial Surgeon. The Rev. R. Knopwood was the principal Chaplain; the rest were influential settlers, Mr. Collins having been the confidential friend of the late and former Governor Collins. Colonial society at that period was very much restricted; but many a happy hour was passed at Mount Waterloo by the members of this club. . . . .

11. THE COMMISSARIAT, EDWARD LORD AND RAMPANT SKULLDUGGERY

EDWARD LORD AND HIS BROTHER JOHN had a well-tested method of getting their own way, evident throughout their careers: making sure necessary people were onside. They offered potentially useful people carrots – friendship, hospitality, assistance, loans – and in return for their help provided unquestioning support; recommending an embezzler to the Colonial Office, for example, as an upright and deserving man. Opponents received the stick: court cases, false accusations, lying reports to the Colonial Office, violence. This was perhaps the way the Owens had been operating for centuries: I'm entitled to have my way and anyone who opposes me gets what he deserves.

In Van Diemen's Land Edward Lord tried to manipulate government officials. While this saga shows governors displaying virtually all faults possible in rulers, they were not alone. Almost all public servants behaved in the same way, having taken these positions for what they could get from them. While this attitude was widespread throughout the British Empire and elsewhere, in Van Diemen's Land it was easier to get away with it. The place was so small and far away.

Coming to government positions in Hobart, men soon realised that whatever they did no one was going to stop them, at least in the short term. No local governor made much attempt. Their superiors, far off in Sydney or even more distant London, found it hard to find out what was going on. Not that many superiors tried, for London governed its remote Australian colonies inefficiently, with officials' actions seldom scrutinised.[1] Besides, if London received reports of misrule, it could threaten but not enforce its threats without going to extremes – dismissal, court martial. These were

Previous pages: The commissariat bought sheep for their meat. Here sheep graze on the excellent pasture at Orielton, two centuries after the Lords' period (James Alexander)

Below: Cattle grazing at Orielton, then as now waiting to be sold (Rebecca Aisbett)

last resorts, for it was difficult to gain evidence and replace officials, while publicity was unwelcome. The result was a stream of officials making hay while the sun shone. Occasionally sinners were brought to justice, but their remarkably lenient treatment merely encouraged everyone else.

Of all government departments, the commissariat or government store was the most lucrative for its staff. As Edward Lord himself wrote, 'nearly all the Public Money of this Settlement must emanate from His Majesty's Stores'.[2] The bulk of the population – all convicts and government employees, many settlers – were 'on the stores', provided with food, clothing and equipment by the commissariat. Its officials bought and allocated huge quantities of goods, playing a central role in the economy. There were no audits, and the commissariat was open to every form of abuse. Edward Lord, leading shopkeeper and stockowner, was in the thick of it.

At the same time, he criticised it. After spending six weeks with him, in 1808 his friend Foveaux wrote that at Hobart (as already quoted), 'a System of the most unexampled profusion, waste, and fraud, with respect to both Money and Stores, have been carried on, almost without the affectation of concealment of sense of shame'.[3]

THE MAN IN CHARGE OF THE COMMISSARIAT was the commissary. Hobart's first commissary was Leonard Fosbrook. His salary was £91 a year, a figure to remember in comparison with amounts embezzled.[4] Fosbrook, a former naval purser, might have started out honest enough, but his clerks were experienced embezzlers, for the only literate men available were convicts, mostly ex-clerks transported for embezzling. Such were Fosbrook's two main subordinates, John Boothman and Francis Shipman. Later, Shipman provided details. As early as 1806, he said, Fosbrook took a bribe of £100 from a ship's captain to accept a cargo of damaged rice, which was later condemned. Presumably for more bribes, Fosbrook bought all the kangaroo meat hunters provided, huge amounts of which were condemned. (Edward Lord was one of the main providers.) Boothman forged receipts worth over £600. This was discovered and he went to gaol, but Fosbrook paid the forged receipts as if they were genuine, fabricating his accounts to correspond.

There was more, said Shipman. Fosbrook took 200 gallons of spirits for himself, putting this down to Deficiencies. He kept £50 paid for government cattle. He forged receipts, with signatures of people unable to write, fictitious or dead. He ran up debts with people who left the colony or were

> GOVERNMENT AND GENERAL ORDER.
> Head Quarters, Sydney,
> Friday, 28th June, 1811.
>
> THE Court of Inquiry, of which Lieutenant Colonel O'CONNELL was President, assembled yesterday for the Purpose of Investigating the Conduct of Deputy Commissary FOSBROOK, respecting the Report in Circulation at Hobart Town of his having granted a Store Receipt to Mrs. Frances Ankers, under Date 30th September, 1810, for 340 Bushels of Wheat, which Wheat had not at the Time been received into His Majesty's Stores, having examined the several Persons summoned to give Evidence in this Case, and having also minutely and strictly examined the several Documents produced by Mr. Fosbrook in his Vindication, have given it as their Opinion, that there is no Ground for the Subject of this Inquiry being brought before a General Court Martial: Which Opinion His EXCELLENCY the GOVERNOR confirms and approves.

Governor Macquarie approves Fosbrook's acquittal, 1811. He is new to the colonies (*Sydney Gazette*, 29 June 1811)

unable to pay, so the debts were never recovered. He paid a man four times the going rate for 200 kangaroo skins, but even then the skins never came into the store. The amount of money involved was enormous: in 1808 alone the commissary spent £13,492. All these frauds were 'committed with impunity, thinking the Distance secures them from Detection', said Shipman.[5]

At first Governor Collins protected Fosbrook, but in 1809 the two men quarrelled and Fosbrook resigned. However, he explained himself to newly arrived Governor Macquarie, who still believed colonial officials, and not only reinstated Fosbrook but made him a magistrate. Fosbrook freed Boothman from gaol and installed him again as storekeeper. Fosbrook sacked Shipman, who returned to England.[6]

In 1810, claimed settler Thomas Keston, Fosbrook infuriated Edward Lord and his partner William Collins by buying almost all of a ship's cargo of clothing, leaving little for their shop. Buying clothing sounds a reasonable action for the commissary: perhaps Lord and Collins had had enough of Fosbrook's rackets, or hoped for a cut? Keston said they put up a notice – the usual way of making public accusations – stating that Fanny Ankers, Fosbrook's fat mistress, was delivered of an enormous amount of wheat, implying corruption. Sure enough, Fosbrook complained that anonymous notices attacked his integrity, claiming he paid for wheat that was not delivered.[7]

Lord went to Sydney and spread the scandal. Macquarie asked him about it. In Hobart it was widely believed, Lord replied, though he himself knew nothing (of course), as he was in Sydney when the alleged fraud happened. Macquarie ordered Governor Murray to send Fosbrook to Sydney if his explanation of the event was unsatisfactory.[8] It was. Lord's agent Matthew Bowden told him the story from Hobart:

As you surmised Fosbrook comes up in this vessel respecting the business of the Store Receipt – <u>Murray utterly denies any knowledge of the transaction</u> and it is avowed and I believe sworn to by D. McCarty that the Wheat as turned into the Stores for Mrs Ankers by him previous to the issue of the receipt – Boothman and Maum accompany Fosbrook to Sydney and he does not scruple to say that he is going up to prosecute you <u>for defamation</u> of Character !!![9]

So Bowden thought Fosbrook guilty, Murray involved and Fosbrook hypocritical enough to threaten Lord with a libel case. Keston also thought Fosbrook's guilt was widely believed. People wondered how he would account for the discrepancy in wheat, and were thunderstruck when he managed to make a 'large complete Patch to cover it all', with witnesses and signed statements proving his innocence. Acquitted, he returned to his lucrative post in Hobart, with rumours that the cost of bribing the witnesses was far more than the price of the wheat. 'You can get plenty in this Country to swear Black is white & that white is no Colour at all for a few Pounds', commented Keston in disgust.[10]

By now Macquarie was disillusioned, and decided both Fosbrook and Murray were 'very deficient in Principles of honor and integrity'. When Governor Davey arrived in 1813, Fosbrook was one of the designing characters Macquarie warned him against. Both he and his storekeeper were corrupt, said Macquarie, but neither could be dismissed until London appointed a new commissary. Then Fosbrook and four other officers in Hobart, all but one on the list of designing characters, asked Macquarie to cancel their debts to government. Horrified, Macquarie not only refused but ordered them to pay at once or their salaries would be stopped.[11]

Fosbrook quarrelled with the next governor, Geils, who found that he was accepting some people's wheat and not others, and cheating when giving out meat. Geils ordered the storeman to give out the proper ration, but the man just laughed. Geils sacked him. Fosbrook objected, and they argued hotly and charged each other with embezzlement.[12] Meanwhile, in England Shipman, penniless, sold his knowledge of Fosbrook's fraud to the government. Dismayed, London told Macquarie to investigate Shipman's claims. Geils' accusation came in handy, and Macquarie ordered Fosbrook to Sydney for a court martial.[13]

Leonard Fosbrook and Fanny Ankers leave Australia in 1814. Discreetly, they publish separate versions of the obligatory advertisement notifying any creditors of their departure (Sydney Gazette, 17 September 1814)

So far, Edward Lord had not been implicated but, just before Fosbrook left, Lord bought from him fourteen acres of land on Macquarie Point for an exorbitant price. Was this a massive bribe to stop Fosbrook implicating Lord? If so, it worked: Lord's name does not seem to have been mentioned (though few details of the case survive). Fosbrook was charged with embezzling large amounts of wheat, rice and meat, and defrauding the store of a large amount of iron by giving it to Daniel Ankers, his mistress's husband. His rambling defence depended on stout denial, a popular tactic. It did not work. The court found him guilty, and he was dismissed and had to repay the cost of the iron.[14] Fosbrook had no one to protect him: no fellow officers, no patron. Such people were vulnerable.

Despite having been found guilty of fraud, Fosbrook asked Macquarie to reinstate him as commissary after eleven years of 'unblemished integrity' and, when this failed, give him free rum for the voyage to England. How Macquarie avoided expiring from apoplexy at dealing with these breathtakingly outrageous requests is not clear. Fosbrook went to England with Fanny Ankers, and presumably they lived comfortably on Leonard's ill-gotten gains. Perhaps he was the Leonard Fosbrook Esquire who died, aged eighty, in 1842, 'universally respected by all who knew him'.[15]

FOSBROOK'S REPLACEMENT as commissary, Patrick Hogan, arrived in 1813. There was also a new storekeeper, ex-convict William Maum. But traditions continued. Big merchants, headed by Edward Lord, monopolised the market, providing most of the wheat for the commissariat. They grew some themselves but bought more from smaller farmers, who had to accept their price and buy at their shops. Hogan made it easy for these merchants. He was a drunkard, 'addicted to inebriety ... so as to render him totally unfit for doing his Duty'. When he was sober, he was more interested in his own concerns: trading, buying cattle and farming speculations. He introduced a new scam at the commissariat, issuing receipts that looked like government documents, so their recipients expected the government to pay them, but which were for Hogan's private expenses. He still ran up huge debts.[16]

Hogan's superior in Sydney, David Allan (himself dishonest and incompetent, eventually dismissed), sent a stream of complaints: Hogan's accounts were irregular, he was not following instructions, he was more trouble than everyone else put together. Macquarie was horrified. If stories of Hogan's drunkenness and negligence were true, he instructed Governor Davey, he must send him to Sydney for trial. In any case he should warn him of the consequences of 'these low vicious courses'. The mind boggles at the picture of drunken, slothful Davey reproving drunken Hogan for neglect and inebriety, but he did it.[17]

Hogan became a great friend of Edward Lord who, in Macquarie's words, 'in a great Degree monopolized the Supply of the King's Store there with Grain and Animal Food'. Hogan patronised Lord's shop, for example buying 2000 gallons of spirits from him. In return, Lord's friend Governor Davey protected Hogan. Some colonists complained to Davey that Hogan would not consolidate the receipts he gave out – that is, they were not being paid – but Davey did nothing. Macquarie claimed he connived at Hogan's dishonesty.[18]

Then things went wrong. One evening at dinner Hogan told Lord's friend John Ingle that he could not repay money he owed the government.

Commissary Hogan lists those whose meat tenders he has accepted. Note who is selling the largest amount
(*Hobart Town Gazette*, 22 June 1816)

Ingle told Lord, who held receipts showing Hogan owed him about £1500. Next morning Hogan's clerk exchanged them for reliable bills on the commissariat at Sydney.[19] Whoever lost money, it was not going to be Edward Lord. Worse, in July 1816 the captain of an American ship complained to Davey of Hogan's incompetence and demanded cash for his cargo. Hogan had bled the commissariat dry and could not pay, so Lord lent him £400. To repay this, storekeeper Maum signed vouchers claiming Lord provided £400 worth of wheat for the stores. Davey passed the captain's complaint to Macquarie, adding that he himself was totally ignorant of these activities (of course).[20] Macquarie dismissed Hogan, ordering him to pay his debts by selling his property. This was only fair, added Macquarie, since he had obtained it through embezzlement. But Hogan could not settle his debts, and Macquarie ordered him to Sydney for a court martial. Macquarie also dismissed storekeeper Maum, and ordered that all receipts issued from the commissariat were to have written on them why, when, for what and to whom they were issued, clearly a novel idea.[21]

The permanent new commissary had to be appointed by London, but Macquarie had to send a temporary man. William Broughton was a protégé of his. Not of the officer and gentleman class, he came to Sydney in the First Fleet as a servant. Intelligent, competent, hard-working, sober and honest, a rare combination in Sydney, he moved to the commissariat. Both King and Macquarie recommended his promotion, but London preferred to appoint its own men. Macquarie could give local promotion, however, and in 1816 he sent Broughton to Hobart to remedy 'the shameful abuses that have so long disgraced the Commissariat Department at the Derwent'.[22]

Broughton was appalled. 'The roguery, which has been carried on at this illfated Settlement, is beyond all calculation', he told Macquarie. 'Crimes are committed with the greatest impunity, while detection is most difficult to come at; but, how can it be expected otherwise, when the very heads, with but few exceptions, set the very worst examples.' He likened Hobart to the biblical cities of Sodom and Gomorrah, home to every species of vice. God promised these cities would be spared if ten honest men were

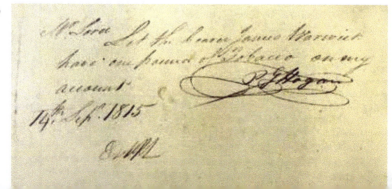

Hogan orders tobacco from Edward Lord
(State Library of Victoria)

GOVERNMENT AND GENERAL ORDERS.

Government House, Hobart Town,
Monday, 23d September, 1816.

His EXCELLENCY the GOVERNOR and COMMANDER in CHIEF having been pleased to appoint Assistant Commissary General Broughton to take the Charge of the Commissariat Department at this Station, and Mr. Broughton having recently arrived here he is directed to assume the Duties of his Office on the 25th Instant.

Deputy Assistant Commissary General Hogan is directed to deliver over to Mr. Broughton all Government Stores, Public Papers, and Government Property of every description in his Charge, on the 24th Instant.

Assistant Commissary General Broughton will not be answerable for any Debts due on account of the Commissariat Department prior to the 25th Instant.

His Excellency the Governor and Commander in Chief having been pleased to appoint William Broughton, Esq. to be a Justice of the Peace throughout the Settlements on Van Diemen's Land, he is to be obeyed and respected accordingly.

By Command of His Honor the Lieutenant Governor,
Thomas Allen Lascelles, Secretary.

William Broughton, his hair in the fashionable windswept style
(State Library of New South Wales)

Broughton takes over the commissariat office
(*Hobart Town Gazette*, 28 September 1816)

found in them; Broughton feared there were not six honest men in Hobart. (He was implying financial corruption, not homosexuality.)

Broughton told Macquarie examples of roguery. The governor's secretary borrowed wheat from the stores for seed, then bartered it for rum! 'This, Sir, is what is called here, *Financiering*; I am sure Your Excellency will find another Name for such a diabolical scheme.' He spoke of 'the want of energy on the part of the Government of this Colony (if so it can be called)', and the lack of shame: people 'boast of their iniquity and glory in their misdeeds. It is really lamentable to see so fine a Settlement as this so mismanaged'. When he arrived, Broughton continued, Davey gave him a survey of what remained in the stores. 'Whether this was done to impress on my mind with what Vigilance and caution he conducted the Public Affairs, I cannot say' – in their private letters, Macquarie and Broughton wrote of Davey with contempt. Broughton noticed a large deficiency of wheat, worth £1293. He estimated that Hogan owed the government £2298.[23]

'M^r. Hogan's defalcation has placed this Colony in a very distressed state', Anthony Fenn Kemp, a leading Hobart merchant, told a Sydney friend. Formerly a friend of Lord, Kemp was now suffering from Lord and Davey's conniving. Kemp had store receipts for wheat and meat worth £1100, but feared he would not see a shilling of it, although Davey had approved Lord's bills for payment. Kemp told Macquarie this, hoping he would pay no bills until Hogan's affairs were investigated, when 'the most nefarious transactions and Robberys in the Store will come out ... M^r. Lord will be a very <u>material evidence</u> in the Court Martial tho' a <u>reluctant one</u> ... Davey appears to have acted in the most imprudent manner in signing Bills in Sydney without calling on the Receipts, but surely the Public are not to suffer thro' the criminality of Government Servants', he wrote hopefully – but, of course, mistakenly.[24]

Hogan was ordered to produce accounts covering his period in office, but did not for nine months from December 1815 to September 1816. Broughton estimated expenditure in this period was between £12,000 and £20,000. These accounts never appeared. Hogan said Maum had them; Maum said he left them in the office when he was dismissed.[25] Hogan's court martial found him guilty of omitting to produce the accounts and fraudulently abusing his power. But this was not made public (so embarrassing, to have a senior official's fraud advertised), and Hogan's only punishment was dismissal. Back in Van Diemen's Land he was given a large land grant, provided meat to the commissariat, became a pillar of the Anglican church and died aged 83. Well into the 1820s the authorities were still trying to recover the missing accounts.[26]

EDWARD LORD'S METHODS of getting the commissary onside become clear when he tried what were presumably tried and true tactics with William Broughton – who sent a full description to his friend and patron Macquarie. Broughton already knew Lord well enough for the men to exchange chatty letters.[27] When Broughton arrived in Hobart, Lord was extremely friendly, inviting him to stay in his house (putting him under an obligation) and offering a loan of £300 (an even greater obligation). Broughton declined, for Lord also told him his debts exceeded £50,000. He also suggested courses previous commissariat officers had taken – presumably hints as to how they could cooperate. But Broughton was no Fosbrook or Hogan. 'His arguments were so at Variance with my principles, and the rule I had laid down for my conduct, that I began to suspect the professions he had made me were not the genuine effusions of friendship.'

As Broughton went about Hobart, he heard complaints about 'the grossly partial manner, in which Grain and Meat had been received into the

Stores', which caused great dissatisfaction. 'A few avaricious individuals' – Lord chief among them – dominated, to the detriment of smaller settlers.[28] Lord managed to persuade him that he was innocent in the affair of Hogan, the loan and the wheat. When the storekeeper asked him to sign the vouchers for the wheat, he suspected all was not right, he told Hogan. He found the wheat had never been put in the store, and declined with horror to have anything to do with the affair – certainly not! 'This I had from Mr. Lord himself!' Broughton told Macquarie. Lord was always plausible, and even eighteen months later when he had shown his hand clearly, Broughton believed Maum misled Lord, though he thought him naïve (Edward Lord!) in allowing Maum to use his name.[29]

Still, Broughton learned enough to feel he must move from Lord's house. Free of a guest's obligations, he set about reforming the commissariat, announcing he would receive wheat and meat only from people who produced them. Merchants were cut out. Settlers were pleased, but the leader of the merchants, Edward Lord, became Broughton's implacable enemy.[30]

First he tried to outwit Broughton. Government salaries were paid by the police fund, which was financed by customs duties. Hobart's police fund was empty, with salaries owing for up to nine months (another scandal). Lord told Davey he would lend him £3000 for the fund, if he could supply the store with £3000 worth of meat and wheat – even though Lord owed the fund £768 for duties on spirits. Davey asked Broughton's advice, and Broughton told him that smaller settlers would suffer, as the store would be full and he could not take their wheat. Swayed as usual by the last person he talked to, Davey tore up Lord's letter.[31]

Lord tried a new tack, and this time persuaded Davey to agree. He would provide the store with wheat to repay the £768, and the money

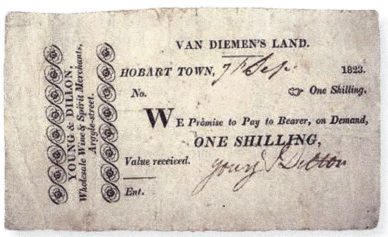

Promissory note for one shilling, issued by the Hobart firm of Young & Dillon, 1823
(W.L. Crowther Library, TAHO)

Promissory note for four Spanish dollars, 1823 (W.L. Crowther Library, TAHO)

would go to the police fund for salaries. Davey instructed Broughton to accept the wheat. 'However distressing it may be to your feelings that the Salaries of the Civil Officers should remain so long in arrears', Broughton replied with irony (Davey had shown no worry about this before), the same argument applied: small farmers would suffer. The other merchants would claim the same privilege as Lord, they would fill the store with wheat and 'the poor industrious Settler' would have no alternative but to sell his grain to the merchants at their price or go to gaol for debt, 'for such is the state of their pecuniary affairs'. Besides, the store already had plenty of wheat. However, if Davey ordered him, he would accept the wheat. Davey did, and cocky Lord wrote to Broughton saying his wheat was ready: 'I am certain you will rejoice with me that such an accommodation has been afforded'. Broughton replied that the store was being thoroughly repaired, and until this was finished he could not accept the wheat.[32] Neither Lord not Broughton was going to give in easily.

The fate of the wheat was not recorded, but all this gave Lord plenty to think about. Broughton, his enemy, was hand-in-glove with powerful Macquarie. Broughton was only commissary temporarily, but could be appointed permanently. Davey was malleable but unreliable, and about to be superseded. The new governor might be of the Macquarie–Broughton stamp. Lord's monopoly was in danger. It was time to get rid of Broughton.

On 22 February Lord wrote Davey a letter attacking Broughton for harming his, Lord's, interests. A stranger in the colony, reading Broughton's orders,

> would naturally observe how happy must this infant Colony be in possessing a Man of such pure principles! how careful he is to the claims of each individual! how feelingly alive to the poor and oppressed! how watchful of the Agricultural interests! how careful of the Public Money!

But in fact, settlers were left 'penny less at the mercy of the Law and their Creditors' (well, no – they would have been paid for their wheat). He, Lord, was the one who was really assisting agriculture in the colony, by exporting so much wheat to Sydney. He had brought £40,000 capital into Davey's government, and when his 'vital interests' were challenged, not by another merchant but by 'an Officer filling a Public Situation ... you cannot wonder that I should feel alarmed'. Lord asked for a court of enquiry, where he would have no trouble proving that under Broughton, corruption existed in the commissariat to an alarming degree.[33] Davey did nothing.

The new governor, William Sorell, arrived. Broughton found him fair and just, but events favoured Lord. Floods in the Hawkesbury region left Sydney short of wheat, and Broughton had to accept wheat from anyone, including Lord.[34]

By now Broughton detested Lord, complaining to Macquarie of 'turbulent persons in this Place, whose sole study has been to oppress the poorer orders of People' – Lord, of course. (This was exaggerated: it was hardly Lord's sole aim, more a by-product of pursuing his own interests.) Broughton asked Macquarie to have Lord's charges against him investigated, groundless though they were. Davey had promised to help him, but 'I want no favour from any one. I am ready to stand or fall on the Merit or demerit of my Conduct ... the shafts of Malice cannot even effect me.' Broughton! one feels like shouting at him across the centuries. Hobart, 1817, of course they can! Macquarie ordered Sorell to set up a court of enquiry to see whether there were grounds for a court martial. Broughton soon started doubting his immunity from malice: the court comprised Lord's friends, and he was worried that they would be prejudiced against him.[35] He was right.

Lord charged Broughton with trading illegally, selling his own wine, clothing and cattle – though Lord himself had assisted Broughton in this and they were tiny amounts. The other charge was malversation: having stated that the price of meat was sixpence a pound, Broughton accepted some for sevenpence. He explained that the contract had been signed earlier and he felt obliged to keep to its terms.[36] These charges were trivial, but they were enough.

Lord's friends concluded there were grounds for a court martial against Broughton, though a Sydney judge thought their procedure illegal and decision unjustified. Macquarie was furious, both at the aspersions cast on an upright man and at the trouble and expense of a court martial. Still, Broughton wanted to clear his name, so Macquarie ordered witnesses brought from Hobart. But he also ordered Broughton back to Sydney, so Lord had won. He did not need the court martial, so refused to attend it.

The plains of the midlands were excellent for running stock to sell to the commissariat, as Joseph Lycett illustrated in his 'Tasman Peak' (Allport Library and Museum of Fine Arts, TAHO)

He was a major witness, and his absence meant the case could not be heard. Even more furious, Macquarie published a general order: Lord's charges were frivolous, and Macquarie was entirely satisfied with Broughton's honorable, meritorious and zealous service. Macquarie summed up Edward Lord to London: there could not be found a more vindictive and implacable man, nor a more malicious one.[37]

Lord had succeeded in his object, getting rid of Broughton, and he continued to succeed. The new commissary in Hobart was Thomas Archer, another competent clerk promoted by Macquarie. He stayed with the Lords and soon became a good friend. Had there been favouritism in the way meat and wheat were received into the store? a settler was asked in 1820. Yes, he replied. Edward Lord received undue partiality. The commissary would make out tenders for less meat than he needed, then ask his friends to make up the quantity.[38] The ingenuity of these officers in coming up with scam after scam is breathtaking.

This settler was not alone in resenting Lord's dominance. In mid-1818 Thomas Birch, a Hobart merchant who had become friendly with Broughton, wrote him a chatty letter. The place was in turmoil; what with one thing and another (mainly acrimonious lawsuits) 'the wole Colony his at war'. It had been better with Broughton: 'We feel the loss of you'. True, as a result of his actions more people were able to sell produce at the commissariat, but the tender for extra needs 'goes into the grate Man's hands that was your gratest enemy' – Edward Lord.[39]

Flight of Fancy:
Governor Davey reprimands Commissary Hogan for drunkenness

Scene: *Governor Davey's office one morning. Hogan has been summoned several times, and has finally arrived.*

Davey: Now Hogan, you must be more careful. We all like the bottle, sir, by Jove we do! But you must be more discreet. Macquarie has been worrying me with complaints. I am to admonish you for drunkenness.

Hogan: Sir, you set a fine example to all your subordinates.

Davey: Aye, that I do! Nothing wrong with a gentleman recruiting his strength, provided he has a hard head. I have as hard a head as any in the British forces. I do set a fine example. Your head, Hogan, is not as hard. I have to say it, not as hard.

Hogan: Sir, I can hold my liquor!

Davey: Well, Hogan, I do not really agree. There you are, thinking you are telling Lord a confidential story, and all along you're telling Ingle! And look what you've just done to me! Sent messages that you've gone out of town, and all the time you're skulking at home, unable to work, unable to speak! Not good enough, not good enough.

Hogan: But sir, I am not alone – you yourself ...

Davey: Pondicherrry! Off with you, sir! I was told to admonish you and I have, so let that be an end to it. And let me have no more complaints of you! Do what you like, get as drunk as you like, but do not let me be badgered from here to Babylon with complaints! I came to this island as a retreat after a noble life entirely given up to His Majesty's service – Trafalgar, the Nore, there's no end to my devotion – and all I get is to be pestered with petty complaints! And now, it's nearly eleven, time for – be off with you!

By the way, make sure I'm down for 5000 pounds of meat in the next allotment. I'm sure I can rely on your storekeeper for, er, constructive arithmetic when my man brings it in. And don't forget, we have a meeting of the Waterloo Club on Saturday. We can have a more pleasant chat there.

Flight of Fancy:
Edward Lord charms William Broughton

SCENE: *The Lord dining room. The two men sip their cognac.*

Edward: William – if I may call you William – I have to admit to you the most terrible mistake. A refill?

William: No, thank you. You were saying?

Edward: You know poor Hogan. Unfortunate man, really – not up to the job. A weakness for the bottle. Between you and me, not the best of organisers. (*Shakes his head sadly.*) London doesn't always send out the best man for the job.

William: I quite agree.

Edward: A while ago Hogan bought goods from an American captain, a rather rough man. He was pressing for his money in that uncouth American way, and Hogan was in temporary difficulties. So I lent poor Hogan £400 to tide him over.

William: I heard something about it, and was going to make enquiries.

Edward: You've come to the right person – I know the whole sad story. Dear me, the dishonest way some people work! It's truly shocking to upright people like you and me.

William: H'm.

Edward: Well, I was to be paid when I sent in my wheat. But Maum, the storekeeper, issued the vouchers for the money before my wheat was delivered! I was horrified when I found out! Cognac to your liking? I have a different bottle if you prefer it.

William: No, thank you, this is excellent. You were saying?

Edward: I was sent the vouchers to sign, and I asked if the wheat had been delivered. Apparently most people just sign without ensuring that their goods have been delivered, so foolish of them! Maum, the rascal – Irish, of course, what can you expect – confessed that not a single grain of wheat had been delivered from my farm! I was utterly appalled! What a rogue! Of course, being in town, I don't know exactly when the wheat is delivered. That's my overseer's job.

William: But you should have ascertained whether or not the wheat had been delivered, before you allowed Maum to make use of your name.

Edward: I know, I know! Mea culpa! I never imagined for a second that he would do such a thing. I would rather lose every penny of my money than stoop to so foul a transaction! Disgraceful!

William: I'm surprised you've retained your standards in this corrupt community.

Edward: It has been a struggle. But I remember what I learnt at my dear mother's knee. "Edward", she used to say, "Never do anything dishonest. Never disgrace the Owen name – well, the Lord name, really – by anything you know I would not approve." And I have stuck by that. Yes, even in this nest of rogues I have remembered those fine words of my dear mother (*voice breaking a little*). I daresay you had the same experience, wise parents whose guidance has stood you in good stead through life?

William: My father was such a one.

Edward (*sympathetically*): Your father? What sort of a man was he? He must have been a fine man, to produce such an excellent son.

William: He was a man of few words, but ...

Edward (*inwardly*): Success!

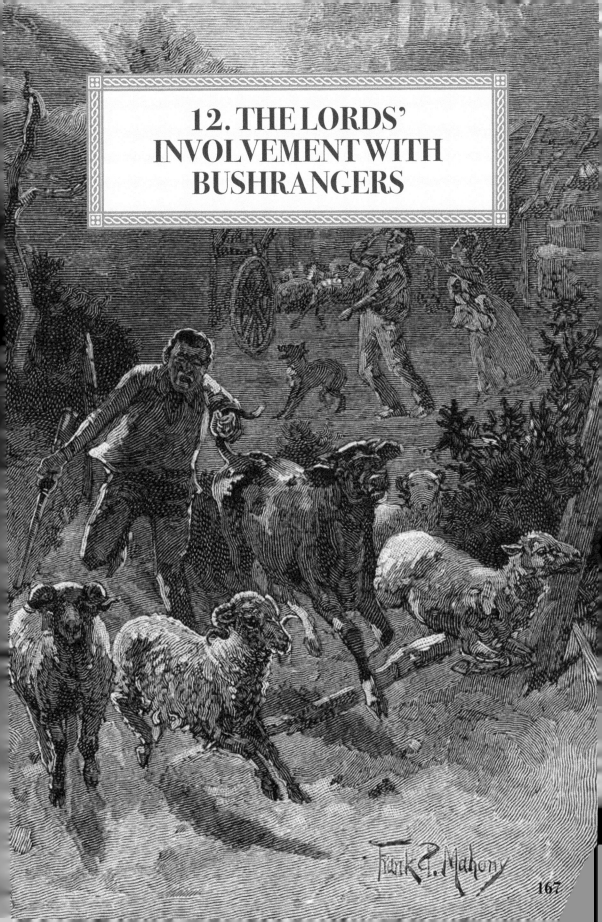

12. THE LORDS' INVOLVEMENT WITH BUSHRANGERS

JUST AS EDWARD LORD TRIED TO ENROL as supporters people who could assist his enterprises, so he tried to neutralise people who could injure them. The main threat came from bushrangers. These outlaws were active in Van Diemen's Land for decades. Usually escaped convicts who took to the bush, they challenged the government by living outside its authority, making a mockery of the whole convict system. Many ex-convicts and convicts under sentence saw them as heroes.

Bushrangers lived by hunting kangaroo and stealing cattle, which they exchanged with their supporters for food, clothing and ammunition. The supporters sold the meat or cattle to the commissariat or other farmers, and helped bushrangers if search parties were after them. Governor Sorell estimated that half the population was involved in this network.[1] Some people enjoyed supporting bushrangers, but this support was not always voluntary. Bushrangers had power. If they ran out of supplies they raided houses or travellers, and some were violent. They became familiar with the bush, and lived in remote, hidden valleys, often moving, constantly on guard. The government found it difficult to capture them, or provide protection against them. Pragmatic settlers came to an arrangement, providing support in return for immunity from being raided: the alternative could have been ruin. The Lords were heavily involved in bushranging in Van Diemen's Land between 1813 and 1817. Their extensive and well-stocked properties were never attacked by bushrangers. In return, Edward seems to have offered them protection.

Left: The Jericho district looks peaceful in this painting by Joseph Lycett – but this was bushranger country
(Allport Library and Museum of Fine Arts, TAHO)

Previous pages: A later illustration which captures the terror of raids by bushrangers
(Tasmanian Archive and Heritage Office)

Was Maria involved? While there is evidence of Edward's activity, her name was never mentioned in contemporary records. There is no evidence for the later suggestion that, being an ex-convict, her contacts and cultural knowledge would have let her come to an agreement with bushrangers.[2] Beside, it seems unlikely. Maria's convict contacts were formed in New South Wales years earlier, and in Hobart she tried to distance herself from her convict past. It seems more probable that affable, masculine Edward initiated the understanding.

It is even less likely that Maria Lord had an affair with the leading bushranger, Mike Howe, as seen in a 2014 opera, *The Bushranger's Lover*. Not only is there no evidence for such an affair, there are strong arguments against it. One is the way Maria tried to ignore her convict past. Secondly, in gossipy Hobart someone would have noticed, as they did a later affair. But nothing was even hinted. In any case – a scruffy bushranger! Edward might prefer the earthy working-class in his sexual partners, of which much more later, but Maria did not.

So, leaving behind this interesting but improbable fantasy, here is the story of the Lords and bushrangers, as contemporary evidence gave it.

BUSHRANGERS TERRORISED COUNTRY Van Diemen's Land from 1808, but at this stage the Lords had nothing to do with them, having no properties in danger of being raided. From 1811 to 1813 they were away. When they returned in 1814 bushranging was rampant. Even Port Dalrymple's surveyor and commissary took to the bush, trying to escape their creditors.[3] Edward Lord was now setting up his country property at Orielton, as well as running cattle inland. These enterprises were vulnerable to attack by bushrangers.

In early 1814, Macquarie ordered Davey to stop bushranging, and to proclaim that if 29 named bushrangers surrendered by December they would be pardoned; if not, they would be exterminated.[4] This merely meant bushrangers could do what they liked until December, as shown in the following story. In August 1814, Captain Fentrill was travelling with a party of soldiers from Port Dalrymple to Hobart. Near Epping Forest they captured two bushrangers. Next day they reached Tin Dish Holes (Sorell Plains) where Edward Lord was running cattle, and had breakfast with his stockmen. One had a musket with Lord's mark on it. The soldiers continued to York Plains, where Lord had stockmen in charge of cattle. Rashly, Fentrill told Lord's overseer he would camp at Jericho that evening.

During the night the soldiers woke to find guns held to their ears, and bushrangers exclaiming 'Lay still you Buggers'. It was a group led by their dreaded leader Mike Howe, who held the musket marked with L that Fentrill had noted. The bushrangers took the soldiers' guns, freed the two prisoners and tied up all the soldiers except one, Craig. They took him with them and it sounds quite amicable, as Howe told Craig he wished the old colonel (Davey) were there, as he would show him how these things were done, and put some buckshot through his paunch.

Howe's men walked to another group of Lord's tents, where Lord's stockmen (all convicts or ex-convicts) had breakfast ready. They were pleased to hear of the soldiers' defeat. Other bushrangers joined them, eighteen in total. Howe told Craig he wanted him to navigate an escape vessel. He knew everything that went on in Hobart and had no intention of surrendering, for his party was growing stronger every day 'and he had not done half mischief enough'. While the bushrangers entertained themselves shooting at a mark, Craig escaped.[5]

His story was worrying for the authorities: the bushrangers' lack of respect for them, their own powerlessness – and the collusion of Lord's servants. But Lord was Davey's friend, and nothing was done. Perhaps Lord had no idea what his servants were up to; perhaps he wanted to make sure his own herds were not raided. He could have been deep in negotiations with the bushrangers, though the musket story is no proof. It was just a musket branded, like cattle, to show ownership, handed to a stockman to protect himself then passed, willingly or unwillingly, to Howe. All that can be definitely said is that Lord's men supported the bushrangers, and who can blame them, isolated, way out in the bush? A hint that bushrangers were at least acquainted with the Lord name came from convict Alexander Laing, who was working for Lord's friend Thomas Lascelles at Pitt Water. Just arrived and still innocent, when Alexander met strangers dressed

'ANOTHER ROBBERY BY THE BUSH-RANGERS': this heading was all too familiar to Hobartians in 1816 (*Hobart Town Gazette*, 23 November 1816)

ANOTHER ROBBERY BY THE BUSH-RANGERS.— The depredations of the Bush-rangers continue to be truly alarming. Scarcely had we mentioned in our last of their audacious attack on the premises of DAVID ROSE, Esq. at Port Dalrymple, then we are again called upon to relate another daring depredation, committed on Monday last, at the residence of MR. THOMAS HAYES, at Bagdad, on the road to Port Dalrymple, by one of those Banditties of ruffians, who have been too long a terror to the peaceable settler & traveller.—MR. WILLIAM THOMAS STOCKER, his wife, and a cart containing property to a considerable amount belonging to them, accompanied by MR. ANDREW WHITEHEAD, and family (the

in kangaroo skins he asked if they were stock-keepers. No, they replied, they were Mr Lord's shepherds, come to see about their tickets-of-leave. Alexander soon realised the truth, but found the bushrangers very jovial, sitting down to dinner with the whole household, asking Alexander to play a tune on the fiddle.[6]

Some bushrangers surrendered in November, but not enough. In Sydney, Macquarie asked Judge Bent what should be done. Bent advised firm action: sending soldiers in pursuit of bushrangers; controlling convicts strictly by frequent musters; establishing a curfew and a pass system for travellers; arresting people who helped bushrangers; and punishing severely anyone involved. The last resort would be martial law but this, replacing civil rule with military, was frowned on by civil authorities. Macquarie sent these suggestions to Davey.[7]

Davey did nothing, until bushranging grew so terrifying he was forced to act. In April 1815 he declared martial law. As well, after sunset convicts were to stay inside, pubs close and no boats be used, though how far this was enforced is not clear – Davey was not a competent enforcer. Parties were sent out, but bushranging only increased. The colony was in a dreadful state of terror, said Knopwood. Then some bushrangers were caught and executed, and the panic died down. Despite the general worry, when three bushrangers were sentenced to execution the inhabitants petitioned Davey to spare two on account of their youth – which he did.[8] A strangely kind act from all concerned, in this otherwise rough society.

Macquarie told Davey he had no authority to proclaim martial law, but did not order him to revoke it. If it worked, its illegality would be overlooked. But outrages by bushrangers continued, so in September Macquarie ordered martial law revoked. Edward Lord, Davey's friend, organised a public meeting to present an address of thanks to Davey for promulgating martial law, such a wise, firm and energetic measure. Davey could brandish this in his own defence, if necessary.[9]

Bushranging continued through 1816, mainly involving Howe's gang. They acted as if they owned the place; Howe actually wrote a letter to Lieutenant-Governor Davey signed 'Michael Howe, Lieut. Governor of the Woods'.[10] They even robbed Davey's farm, taking the new trousers off the legs of his overseer and asking for a dictionary. They said they would be free and safe in Hobart in five months, for they had seen a gentleman who promised to take up their cause. He sounds like Edward Lord, for shortly afterwards a bushranger claimed 'that Mr. Edward Lord was going up to the Governor in Chief [Macquarie], and that he would do every thing in his power for them, and get them in' (pardoned).[11] This strongly suggests that Lord was offering protection to protect his own operations. Not that he did get the bushrangers pardoned. He achieved his aim, the safety of his properties, so that was that. It was one of several instances when he did not make good his promises.

William Broughton reported to Macquarie that the government lacked energy in dealing with bushrangers. It was the industrious settlers who suffered – the others were in league with the rogues. 'These fellows are assisted by many of the Settlers,' wrote Broughton; 'indeed I sometimes think they are encouraged by those, who wished to justify the necessity there was of establishing Marshal Law' – Davey and Lord?[12]

In December Howe's gang sent Governor Davey an extraordinary, rambling but quite well-spelled letter (perhaps the reason for stealing the dictionary). They complained they had been kept in the dark. They wanted to know whether Davey was for them or against them. 'He who Preserved us from your plotts In Publick will Likewise Preserve Us from them In secret': Edward Lord again? They could destroy all the parties Davey sent out to capture them, as he would find if he did not give them 'A Little Quietness'. They demanded an answer by their messenger, but Davey was not to think of defrauding them by sending out a party of soldiers: 'We Will Be watching'. He should weigh the consequences of his action 'for the Good of the Peaceable and Weell Desposed Inhabitants'. Enough to drive Davey to drink – on one hand Macquarie was telling him to care for industrious settlers, and now here were bushrangers giving similar orders! He replied to the bushrangers mildly, telling them that 'good Conduct is the Surest way to Favor'.[13]

Macquarie continued to urge action. There were only a dozen bushrangers, and Davey should send soldiers to catch them. In March a party killed

The signatures of Mike Howe's band of bushrangers on a letter to Davey, though many of them signed only with their mark (author's collection)

Government & General Orders.

Government House, Hobart Town,
Monday, 20th October, 1817.

WHEREAS Michael Howe, a Crown Prisoner now at large, stands charged in addition to his former Offences, with the Murder of William Drew (commonly called Slambo), on Friday the 10th Instant. In addition to the Reward of One Hundred Guineas already offered for the apprehension of the said Michael Howe, His Honor the Lieutenant Governor is pleased to declare that he will Recommend to His Excellency for a Free Pardon and his Passage to England, any Crown Prisoner who shall be the means of apprehending the said Michael Howe.

By Command of His Honor the Lieutenant Governor,
W. A. Ross, Secretary.

Governor Sorell tries desperately to secure Mike Howe (*Hobart Town Gazette*, 1 November 1817)

two. But outrages continued, especially from Mike Howe. A party of soldiers caught sight of him and his Aboriginal companion, Mary Cockerill. Fearful that she would slow him down, he shot at her; furious at being betrayed, she helped the soldiers track him, but after some days they lost the trail.[14]

April 1817 saw the arrival of the new governor, William Sorell. He had spent time with Macquarie in Sydney and had, no doubt, been fully briefed. Stopping bushranging was his first aim, and he implemented Judge Bent's advice: send parties to catch them; control convicts with musters and passes; punish bushrangers' supporters; offer substantial rewards for their capture. Howe offered to surrender, and Sorell promised him a pardon. Howe came to Hobart but gave little helpful information – except to implicate the clergyman, Knopwood, as abetting the bushrangers. Murky intrigue was implied, but Sorell had difficulty pinning down any information. There were plenty of hints that Knopwood was involved, but when Sorell ordered an investigation it pronounced Knopwood innocent, a decision 'rendered certain by the absence of all Evidence', Sorell wrote drily.[15]

At first Sorell had little success against bushrangers. Soldiers failed to catch them through incompetence and inexperience. Sorell stationed eight men under Lieutenant Nunn at Pitt Water, and they had their chance. Nunn heard that a group of bushrangers was at Orielton, Edward Lord's house. He marched his party there and the bushrangers hastily escaped, leaving their knapsacks behind. They gathered at the edge of the bush, and apparently shot at the soldiers, for Nunn was slightly wounded. This, a lack of ammunition, and the soldiers' reluctance to advance meant that Nunn fell back. The bushrangers returned to Orielton for their knapsacks, then made off.

Sorell was deeply disappointed: 'a more favourable opportunity for taking or killing some of the Banditti could never occur'. He was uneasy, as well he might be. There is no evidence that the bushrangers were actually attacking Orielton; it sounds as if they were resting there, perhaps even having dinner. They stole nothing – some flour was mentioned, but this would hardly be stripping the house bare, and could have been a gift – and no one from the house tried to catch them, or thought of hiding their knapsacks, so vital to them. It seemed that Lord and/or his men were protecting them, as Sorell hinted: 'their indirect connexions are so widely ramified, that they are still *too well* received in many Settlements; and they have been so long tolerated' that they were seldom opposed.[16] They were cautious and even judicious in supporting each other, he mourned. Their toughness and perfect knowledge of the country made them a difficult enemy, while the young soldiers were 'not *knowing* enough' to catch them. Even worse, Howe escaped – Knopwood always thought Sorell was too trusting, he wrote bitterly. Once Howe was safe in the bush, Hobart gossip reported that he sent Sorell a note bidding him 'wipe his A– with his Pardon'.[17]

But times improved. An energetic captain inspired the troops, and this time when they found a band of bushrangers they killed one, captured two and seized all the knapsacks and dogs, which crippled the rest. Sorell held a public meeting to ask for funds so he could reward captors of bushrangers. A large amount was enthusiastically offered, so worthwhile prizes could be offered. Knopwood gave generously; whether Lord did is unknown, but he

The *Hobart Town Gazette* was no supporter of bushrangers, describing them as 'a pest and a disgrace to their species', and appalled at Howe's escape from custody (*Hobart Town Gazette*, 2 August 1817)

was probably to the fore with his money.[18] Not necessarily hypocritically: if bushrangers held power he made sure they did not harm his interests, but he probably preferred them captured, since they disrupted commerce.

Sorell's measures were effective, and by September bushranging was nearly annihilated. Instead of twenty desperadoes in the bush, there were only two: Mike Howe and George Watts. Their stories are studded with hints that Edward Lord was involved with them.

MICHAEL HOWE ARRIVED IN Van Diemen's Land as a convict in 1812. Assigned to Lord's friend John Ingle, he absconded and joined a band of bushrangers. Tough and brutal, after escaping from Sorell he lived alone, not trusting accomplices. But even he had his admirers, one claiming his only fault was 'loving liberty, as much as any of us'.[19] George Watts was cast in a more heroic mould. Transported to Sydney, he arrived in Hobart in 1804. In his memoirs, Fawkner described Watts as a pleasant, goodlooking man who worked hard. Briefly a bushranger during the famine, he was captured and returned to life as a convict. He was attracted to beautiful Peggy Eddington, teenage mistress of 52-year-old Governor Collins, and 'a friendship anything but platonic resulted'.[20]

George and Peggy married in 1811, and their daughter Mary was baptised in 1812. Then the villain entered the story. Fawkner made it a morality tale, noble convict hero versus wicked gentleman. Watts, he said, continued his exemplary conduct until tortured past bearing by 'the Man who should have shielded him from tyranny': Old Bobby – the chaplain, Robert Knopwood.[21]

Knopwood, said Fawkner, was lusting after Peggy Watts. The 'wine bibbing parson' was a drinking companion of Governor Murray, and George found himself working out of town, with his overseer told to keep him from Hobart. But the overseer liked George, and looked the other way when

Above: Mike Howe arrives in Van Diemen's Land, 1812 (Tasmanian Archive and Heritage Office)

175

The Rev. Robert Knopwood, painted by a friend and looking the picture of the jolly, innocent clergyman (Anglican Diocese of Tasmania)

he spent weekends there. One day George came home to find Knopwood urging himself on Peggy. George thrust him out of the house. Knopwood organised a trap, to catch George leaving work illegally. George was warned, and he and his wife Peggy met secretly in the bush. They got away with it once; they got away with it twice; but as in all good stories the crunch came at the third time. George was caught, and magistrate Knopwood sentenced him to 50 lashes.[22]

To escape a flogging George returned to the bush and went in for large-scale sheep stealing, selling the meat through well-wishers. In 1813, he was caught and sentenced to seven years at Newcastle, a brutal penal station. He escaped and returned to the Derwent, where he became a bushranger again. It was difficult for Peggy, married with no husband, and with young children. She managed, with help from the Lords. Edward assisted her in business, as seen below, and she sold large amounts of meat to the commissariat. Where she obtained it is not known; she had no farm. Her brother John was also a protégé of Edward Lord, riding in horse races at Orielton and becoming licensee of Lord's pub, The Bird in Hand.[23]

Whether anything happened between Robert Knopwood and Peggy Watts is unknown. His diary is silent, of course; his few mentions of her are not romantic. On 5 January 1816 she was one of several women who came to eat fruit in his garden; a few days later she and Edward Lord visited Knopwood on business, and later when he was out, 'Mrs. Watts and two children, Mr Lassells, Mrs. Hogan, Mr. Collins and Lieut. French came and took fruit when I was out – in short it is impossible to keep any fruit in the garden till it is ripe'.[24] Hardly the words of a lover.

In 1817 the authorities offered a large reward for Watts. By now, said Fawkner, he was tired of life in the bush, wanting to live with his family.

A friend suggested he earn a pardon by capturing Mike Howe. Watts engaged a servant of Fawkner's called Drew and they got Howe drunk, captured him and started to walk him to Hobart. But Howe freed his hands, plunged a knife into Watts, seized his gun, shot Drew dead and escaped. Watts struggled to Hobart to report.

He gained his pardon, but not freedom. Sorell sent him to Sydney, afraid he would escape if he stayed in Hobart: 'From the numerous friends which this Man Watts has, the property they possess, and the ramification of his connexions throughout this Town and Settlement, and also from his desperate Character ... such are his Connexions and influence that *I could depend* upon few people here for his safe Custody'. Naming no names, of course – but it would not be surprising if these 'connexions' were led by Edward Lord. Watts arrived in Sydney, but died three days later.[25] No reason was given, but it was a handy death for the authorities.

Meanwhile, Howe was alone in the bush. Many stock-keepers were afraid of him or sympathetic, noted Sorell, and either would not or could not try to catch him. Finally, in 1818 a man suggested to a convict stock-keeper of Edward Lord's that they capture him. They enlisted a mainland Aborigine and a soldier. The venture sounds at least semi-official; was Edward Lord involved, or was his stock-keeper acting on his own initiative, perhaps wanting a pardon? At any rate, the men found and killed Howe; Alexander Laing reported that Howe's head was cut off by 'Drummond, Mrs. Edward Lord's butcher at the River Shannon' (note that he is Maria's butcher, not Edward's).[26] The bushranging menace was over, for the time being. Edward Lord played an important but background part, his name continually cropping up on one side or another. He was following his guiding principle – doing his best for his own prosperity.

The challenging task of chasing and trying to capture Mike Howe (*Hobart Town Gazette*, 12 April 1817)

On Thursday returned to Town a small party of Capt. Nairn's Company of the 46th Regt. who were lately sent in quest of the bush Rangers; the following particulars of their pursuit we lay before our Readers:—

After a diligent search in the woods the party at Jericho perceived *Michael Howe*, accompanied with a Native Black Girl, named Mary Cockerill, with whom Howe cohabited. On the approach of the party Howe darted into a thicket, and effected his escape, after firing at the native girl, who, from fatigue, was unable to keep pace with him in his flight, and was taken. Howe being so closely pursued, threw away his blanket & knapsack. The native girl then led the party to ⸺ River, a distance of 11 miles from Jericho, where they found four huts, which they burnt. 'While thus employed, they perceived three of the bush-rangers (Howe, Septon, & Geary) at the side of a high hill, contiguous to the river.

Flight of Fancy:
Edward Lord contacts the bushrangers

SCENE: *Somewhere in the Van Diemen's Land bush, perhaps out the back of Oatlands. Edward Lord is officially inspecting his cattle, but on the way he has a small diversion. Earlier he had sent a trusted servant to find the bushranger Mike Howe and set up a meeting.*

Lord: About here, in this clearing, Tom? We were to meet here at midday?

Tom: Yeah.

Lord: Ah, well, we'll wait. (*Dismounts, finds a handy fallen tree for a seat, and takes out his pipe and a bottle of rum. It won't hurt to have Tom a bit fuzzy, unable to remember clearly what happens.*

An hour or so passes. Suddenly there is a clatter of hooves, and four bushrangers ride up. They are wearing a mixture of old clothes and kangaroo skins, inexpertly fashioned into jackets and trousers – an alarming sight. Mike Howe, tough, acute, suspicious, is in the lead.)

Howe: Edward Lord?

Lord: Yes, that's me, and you're Howe? Very glad to meet you! (*They shake hands, and despite the lack of formal introductions Lord continues with the other men – he knows when to leave aristocratic convention behind.*)

Lord: Now, my men, down to business. (*Pulls out another bottle of rum and hands it round.*) Very understandable that you escaped from convict labour, very understandable indeed! And now you're living out here – and you look very well on it. Flourishing! (Keep passing that rum bottle round, Tom.) But what are you thinking about for the future?

Howe: We want pardons. We're never going to surrender. I don't trust that drunken idiot Davey.

Lord: An excellent decision. I agree with you entirely. Now, I think we can make a bargain. I can help you. More rum, anyone? When I

	next go to Sydney, I can see the governor-in-chief up there. He's a reasonable man, much better than Davey, and he's in the palm of my hand. I can ask him for pardons for you, tell him you only want a chance to give up bushranging – very uncomfortable, after all, especially in winter. You want to live normally, with women, a house, a fire – a cosy life. I'll arrange it.
Howe:	That's good. That's what we want, isn't it, boys? (*They grunt assent.*) How do we know you'll do it?
Lord (*looking offended*):	My good man, you have my word! A Lord never breaks his word! Of course I keep my promises. I'll be going to Sydney quite soon, in a couple of months, and I'll see Macquarie then.
Howe:	Good. Make sure you do.
Lord:	In return, leave my properties and cattle alone. You might find some extra supplies useful, tea and sugar, ammunition, guns, I'll send them up. Just don't touch my cattle. Or else (*menacingly*). I have power. (*Frowns at the circle. There is some shuffling of feet.*)
Howe:	Yeah. All right.
Lord:	A bargain! Good! We need to seal it – another couple of bottles from my saddlebags, Tom! (*And so it goes on.*)

Funnily enough, Macquarie is absent on a tour of inspection when Lord visits Sydney ...

HOBART TOWN, SATURDAY, AUGUST 30 1817.

SITTING MAGISTRATE.—Rev. ROBERT KNOPWOOD, A. M.

SHIP NEWS.—On Wednesday arrived His Majesty's colonial brig Elizabeth Henrietta, Mr. WATTS Commander, having on board 30 male and 50 female conv8ct;:—A part of the latter are to be re-shipped on board the Governor Macquarie for Port Dalrymple; and we understand some of the male prisoners likely arrival will shortly be sent to that settlement.

The Elizabeth Henrietta will sail for Sydney early in the ensuing week.—She takes up several respectable persons, who are (whether) on the (Acensal Crt at Marshals about to take) place. They (Lieutenant) for the trial of Deputy Assistant Commissary General the General, Mr. Assistant Surgeon YOUNG, both of this settlement, also others remain in the harbour, His Majesty's colonial brig Kangaroo, Henrietta; also the brigs Governor Macquarie, Jupiter, and Sophia, and the cutter Neried.

In consequence of strong information being given (that) a young Lady in Hobart Town considered under circumstances of peculiar gestation, had been secretly delivered of a child, an inquiry was held a day since on foot, which led to the discovery that a male grown male child had been privately interred in a box in the burial ground, under circumstances creating so much doubt, as to the infant's having come fairly by its death, that, after consulting the Medical Gentlemen, a Coroner's Inquest was deemed necessary. The Corpse remaining the infant having been removed to the General Hospital, a Jury of the most respectable Gentlemen and settlers of the Colony, amongst whom were two Magistrates, were called and a full enquiry was commenced before A. W. H. HUMPHREY, Esq. Coroner; in the course of which it appeared that Miss MAXFIELD, lived in Mr. Drummond, and living in the house of Mr. Drummond, had been delivered of the child without any medical assistance; and that it was privately buried, with a trowel in the night, by Mr. Drummond. The sittings continued several days, and after a most minute and laborious investigation, the Jury found Miss MAXFIELD Guilty of Wilful Murder; and JOHN DRUMMOND, ESQ. and MARY EVANS, a servant, guilty of aiding and abetting in the same.—A.—B.—A—The parties are in custody, and will be sent to Sydney for trial in a few days.

This transaction has caused a great sensation in the Settlement; the more so from the relative situation of the parents of the child; and much feeling of commiseration for Mrs. Drummond and infant family.

HOBART TOWN; SATURDAY, AUGUST 30, 1817.

SITTING MAGISTRATE—Rev. ROBERT KNOPWOOD, A.M.

13. INTERLUDE: APPALLING ACTIVITIES IN THE NAVAL OFFICE

on the General Court Martials about to assemble at Head Quarters for the trial of Deputy Assistant Commissary General H. G. and Mr. Assistant Surgeon YOUNG, both of this Settlement of Jerusalem.

Remain in the harbour, His Majesty's colonial brig Elizabeth Henrietta; also the brigs Governor Macquarie, Jupiter and Sophia, and the cutter Mermaid.

In consequence of strong suspicions being entertained that a young Lady in Hobart Town, considered under respectable protection, had been secretly delivered of a child, an enquiry was a few days since set on foot, which led to the discovery that a full grown male child had been privately interred in a box in the burial ground, under circumstances creating so much doubt, as to the infant's having come fairly by its death, that, after consulting the Medical Gentlemen, a Coroner's Inquest was deemed necessary. The box containing the infant having been removed to the General Hospital, a Jury of the most respectable Gentlemen and Settlers of the Colony, amongst whom were two Magistrates, were called, and a strict enquiry was commenced before A. W. H. HUMPHREY, Esq. Coroner; in the course of which it appeared that Miss MAKILLER, sister to Mrs. DRUMMOND, and living in the house of Mr. Drummond, had been delivered of the child without any medical assistance; and that it was privately buried, with a trowel in the night, by Mr. Drummond.

The sittings continued several days, and after a most minute and laborious investigation, the Jury found Miss MAKILLER Guilty of Wilful Murder; and JOHN DRUMMOND, Esq. and MARY EVER, a servant, guilty of aiding and assisting in the same.

The parties are in custody, and will be sent to Sydney for trial in a few days.

This transaction has caused a great sensation in the Settlement—the more so from the relative situation of the parents of the child; and much feeling of commiseration for Mrs. Drummond and infant family.

T HE STORY OF EDWARD LORD'S activities makes him sound like an unprincipled rogue – but he was by no means alone. Such behaviour was frequent in Van Diemen's Land's first twenty years. The public service was an especially fertile field, with one or the other of its officers committing every possible offence.

Hobart's public service comprised six tiny departments, headed by the commissary, the chaplain, the judge advocate, two surgeons, the surveyor and the naval officer. The chaplain was Robert Knopwood, who did little to promote religion, morals or respectability – with strong suspicions about his own honesty. Macquarie described the first judge, Samuel Bate, as 'much addicted to Drunkenness and low Company, totally Ignorant of Law, and a very troublesome, ill-tempered Man'. Bate's successor, Major Abbott, had little knowledge of the law but used his common sense. He proved one of the better civil servants, merely favouring his own family.[1]

Surgeons were often young, inexperienced, inadequately qualified, drunken, or even all four. The worst, Henry Younge, was 'exceedingly Ignorant as a Medical Man, being almost destitute of common Understanding, and very low and Vulgar in his Manners' (Macquarie again). He drank with convicts in pothouses, and was once picked up drunk and naked in the street. Suspended from his position, Younge tried to escape in a whaler, but was discovered, disguised, in the hold. The list continues: Dr Mountgarrett was suspected of assisting bushrangers, stealing cattle, misappropriating medicines and desertion from duty; Dr Luttrell was 'Very Unfeeling and Criminally inattentive to his Patients ... extremely Irritable and Violent in his Temper and Very Infirm from Dissipation'.[2] The first surveyor, George Harris, was honest but untrained, more interested in natural history than surveying. His surveys had to be redone. His successor, George Evans, was open to bribery (money or, in one case, a piano) if an applicant wanted extra land, or indeed any surveying done.[3]

The naval officer's task was to collect customs duties. The first, Edward Lord's colleague William Collins, avoided overt trouble, but Macquarie included him on his list of dubious characters. Lord himself was briefly naval officer until 1810, when the position was abolished to save money. Its next holder, Lieutenant Campbell, colluded with Fosbrook and took a 5 per cent commission from duties he collected. In 1814 he was replaced by James Gordon, who was deplorably lax (if not worse) in his record-keeping,

Previous pages: The sensational newspaper report (*Hobart Town Gazette*, 30 August 1817)

and also took the 5 per cent commission. Furious, Macquarie made him repay it.⁴

The warnings Macquarie gave his subordinate governors show the situation. In 1814 he warned Davey against Knopwood (chaplain), Fosbrook (commissary), Humphrey (mineralogist), Bowden (surgeon) and Boothman (storekeeper). In 1817 he warned Sorell (apparently) against Edward Lord, William Collins, Kent, Ingle, Knopwood, Humphrey, Luttrell and Mountgarrett – nearly the whole roll-call.⁵ However, of this disgraceful collection of public servants, the prize for creating the most shocking public scandal – against stiff competition – would have to go to John Drummond. The Lords had a cameo role in his story, as they did in virtually every story in Hobart at this time.

ON 30 AUGUST 1817 THE *Hobart Town Gazette* published the following fascinating paragraph, in one long, breathless sentence:

> In consequence of strong suspicions being entertained that a young Lady in Hobart Town, considered under respectable protection, had been secretly delivered of a child, an enquiry was a few days since set on foot, which led to the discovery that a full-grown male child had been privately interred in a box in the burial ground, under circumstances creating so much doubt, as to the infant's having come fairly by its death, that, after consulting the Medical Gentlemen, a Coroner's Inquest was deemed necessary.

'This transaction has caused a great sensation in the Settlement', added the *Gazette*. The whole town was agog, waiting for the result of the inquest. It fulfilled their worst fears (or possibly hopes):

> Miss MAKELLER, sister to Mrs. DRUMMOND, and living in the house of Mr Drummond, had been delivered of the child without any medical assistance, and that it was privately buried, with a trowel in the night, by Mr. Drummond.⁶

Like almost everyone else in Hobart, John Francis Drummond – who liked to call himself Sir John – came to the colony under a cloud. He had an upper-class Scottish background, and sounds like a hot-headed, rash, not to say faithless young man, whose imprudent marriage to the daughter of a convict led to his exile. Ensign Neil Mackellar had arrived in Sydney in 1792 and, after a chequered career that included murdering Aborigines,

Drummond writes to his friend John Piper in Sydney, complaining of the poor standard of 'Society' in Hobart. He himself was soon to lower it further (State Library of New South Wales)

was promoted to captain. His convict mistress Sarah Cooley bore him two sons and three daughters. Captain Mackellar set out for Britain in 1802 with despatches, but his ship vanished and he was presumed drowned. Sarah inherited his farm on the Hawkesbury, but died in 1812.[7]

The Mackellar daughters went to London, where in December 1813 Sir John Francis Drummond married Elizabeth Mackellar. His father was displeased; strings must have been pulled, and in 1814 John was appointed naval officer in far-off Hobart. John, Elizabeth and their baby son arrived in Sydney in January 1815, with Elizabeth's younger sisters, Lilias aged about seventeen and Isabella, sixteen. John Drummond lost no time in asking Macquarie for 'the usual per Centage' on duties he collected.[8]

In July they reached Hobart. The naval officer was meant to collect duties and stop smuggling, but since under Davey smuggling was widespread it does not sound as if Drummond was successful, while in the Jeffreys saga (see chapter 16) he appears a coward, fleeing from trouble instead of supporting a man who had offered to help him. Like Edward Lord, Drummond was a member of Davey's convivial Waterloo Club with its drunken dinners in the bush, but he was not particularly friendly with Lord. Shortly after his arrival he fought a duel for an unknown reason with Lord's friend Lieutenant Lascelles. Both fired but missed. In 1816 Elizabeth bore John a second son and her younger sister Isabella married Richard Lewis, a free settler who worked for the Lords as a clerk, then became a prosperous merchant. Edward and Maria Lord were friendly with the family, asked to be godparents of the Lewises' first child.[9]

How Hobart must have gossiped as it became evident through 1817 that Lilias Mackellar was pregnant. There was even more gossip when she was seen in public 'divested of such appearance', but with no baby. 'Many suspicious Circumstances it appeared were operating on the minds of persons here, who best know the family, as to what had really occurred', Sorell told Macquarie. The police magistrate made delicate inquiries of two doctors, whose replies confirmed the gossip. Pressed for an explanation, Drummond admitted that Lilias Mackellar had given birth to a child, delivered secretly. It was born alive but then died, he claimed, and he buried it at night. This was disreputable, but at least legal. However, when the authorities dug up the little corpse, suspicious circumstances (marks of strangulation, suffocation?) made an inquest necessary. The jury found Lilias Mackellar guilty of wilful murder, and John Drummond and Mary Evans, a servant, guilty of aiding and abetting her. Presumably they found Lilias rather than John guilty of murder due to gruesome revelations, perhaps by the servant. The three were sent to Sydney for trial. There was, concluded the *Gazette*, 'much feeling of commiseration for Mrs. Drummond and infant family'.[10]

Elizabeth Drummond accompanied her husband to Sydney for the trial; 'they have relinquished everything here', Sorell reported. There are no records of the trial and the accused were acquitted for lack of evidence, officialdom perhaps anxious to whitewash the case. But it looked suspicious, while Drummond had clearly had sexual relations with his sister-in-law. Governor Macquarie was horrified, especially when Drummond asked to

As soon as Captain Siddons arrived in Hobart he was no doubt questioned eagerly for news. He reported not only the Drummond acquittal, but the death of George Watts, while the Lords' ship *Jupiter* had just brought Huon pine from the west coast (*Hobart Town Gazette*, 13 December 1817)

be reinstated as naval officer. Macquarie, already appalled by Drummond's cowardly behaviour in the Jeffreys saga, was sure he was guilty of this new offence. His reply lamented the 'distressing and embarrassing Circumstances in which you have involved your family, and the disgrace thereby entailed on them'. There could be no question of reinstatement, for this would disregard society's established rules and encourage 'abandoned and vicious habits'. Macquarie suggested that Drummond leave Sydney at once, 'well assured that recent circumstances must cause you to be viewed by every well-disposed person in the Colony with horror and disgust'.[11]

Elizabeth Drummond remained with her husband: with no family or money she had no alternative. The Drummonds returned briefly to Hobart, where their house was stripped bare by thieves, Elizabeth gave birth to a third son, and the former naval officer was reduced to providing his successor with glazed hats for the boat crew. In 1819 the family returned to England and settled in Surrey, well away from Scotland and John's father.[12]

Lilias remained in Hobart and in 1820 married Nathan Elliott, an upright and prosperous free settler. She bore him a son, whom she named (rather insensitively) John Francis after her former lover, implying fond memories. The Elliotts lived quietly on their farm; Nathan died in 1862, their son died childless in 1885, and Lilias lived to her hundredth year.[13]

Meanwhile, in 1830 convict Mary McLachlan was executed for the murder of her baby, on much the same evidence that had seen officer and gentleman John Drummond acquitted.

The Drummond story shows that it was possible to go too far in Hobart. People were resigned to financial corruption, but adultery and likely

There must have been interesting chat on this trip to Sydney, with the passengers including the Drummonds; Edward Lord; his enemy Loane; Thomas Kent and Lucy Murray, in an adulterous relationship; and a clergyman to read them all Sunday prayers
(*Hobart Town Gazette*, 12 June 1819)

murder did shock them. Their sympathy was with one of the victims, Elizabeth Drummond, and Macquarie's reaction was probably typical of the whole community: disgust and horror. There was no welcome for the Drummonds when they returned to Hobart. They left, but Lilias Mackellar stayed; probably she had no option if, as seems likely, her sister Elizabeth refused to take this home-wrecker to England. But then Lilias married well. Did no one tell newcomer Nathan Elliott of her past, did good looks outweigh it, or were women in such short supply that Elliott was prepared to overlook it? Certainly the whole disgraceful saga – convict mother, sexual betrayal, possible murder – was hushed up. It was never mentioned, at least publicly, when Lilias' great-nephew, Neil Elliott Lewis, became premier of Tasmania in 1899.

Right: Absolute respectability: Neil Elliott Lewis, premier of Tasmania and great-nephew of this disreputable family
(Allport Library and Museum of Fine Arts, TAHO)

Below: Mount Dromedary and the River Derwent, by Joseph Lycett. The Elliotts' property was in this district
(Allport Library and Museum of Fine Arts, TAHO)

14. GOVERNOR SORELL

Above: Hobart during Sorell's period: ships in the harbour, men with guns on the near shore
(Allport Library and Museum of Fine Arts, TAHO)

Previous pages: Mount Wellington from Sorell: Macquarie named the town after the governor, whose name has therefore been remembered in the island (Allport Library and Museum of Fine Arts, TAHO)

BY THE END OF DAVEY'S PERIOD as governor, Edward and Maria Lord were flourishing. How much money they had made is not known, but other merchants made tens of thousands, and the Lords were better placed than anyone else, with their country property, extensive business and ships. Even so, there were problems. Edward Lord said he had £50,000 worth of debt, though it did not seem to worry him (and who knows why he said it, or how accurate the claim was). Perhaps a more difficult problem was that Davey's weak government led to a lawless society, not good for commerce.

In the colonies, much depended on the governor, and the Lords must have been keen to see what the next one would be like. Eventually, the British government had to act on Macquarie's despairing reports of Davey's total unfitness for the position, and in 1816 Bathurst told Macquarie that Davey would be replaced. When 'the state of society is good', he wrote, the governor's immorality did not matter (an astonishing claim), but in a convict society 'a bad example in a commanding officer has a direct tendency to defeat the object for which the colony was formed'.[1] For goodness' sake, Macquarie might well have thought, you're telling *me* this utterly obvious observation, *now*? Why didn't you think of it when you appointed a drunkard to the position? But finally Davey went. Though he owned 8000 acres in Van Diemen's Land he could not prosper, and he died bankrupt in a London boarding-house in 1823.

In March 1817 the new governor arrived: Colonel William Sorell. By now the population of Van Diemen's Land comprised four distinct groups. The Aborigines, a peaceful people, had retreated to the interior, and had little interaction with whites except those on the frontier. These men, mainly convict stock-keepers, often treated the Aborigines brutally, taking women and killing men; but for the time being this violence was distant, and Hobart officials could ignore it.

Convicts serving their sentences formed nearly half the white population. Most worked as assigned servants for settlers, living in the community relatively peacefully, though some men worked for the government. A small number at any time were undergoing punishment, mostly in gaol or in gangs working on government projects, such as roads. Once convicts had served their sentences, about half left the colony as soon as possible, but the remainder settled down as labourers, farmers and tradesmen (men), or servants, wives or partners (women). These ex-convicts and their children formed another 40 to 45 per cent of the population, looked down on by the elite for their convict connections. A small group, perhaps a tenth of ex-convicts, formed a subgroup of vagabonds, criminals and bushrangers, living outside the general community.

The remainder of the population, a tiny elite of under 10 per cent, were in the prized position of 'always free' with no convict taint: free arrivals, marines and government officials. The more successful among them, perhaps 1 per cent of the whole community, were the influential people, the ones with power, money and position. Their leader was Edward Lord.

Everyone in the free elite liked William Sorell. In Sydney, Macquarie thought him 'a Man of good Understanding Energy and Firmness ... Honor and Integrity'.[2] A competent governor at last! People in Van Diemen's Land were just as impressed. Sorell quickly showed himself efficient, putting down bushrangers, building public works and so on. Affable and charming, with a distinguished military career, he seemed the ideal governor. What, the cynic might ask, was this paragon doing in Van Diemen's Land, where virtually everyone had a shady past?

He had one, of course. At the end of 1817 astonishing news arrived: Governor Sorell, the king's representative in Van Diemen's Land, was – the stunned inhabitants of Van Diemen's Land told each other – 'living in fornication with another Man's Wife'. There was great debate, said a contemporary, and 'some would have it that if he was not married to her his Majesty's Ministers would not have appointed him Lt Govr of such a Colony where the strictest Morality was wanting'. But, once more, patronage triumphed over principle. To the great surprise of everyone in Hobart, London newspapers told of a court case, in which William Kent sued William Sorell for taking away his wife.[3]

Governor Sorell (Tasmanian Archive and Heritage Office)

Official and unofficial biographies of William Sorell differ. Officially, he was born in 1773, the son of a general. Joining the army himself, he saw much action and was promoted to major. Unofficially, his great-granddaughter reminisced that he had the morals of a tomcat. Wild and dissolute, he joined the circle of the equally dissolute prince regent, giving his father much trouble with his gambling and women – one of whom, Harriet Coleman, bore him seven children. She was an illiterate working-class woman, perhaps Sorell's 'rough trade'.[4]

In 1807 Sorell was ordered to Cape Town as deputy adjutant-general. A novelist would relish the dramatic scene where General Sorell thundered to his son that he had paid his debts for the last time. He had found him a position thousands of miles from his frightful friends. He was to marry this mother of his children and provide for them, then go to South Africa and behave himself. Whether this scene happened or not, William did marry Harriet, promised to pay her half his salary and went to South Africa.[5] There he posed as a bachelor and met Louisa Kent, née Cox.

Not many people delving into their family trees will find such an interesting story as Louisa Cox's. She was the great-great-granddaughter of James II, whose nineteen-year-old illegitimate daughter bore a son to the 56-year-old married Duke of Buckingham. Louisa, born in 1780, was this son's granddaughter, 'a young lady of great beauty, elegant accomplishments and most prepossessing manners'. But she had little money and in 1804 married William Kent, an obscure army lieutenant. Louisa bore him two children, one dying young. In 1807 they were sent to Cape Town, where they enjoyed a lively social round, he a 'most anxious kind husband and father', she 'a very pretty interesting little woman', 'doatingly fond of her children'.[6] Or so said witnesses in the later court case.

The Kents became friendly with Colonel Sorell, who took a special interest in their next two children, asking to be godfather to the second. Was he its father? Perhaps, for he and Louisa were having an affair. Those witnesses were surprised at the news. Sorell, said one, was reserved and serious, 'the last person he should have suspected of the least dishonourable intentions'. 'A rather grave middle-aged man', agreed an officer's wife.[7]

In 1811 William Kent returned to England. Louisa and the two children – another had died – went with him; but Sorell followed her and she left her husband for him. She signed her social death warrant. No respectable woman could acknowledge her (as Jane Austen showed in *Mansfield Park*), and William had to resign his army commission.[8] Louisa bore him three more children and he abandoned his legal family.

Doubtless the families of both William and Louisa preferred them to continue their immoral lives out of the country. When a new governor was needed for distant Van Diemen's Land, wrote their great-granddaughter, the

Cape Town, by W. Hodges (National Library of Australia nla.pic-an7691838)

> **GOVERNMENT AND GENERAL ORDERS.**
>
> GOVERNMENT HOUSE, HOBART TOWN,
> Thursday, 10th April, 1817.
>
> CIVIL DEPARTMENT.
>
> I. IT being necessary that the exact state of the Public Stores should be ascertained and reported at the Period of a Transfer of Authority in this Settlement, a Committee of Officers will assemble on Monday Next, the 14th Instant, at Ten o'Clock in the Forenoon, for the purpose of taking an exact Survey of all Naval and Military Stores, Provisions, Spirits, Grain, and Cattle belonging to the Crown, or in the King's Stores at Hobart Town, and will make a Report in the usual way to the Lieutenant Governor.
>
> MEMBERS OF THE COMMITTEE:
> Captain Nairn, Inspector of Public Works;
> Mr. Drummond, Naval Officer;
> Mr. Gordon, Magistrate.
>
> Mr. Acting Assistant Commissary General Broughton will afford all necessary Information to the Committee of Survey.
>
> II.—His Excellency the Governor in Chief having been pleased to give it in Instruction to Lieutenant Governor Sorell, that all Public Accounts up to the Day on which he should assume the Command of the Settlements in Van Diemen's Land should be settled, liquidated, and closed by Lieutenant Governor DAVEY, his Predecessor; His Honor Lieutenant Governor SORELL apprizes the Inhabitants generally, and all Persons concerned, that he is to be considered responsible for no Claims or Demands whatever upon Government for Grain, Animal Food, or other Articles delivered to the King's Stores, or for any Work done for Government prior to the Date of his taking upon him Authority as Lieutenant Governor in Van Diemen's Land.
>
> *By Command of His Honor the Lieutenant Governor,*
> W. A. ROSS, *Secretary.*

Sorell introduces order and method to Van Diemen's Land's government as soon as he arrives
(*Hobart Town Gazette*, 12 April 1817)

prince regent put in a word and Sorell was appointed. 'When the Governor went to have his farewell audience of the Prince Regent, the Prince pulled a diamond ring from his finger and gave it to him as a keepsake. That ring was afterwards my mother's wedding ring.'[9] The wedding ring tale has a convincing air, and this story would explain why, after Bathurst specifically stated that the governor of a convict colony needed to set a good example, an adulterer was appointed. Surely only really superior, royal patronage could achieve such a result.

William, Louisa and four children – their three and one of the Kent girls – left England in September 1816. They travelled as husband and wife: the children's nurse complained that she had been tricked, employed to accompany 'His Honor's *Wife*', and William introduced Louisa to everyone as Mrs Sorell. The family arrived in Hobart in April 1817.[10]

SORELL HAD HARDLY SET FOOT in Hobart before Edward Lord began his usual charm offensive. The owners of four ships, *Spring, Jupiter, Harriet* and *Cochin* (that is, Edward Lord and two other men), gave a 'splendid and elegant' welcome dinner to Sorell: 64 gentlemen, a lavish spread, guns firing continually 'as the merry glass went round', and *Cochin*'s captain singing whimsical songs. It seems likely that Edward Lord organised and largely paid for this festivity; the other ship owners had little interest in conciliating Sorell. Lord also paid the duties he owed the government and dropped Davey, since Sorell thought poorly of him and Davey was now powerless.[11]

It needed more than this for Edward Lord to gain Sorell's approval. In Sydney, Macquarie had briefed Sorell, doubtless telling him of Lord's iniquities. A list of names Macquarie wrote, presumably a warning against designing characters like that he had written for Davey, was headed by Edward Lord. In Hobart Sorell shunned Lord. He and Macquarie criticised him over the Broughton case, and Knopwood's diary shows Lord attending no dinners at government house.[12] Sorell's opinion of Lord sank further after the Jeffreys saga.

'In no part of the world is Smuggling carried on to a greater extent' than in Hobart; 'there have been whole Cargoes smuggled of 4 to 5,000 Gallons of Spirits at a time', wrote observers.[13] Hobart was well sited for smuggling, with the winding Derwent estuary with its secluded inlets giving captains plenty of opportunity to land cargoes secretly. The huge demand for rum encouraged a thriving trade.

In 1814 Lieutenant Charles Jeffreys R.N. arrived in Sydney with a government brig, *Kangaroo*, provided by London for colonial use. Much of Jeffreys' work involved taking cargoes to and from Hobart, where he and his wife became friendly with the Lords. On one voyage Jeffreys sold Edward Lord a large amount

This sheltered bay in the River Derwent would have been a good spot for Jeffreys to land his contraband
(Allport Library and Museum of Fine Arts, TAHO)

of spirits on which Davey remitted the duties, claiming it was supplied to government. Macquarie was forced to allow this fishy-sounding transaction. He disapproved of Jeffreys as vain, ignorant, negligent and totally unfit for command (one of his Sydney–Hobart voyages took over three months), and in 1817 ordered him to return to England in *Kangaroo*, without stopping on the way – perhaps after hearing rumours about smuggling.[14]

From Sydney Jeffreys took, legally or illegally, a mixture of passengers: several stowaways; Garnham Blaxcell, a merchant who owed the government £2385; and Thomas Hassall, a devout young man sailing to England to be ordained a clergyman. Despite Macquarie's instructions, Jeffreys stopped at Hobart, saying he needed repairs. Sorell helped him – to hasten his departure, he told Macquarie. The disreputable Blaxcell was another friend of the Lords, having done business with them since 1812.[15] What a trio, Sorell might have thought: Lord, Blaxcell and Jeffreys, each as bad as the other.

Drama erupted when Jeffreys was about to sail. Not only did the usual searches find convict runaways on his ship, but Sorell heard that he intended to anchor downriver, smuggle spirits on shore and pick up more runaways. Sorell, a newcomer, could not believe that a Royal Navy officer would smuggle spirits, but everyone else in Hobart did, telling him Jeffreys had done this before. (Who received the spirits? Jeffreys' friend Edward Lord?) Sorell forbad Jeffreys to stop downriver. Jeffreys answered rudely and anchored three miles downstream.[16]

Sorell ordered the naval officer, John Drummond, to row around *Kangaroo* all night, the only way of stopping communication with the shore. Captain Jones of Lord's ship *Jupiter* volunteered to help with his ship's boat. At 11 p.m. Jeffreys and some of his crew in their own ship's boat attacked Jones with drawn cutlasses, Jeffreys shouting, 'You damned scoundrel, I'll cut you down'. The men seized Jones, cut him on the head and beat him severely. Jones called for help to Drummond, who rowed away. Jeffreys and his men dragged Jones and his crew on to *Kangaroo* and put them in irons. Sorell sent a note ordering their release and finally, numb with cold, they were freed. Jones told Sorell that everyone on board was drunk, including the chief constable who brought Sorell's note.[17]

Shocked at this attack by a Royal Navy vessel, Sorell prohibited all communication between Jeffreys and the settlement. Despite this, next day Edward Lord and Garnham Blaxcell were rowed from Hobart to *Kangaroo*. Lord planned to sail to England with Jeffreys, Sorell reported, but at Maria Lord's request Sorell sent an officer to bring him on shore.

Apparently Edward obeyed; if so, it is one of the few known examples of Maria's influence over him. Jeffreys hung about the mouth of the Derwent for days and, with Drummond's guard probably ineffectual, could have landed his spirits and taken runaways on board. Finally he left for England, with not only Blaxcell but two of the Lords' children. Blaxcell died of drink on the way, the one aspect of this story that might have given Macquarie some grim satisfaction.[18] Various versions were told, but plainly Jeffreys challenged Sorell's authority and Edward Lord was friendly with him, the most likely purchaser of the smuggled spirits. Sorell continued to shun Lord for the rest of the year.

But in the end Lord succeeded in winning Sorell over, with four reasons possible. One was his tried and tested charm, affability and aristocratic background, which worked with almost everyone, except Macquarie and Bligh. Then he was useful, providing at a moderate charge goods such as a cargo of Huon pine Sorell needed. Thirdly, Sorell soon found worse villains, complaining of, for example, Roland Loane, whose 'egotistical, absurd and ungrammatical' complaints masked a career of insolence and disrespect never exceeded in any colony; Anthony Kemp, the most seditious, mischievous and undeserving man in the island; and the totally appalling Major Stewart at Launceston.[19] Fourthly, the arrival of the news of the Kent v. Sorell court case meant that Sorell was vulnerable. As things stood, the British authorities could claim ignorance of his adultery, but one official complaint from a disgruntled colonist would mean they had to act. Sorell had to keep important men onside. The news arrived about the end of 1817. In January 1818 he was writing to Lord in a friendly manner, one ally to another, and Knopwood first noted Lord dining with Sorell in March 1818.[20]

Once Lord had his feet under the table, his winning personality did the rest. Sorell and Lord became good friends. They were similar, both using their personal attractions to get their own way, both convivial and hospitable, both having female partners with dubious pasts. Lord could have lent Sorell money, putting him in his debt. Found guilty in the court case against Louisa's husband, Sorell had to pay £3000 damages, almost four times his annual salary: a loan would have been helpful. For whatever reasons, Edward Lord won over the new governor. Maria Lord commented that 'M^r. Lord & our very excellent Lt Govr continue on the best Terms', and Sorell conferred signs of approval, such as in 1818 making Lord a member of the governor's court of civil judicature.[21] He was free to continue making money without official obstructions.

Edward Lord tells his friend Piper about his support for Sorell
(State Library of New South Wales)

In return, he supported Sorell. In July 1818 he told a friend that a group opposed Sorell:

> I believe I have given great offence to them in not joining the discontented; but as I always hope to act from principle I should have done great injustice to my own Sentiments had I in the slightest degree have concurred; being fully persuaded that Governor Sorells conduct is entirely actuated from the purest and most disinterested principles of doing justice to every Individual, and promoting the real Interest and welfare of this Settlement by every means in his Power[22]

How Macquarie and Broughton would have spluttered had they read this, Lord claiming he always acted from principle! But, like many others, Lord never minded a little hypocrisy.

Sorell helped Lord in another way. An excellent administrator, he stopped bushranging; provided infrastructure such as public buildings, bridges and roads; encouraged farming; tried to enforce obedience to the regulations; and brought a measure of law and order to the colony – but did not impinge on the rights of leading colonists or try to stop corruption, because to do so would have made enemies. This was the most encouraging situation possible for merchants.

As the colony grew and a few individuals started enterprises, Van Diemen's Land's free economy gradually developed. This trend accentuated from 1820, as immigrants arrived from Britain. That year a description of Van Diemen's Land was published in England. Some time previously surveyor George Evans decided to encourage emigration by writing a glowing tribute to the island, describing it as ideal: beautiful, with not only the most salubrious climate in the globe, but fertile land, free labour and government support. He ignored disadvantages, such as the presence of convicts – quite a feat, considering Van Diemen's Land was primarily a convict colony. However, Evans made the mistake of travelling to Sydney with Lieutenant Jeffreys, and complained that Jeffreys stole and copied the manuscript. Jeffreys (who had few chances to acquire such knowledge) published a book about Van Diemen's Land in London in 1820, and it contains many passages almost word for word with Evans' book. Evans could not get his version published until 1822.[23]

Britain was suffering economic depression after the end of the Napoleonic War, and Jeffreys' book inspired a number of respectable, god-fearing people to migrate, a change from the shady characters of the past. They had more money, they aimed to start a new life, they were more likely to stay than the previous birds of passage and, being hard-working and sober, they were more likely to establish successful farms and businesses. All these changes were promising for an ambitious couple like the Lords. (Jeffreys received his comeuppance. His book, the first, was in the firing line when reality did not live up to his description. Migrants blamed him as 'an author of lies'.[24])

All this time, the Lords could have suffered if Macquarie had acted firmly against Edward. Macquarie had enough reason to, but he never called him to account, probably because he had so much influence in London through his brother. Macquarie himself was an outsider in London, a Scot from a lowly background without a patron: he obtained the position of governor only because the man first appointed (high-ranking army officer, protégé of Wellington, natural son of a marquis, influential wife) decided the pay was inadequate. Macquarie, his second-in-command, was appointed because the only other applicant was even less impressive. So like Sorell he was vulnerable, and had to treat influential people with caution.[25]

SORELL WAS PRESUMABLY DISMAYED when London newspapers arrived in Hobart with news of the Kent v. Sorell court case. Yet the effect was less than he might have feared. By now he had been in the colony for the best part of a year and most people liked and admired him as an efficient governor. After such a run of incompetents this was welcomed – at least by the upper classes. Thomas Keston, small farmer, was not so keen. He was horrified at

> the whole account of the scandalous & ungentlemanlike manner he seduced the young Woman from her Husband & he an old

lantern jaw'd man, old enough to be her great grand Father, for she was 22 y^{rs} of age when seduced from her Husband & his Honor upwards of 60 Years of age

The age difference was not really so great: though prematurely grey, Sorell was only 44, while Louisa was 37. But Keston could hardly ask them their ages, and instead reported gossip flying round the colony. It was a very bad example, he continued:

> When a pair come together without being married & any one speaks to them about it they say what is the Harm for us to live together without marrying any more than our Lt Govr for he is not married to his Woman and mine is not another Man's Wife, & if she was have not we as much right to live together as they have we are not sent from England to teach Morality.[26]

Keston accused Sorell of trying to make money dishonestly, selling tickets-of-leave for example. No one else claimed this and it seems unlikely, but perhaps no one else would have written it down.

Sorell did not care about such opinions – no member of the elite took any notice of what the working class thought – and continued to govern the colony competently. When Macquarie arrived on his second visit to the island in 1821, he was thrilled with its progress. Hobart's wretched huts of 1811 had been converted into substantial buildings set on regular streets, and Sorell had encouraged the prevailing spirit of industry, he wrote.[27] Besides being genuinely pleased, Macquarie was not going to criticise Sorell – it would have been foolish to make problems for a friend of the prince regent.

From stories told about Sorell, he sounds charming. He would stroll about the gate of government house, chatting with anyone, pleased to hear anyone's petition – but, unlike Davey, he always kept his dignity. He was no strict disciplinarian, but wanted everyone happy, settlers, convicts and all. Edward Abbott accompanied Sorell to inspect the highway to Launceston, whose construction Sorell was pushing ahead. They came upon a road party, which consisted of a line of convicts comfortably seated breaking stones, 'the work being done in the most approved and orthodox of the "Government stroke" method' – that is, slowly. No one recognised the governor.

Opposite: Macquarie expresses his pleasure at Sorell's excellent government *(Sydney Gazette,* 21 July 1821)

and arrived at Hobart Town, on the River Derwent, in Van Diemen's Land, on the Morning of Tuesday the 24th, after a Voyage of Eleven Days.

His EXCELLENCY's Arrival being expected, his Landing was marked by every Degree of Attention and Respect by His Honor Lieutenant Governor SORELL, the Civil and Military Officers of Government, and the principal Inhabitants, which His Station, or personal Regard, could dictate.

2. It was, with much Satisfaction, His EXCELLENCY beheld the numerous Changes and Improvements which Hobart Town had undergone, since the Period of his former Visit, in 1811. The wretched Huts and Cottages, of which it then consisted, being now converted into regular substantial Buildings, and the whole laid out in regular Streets; several of the Houses being two Stories high, spacious, and not deficient in architectural Taste. The principal Public Buildings, which have been erected, are—a Government House; a handsome Church; a commodious Military Barrack; a strong Gaol; a well-constructed Hospital; and a roomy Barrack for Convicts, which latter is now nearly completed.

The GOVERNOR had the Curiosity to ascertain the Number of Houses and Population of the Town; the former he found to consist of no less than 481 Houses, and the Inhabitants to amount to upwards of 2700 Souls.

On the Stream, which passes through the Town, there have been four Water Mills erected for the Grinding of Grain, and a neat Battery has been constructed on Mulgrave Point, at the Entrance of Sullivan's Cove; and, on Mount Nelson, a Signal Post and Telegraph have been established. The GOVERNOR observed also, with much Pleasure, the well-directed Attention which has been displayed towards the Accommodation of the Shipping Interests, in the Planning of a large substantial Pier, or Quay, which is now in Progress in Sullivan's Cove, for the Convenience of Ships or Vessels trading thither, in the Loading and Unloading of their Cargoes; which Work, combined with the natural Facilities of the Place, will render Sullivan's Cove one of the best and safest Anchorages in the World.

3. The Industry and Spirit of Enterprize, exhibited generally by the Inhabitants of Hobart Town, bespeak a favorable Opinion of their Manners, and the numerous Comforts enjoyed by them, as the Result of their Application mark the certain Reward which will ever be attendant on persevering Industry; whilst the prevailing Desire for the Improvement of the Town, bids fair to render it one of the handsomest and most flourishing in Australia.

'Where is the overseer?' Sorell asked the nearest man.

'Kangarooin'', came the reply – the overseer was out hunting kangaroo, leaving the convicts to break stones unsupervised.

'Kangarooing! Why, is this the usual thing for him to be doing?'

'Oh yes', said the roadman. 'We likes a bit of fresh meat occasionally.'

'You seem to be comfortable', remarked Sorell.

'Yes; can't grumble.'

Looking along the line of men, Sorell noticed one whose hammer rose and fell particularly slowly. 'Hi! my man', shouted the governor, 'you'll break that stone if you're not careful.'

'No fear o' that', was the reply. 'I've got to make that beggar last me all day!'[28]

This story probably grew each time Abbott told it after dinner to roars of laughter, but the gist is clear: the governor found a party of convicts unsupervised, working slowly, making little progress on his cherished road – and enjoyed the humour of the situation. No wonder he was popular.

Meanwhile, the British government had been told of Sorell's adultery. Harriet Sorell complained to them that she had no support from her husband since 1814. Fire crippled her, she had to go to a workhouse, two daughters had to work in factories and one child had died. And 'I am Sorry to Say Col. Sorell is at this moment living with the wife of Cap. Kent of the 21 Dragoons, by whom he has a Family or 4 or 5 Children'. Could some of Sorell's salary support her and their children? Bathurst sent her £100 of Sorell's salary, sure he was only anticipating Sorell's wishes, as he wrote to Sorell – who agreed (he had no option) and, rashly one feels, tried to explain to Bathurst: since Harriet had refused to be separated from the children he felt justified in abandoning them, while though he had made 'one great error of conduct',

A group of convicts, by French visitor Dumont D'Urville
(Allport Library and Museum of Fine Arts, TAHO)

he still had the protection of distinguished persons (was he threatening: keep quiet or I'll complain to the prince regent?). So he had to pay Harriet something, but in 1821 she was earning a living as a fruiterer, so it does not sound as though he helped her much.[29] However, the government had been alerted, though only privately, and for a time they could ignore the situation.

In the colony William and Louisa continued to live together, William telling a visitor that Mrs Kent's claims on him had as much force as if they had received the most solemn sanction: marriage. Not that this was much to go by as far as he was concerned. Louisa bore six more children, a daughter Matilda and five boys. Three died young, leaving her seven children to care for.[30]

In 1820 Commissioner Bigge, upright and respectable, arrived in Australia to enquire into the colonies. Like Keston, he thought Sorell's immorality had a bad effect, injuring the moral feelings of the respectable and giving the 'worthless' a pretext for adultery. Respectable immigrants arriving from 1820 were also shocked. Finally Anthony Kemp, whom Sorell found so undeserving, complained to London about Sorell's immorality, in retaliation for Sorell trying to curb his, Kemp's, misdoings. This was hypocritical, as Kemp too had an ex-nuptial family whom he treated cruelly. But the complaint had its desired effect. The British government had to recall Sorell; according to the family, his former patron, now King George IV, lost interest in him, possibly feeling he could hardly champion such a flagrant adulterer. Bathurst dragged it out as long as possible, but in 1823 told Sorell he was forced to dismiss him.[31] Back in Britain, Sorell received a pension but no paid work. His property in Van Diemen's Land went to pay a gambling debt. The family moved to the continent, cheaper and less censorious than England. The sons joined the army, but illegitimacy was now a handicap and three remained single. In 1839 William and Louisa were able to marry, both their spouses having died. William himself died in 1848, aged 74, and Louisa and Matilda lived in genteel poverty. Matilda disliked her father, who had not allowed her to marry the man she loved, telling her it was a daughter's duty to look after ageing parents.

Only one of William and Louisa's children married, to a Russian heiress. Like father, like son: he went through her enormous dowry in five years. Their four children produced only one grandchild, who died childless. So, despite their large family, William and Louisa have no descendants today.[32] It is Harriet's who continue the family name.

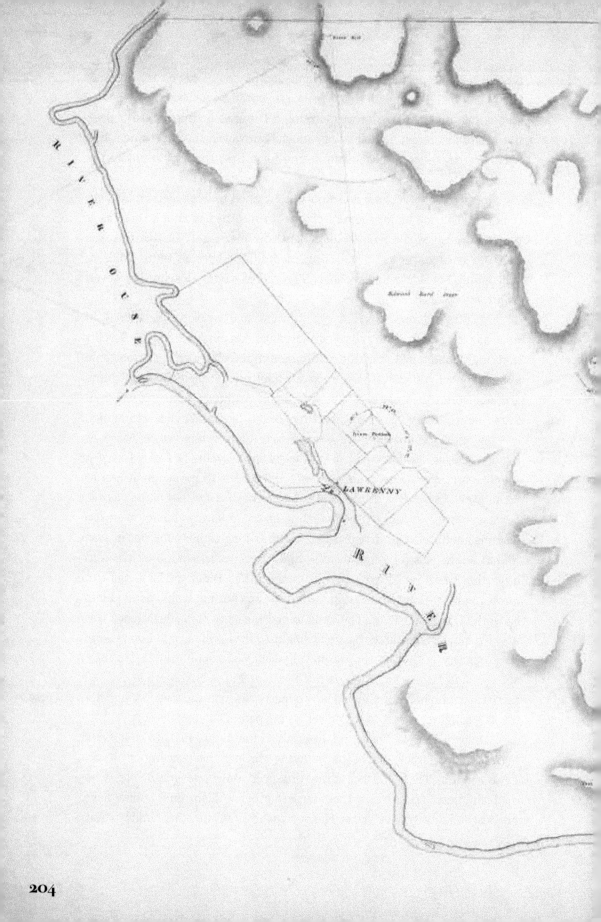

15. EDWARD LORD, ENTREPRENEUR

IN THE YEARS FROM 1817 TO 1823, the Sorell period, the Lords' success reached its zenith. Edward Lord became known as the richest man in Van Diemen's Land, in 1823 estimating he was worth £200,000. Gossip magnified this to £500,000, an astronomical amount.[1] To achieve this, the Lords tried every enterprise possible: landowning and grazing, selling wheat and meat, lending money, shopkeeping, shipowning, exporting, sealing, whaling, harvesting Huon pine. They seldom thought of anything new themselves, but took up any idea suggested by others. By 1822 they owned a large network of interests with tentacles throughout the colony.

Edward and Maria apparently worked together well to achieve this result. They specialised in different areas. Maria remained in Hobart, running the shop and organising the local side of all the business. Her activities are described in the following chapter. Edward's strength was public relations: gaining land grants, completing deals, hobnobbing with the governor and other useful people, becoming a civic leader, travelling, socialising.

Lord's activities show that he had two main aims. The overriding one was to advance his own interests. The minor aim, which he was happy to pursue as long as it coincided with the first, was to advance Van Diemen's Land, especially by establishing exports. It was all very well relying on British government finance at first, paying commissariat bills for example, but for the colony to develop, an independent source of income was necessary. This could come only from exports. Lord had shown himself an ardent Van

Below: A modern photograph of Lawrenny, showing the house (built after the Lords' day) beside the River Derwent, and cattle grazing on the rich river flats (Rebecca Aisbett)

Previous pages: Surveyor's map of Lawrenny and its three rivers: the Ouse to the west, the Derwent to the south, and the Clyde to the east (Tasmanian Archive and Heritage Office)

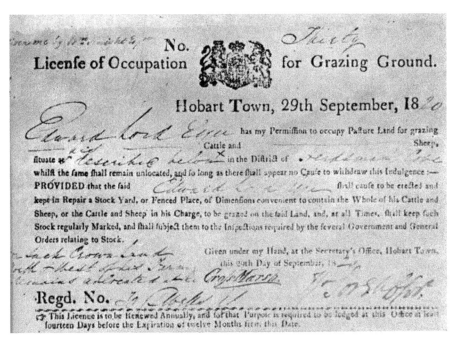

Edward Lord's grazing licence issued by Sorell in 1820, giving Lord permission to graze his stock on any unallocated land north and west of his land at the Cross Marsh (author's collection)

Diemen's Land patriot as early as 1812, and claimed he was always trying to advance the colony. However, he had no apparent trouble shedding his patriotism after 1824. Perhaps he had always been more interested in the advantages it brought him: sounding public-spirited, boosting his image as a high-minded community leader.

EDWARD LORD'S STATUS came largely from his landholdings. In Britain the gentry's vast acreages provided this, and what went for Britain, went for the colonies. By the early 1820s Lord owned or leased 30,000 acres, a huge area.[2] Part of this came through a major coup. The government decided to acquire Macquarie Point, a central headland in Hobart. It belonged to Lord, and his friend Governor Sorell agreed to exchange it for 7000 acres inland near Hamilton. Lord turned this into the grazing property Lawrenny (after a second Owen property in Wales), adding to it a 3000-acre grant his brother obtained for him. He tried a similar coup by quietly buying the block adjoining Macquarie Point, which Sorell agreed to exchange for a further 3000 acres. Higher authorities negated this outrageous deal.[3]

Lord also bought land, such as that of his colleague John Ingle who returned to England, or farms people were forced to sell cheaply. He took over properties in payment for debts, and leased large areas from the crown.[4] His friend Sorell gave him a licence to graze his cattle on all

A typical stock-keeper's hut, built of mud and thatched with grass. This one, on the Macquarie River, was drawn by surveyor Thomas Scott in 1821 (State Library of New South Wales)

unallocated crown land between Lord's own land at the Cross Marsh and the High Plains beyond New Norfolk, in effect anywhere not owned by another person.[5] Lord's land stretched from Orielton in the southeast up to the northern midlands (in an 1821 case of murder near Ross, the nearest hut housed Lord's men), and west across to Lawrenny, though in fact his cattle grazed at will in the interior of the island. They ran wild, in herds of thousands. No one knew how many there were, or where they were. Explorers found wild cattle in all sorts of obscure places – as far away as Cape Grim in the northwest – and assumed they came from Lord's herds. One writer claimed Lord's stock grazed 'over nearly the whole island'.[6]

There were few buildings on Lord's land except for some stock-keepers' huts and stockyards.[7] The only regular farm was Orielton, which was one of the colony's two farms with fences. The 1819 muster showed that the Lords grew 80 acres of wheat, probably at Orielton, the best wheat-growing area.[8] The rest of the land was used for grazing, mainly cattle. Maria Lord had some involvement, buying expensive merino rams to improve the flock's wool.[9] However, the land was generally Edward's interest.

Reporting on land use in 1826, three land commissioners were scathing. They visited property after property that had belonged to someone else, but were now Lord's. His 30,000 acres could be divided into productive farms, but he was 'one of the greatest destroyers of the prosperity of this Colony', for his acres were 'nothing but Stock runs, occupied by ruffians of Stock keepers under no control, galloping after wild Cattle in every direction', while would-be farmers left the colony because they could find no land.[10]

In fact Lord's land was not all arable, but doubtless more could have been used for farming.

Lawrenny was praised as superb, 'the gem of Van Diemen's Land', its park-like glades studded with noble woods, encircled by three rivers so it always had good water.[11] In 1821 immigrants George and Robert Dixon became Lord's overseers at Lawrenny, in charge of fourteen stock-keepers, almost all convicts, whose job was to choose fat cattle and send them to the commissariat. Later, Lord moved the Dixons to a farm at Pitt Water he had bought for a trifle, but they soon left. George wrote that some articles were stolen, Maria Lord held him responsible, they 'had some words' and he resigned. Not surprisingly; in a letter to him she expressed surprise that 'my farm of Orielton Park' had been robbed due to his careless way of leaving property exposed at night. He was liable for everything stolen. She hoped for his sake that the goods would be found, but even so the waste of time caused loss. 'I trust it will be a lesson to you to be more careful & attentive to my interests in time coming. And I beg further the more frugality & economy will regulate your conduct.' Shortly afterwards, Robert Dixon also resigned.[12] The Lords hardly sound like considerate employers.

Nor were they ideal neighbours. Newcomer James Ross took up land near Lawrenny, but found his farm surrounded by Lord's land, he wrote

After he left the Lords, George Dixon farmed on his land grant on the River Clyde, near Lawrenny. His painting of his property, Green Valley, shows a typical successful farm in the 1820s
(National Library of Australia nla.pic-an4911393)

W.C. Piguenit's painting of the River Shannon
(Allport Library and Museum of Fine Arts, TAHO)

bitterly. Once a herd of Lord's cattle appeared, and Ross's four bullocks broke their tethers and joined them. He and his men looked for them among Lord's herds, but days of searching produced nothing. He did see picturesque scenes, such as

> one of those heavenly lawns or plains, so common in this part of the island, sweetly diversified with picturesque clumps of trees or shrubs, with perhaps a herd of Mr Lord's cattle quietly grazing at one end, and the Shannon washing the other over its stony bed, with its silvery glittering waterfalls …

But he could not find his bullocks. 'I wished Mr Lord's cattle and himself and Sir John Owen too, a hundred times back at Lawrenny or anywhere else in the remotest and most miserable part of Wales.'

Thirteen of Lord's stockmen rode up to collect cattle for market and promised to help Ross, but did nothing. On the advice of a neighbour Ross offered a reward, and next day the stockmen delivered the bullocks. They had found them the first day, Ross was told, but hid them until he came good with the reward. That was not the end of it. Ross's wheat looked beautiful, until Lord's cattle discovered it. Ross chased them away, but they had already eaten half the crop. He was powerless: he could not impound them as he could not get hold of them without the help of Lord's own men, and going to law was impossible as the colony's one lawyer was in Lord's pocket. And no sooner had he chased away the cattle than they returned.[13]

Ross was not the only one to criticise Lord's herds of wild, unmanageable cattle; there were sporadic complaints for years. Many small farmers resented rich graziers' domination, as they influenced the police, had settlers' stock impounded or set up false claims of damage. 'A kind of black mail was levied on the [small] settlers to preserve their stock from molestation', wrote John West, naming the Lords as major culprits.[14]

Edward Lord did not have everything his own way. Stock theft was rife, and he often lost sheep and cattle. Only a few thieves were caught. In 1818, three men were tried for stealing over a hundred sheep from Lord and others, and a newspaper regretted that their punishment did not deter others.[15] In the north, farmer David Gibson was caring for a flock of sheep owned by him and Edward Lord, and in 1817 found 150 missing. They were discovered in the flocks of the notorious Tremby family, who had for years been suspected of large-scale sheepstealing. Now the authorities had proof, such as the brand 'L' awkwardly converted into 'T'. Three Trembys were severely punished, but stock theft continued. In 1822 Lord offered a large reward for information about 'a Conspiracy ... to defraud the Undersigned of Cattle and other Stock, under Colour of *Marking the Young by Mistake*' – taking unbranded calves and putting your own mark on them.[16] It was tit for tat in the backwoods of Van Diemen's Land.

There were other problems. The land commissioners reported that Orielton had indifferent water, so drought was a possibility. Convict servants could be unreliable, and Maria Lord complained that stock-keepers left their posts and came to Hobart without permission. Some convicts worked well, however. In 1824 the Agricultural Society presented an assigned servant of Lord's with money and a suit of clothes for his excellent care of a large flock of sheep for over five years, and a decade later the manager of Lawrenny praised another employee who had been a long time in Mr Lord's service, and was well acquainted with the cattle and the country.[17]

The Black War had not yet broken out, and in 1818 Edward Lord employed two Aborigines: an eighteen-year-old boy, Charles Frederick Van Diemen, about whom nothing else is known; and Musquito, who was born at Sydney in about 1780, exiled to Norfolk Island for raiding settlers'

Surveyor Thomas Scott's sketch of 'Natives of Van Diemen's Land' (State Library of New South Wales)

properties, and in about 1807 came to Van Diemen's Land, where he worked as a tracker for the government – he spoke good English. In 1818 Lord advertised that he was taking Musquito on his voyage to Mauritius: because Musquito was useful, good with cattle? because Lord liked to have a native servant, as was fashionable in England? or as a kind gesture, to extend Musquito's knowledge? Nothing more is known of Musquito in Lord's employment. Later that year he helped to kill bushranger Mike Howe, but he soured towards whites because convicts ostracised him and Sorell did not keep his promise to send him home to Sydney. He led Aborigines in guerilla warfare until he was captured and hanged in 1825.[18] His connection with the Lords hardly helped him.

Edward Lord's stock-keepers would have had more to do with Aborigines, but their stories were rarely told. Stock-keepers in the interior, far from any white women, were notorious for capturing Aboriginal women and treating them appallingly, and since the Lords employed many stock-keepers, it is likely they were involved. At least one example is known. A government enquiry heard that in 1824, 'a stock-keeper belonging to Mr Lord, named Jenkins, seized a native woman and kept her confined for some days in his hut, always chaining her with a bullock chain to his bed post whenever he went abroad'.[19] This was probably just the tip of the iceberg. The Lords' attitude is unknown. It would have been hard for them to control their stock-keepers out in the bush, but there is no evidence that they tried, and they must bear some responsibility for their employees' actions. They and the government would have realised, had they thought

Sheep grazing at Lawrenny (Rebecca Aisbett)

about it, that sending single men into the Aborigines' land would almost certainly result in Aboriginal women being raped; but this consequence probably did not cross their minds. In early Van Diemen's Land, few whites bothered about Aboriginal well-being.

In 1823 Lord's manager reported an amazing story from country near Orielton. A valuable horse of his had been missing for several days, when suddenly it was seen – being ridden bareback at full gallop down a valley by 'a black native girl'. A servant was sent after 'the fair Tasmanian jockey', as a newspaper put it, but despite chasing her for four days he could not catch her.[20] This is one of the few stories showing an Aborigine gaining the better of whites.

PROFIT FROM LAND came from selling wheat and meat, and the best customer was the commissariat. Maria organised most of the day-to-day transactions here, but Edward was involved in high-level negotiations. The land commissioners disapproved of his involvement. 'Job' implied corruption: 'any Job Mr E Lord wished to carry, it was done, so long as he had Meat or Wheat to send into the Store, no Settler could get a tender, in short, Corruption was the order of the day'.[21] Lord's activity under Davey was described in chapter 11, with him having everything very much his own way. However, he received his comeuppance. In 1821 a new commissary arrived, Affleck Moodie. Unusually, he was honest. Lord did his best to control him. In 1822 the governor of New South Wales, Thomas Brisbane, agreed that Van Diemen's Land could export a large cargo of wheat to the Cape of Good Hope. Moodie organised it and Lord tried to bribe him, as Moodie told his superior in Sydney:

> Finding no argument could prevail with me to prevent the exportation of the Wheat to the Cape in the manner suggested, he spoke about a "Reciprocity of Interest" (a term I believe made use of by the same Individual to yourself) and in direct terms said that if for instance I would agree to take the Wheat in question and give Treasury Bills for the same, he would willingly pay me <u>a per centage</u> on the amount.
>
> I replied that his ignorance of my character from the little intercourse we had had together was the only apology that could be made for making such a proposal to me – That he mistook me much – that I had never been concerned in such dishonorable action, and trusted I never would.

Horrified, Brisbane suggested to London that Lord with his 'sordid interests' be removed from the magistracy. He could not charge Lord with trying to bribe a government official, however, because he had left the colony – a place, Brisbane wrote, whose 'peculiar circumstances [were] so enticing to every act of corruption'.[22]

Lord explained Moodie's charge to Bathurst in London with one of his high-flown letters which not only entirely justified his actions but went on the attack: 'you have completely misunderstood the charge against me' and it was Moodie who behaved disgracefully. He, Lord, had nobly offered to provide wheat at a loss to himself, 'because it has been my invariable endeavour during the whole period of my long residence at V.D. Land not if possible, to run counter on any occasion to the wishes whether expressed or implied of the local Government'. But Moodie broke the contract, to Lord's horror – such a base and ungentlemanly action![23] By now the authorities had learnt to be sceptical of such letters from Edward Lord: Moodie retained his position and the government's confidence.

THE LORDS' ORIGINAL BUSINESS VENTURE, the Hobart shop, was flourishing. Other shops came and went, but theirs was the biggest and best, *the* trading establishment. Maria ran it but Edward was involved, mainly in obtaining goods. In 1816 he bought cargo from a ship's captain – vinegar, tea, lead, rice, arrack and iron pots – for the large sum of £1526. He paid mainly in wheat, but partly in oil and cash. An agreement between Lord and merchant Roland Loane saw Loane buying a cask of glass and running the risk of breakage, while Lord received a cargo of iron, the difference to be paid in cash by either party when the amount of iron was ascertained – a risky venture on both sides, but merchants had to obtain goods where they could.[24]

Lord moved into salvage. In January 1821 Captain Peter Dillon sailed from Calcutta. It was a horrific, slow journey, for the ship leaked badly and in July was wrecked off the northwest tip of Van Diemen's Land. Most of the cargo was rescued, and Dillon put it and the ship up for auction in Launceston, but received only paltry bids. Then 'Edward Lord Esq., of Hobart Town, was kind enough to take upon himself the Management of the Wreck'. He auctioned the cargo at his Hobart premises: rum, guns, ships' stores and other goods ranging from curry powder to castor oil. (Dillon lost three ships through wrecks, but made his name by discovering the fate of French explorer La Pérouse, finding relics on a remote Pacific island.)[25]

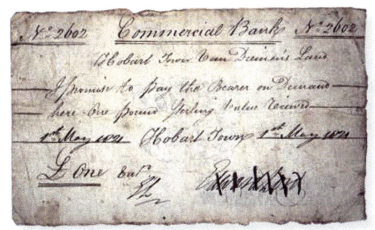

A promissory note for £1 issued by Edward Lord in 1821
(W.L. Crowther Library, TAHO)

As before, a large part of the shop's business involved alcohol, and here Edward's friendship with Governor Sorell came in useful, especially in avoiding paying customs duty. In 1821 Sorell explained to Macquarie why Lord should be exempted from paying £300 duty on rum. Before Sorell's arrival (so it was not his fault) Davey allowed Lord to import 15,000 gallons. There was no room in the government store, so Lord kept it under bond in his own store. It was an established practice, continued Sorell (again, nothing of his doing) to levy duty on spirits only when they were released from bond, but Lord's were found to have had heavy loss from leakage, £300 worth, and the naval officer agreed he should be exempt. Macquarie must have found this story fishy, but without ordering an enquiry in which Lord would surely have a watertight case, he was forced to accept it.[26]

All these activities made money – and cost money. At a time when a small farm could cost £33, Lord paid enormous amounts for goods. In 1821 he bought nine bales of slops (clothing) for £834 – paying as well as a surcharge, customs duties, shipping charges, insurance, freight and primage (handling costs) which totalled £481, over half the original value. However, by buying in bulk Lord saved money; a merchant sold him sixty chests of tea at £9 each, instead of the usual £12.[27] Since the colonists' appetite for tea was almost as insatiable as for rum, this speculation was safe, but sales of other goods depended on the market. Perhaps this risky aspect appealed to the gambler in Edward Lord.

The large amount of money coming in and out is indicated by an advertisement in 1818, when the House of Lord offered a reward for a brown paper parcel dropped by some careless person leading a horse. It contained 35 notes of hand and drafts drawn on the Sydney commissary. Most, 32, were in favour of Edward Lord and were worth £993; there was one for Maria, worth £18, and three for other men.[28]

Though details were rarely given, there are hints that Edward Lord was involved in dishonest practices. In 1820 Commissioner Bigge conducted an inquiry into the colony, and among the enormous amount of self-excusing, vague, contradictory and incorrect information given to him were several mentions of Edward Lord – who was absent, so could not give evidence himself. Scams were suggested, mostly involving alcohol: Lord had not paid his duties for spirits; Lord was allowed to land 7000 gallons of rum; Lord was allowed to take spirits out of the store on giving security, as much as he could. And so on.[29]

AT THIS STAGE, THERE WAS NO BANK in Van Diemen's Land, and merchants often acted as unofficial lending institutions. This was a racket, complained new arrival Peter Harrisson in 1822. He started farming at Jericho, and was determined to avoid 'the gulph that swallows up the means of many settlers': borrowing money. Those without money had no income until their crops were ready, and were obliged to borrow from the merchants. This meant settlers were

> obliged to take goods on credit of [merchants], for which they charge enormously, and it is next to impossible to get clear of them when once you have commenced a credit account, as it is their interest to keep you on their books, being well aware you cannot have goods of any body else while you are their Debtor, and must pay them any price they demand

This, said Harrisson,

> is the chief cause that keeps so many poor, from shortness of capital in the first onset or from want of prudence, a great many get into this situation, until at last the merchant gets the land and every thing into his possession as security for his acct, and reduces his Tenant to a complete state of dependence.[30]

Chief constable and farmer John Wade agreed. Merchants often lent farmers money, he stated, and they were caught in a spiral of debt. Two-thirds of the settlers were insolvent, not because they were dissolute (as the upper classes assumed), but because of these practices.[31]

The Lords had a number of these 'dependants'. This was not entirely to their advantage, since it was difficult to get debts paid. From the time a newspaper started in 1816 the Lords printed a stream of advertisements calling in their debts.

Tactful Maria made courteous requests:

> MRS. LORD acquaints the numerous Settlers indebted to EDWARD LORD, Esq. to whom Indulgences on their old Accounts, Notes of Hand, and other Obligations, have been long extended, that she is desirous to afford them every Facility in discharging their Embarrassments.[32]

Impetuous Edward was tougher:

> MR. EDWARD LORD, of Macquarie street, having in his Commercial Concerns given Credit (in an unlimited Manner) to many little deserving such Favor, which is proved by a Regardlessness of Payment, is now reluctantly compelled to resort to coercive Measures, unless their respective Amounts are immediately paid.

These undeserving people did not pay up, for the next week:

> Mr. EDW. Lord having in last Week's Gazette announced his Intention of resorting to the most rigid Means to Recover Debts due to him, is now determined to be trifled with no longer.[33]

Richard Lewis, now an auctioneer, sells a farm which Lord acquired after a debtor's death, 1819
(State Library of Victoria)

But the advertisements, and therefore the debts, continued. Nothing worked, not tact nor firmness nor threats. The Lords' only 'rigid Means' was court action, which they rarely took. The colony's wealthiest man suing a destitute farmer was expensive, troublesome and appeared grasping and mean. However, at least these debtors were under the control of the Lords.

THE LORDS EXTENDED THEIR shipowning interests. They already owned *Spring*, but Edward sold it to his friend John Ingle for his return to England.³⁴ In 1817 the Lords bought the brig *Jupiter*. In 1820 Edward sailed back from England in a new purchase, *Caroline*. The next year the Lords bought a colonial schooner, *Victorine*. Brigs and colonial schooners were similar, two-masted vessels with smallish crews – *Jupiter* averaged ten men.³⁵

Jupiter and *Victorine* were workhorses, transporting whatever cargo the Lords could find – *Jupiter* made seventeen voyages between 1816 and 1823. They took wheat from Pitt Water, Hobart and Port Dalrymple to Sydney, with other local produce such as whale oil, beef, pork, tongues, tallow and potatoes. They also carried passengers and freight. They went to the island's west coast for Huon pine, took equipment to the east coast for settlers, and delivered goods to Lord's partner in Launceston. They went sealing, mainly to Kangaroo Island off South Australia. Edward – but not apparently Maria – liked sea voyages. He went in *Victorine* to Port Davey for Huon pine, and took *Jupiter* on a trip to help his asthma.³⁶

Ships did provide problems. Expense: an invoice for *Jupiter* lists payments for wood, water, clearance, bonds, pilotage and wharfage, and there were also wages, repairs, stores … Crew members drowned, resigned, deserted or were sacked, and crew lists show names constantly changing. Advertisements for steady, sober men imply that drunkenness was a problem (hardly surprising). The Lords' captains tended to remain longer, in this better-paid position.³⁷

Sailing ships were at the mercy of the weather. Winds were unpredictable, and the Lords' ships took between four and 31 days to sail between Sydney and Hobart. On the 31-day trip, *Jupiter* reached the entrance to the Derwent in a fortnight but was forced out to sea by a gale, and did not make Hobart for another sixteen, doubtless frightful, days. Even worse, one winter's evening, taking seventy convicts from Sydney to Hobart, *Jupiter* ran into a heavy thunderstorm: 'the evening very dark, the thunder awful, the lightning excessively vivid, and accompanied with torrents of rain', as the newspaper description ran. Lightning struck the ship, setting a mast on fire and running down the mast to the deck, killing one of the convicts. It jolted the ship badly, making a tremendous cannon-like bang; the convicts panicked, thinking they were being attacked. A second bolt of lighting produced such a violent thump that everyone was thrown flat on the deck, as the lightning fire-ball darted over the bows with another cannon-noise. Everyone feared the ship would sink, but it limped into Twofold Bay for repairs, then returned to Sydney. Shortly afterwards it left again for Hobart with eighty convicts, in convoy with a government ship for safety.[38]

Enterprises could be unsuccessful. In 1818 *Jupiter* ran into bad weather at Kangaroo Island and returned with only a small quantity of salt. At other times, ships had to hang round ports for months waiting for cargo. Plans would fall through: in 1818 a Hobart merchant chartered *Jupiter* to take wheat to Sydney, but then it was announced *Jupiter* would go to the Gordon River for pine, and in fact it sailed to Port Dalrymple.[39]

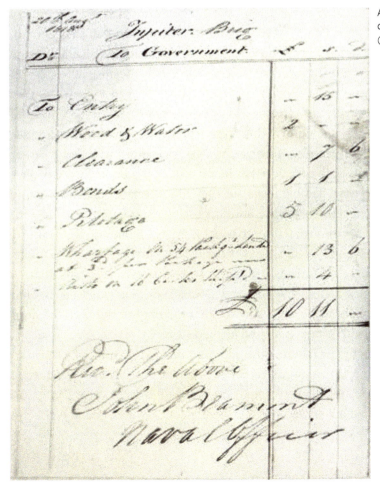

An account for *Jupiter*'s owner, 1818
(*State Library of Victoria*)

There were fewer problems with *Caroline*, which was an aristocrat of a ship, pretty, fast and comfortable, with two state cabins complete with water-closets – top-of-the-range transport. The Lords kept this 'remarkable fine fast sailing ship' for the Hobart–Sydney run. Once it left Sydney on a Wednesday and arrived in Hobart on Sunday, a record four-day trip.[40] This was excellent for special livestock, such as 'a most famous horse' and merino rams, and special passengers: on his 1821 visit to Hobart, Governor Macquarie was so impressed with the four-day trip that he chartered *Caroline* for his return. This voyage was not quite so fast, for *Caroline* had to shelter from adverse winds in Oyster Bay until a strong southerly gale provided a quick but boisterous passage to Sydney, thirteen days in all. But *Caroline* was expensive, and could not gain enough work on the Sydney–Hobart run. In 1821 it left on a whaling and sealing voyage in the South Shetlands, off South America, its water closets wasted on a whaling captain and his mate.[41]

EDWARD LORD had even more expansive ideas, wanting to establish exports for Van Diemen's Land. In 1818 he chartered the ship *Frederick* to take 61 cattle to Mauritius, where they were in demand. One day Knopwood accompanied Edward and Maria to Kangaroo Point (Bellerive), where they had a picnic in the bush and inspected cattle being loaded on the ship. A fortnight later Edward sailed on *Frederick* to Storm Bay to take on grass for the cattle.[42] Not enough, as it turned out.

The ship finally got away on 18 March, after first trying to leave without a port clearance, and taking three stowaways – underhand activities dogged Lord's enterprises. However, 14 May saw him back, bad weather having slowed the ship so much that he ran out of fodder in King George's Sound. Though Lord had big ideas, he sometimes lacked organising ability in carrying them out: delays are always possible, and surely a competent person would carry enough fodder to cope? Lord lost money on this venture, but others had even more disastrous experiences. His friend William Collins took another ship to Mauritius, sailing via Torres Strait to avoid the Roaring Forties. The stock died in the heat and Collins' ship was wrecked. He and five other survivors made their way to Timor, living on the hides of dead cows, but his health was so impaired he died there.[43]

Never daunted by failure, Edward Lord pressed on. In 1819 he sailed to England. His ship took a cargo of colonial produce, possibly his. He returned to Hobart in 1820 in his new ship, *Caroline*, with a large cargo. As usual, the first items he advertised for sale were alcohol: wines, brandy, gin and

Scrimshaw on whalebone: whaling in the South Pacific Ocean (W.L. Crowther Library, TAHO)

rum. There were also sugar and tea, broadcloths and cambric, cheese and brown stout: not as complex a list as in 1814. Maria had advised him to bring clothing for convicts instead of European goods, with which the market was glutted; perhaps this is one of the rare examples of Edward taking Maria's advice.[44]

Edward was always looking for opportunities, and while in England sold 300 cattle in Van Diemen's Land to an immigrant, promising to take all the butter he made for three years. Lord was considered to have made a 'very great bargain'. It is not clear whether this operation eventuated, but he would not have lost money whatever happened.[45]

In 1822 Lord planned another voyage, exporting colonial produce. He left in May with large amounts of wheat for Cape Town and wool for England. As usual, he did not originate this idea – others had tried to export wool – but took it up on a large scale. He advertised to buy wool, and Maria noted in June 1822 that the resources of Mr Lord's estate were momentarily exhausted in preparing for this voyage.[46] But if it were successful, it could make their fortune.

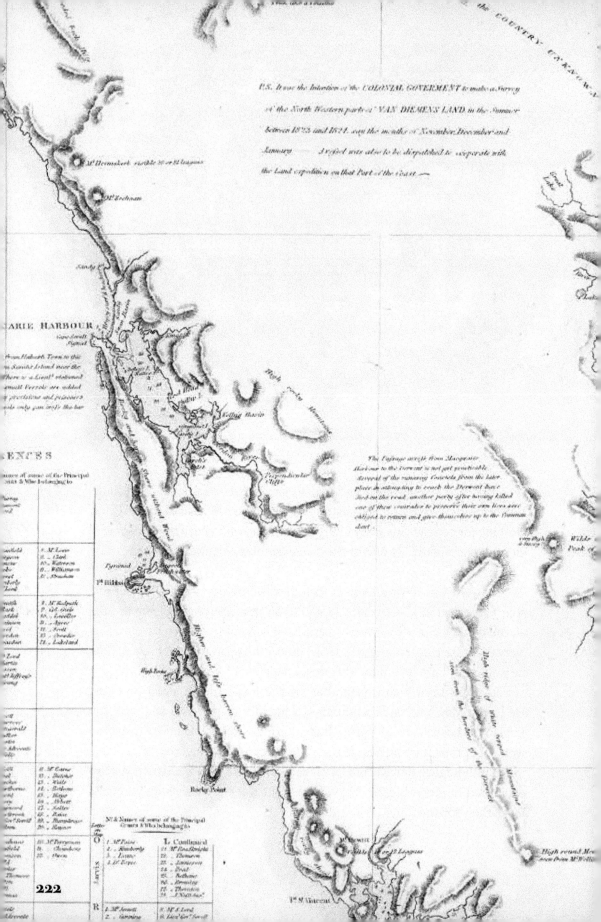

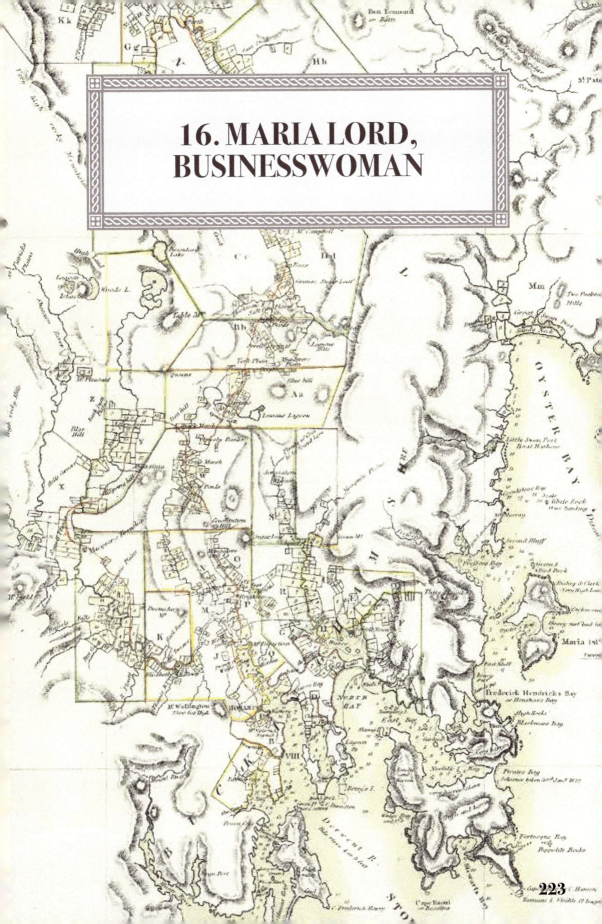

16. MARIA LORD, BUSINESSWOMAN

WITH ONE VOYAGE OR ANOTHER, Edward Lord was absent for half the seven-year Sorell period. While he was away, and sometimes while he was in Hobart, Maria Lord ran the entire business – most capably. This implies that she was an equal partner with him, knowing enough to take over automatically. Theoretically, however, Edward owned it all. It was a huge enterprise: the 1819 muster listed Maria (as Edward's agent) in charge of 6974 acres, 3400 cattle, 4500 sheep, 41 horses and 75 servants, and this was before the Lords owned Lawrenny. John Pascoe Fawkner saw Maria as the brains of the Lord partnership, while Edward wasted the profits. Or, as an admirer of Edward wrote, while he was 'universally beloved in the Colony', his wife was 'a cruel unfeeling woman' – calling in debts, driving hard bargains.[1] From opposite points of view, both comments show that Maria made the money and Edward enjoyed the more pleasant side of business.

So powerful did Maria become that Commissary Hull described her as 'the person possessing the greatest local influence in the Colony'.[2] No one seemed surprised that this person was a woman. People seemed to accept it: she was Mrs Lord, not to be trifled with, and they dealt with her just as they would have with a man. It says much for her strong personality that this occurred at a time when women were expected to stay at home, at most assisting their husbands in a subordinate role. Instead, Maria was firm, tough and decisive. Though a woman in a man's world, she was completely in her element.

Maria's business personality is seen in two letterbooks, containing instructions she sent to clients, customers, agents and colleagues. Major themes run through them. Frugality and economy are to be observed. Agents are to find the best markets, sell at the highest price. People are to obey, at once ('You will of course use every possible dispatch'; 'you will of course dispose of this Article to the best advantage'). No excuses are

BIRTH.—Laſt Saturday, Mrs. E. LORD was ſafely delivered of a fine Boy.

Maria Lord did not let unavoidable family activity hamper her business activities
(*Hobart Town Gazette*, 19 July 1817)

Previous pages: Map of Van Diemen's Land in 1824, by Thomas Scott, showing the extent of the farms with which Maria Lord dealt
(Tasmanian Archive and Heritage Office)

allowed. But at the same time, the words 'fair' and 'just' recur: 'wishing every equitable and fair arrangement', 'a just consideration'.[3]

Edward Lord was away for the initial fifteen months of the first letterbook (which covered August 1819 to February 1821) and Maria was in charge of everything. Her 53 letters show her as extremely competent, every detail at her fingertips. She sometimes mentioned Edward, but she was in charge: it was 'my ship', 'my sheep', 'my servant'. She wrote to eighteen recipients, mainly about selling goods in Hobart, Sydney or Port Dalrymple, buying goods, or renting out properties in Hobart. Five recipients were told to pay debts or provide information, and one farmer was directed to return sheep. This letter is a good example of Maria Lord's no-nonsense style:

> February 6th 1820.
>
> Sir,
>
> My Servant having reported to me that you have detained two of my Sheep under the plea that Two of your's have on some occasion joined mine; I have to express my extreme surprise at the proceeding, and especially that my Stock should be detained without reference to myself.
>
> If at any time Sheep of yours may have joined any Flock of mine they would doubtless be taken away again, or remain to be taken away; nothing of the kind, however, was ever reported to me; and I cannot for a moment suffer my Sheep to be detained on such a representation, or without that notice the Case required.
>
> The bearer has my Instruction to deliver this to you and to demand the Sheep detained, or any other bearing my Mark, which may have strayed or got amongst yours.
>
> ML [initials only, in the office copy][4]

The letter was actually written by a clerk, and possibly the wording was his, expressing his employer's wishes. However, since all letters Maria Lord signed have a similar forceful style, though written in different hands, at least the basic wording must have been hers. Two letters seem to be in her own handwriting, which indicates she could write, though more awkwardly than the clerks.[5] The direct, commanding style is just the same.

Business was business, and people received no special treatment because of their rank. The ex-convict wrote forcefully to the governor after horses she lent were returned late, in poor condition, with the stallion's tail docked. Will the king's representative pay her compensation, or must she go over his head to his superior in Sydney?

> Mrs Lord has ascertained that the entire Horse is at hand, reduced to the lowest state of condition; that the unwarrantable liberty of docking him has been taken by, or under the direction of M[r] O'Brien, to whom if the Deputy Commissary entrusted the re-delivery of the Horses no right of use could be transferred or was ever sanctioned by Mrs Lord; that her Servant, who was at Port Dalrymple a Month ago desired to be allowed to bring the Horse home with him, which was refused; and Mrs Lord respectfully has to add, that the unauthorized detention of the Horse & Mare, besides their reduced and present useless state, has put her to great loss in hiring carting which they would have performed.
>
> Under all the Circumstances Mrs Lord respectfully solicits His Honor may be pleased before she takes over possession of the Horse to direct that she shall be informed whether any compensation for the loss and damage on the case will proceed from the local Government; or that she must claim on the Deputy Commissary General.[6]

The outcome is not known, though surely she gained her compensation.

Many letters were to the Lords' agents. A competent merchant like Maria Lord could seldom find agents of her own ability, though it cannot have been easy for them: she was a hard taskmaster, never praising, only criticising. The Lords' agent at Port Dalrymple was told to collect cargoes and sell goods, but proved a poor businessman, not answering letters ('Do not fail to write by return' – but he did fail), not sending money ('remittances entirely failing this year'), not telling Maria when his stock of spirits was low.[7] Just as exasperating were the Sydney agents, Jones & Riley, the town's leading merchants. Governor Macquarie was unimpressed with 'this sordid Rapacious House'; so was Maria Lord. She employed them to sell goods she sent to Sydney, and send to Hobart goods she ordered, but they too did not obey orders: they overcharged, omitted to acknowledge receipt of goods or return empty casks; they set up accounts the wrong way. 'I calculate upon a liberal consideration of these points as essential to our good understanding and continued dealings', she informed them.[8]

The River Tamar, with ships travelling to do business in Launceston
(Allport Library and Museum of Fine Arts, TAHO)

The really vital imports were 'India goods' – sugar, tobacco, tea and rum – and the Lords had an agent in Calcutta, William Walker. Maria Lord dealt amicably with him, ordering goods and exchanging commercial news. However, in 1820 he joined Jones & Riley in Sydney, and Maria's letters became curt. Ships arriving in Hobart were offering her better goods at lower prices, and unless Jones, Riley & Walker lifted their game and stopped sending inferior goods such as sugar that even stock-keepers refused ... A change of agents seemed likely.[9]

In 1820 John Duncan arrived in Hobart, sent from England by Edward. Once Maria had cut his demands down to size ('The Salary part of the emolument much exceeds what the nature of the situation would for some time warrant me in agreeing to – and I cannot bind myself to an engagement for so long a period as that you stipulate') she employed him to carry out her business in Sydney. She sent him there in *Jupiter* with strict instructions: sell the cargo, pay off the crew, refit the vessel, fix up the accounts with Jones, Riley & Walker, obtain relevant documents, and bring back those empty casks! She did not have enough casks in Hobart to salt more meat.[10] Her exasperation at these inadequate agents comes through strong and clear.

Maria had other problems. Letters went astray. Markets were uncertain. A ship might glut the market with a certain item. Competitors undercut her: Maria was contemptuous of a local dealer who was content with small profits. Ships were delayed by weather: the cargo of fresh meat for Sydney might go off. Then there was cash. With no bank in Van Diemen's Land, the only sterling currency was what people happened to have. It was not enough. To provide more, merchants issued promissory notes. In 1824 during a trial a publican's wife stated that she gave as change for a ten-dollar note 'two of Mrs. Lord's 4-dollar notes' – Maria's business was part of the fabric of Hobart.[11] She mentioned several times that she was short of cash. 'Extensive as [Mr Lord's] property here is, the unconvertible shape of the great bulk, together with the uncertainty of Markets for produce, and the little Money on the Island, frequently leaves us with little more Cash than local demands require'; 'I am extremely pushed for Money, as of course I must be for a long period, and I am expecting a Ship from England very shortly which will put me under a heavy pressure'; Mr Lord's ship was expected daily and 'her arrival will greatly increase my immediate demands for cash' – perhaps to pay the crew and port charges.[12]

Hobart in 1819 by George Evans: the centre of Maria Lord's activity. The Lords' house is the pink building almost exactly centre, with ten windows facing Argyle Street and a blank wall facing north-west
(State Library of New South Wales)

Promissory notes were a poor replacement for actual cash
(Hobart Town Gazette, 22 January 1820)

MRS. LORD requests all Persons holding Promissory Notes, signed by herself or EDWARD LORD, Esq. will present them for Payment at her Office at the Veranda House; and, in Consequence of the recent Detection of a Forgery, as well as of Mrs. Lord's having some time discontinued issuing or re-issuing Cash Notes, she will feel obliged by any Inhabitant holding Notes as above described not to negociate them, but to send them in for immediate Payment.

FOR FREIGHT AND PASSAGE.—The Brig JUPITER will positively sail for Port Jackson in the Course of 14 Days from this Date.—For Freight or Passage apply to Mrs. LORD, Macquarie-street.

Mrs Lord organises a trip for Jupiter
(Hobart Town Gazette, 12 August 1820)

Mrs Lord asks debtors to pay up
(Hobart Town Gazette, 9 September 1820)

MRS. LORD acquaints the numerous Settlers indebted to EDWARD LORD, Esq. to whom Indulgences on their old Accounts, Notes of Hand, and other Obligations, have been long extended, that she is desirous to afford them every Facility in discharging their Embarrassments which Circumstances Place in her Power, as Agent to Mr. LORD; and that she will receive during the next three Months good storeable BEEF and MUTTON to the extent in Quantity of 150,000 Weight, at Six-pence per lb. in Liquidation of their Debts.

Mrs. LORD reminds Cultivators, and those who are under Engagements to deliver Wheat this Season, especially those to whom in the early Part of it she had engaged to allow Store Price, that 10s. per Bushel being given no Excuse will be admitted for any Breach of Engagement this Year; and generally, Mr. Lord feels it a Duty belonging to her Agency to state that if the present Opportunities be not embraced by the old Debtors to Mr. Lord's Estate, she will not allow the expected Circuit of the Supreme Court to pass without resorting to that and the Lieutenant Governor's Court, as the Case may require, to compel Payment of their several Obligations.

Macquarie-street, Sept. 9, 1820.

Hobart Town
August 28th 1819

Sir!

The Brigg Jupiter has this day cleared out for Port Dalrymple and Sydney and will sail tomorrow wheather permitting, She conveys to you the Goods as per enclosed invoice, amongst which are 15 Casks of Lime, charged at 5/ per bushel — at which rate the labour and freight are little more than covered; you will of course dispose of this Article to the best advantage for the concern; should the casks not be returned an allowance of £3 per Ton must be made, as well as upon all other empty casks. The Pannel'd Doors and Window Frames are also on board; and these having been got up at considerable trouble as well as advance of ready money for Materials and Labor, will be expected to be paid for on delivery, or at all events settled for by a note of hand bearing Interest.

You will find one bag of Shot more than is invoiced to you, which you will deliver to Mr Brumby.

As the taking wheat in payment for goods is so much more disadvantageous than Cash, inasmuch as it cannot be reckoned to produce more than 5/ per bushel upon an average after Expences are paid) it will be necessary to calculate your prices in sales to cover this heavy discount.

This letter was probably written by Maria Lord herself. The writing is not as flowing as the clerk's, and there are some spelling mistakes, but the author definitely knew her own mind
(State Library of New South Wales)

Even worse was the incompetence of Maria's husband and nominal superior. 'Mr Lord having omitted to send an account of his sales or disposal of the Goods which accompanied him to Sydney', can you tell me if you sold the skins and tallow, or did he take them with him? she asked her Sydney agents. Can you give me a copy of the account he paid, and the account current? Other examples of Edward's incompetence abound. How much money had been received from the Luttrells, 'Mr Lord having mentioned £300, but Mr Luttrell stated a larger Sum'? Lest Mr Lord omitted to forward an invoice, she sent a duplicate; if Mr Lord forgot to order sugar, could she do so? An account itemising contents of a box did not agree with Mr Lord's list, 'which I attribute to M^r L–'s having perhaps taken home [to England] some part' – without telling her.[13] So Edward was not businesslike, he did not keep her informed, was slack, forgetful: all extremely exasperating, making it difficult for his wife to run the business properly.

While Edward was in Britain, Maria sent a letter to his brother Eyre in London about business concerns, seeming to take it for granted that he was more businesslike than Edward – but also telling him that she could not liquidate a mortgage at only 5 per cent interest. If he offered 7 per cent, she could liquidate it at once.[14] Family received no special consideration. There are no letters from Maria to Edward, so her tone in writing to him is unknown.

By way of general news, in various letters Maria mentioned that she was building a new store, which would be run under a proper system (unlike the system set up by Edward?); entering into a bond to deliver cattle to enable someone to leave the colony, a kind action; and helping settlers. When the price of wheat was low in Sydney she told those with the largest debts that they could send their wheat there at their own expense and pay her back; now the price was improved, and in all fairness 'I cannot but give them the advantage'.[15]

In November 1820 Edward Lord returned to Hobart, and took over in the office. His writing style was far more obscure than Maria's, and it is easy to see who had the superior business brain. But they remained a united couple running the business, as a letter of 1821 showed. Robert Ogilvie wanted to know the origin of the false and malicious report 'that so enrages your lady and you against me. Mrs Lord told me in your presence that I was infamous and made away with all my late uncle's property and then ran away'.[16] It would usually be the man doing the scolding, while the woman watched – but not when Maria Lord was involved.

THE SECOND LETTERBOOK started in December 1821. Though it was only eleven months later, much had changed. Edward had appointed two new agents, both 'gentlemen' ex-convicts. Neither proved much use to the firm, but perhaps Edward felt happier employing men with this background. Thomas Wells used his position as Governor Sorell's clerk to profit through corruption. Extravagant and haughty, he hardly sounds Maria's soulmate, but Edward made him joint agent in Hobart.

As a secondary agent, Edward appointed Robert Lathrop Murray. Rumoured to be an illegitimate son of George III, Murray joined the army, married three times trigamously, went bankrupt, and in 1814 visited Napoleon in Elba, with intrigue suggested. In England he was charged with bigamy. Transported to Sydney, he gained his freedom suspiciously quickly, and in Hobart his old schoolfriend Governor Sorell gave him an enormous land grant. He dabbled in many activities and married yet again, but was best known for virulent journalism.[17]

Clerk to the agents was Charles Robinson, a meek man, probably an assigned convict, who did as he was told. He wrote to Mrs Lord telling her he had received her instructions, 'to all of which I shall pay strict obedience and attention', and wished her a speedy recovery, the only hint of illness throughout Maria Lord's long life.[18]

There were also new agents in Launceston and Sydney. In 1820 Edward Lord brought Thomas Simpson to Van Diemen's Land. Simpson married Maria's sister Catherine – perhaps from love, perhaps as a link to the wealthy Lords. Edward established Simpson as his partner in Launceston. It was not a partnership of equals, with a letter from Edward instructing Simpson to obey him and observe all instructions.[19] In Sydney, Lord engaged engineer, manufacturer and grazier John Dickson Esquire as his agent.

When the letterbook opened in December 1821, Edward was in Hobart, busy gathering produce to take to England, raising money by selling his

Maria Lord's signature: not the easy writing of someone schooled in childhood
(State Library of New South Wales)

New South Wales property. Maria Lord and Thomas Wells signed all letters, but since they had just the same tone as before – you will do as you are told – and 'my' was used often about property ('my farm of Orielton Park'), it seems that Maria was still in charge. The need for cash was dominant. Maria mentioned pressing claims, presumably Edward's voyage expenses. Debtors must pay at once; sometimes Maria threatened legal action. Clearly Peter Harrisson's claim was correct, with many farmers so deeply indebted, it was almost impossible for them to clear their debts. One debtor was in deep trouble, having already caused the Lords 'disappointment' when his wheat did not appear, even after he had the vessel delayed for it. He was to fulfill his debt immediately, and would receive no further indulgence (time to pay). Even a friend of Edward's, Thomas Lascelles, was told firmly that he had promised to deliver 500 bushels of wheat by 30 April and must do so.[20]

As before, the firm bought goods – haggling over prices, successfully – and Maria sent captains of the Lords' ships decisive orders: organise return freight without delay, immediately tender to the commissariat for conveying stores to Hobart, advertise at once for freight and passengers. 'You will of course incur no expense at Sydney that can be avoided having been amply supplied here.' Maria was more polite to their socially superior agent in Sydney, John Dickson Esquire, though he too was told to spend no unnecessary money.[21]

Simpson in Launceston did not receive the polite treatment. Brother-in-law or not, Maria thought poorly of him. She instructed the supercargo to be strict: 'Under the present circumstances no inconvenient delicacy can be expected'. She told Simpson that he was responsible for articles he selected; he should not have shipped that wheat, and must bear any loss; he must include bills of lading. Simpson must have objected, as a conciliatory letter followed. The House did not think it had written in a dictatorial manner. Why was Simpson taking umbrage? Later letters were more polite, though still firm.[22]

Maria also ignored 'inconvenient delicacy' in dealing with her brother John, who arrived in the colony in 1819. He worked for the Lords, running a butcher's business, among other activities:

> Sir
>
> I have sent repeatedly to the Butchers Shop for the Books & Accts of that concern but all my endeavours to obtain inspection

of them have failed of success. I am therefore under the necessity of demanding that you will on Monday morning next the 22^d inst order the said Books & Accounts to be sent to the Office here in order that they may be examined by M^r. Lords agents, and as the Cash Keeper of his Concerns I cannot admit of further delay,

 I am Sir

Your most obed^t Servant

(Signed) Maria Lord[23]

Staff received even firmer letters: 'if Goods be stolen in consequence of the inattention of those whom I employ to take charge of them I must hold such persons liable for the value. I request therefore you my keep my property as securely as possible'.[24]

Once Edward had gone, Maria got rid of both new agents in Hobart. In mid-1822 she had a falling-out with Wells after he took money from the office. Debtors were told that no receipts were valid without Maria Lord's signature, and she told the clerk to give money to no one but her. Wells went, and was soon bankrupt.[25] Murray also had his contract terminated:

> I request you may deliver over to me with as little delay as possible all my documents and papers of whatever description, and I beg you may at the same time furnish me with an abstract of your account in order that it may be settled, and all matters between us brought to a close,
>
> I am Sir
>
> Your most obedient Servant
>
> (Signed) Maria Lord

Murray must have answered that she had the papers and made impertinent comments, for she replied: 'I beg to remind you that you have in your hands M^r. Thorntons papers and M^r. Merediths papers. The whole of those I now wish to look into & request you may sent them by the bearer'. The rest of his letter 'I have neither inclination nor time to notice'.[26] That put Murray in his place – but turned him into Maria's enemy and Edward's champion.

> at Port Dalrymple, will be held at the New School House, Launcefton, on Monday, the 5th of August, at 11 o'Cock in the Forenoon. R. DAY, Affiftant Secretary.
>
> NOTICE.—All Perſons indebted to the Eſtate of Edward Lord, Eſq. are defired to take Notice, that no Receipts given for Payments made to that Eſtate are valid, without the Signature of the underfigned. MARIA LORD.
>
> NOTICE.—Edward Lord, Esq. having executed General Powers of Attorney to Mrs. Maria Lord and Mr. Thomas Wells, of Hobart Town, to act Jointly in all Matters relating to his Estate; which Powers, bearing Date 21st March 1822, have been duly verified and acted upon; all Perfons concerned in Van Diemen's Land, New South Wales, or elſewhere, will govern themſelves accordingly.—Macquarie-street, July 27, 1822.
>
> MR. R. L. MURRAY, in repeating his Notice of Departure for Sydney, by the Castle Forbes or fome other early Opportunity, requests that fuch Perfons as have fignified their Intention of placing Agencies in his

Maria Lord and Thomas Wells both assert their position in the press. Maria won
(Hobart Town Gazette, 27 July 1822)

MARIA'S POWER IS SEEN in her dealings with Commissary George Hull, who arrived in 1819 when Edward was away. She continued the family policy of hospitality: three days after the Hulls landed, Knopwood dined with them at Maria Lord's. Perhaps Edward's bonhomie was necessary for such hospitality to work, however, for she and Hull had several fallings-out, Hull resenting her extensive influence.[27]

One of the commissary's tasks was to call for tenders to provide meat. Hull made several changes. First he asked settlers to sign bonds against their failure to provide the meat. Then in January 1820 a large quantity of meat slaughtered at Orielton was putrid on arrival in Hobart. Hull ordered that animals be brought alive to the store for slaughter. In August he called for tenders, and Maria Lord replied that she would not sign bonds, which had not been necessary before. After this session of tendering, she would look for a better price for her meat, since it cost time and money to drive 'Cattle comparatively Wild' to Hobart. The Lords owned or controlled between a third and a half of the colony's storeable meat, wrote Hull. He believed Maria was trying to create a monopoly. She continued to refuse to sign bonds, and in the end Hull had to accept her tender, so she won that round. He bought huge amounts from her, about a third of his total purchases, since she controlled so much meat and was able to fill his quotas if other settlers failed.[28]

Maria Lord was just as active in the wheat market. In 1820 Hull reported that he feared 'a sort of competition' by Mrs. Lord, 'now for the first time shewn with an apparent view to create a Monopoly, where it was once the least expected'. Where it was once least expected: Edward Lord

A later photograph of Hobart shows the Lords' Verandah Stores, on the corner of Collins and Elizabeth streets: centre far right beside the tree, with thin posts holding up the verandah roof. The building is a much older style than the others (Charles A. Woolley collection)

was away, and perhaps this was Maria's idea. She controlled most of the wheat in Van Diemen's Land, Hull found, and the 'competition' involved refusing to sell to him. To defeat her, he advertised that he would accept anyone's wheat, whether they tendered or not. 'A strong probability exists in another year, the principal part of the Settlers being much at the Mercy of Mrs. Lord and one or two others, the Stores will be at the Mercy of them if any considerable demand should be made from Sydney', he added. Despite this worry, in an emergency the authorities had to turn to the Lords for wheat. In January 1821 Macquarie urgently wanted more, so Sorell agreed with them to provide an enormous amount.[29]

Maria Lord and Hull had an up-and-down relationship, each wary of the other but having to co-operate, she to sell her goods, he to buy enough for the colony. Maria Lord sold him other goods besides meat and wheat. Once when Hull needed rum, he found that two merchants, Mrs Lord and Kemp & Co., had cornered the market. Their prices were the same, and he chose to deal with Mrs Lord – why, he did not state.[30]

AMONG THE TOWNSFOLK, MARIA LORD was best known for her shop, 'the best shop in Hobart Town'.[31] She traded in everything she could: imported goods; local produce; real estate; freight or passenger tickets on ships. She provided the government with furniture, greatcoats for constables, and articles for the church, courts, boat crews and a funeral. She leased buildings, organised freight and (never one to let slip an opportunity) when Commissioner Bigge visited, leased him her house, the best in Hobart.

By January 1819 the Lords had opened a new shop on the corner of Collins and Elizabeth streets, calling it Verandah Stores. It was part of a large establishment, Verandah House, which included the New Inn and rooms for rent – Hobart's first lawyer set himself up there, perhaps at reduced rent to put him under an obligation. Maria (but not apparently Edward) had an office there: in 1820 she advertised for those holding the Lords' promissory notes to present them to her office for payment.[32]

All shops charged high prices, as all visitors to Hobart noted: 'every thing is *dear* beyond all calculation'. No one complained about Maria Lord in particular; she would have been far too canny to price herself out of the market. She supplied Knopwood with goods ranging from foodstuffs such as sugar, mutton and coffee to paint, clothing and a white feather, but mostly rum, three gallons every couple of weeks. She also paid bills for him and fixed up other transactions: 'Mrs Lord Please let Mrs Clissoll have to the amount of two Pounds on my account', ran one note.[33]

As in the earlier period, a stream of notes to Maria Lord indicate her activities. They were polite: Mrs Lord was a person to be addressed courteously.

> Hobart town 8th Feby 1821
>
> Please to give the bearer four yards of Ribbon on account of
> Mr Loane
>
> M Dhotman
>
> To Mrs Lord

Madame Dhotman, Loane's mistress, was one of Maria's friends. Strange that she did not specify a colour for the ribbon – but perhaps the bearer was to choose it.

Customers' level of literacy and spelling varied, from:

> Pleasant Banks Port Dalrymple
> May 30th 1821
>
> Mrs Lord
>
> Be so good as let Mr Evans have Thirty Pounds of Butter out of the Cask I have now sent over
>
> James Brumby
>
> Witness David Gibson

to:

> Mrs Lord Pleas to Lett the Bearer My Sun have Six Pounds of Sugar and Six of Salt and half a Pound of Tobbaco and Place The Sum to My Account
>
> William Cockerell

As before, most orders involved alcohol:

> Mrs Lord
>
> I Shall take it as a Particular favour if you will oblige me with half a gallon of Wine and send me word what the Price is
>
> Your obt Servt
>
> Wm Rayner Junr
>
> 29th Sepr 1820

Some notes did not involve purchases. David Rose apologised for leaving his small debt so long unpaid, but it was not his fault – how often must Maria Lord have heard that excuse. Then there were agreements:

> July 29th 1820
>
> Mem[oran]dum
>
> I agree to give Six shillings & nine pence per Bushel for 400 Bushels of Barley to be deliver at my House.
>
> Maria Lord
>
> I agree to sell Mrs Maria Lord 400 Bushels of Barley at six shillings & nine pence pr Bushel to deliver it at her House on her Orders.
>
> Richard Troy[34]

Though it seems to be mainly Edward who made loans, Maria did make some herself, possibly when he was away. Again, she was treated politely. John Pascoe Fawkner replied humbly to her request to pay up:

Launceston, October 11, 1820

Honored Madam

I herewith send send [sic] you the Receipts I have Had of Mr Baker [Maria Lord's agent] for Monies Paid to him on your Acct And I have further Sold a Bullock for 25£ which Is To Be Paid Next week to Mr Baker and I shall Continue to Pay into his hands what money or Wheat I can Collect I therefore hope you will not Compel me sell anything which may ultimately Ruin Me as I am striving the utmost in My Power to Pay you. [there follow more details of his efforts to pay up]

I Remain Honored Madam with the Greatest Submission your Most O[bedient], H[umble], Servant

John Fawkner Junior[35]

Maria also showed her efficiency in running the shop. An advertisement informed customers at 'her meat stores' of new, competent-sounding regulations about delivery and payment, with a discount for cash. In a convict colony theft was so frequent that shopkeepers felt obliged to sleep on their counters to deter robbers, but only one robbery was reported from the Lords' store, when thieves entered the upper storey by a ladder placed on an empty cask and stole goods worth £400.[36]

SINCE IT WAS SUCH A LARGE OPERATION, the House of Lord was seen as the leading business of Van Diemen's Land, and Edward the richest man in the island. How much was due to him and how much to Maria? The growth between the 1819 muster and the early 1820s was huge – and Maria must take much of the credit, for Edward was often absent. But they were both necessary: he providing the initial money and land grants, building the connections, having the big ideas; she with her excellent business brain. In 1822 the Lords' business looked flourishing and, with Edward's huge export of wool and wheat being gathered, about to expand even more.

Much of this success was due to Edward Lord's corrupt activities, as shown in his dealings with successive commissaries. But there is no evidence that Maria was involved. Instead, in her letters she emphasised her desire for fairness, and later boasted of her integrity. No writer of the period suggested she was corrupt. Could it be that the convict thief turned out honest, while the gentleman was the crook?

Edward Lord's family saw superior social status as obviating any need for honesty. His brother John was also corrupt, proved guilty of electoral fraud. Maria Lord probably came from the respectable working class, which was more likely to be honest, either by conviction or to distinguish themselves from the shifty lower working class. She had one slip, in her early twenties, but possibly after that she went straight. To distance herself from her convict origin, to show her integrity so that she could maintain her credit? Surely as Edward's partner this intelligent woman knew what was going on, but she seems to have kept out of it herself.

What does the evidence say about the characters of Edward and Maria Lord? Edward had abundant, affable charm. A range of people liked him, from Governor Sorell to upright Congregational minister John West, who travelled with him from England in 1838. Lord's gentlemanly deportment made the voyage pleasant, wrote West – no small feat, in a cramped sailing vessel for three months or more.[37] Lord undoubtedly preferred to use his charm, hospitality and offers of help. However, if people like Broughton stood in his way, he was ruthless, with a dark side that was vindictive and selfish.

Maria was a tough businesswoman, efficient and organised. Unlike Edward, she started out with nothing but her own personal skills, though these did include the strength and self-confidence which can come from a stable home background. A strong, brave woman, a survivor, she became skilled in making the best of a situation. A descendant of her brother John Riseley said Maria was known in the family as 'very good with figures, very good at business, and as mean as they come, like all the Riseleys'.[38] This seems fair comment.

THE OTHER FEMALE CONVICT to become an outstandingly successful businesswoman in early Australia was Mary Reibey. She and Maria had similar backgrounds: born in rural England, to respectable families, though Mary was orphaned early. Both committed one crime only. Mary ran away dressed as a boy, and as 'James Burrows' was caught trying to sell a stolen horse and transported for seven years. She arrived in Sydney in 1792 and married Thomas Reibey, a naval officer who became a successful trader. Mary gave birth to seven children and

Mary Reibey in her respectable old age
(State Library of New South Wales)

was closely involved with Thomas in the business, managing it when he was away. So far Maria and Mary's stories are remarkably parallel.

Their stories diverged owing to the men they married. Thomas Reibey was steady, did not become involved in politics and was not known to be dishonest. He died in 1811 and Mary ran their business successfully, extending it considerably – in 1816 she was said to be worth £20,000. Very respectable, she was a favourite of the Macquaries, though her respectable appearance was marred when she was found guilty of assault on a debtor, reminiscent of Maria's strong character. In the 1820s Mary lived on her investments and busied herself with charitable activity. Once Maria was free of Edward, she lived in much the same way.

Both women tried to minimise their convict pasts. In the 1828 census, Mary Reibey claimed that she arrived free in 1821 – as she did, though she had not been free on her first arrival. But as with Maria, people knew. In 1838 Lady Franklin, the governor's wife, reported that Thomas Reibey was one of the island's largest landed proprietors, but 'his mother is said to have been transported to Sydney for horse stealing, and to be now living there in affluence, driving a phaeton with two white ponys about the streets'. Lady Franklin was horrified to find that Governor Arthur's nephew had married Mary Reibey's granddaughter. The girl was very pretty, quiet and modest, with a rich father, but 'I cannot conceive how the Arthur family can have been satisfied with the match'.[39] Mary and Maria had both risen to prominence, so they and their stories were well known. They could never leave their disgraceful convict past behind.

17. LIFE OUTSIDE BUSINESS

Though business obviously took up much of the Lords' time, both enjoyed other activities. Even for hard-working Maria Lord there were 'parties of pleasure' upriver to the Lords' property at Glenorchy, while in the 1820s stories were told of her enjoying walks in the bush, which she surely did not start in her fifties.[1] All this activity took place on or around Lord properties, however: Maria was probably combining pleasure with business.

Edward needed no excuse to enjoy everything life offered. He relished being Van Diemen's Land's foremost citizen, and led society wherever possible. In 1820 the church of St David's was opened. Pew numbers had nothing to do with religious devotion and everything to do with social status: the Lords scored pew no. 1, second only to the governor. Then Governor Macquarie visited again. At a public meeting to prepare an address of congratulation, Edward Lord ensured his version was accepted. A deputation of gentlemen presented the address to His Excellency, and Edward Lord Esquire delivered the address: '... sincere and respectful congratulations ... most grateful Thanks ... beneficent and distinguished administration of Your Excellency ...'. How Macquarie must have inwardly writhed, at the detested Edward Lord mouthing such sentiments. As before, his diary mentioned only those he could praise, and Lord was omitted.[2]

Then news arrived that Sorell was to be superseded as governor. Another public meeting led by Lord resulted in an address to Sorell, again given by Lord. A group of gentlemen decided to form an agricultural society: Edward Lord, clearly the instigator, was elected president. Lord supported charities such as the Auxiliary Bible Society, and his office accepted subscriptions for a Catholic church, an unusually tolerant attitude for an Anglican gentleman. Meetings to establish the Bank of Van Diemen's Land were held at the central Lord house, though Edward himself was away

Left: Surveyor Thomas Scott's sketch of a waterfall on the upper Derwent River. Maria Lord enjoyed exploring these areas
(State Library of New South Wales)

Previous pages: A landmark on the long trek to Port Dalrymple: Handsome Sugar Loaf at York Plains, drawn by surveyor Thomas Scott in 1821
(State Library of New South Wales)

St David's church, where the Lord family had pew no. 1
(Allport Library and Museum of Fine Arts, TAHO)

and this was probably at Maria's invitation. He (or perhaps Maria in his name) bought shares in the bank.³

This was all most respectable, even statesmanlike, but Edward Lord's private life was not so commendable. In 1819 he was sued for assault. Roland Loane, a merchant with the usual shady past (his claim to have been a naval officer was false) was a difficult man, quick to feel injured. He became embroiled in several court cases, one against Lord's friend Gunning concerning cattle. Loane was bound over for £1200 to keep the peace. Lord came to his house (complained Loane) and called him a rascal and a scoundrel. Loane told Lord he deserved horse-whipping, on which, said Loane:

> he turned round and made use of the most Scandalous and disgraceful language, which induced me to shove him out of my house, and shut the door against him; he was no sooner out side than he turned round and committed a most violent assault and battery by breaking my Windows with a large Bludgeon that he brought with him, at the same time making use of the most vulgar expressions

Loane was convinced Lord was trying to goad him into breaking the peace and forfeiting his bond. He won the court case,⁴ but another merchant had a different version ('his' can mean 'is'):

> that Bad fellow R. W. Loan his sentenced by a Bench of Magastrates to be tride at the Supreme Court for Robbing Gunning of his Cattle wile he [Gunning] was in Jail and R.W. Loan his going to enter an action against that [gentleman], E Lord, for taken a Challenge from Mʳ Archer and because he would not receive it he turnd too and broke all his windows with his stick⁵

245

Whatever happened? Who was receiving a challenge – to a duel? Some skullduggery was going on, and Lord did break those windows. But he was safe from trouble. A month later Loane asked Lord's friend Knopwood, a magistrate, to issue a warrant against Lord. Knopwood refused, and Governor Sorell backed him. The judge too asked Knopwood to sign the warrant but he again refused, giving as a reason Lord being 'so unwell that he could not speak' (asthma presumably): Lord's network saving him from possible trouble.[6]

During this period he was often away. As already mentioned, in June 1819 he sailed to Britain, taking his stepdaughter Caroline, aged fourteen. They suffered 'one of the most unpleasant Voyages I ever experienced', owing to the blackguard of a captain; 'but I hope we shall yet make him suffer', wrote Lord vindictively. More hopefully, he continued, 'I expect much good to accrue from my presence here': loans, land grants, a word to those in power.[7]

Family tradition says Edward put Caroline in a 'finishing school', a seminary for young ladies, to learn as many English manners as possible in the next few months. She visited her humble Riseley relations, and perhaps saw the other, dazzling end of society: her Owen in-laws, cutting a dash in London society in the best tradition of regency novels. Lady Owen was even patroness of an institution which rivalled the famous Almack's assembly rooms. Each year she appeared at court, in 1816 wearing a satin petticoat richly trimmed with gold fringe; 'curiously wrought' draperies of French gauze with superb gold bullion cords and tassels; a 'body' of gold tissue and white satin, and a satin train looped up in the most novel and elegant style – a magnificent (and expensive) spectacle. Every season the Owens gave wonderful entertainments, such as a masked fete – rooms brilliantly lit, select company, Lady Owen looking 'fascinating in the extreme', dancing, supper, more dancing. A composite beautiful woman invented by a newspaper included the Duchess of York's foot and Lady Owen's shoulders.[8] Edward's 1820 visit included the London social season, and he could have attended a wonderful fancy ball in London with his brother and sister-in-law, and the concerts Lady Owen hosted, with up to five hundred 'visitors of the first distinction' at each.[9] Doubtless Edward Lord, with his love of conviviality, enjoyed such occasions to the full.

The beautiful Lady Owen
(Roy Precious)

He had plenty of other activities. He showed his diplomatic skills in a letter to government, asking that convicts be sent direct to Van Diemen's Land from England instead of via Sydney – not for Hobart's benefit (Lord's undoubted real aim, but one which would not interest London) but for monetary savings to 'the mother Country' (a dubious claim). The government replied that this was already decided. Edward organised his brother Sir John to ask for a government position for him in the colonies (unsuccessfully);[10] requested his salary as governor from way back in 1810 (apparently unsuccessfully); applied to become the Hobart agent of Lloyd's insurance company (successfully); and tried to protect himself from his enemy, Governor Macquarie. He sent Lord Bathurst a long memorandum:

> My Lord
>
> Having embarked a very extensive Capital in Van Dieman's Land in the confident Reliance of receiving Protection & Encouragement, & having been injured to an almost incalculable Amount by the harsh & unjust Proceedings of the Governor General Macquarrie, I am very reluctantly compelled to trouble your Lordship with a Statement of some of the Injuries I have received, & to solicit that Redress from your Lordship's Justice I cannot otherwise obtain, in Opposition to the arbitrary Will of the Governor.

Macquarie had not allowed him to sell his cargo in Hobart in 1813, or his wheat in Sydney; revoked martial law against bushrangers in 1814; defended Broughton; and imposed unjust duties which Lord had to pay or face being sent to work in the coal mines in chains (a gross exaggeration).[11]

Bathurst did not answer, and a fortnight later Sir John Owen pressed him: 'As a sincere and steady friend to present minister I wish to obtain redress only through the medium of the government'. A threat? Bathurst replied next day – firmly. He needed more information, and in some points Lord was inaccurate. This would have stopped most people, but not Sir John Owen, who asked Bathurst to give Edward a 3000-acre land grant and an appointment as a magistrate (presumably Edward's aim all along). Bathurst refused, merely recommending Sorell to give Lord every consideration he deserved. Sorell, Lord's friend, translated this into the grant and the magistracy owing, he said, to Lord's unexceptionable conduct towards the colony's government.[12] The Broughton and Jeffreys affairs notwithstanding

– but doubtless colonial governors often found it expedient to have short memories.

Meanwhile, Edward bought a ship he called *Caroline* after his stepdaughter, and a large cargo. Taking a group of Maria's relations at her request, he left Plymouth in August 1820 and arrived in Hobart in November. He was very pleased, writing to his friend Piper in his usual breathless style:

> We arrived here in the Ship Caroline on Monday week after a Passage of three months and Sixteen Days from Plymouth and as we were very deep [low in the water from cargo?] it might be considered a very expeditious one we were compleatly full with very respectable Settlers for this Island[13]

Not all were so respectable. Among them was William Williamson, a young lawyer who had defrauded his sister Agnes and his aunt of all their money. He had a very pleasant journey, he wrote to Agnes, rather tactlessly. 'For three days we had a rough gale when the sea ran mountains high but being in a most excellent little ship we suffered no inconvenience whatever. I was only sick about half an hour and suffered no inconvenience further than just throwing up.' The ship's livestock provided fresh meat all the way – an unusual treat for passengers, but Edward Lord liked his creature comforts. Williamson was particularly struck by Caroline Lord, describing her as a very beautiful young lady. (Sir John Owen's scheming is shown in a letter he wrote to the Colonial Office vouching for Williamson the embezzler, describing him as a very respectable man, with capital exceeding £8000. Williamson himself admitted he had not £15.[14] Sir John was either naïve or dishonest, and he does not sound like a naïve man.)

IN HOBART, SOCIAL LIFE WAS DULL. Since Governor Sorell lived in adultery, respectable ladies could not attend functions at government house, and no big parties or balls were held. Dinners were the main social activity. Knopwood's diary shows Edward Lord often out to dinner, while the Lords asked many people to dinner themselves. Knopwood never mentioned that Maria left her own house, except to visit him occasionally; but despite this restricted social life she remained cheerful. 'The People here go on much as usual, the Town improving fast and the Settlement likely to be of consequence', she commented in 1820.[15]

She had one great success, when Governor and Mrs Macquarie visited Hobart in 1821. They believed that ex-convicts should be treated like other free people, and encouraged deserving emancipists. Maria Lord, successful businesswoman and well-behaved wife and mother, was just the sort of convict-made-good they appreciated. A Hobart woman reported that 'wile Governor McWharie and his lady were here paying there last visit Mrs Lord was Mrs McWharies most intimate friend'.[16] Perhaps gossip magnified the closeness, but intelligent, tolerant Elizabeth Macquarie could well have liked Maria's similar intelligence. Social success at last!

However, the Macquaries returned to Sydney, and the Hobart elite did not share their views. Although respectable ex-convicts were accepted as community members, the elite never accepted them socially. This did not matter much when this elite was numerically negligible and people like Governor Davey fraternised with anyone, convict or not, but from 1820 new immigrants increased the elite's number and influence. Three of them described the Lord family. All were hostile to Maria. William Williamson was a traditional ne'er-do-well immigrant, but ranged himself with the respectable gentry. People in the colony were the biggest rogues and scoundrels in the world, he wrote, 'a set of vultures preying upon each other with the greatest rapacity', though fortunately his own crime remained unknown. Falling under Edward Lord's spell, he described him as 'universally beloved in the Colony', but continued (omitting names, though his meaning is clear):

> his Wife has the worst name of all – she is very ugly and I cannot conceive what could induce such a man as Mr [Lord] to marry her. She was a convict girl – a common prostitute I have heard in Sydney, taken in to keeping by Mr [Lord] & afterwards married her. By all accounts she is a cruel unfeeling woman.

Another young man made this comment about Maria: 'she can't read, and <u>can</u> put herself into most <u>original</u> passions and curse and swear'.[17]

What are we to make of these accusations? Maria was in her early forties, had borne eight children, and had spent the last fifteen years

Above: Elizabeth Macquarie, who made an 'intimate friend' of Maria Lord
(Tasmanian Archive and Heritage Office)

immersed in the worries of business. No doubt her looks had lost their earlier freshness, especially to a critical youth. She could read and write, though her writing did not have the elegance of one taught at school, and the other accusations might have been exaggeration. A hot temper: this is the only mention, so she usually kept it under control. Cursing and swearing: it could have been mild. Ladies were not meant to swear, and even 'damn' would have raised Jane Austen's eyebrows. 'Cruel' and 'unfeeling' sound like debt-collecting, though advertisements show that Maria did this more tactfully than Edward. Did antagonism grow because a woman was so successful in the man's world of business, not the domestic angel men desired?

'Her sister Mrs .... is just as bad', continued Williamson. 'She pretends to set up for a fine Lady but neither her manners or her language are ladylike – vulgar in the extreme can neither read nor write I wonder what could induce anyone to marry her.'[18]

It sounds as if Catherine did not, or could not, capitalise on marrying an officer by picking up the behaviour of the gentry. Williamson was naïve in wondering why anyone married her, however: the sister-in-law of Edward Lord, the colony's richest man, was a good match whatever her manners.

Janet Ranken and her husband had grand relations, but Janet knew why they were in the colony: 'We are all come here to make money and money we will have by hook or by crook'. However, she intended to maintain her standards, as she told her sister:

> The society here is abominable. Mr Lord a man worth half a million money is married to a convict woman. The Leut Governor Mr Sorell is married but he left his own wife in England and brought another mans wife with him in her stead. Mrs Lord sent her daughter Miss Lord and her sister Mrs Simpson to call upon me when I came here but I have never returned the call yet nor shall I.

So the first thing both newcomers, Williamson and Ranken, were told about Maria Lord was that she had been a convict. She could never escape it. The Macquaries might have had the poor taste to socialise with her, but Janet Ranken did not intend to: 'I have been advised to visit [Mrs Lord] but they say "evil communication corrupts good manners" so I shall rather be without the kindnesses that Mrs Lord has in her power to show me than visit her'.[19] Those kindnesses presumably being hospitality, perhaps a loan, help with accommodation – assistance usually valued by a newcomer.

Poor Maria Lord! She had committed theft two decades earlier, but she had served nearly all her sentence, surely enough punishment. Since Edward had chosen her she had run his house and his business, and borne his children. She had not broken the law, committed any scandals or made any discernable mistakes – in fact, she could have been one of the few people in Van Diemen's Land to go straight. However, her convict past and her relatively humble background condemned her to be deemed unacceptable by pert young pieces like Janet Ranken and blackguards only one step ahead of the law like William Williamson.

Why did she even try to establish contact with Janet Ranken? It was probably the Lords' customary way of getting people onside: welcome, offer hospitality, show 'kindnesses'. The many dinners they held indicate that this tactic was often successful. It seems unlikely that Maria was actually trying to make friends with Janet. She was so tied up in business that she did not have much time for friendships, though she was close to a few people. Knopwood often dined with both Lords, or just Maria when Edward was away (though there is no suggestion they had an affair). Maria helped him when he was ill, held celebratory dinners on his birthday, and invited him to family occasions such as a daughter's birthday. In his diary he usually listed guests at dinners; several women dined with Maria, though none of particularly high social standing.[20]

A few glimpses of Maria fraternising within the merchant group show a warm and self-confident person. In 1838 she gave evidence in court when Thomas Birch's will was challenged. She had known Birch since he arrived in the colony in 1807 as a clerk, she said; he was in her employ and was a keen, shrewd man. After he set up his own business she became a family friend. In 1821 Birch was taken ill and Maria often came to the house, supporting Thomas' wife and

A thoroughly respectable citizen: Maria Lord is foremost among those donating to the Wesleyan Sunday School
(Hobart Town Gazette, 12 October 1822)

THE Treasurer of the Wesleyan Sunday and other Schools thankfully acknowledges the Receipt of the following Benefactions, in addition to those already advertised.

	£	s.	D.
Reverend R. Knopwood, M. A.	. 1	1	0
Dr. Westbrook	. 1	0	0
His Honor Lieut. Governor Sorell	1	1	0
Mr. Secretary Robinson	. 1	0	0
Mrs. M. Lord	. 1	0	0
W. A. Bethune, Esq.	. 1	0	0
Mr. John L. Roberts	. 1	0	0
Mr. Knox	. 0	10	0
Mrs. S. Birch	. 1	0	0
Mr. E. Hodgson	. 0	10	0
A. W. H. Humphrey, Esq. J. P.	1	1	0
A. F. Kemp, Esq.	. 1	0	0
Mr. R. Barker	. 1	0	0
Mr. J. Fawkner	. 1	0	0
Mr. J. Williamson	. 0	10	0
T. Wells, Esq.	. 1	0	0
Mrs. Wells and Miss Wells	, 1	12	6
Captain Hunter	. 1	0	0
G. W. Evans, Esq.	. 1	5	0
George Frederick Read, Esq. J. P.	1	0	0
Dr. Margetts	. 1	0	0
Dr. Bromley			
Mr. John Lakeland			
Captain Pickersgill, Bengal Army	5	0	0

The outskirts of Hobart, showing the road to Port Dalrymple, a settler's homestead, and Mount Wellington, a welcome sight for weary travellers (Allport Library and Museum of Fine Arts, TAHO)

visiting Thomas in his sickroom, discussing business matters and joking with him to try to raise his spirits. Maria Lord and two businessmen were chosen to witness his will, 'witnesses, in every respect disinterested and of unimpeachable veracity', claimed the lawyer.[21] Birch's letters to William Broughton show contempt for Edward Lord, but he kept up his friendship with Maria.

Maria had at least two close women friends. Though Roland Loane was difficult, his mistress Margaret Dhotman, a 'woman of colour' he brought from Calcutta, was widely liked for her kindness. Maria was intimate with her from her first arrival in 1809, she testified – no colour prejudice here. Then there was Jane Jeffreys, wife of the underhand Charles Jeffreys. In 1820 the family returned to Van Diemen's Land. Knopwood's diary shows Maria and Jane often together, calling on him, dining at Maria's.[22]

Another friend was Richard Dry, to whom Maria sent warm personal letters, unusual in her letterbooks. He too was an ex-convict, a farmer and businessman in Launceston. Maria wrote to him that she would be coming to Launceston on business for a fortnight; could he engage lodgings for her and her daughter Caroline? She would be happy to take his daughters to Launceston and back to Hobart if he wished (presumably they were at school in Hobart). 'At this moment I am much engaged at home, but in about a fortnight I hope I shall be able to undertake the journey.'[23]

There was a great deal to keep her engaged at home. Not only was she running a complex business, but a large house and family. This meant employing female convicts, many of whom were unwilling servants, so instructing them and keeping their noses to the grindstone was an uphill battle. The reader is torn between sympathy for these forced domestic skivvies and for the mistress, obliged to cope with them neglecting their work, answering back, getting drunk and so on. Few convicts stayed long in one household, and the mistress's overseeing work was onerous. Records were scanty at first, but from 1817 they show a stream of servants coming and going at the Lords', committing typical offences and gaining typical punishments. In 1819 Maria charged Mary Ryan, a middle-aged Irishwoman, with neglect of duty (punishment: a week's solitary on bread and water), refusing to work (a fortnight's solitary) then stealing four rings. Rings were valuable, and Mary was sent to the dreaded penal settlement at Newcastle for further punishment.[24]

On 22 June 1820 Elizabeth Lovett, a newly arrived 24-year-old convict, was assigned to Mrs Lord. On 27 June she was punished with fourteen days' solitary for absconding repeatedly – fast work, in only five days. She had barely returned from her punishment before on 15 July she absconded again: a month in solitary.[25] Other servants of the Lords were punished for being drunk, insolent, disobedient and in one case, after she left the Lords, receiving a piece of Irish linen stolen from Edward Lord – by a former colleague? Petty enough offences, but a mistress would always be wondering when the next would occur. Some convicts were more obedient. Ann Wilson, a London mantua-maker, was drunk, disorderly, insolent and absent without leave with other employers, but committed no offences while she was with the Lords.[26] The Lords also employed male convicts, and they too were accused of offences: drunkenness, being absent, theft.[27]

As well as running the house, Maria had her children to care for, with the physical burden of pregnancies and breastfeeding (one imagines her, holding a baby at the breast with one arm, with the other reaching for the day's letters, while dictating replies to the clerk). In 1815 the Lords had five children: Caroline (born 1805); Eliza (1808), John (1810), Edward Robert (1812) and Corbetta (1815). Maria bore two more: William Henry in 1817, called after Edward's older brother; and Emma, another Owen family name, in 1819. Pregnancies did not seem to bother Maria, and she made the long, uncomfortable trip on horseback or by jolty carriage from Hobart to Port Dalrymple when she was four months' pregnant. A hint that her life could be adventurous was her pistol, a tiny six-cylinder silver and black weapon, small enough to fit into the palm of her hand.[28] Did she ever have to use it, against bushrangers, thieves or even difficult debtors?

The children did not necessarily mean Maria was busy, for their father sent them to England. John had left in 1816, aged six, and the others followed. Despite Macquarie thinking poorly of Captain Jeffreys' seamanship, and all the carousing and smuggling on board, Edward Lord entrusted Eliza and Edward Robert, aged nine and five, to Jeffreys' care on his return to England in 1817. Among the passengers were Maria's friend Jane Jeffreys, who presumably looked after the children, and Thomas Hassall, a young trainee clergyman, who also helped them. Five years later Corbetta and William, aged six and four, accompanied their father to England. What Maria felt at having her children whisked away from her is not recorded. The only hint that she missed them came in a comment in Knopwood's diary, when he dined with her on 29 May 1829: 'Corbetty's birthday'.[29] Maria remembered.

The trip to Port Dalrymple took several days, and parties often had to camp on the way. This is surveyor Scott's camp near Spring Hill in 1823 (State Library of New South Wales)

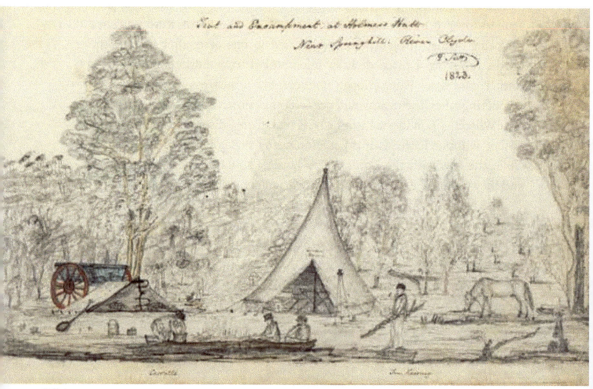

Corbetta was turning fourteen, and her mother had not seen her since she was six. However, although she must have missed her children, she could well have approved of their going to Britain to be turned into ladies and gentlemen, a destiny impossible for Maria herself and difficult to achieve in Hobart, with its dearth of the genuine article. The children were cared for by Edward's large family, and the initial plan was for them to come back to Hobart.

In 1821 Eliza wrote to Thomas Hassall. The thirteen-year-old girl thanked him for his kindness to her and her brother on the voyage four years earlier, and hoped 'the good instructions you used so frequently to give us, will never be forgotten'. Dear Papa had visited last winter, she continued, and Eliza would return to Van Diemen's Land with him: 'what joy shall I have in again seeing my dearest relations from whom I have been so long separated!' Meanwhile, she was spending the Easter holidays with dear Grandmamma, Edward's mother (his father had died in 1801).

Edward, now nine, would be delighted if Mr Hassall would visit him, wrote Eliza: he and John were at Mr Wallace's Academy, at Cheshunt in Hertfordshire, where Mr Wallace advertised that 'Young Gentlemen are thoroughly grounded in the Classics, and prepared for the Public Schools'.[30] Hertfordshire, just north of London, is a long way from Pembroke, but perhaps Edward had chosen it as reasonably near relations in London.

Eliza sympathised with Hassall on the death of his father: 'no doubt Sir, you know how to bear with pious resignation so great a trial, for it is what we must all endure sometime'. Someone was bringing her up well. 'I have many Relations here who are very kind to me', she continued (thank goodness, one feels), and

> when I return to my beloved Papa and Mamma I hope to prove, that during my absence I have not been unmindful of the parental advice they so lavishly bestowed upon me, when I left them, and that I have learned to be [hole in page, probably 'as they'] so much wished, a good and useful member of Society, as I hope to make it the study of my life, to promote their comfort and happiness, as a trifling return for what they daily do for me.

This is worthy indeed from a thirteen-year-old, but perhaps a teacher was looking over Eliza's shoulder. She concluded by wishing Hassall 'prosperous gales', and hoped that when they next met, he would find 'your "old Scholar and Shipmate" has not passed her time at School in vain'.[31]

HOBART TOWN.

Sitting Magistrate.—Rev. R. Knopwood, M.A.

SHIP NEWS.—On Monday last arrived from England, the ship *Caroline*, Captain Taylor, with a valuable cargo of merchandize.—This vessel left Plymouth the 11th August, and touched at no port on her passage.—Passengers, Edward Lord, Esq. of this Settlement, the owner, Miss Caroline Lord, Mr. and Mrs. Simpson, Mr. and Mrs. Margett, Mr. Talbot, Mr. Williamson, Mr. Cartwright, Mr. Eldridge, Mrs. Risely, Miss Stagg, Miss Saunderson, and Master and Miss Piper.

Caroline arrives in Hobart: major news
(*Hobart Town Gazette*, 2 December 1820)

Maria and Edward sent funds annually to meet the children's expenses, and in 1820 Maria sent an accompanying letter, thanking Edward's brother Eyre for 'your constant goodness in attention to my dear Children'. Could he tell her 'in what manner they landed as to equipment, Clothes &c; a very large Sum having been expended to fit them for the voyage, in provisions and for their appearing before Mr Lord's friends' – not everyone would be so frank, admitting the necessity for bumpkin colonials to make a good impression. Maria also asked for Eyre's help in 'getting out' to the colony her brother John's wife, her sister Catherine, and her daughter Caroline, who had gone to England with Edward.[32] Was Edward not reliable enough to ensure Caroline's return?

At either Edward or Eyre's instigation, quite a family group returned in *Caroline* with Edward in 1820: not only Caroline, but two of her aunts and two cousins. John and Catherine Riseley were twins, born in 1796, eighteen

Sheep at Orielton: a large part of the Lords' fortune (Rebecca Aisbett)

years younger than Maria, and only five or so when she left Catworth. Maria had already seen Catherine when Edward Lord brought her to New South Wales in 1813. She married Lieutenant James Taylor of the 73rd regiment, and in 1814 they went to Sri Lanka where Catherine bore two sons. James died in 1817, and Catherine took the boys back to England. As Maria requested, in 1820 Edward brought them to Van Diemen's Land. Catherine enjoyed a romance on board with fellow passenger Thomas Simpson, and they married the day the ship crossed the equator. In Van Diemen's Land, they lived in Launceston.[33]

Maria's youngest brother John had already joined her. By the time she was in a position to offer help to her family, the oldest of her brothers and sisters were no doubt settled, with no wish to emigrate across the world. But John, still in his early twenties, married with a baby, decided to go to Van Diemen's Land where these rich relations could assist him. He applied to the government for a land grant, stating that he possessed some property and had been brought up to farming. It was unlikely that he did have much property, but doubtless the Lords advised him on what to say. John reached Hobart in 1819. A brother-in-law experienced in farming was useful, and Edward made him manager of Orielton. In November Governor Sorell, Parson Knopwood and other gentlemen attended the

A scene at Orielton (Rebecca Aisbett)

muster in the district. 'Mr. Riseley of Orielton Park, belonging to E. Lord Esq.' (note the difference in status) dined with the governor, Knopwood noted, and everyone rode to visit Orielton, 'a very fine place'. At one muster a neighbour, George Gunning, sent Maria Lord an urgent letter: he had just heard that the governor and his suite would have breakfast with him the next day. Could she send some lump sugar, a dozen large breakfast cups and saucers, two dozen glasses, a cream jug, two basins, a little coffee, two gallons of brandy and two bottles of wine?[34] It was alcohol at every meal in Van Diemen's Land in 1819.

In 1820 Edward brought out John's wife Sophia. John was prospering, with his own farm, Kimbolton Park, beside Lawrenny (Kimbolton was a village near Catworth). Edward made John joint manager with him of Lawrenny, John managing both properties when Edward was away. When the Agricultural Society held its one and only show, John Riseley won its medal for sheep, for ten fine-woolled ewes he had bred. He sold large quantities of meat, signed an address to the governor, gave to charities, employed convicts and started to build a large stone house – well on the way to making his fortune.[35]

In 1822 John's parents dictated a letter to him – they appear to have been illiterate. They had just received John's letter of December 1821 and were pleased all was well, but why didn't more people write? Sophia's father had received a short letter from Caroline Lord with news that John and Sophia had a baby, but Sophia herself had not written, and a clergyman was 'in a Deale of Trouble' through not having received a letter Edward Lord had promised – another hint that Edward, though generous in offering help, did not always deliver on his agreements.[36] The family does not sound very

Port Dalrymple on the 21st ult. with merchandize from Port Jackson.—Passengers, Dr. Cameron, and Mr. Thomas Collicot.

Sailed on Wednesday last for England, via the Cape of Good Hope, the ship Royal George, Capt. Powditch; having on board a cargo of colonial produce, amongst which are 40,000lbs. weight of wool of Van Diemen's Land, and 6 thousand bushels of wheat, the latter being for the Cape.—Passengers, Edward Lord, Esq. and two children, Dr. Doak, R. N. late Surgeon Superintendant of the ship Lord Hungerford, Gregory Blaxland, Esq. Mrs. Drennan, Miss Walsh, Mr. G. R. Ross, Mr. Henry Heylin, Mr. James Canton, Mr. Edward Clark and wife.

Sailed on Sunday week for Sydney, the brig

In 1822 Edward Lord leaves Maria, again, taking two of their children
(*Hobart Town Gazette*, 4 May 1822)

close, and from Maria's terse letter to John in 1821, and Catherine being in Launceston, it does not sound as if the siblings were any closer in Van Diemen's Land. Of all Maria's family, her daughter Caroline appeared most important to her.

And what of her relationship with her husband? This can only be inferred from occasional details. There must have been great initial attraction for Edward Lord to select her in 1805 and marry her, a convict, in 1808 – and to her, he must have appeared a knight in shining armour, her escape from the humiliation of a convict's life, though Fawkner did use that uncomfortable word 'slave' to describe her. They seemed to settle down happily enough, conceiving their numerous children, and there is no suggestion that either had outside affairs. Until 1819 Knopwood's diary often mentioned them together: 'I breakfasted with Mr. & Mrs. Lord', 'in the eve Mr. & Mrs. Lord drank tea with me'.[37] Their different roles in their business enterprises did not seem to create friction, though since Maria was the woman, the dependant, she probably had to bite her lip at Edward's impulsive gestures, unwise loans and extravagances.

In 1822 Knopwood showed Edward and Maria often apart. In April Edward went to England. Maria's subsequent actions showed that her period of being a devoted, grateful wife to Edward was over, and possibly her attraction for him had also waned. She was ageing, her looks fading, and as Edward became Van Diemen's Land's leading citizen, Maria's past as a lower-class convict could have become an embarrassment. In these circumstances, he would not have been the first or last man to look elsewhere.

Maria's attitude is also understandable. Since 1805 she had not put a foot wrong. She had supported Edward, borne his children, run his business. She coped with his follies and, despite her temper, she was not the one who insulted people publicly and broke their windows. As far as is known, she behaved impeccably: for what reward? Her children were almost all taken from her. Edward was off on another jaunt to the enjoyments of sophisticated Britain, including visiting their children, while she slogged away in the office in obscure Hobart. Newcomers slighted her. Whatever she did, however much she turned herself inside out for them, they were not going to accept her because of her convict past. She was 44, still in the prime of life, even if whippersnappers like William Williamson thought her old and ugly. She could be justified for feeling: is this all life has to offer?

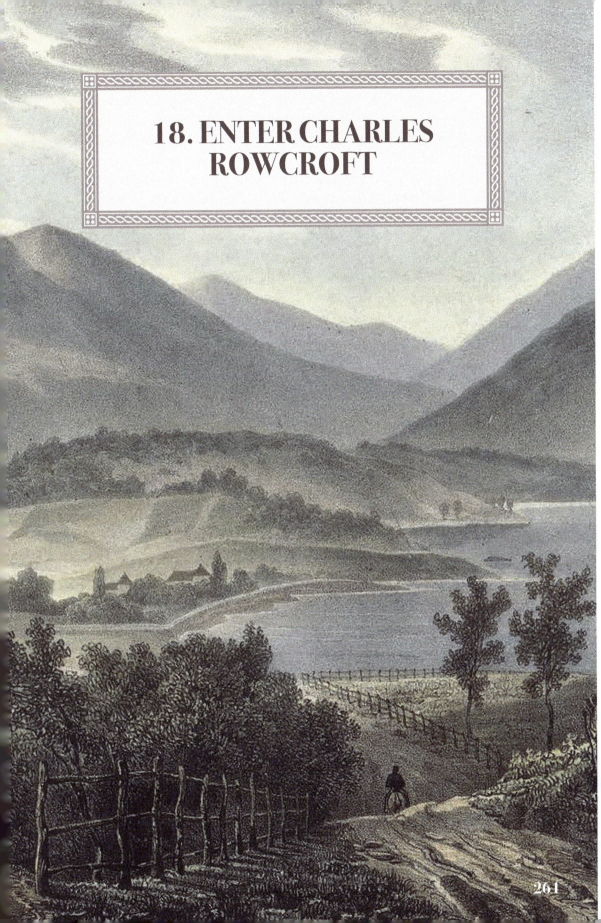

18. ENTER CHARLES ROWCROFT

CHARLES ROWCROFT WAS BORN in London in 1798, son of a wealthy merchant and alderman. He attended Eton, England's most fashionable boys' school, but did not think much of it: 'I was surrounded by bad examples on every side; the getting into debt was the habit of the whole school'.¹ What he did after leaving school at thirteen is unknown – clearly nothing successful – and in February 1821, aged 22, Charles arrived in Hobart with his younger brother Horatio. He was unimpressed. The country looked dry and desolate, Hobart a straggling township of rude huts. 'I felt very queer myself among the convicts'; chain gangs, men in irons working on the roads, made the place look 'not very respectable'.² This concern for respectability was to prove short-lived.

The brothers claimed impressive assets, and Governor Sorell gave them large land grants and made Charles a magistrate. Horatio worked

Previous pages: New Town, a charming residential and farming area (Allport Library and Museum of Fine Arts, TAHO)
Below: The Hobart Town chain gang, which so horrified Charles Rowcroft (Tasmanian Archive and Heritage Office)

on his land, but Charles preferred easier ways of getting ahead.[3] Edward Lord enjoyed extending his patronage to promising young men, and seems to have taken up Rowcroft. So thought Maria's brother John Riseley, who detested Rowcroft and induced Robert Lathrop Murray to write a 'squib' or lampoon about him. A spunger, or sponger, is a contemptible creature who cadges off others:

The Spunger

Who, was it lately that from England came
Bankrupt in reputation, fortune fame!
Seeking to find amongst us Golden Game
　　　　　　　　　　The Spunger ...

Who, when he landed, Conscience, nothing Loath
Swore to three thousand pounds a solemn Oath
When not worth thirty pounds were Brothers both
　　　　　　　　　　The Spunger

Claiming fictitious capital to get a land grant, as immigrants routinely did.

Who (Noble Diddler) looked about the Town
To see where easily the Dust would down
Content if he could raise but half a Crown
　　　　　　　　　　The Spunger

Who, when with L[or]d acquainted full of Bows
With fauning Compliments, and ifs and hows,
Sold his old Carravans for Twenty Cows
　　　　　　　　　　The Spunger

'Old carravans': what they were is not clear, but they were clearly not worth much. Rowcroft made a good bargain, with Edward Lord hoodwinked, to be pitied:

Who, when he thus poor L[or]d had once got round
And to his plenteous Board the Way had found
Modestly asked him for five hundred pounds
　　　　　　　　　　The Spunger[4]

And he might have received a loan; he told his father of 'the kindness I have received from Mr and Mrs Lord'.⁵ He certainly enjoyed their 'plenteous board'. Knopwood first noted him dining with Mrs Lord in March 1822. In the next few months he dined with the Lords several times, and attended the gentlemen's dinners that were the colony's chief social activity. In April it was all bustle as Edward Lord prepared to go to England on *Royal George*, taking his children Corbetta (six) and William (four), and his large cargo of wheat and wool. The ship had to wait for a fair wind, but on 30 April, wrote Knopwood, 'at 12 the ship fird a gun and made sail with a fine breeze for the Cape and England'.⁶ Maria was left with her eldest daughter Caroline and her youngest, Emma, a toddler. She never saw Corbetta or William again.

During the next year Knopwood often dined with Maria, and Charles was mostly there. So were others, such as Caroline, and Mr and Mrs Jeffreys of *Kangaroo* notoriety, returned as settlers; but Charles was the most frequent guest, possibly staying in the house. In June 1822, Maria celebrated Caroline's seventeenth birthday with a dinner for seventeen people, including family friends like Knopwood and Charles, who was a fixture by this stage. More guests came for tea, a ball and a supper, the first ball held in Hobart for many years. Three days later, Maria entertained 22 guests at another big dinner which was followed by tea, dancing and an elegant supper.⁷

The next month, Maria took the unusual step of putting her two-year-old daughter Emma in a boarding school. Her education could hardly have been an issue, but perhaps Maria wanted her out of the way, for she then spent several weeks at Port Dalrymple with Charles.⁸ Murray's squib about Charles shows his methods:

> *Who, the best way his Interest to maintain*
> *Strutted flourished and bowed with might and main*
> *And presented Mrs L[or]d with a Copper Chain*
> *The Spunger*

A copper chain, worth next to nothing. But a gift, apparently received with pleasure, along with all those flourishings, bowings and (perhaps) expressions of everlasting love and devotion. John Riseley accused Charles of trying anything to gain money, 'all other ways of Diddling', selling his old spoons and other trash and cheating John over some cows. And then:

Who, when all other Trade, were found to fail
Became (Reader I see your Cheek grow pale)
Petticoat Pensioner!!! Oh Wretched Tale
The Spunger

Petticoat pensioner: lover, or merely sponging on Maria? No evidence remains, though there was enough in the eventual court case to prove to the judge that Charles Rowcroft became that laughable figure, the young lover of a much older woman. Maria can be described as anything from a mature woman enjoying her attentive 'toyboy', to a wife betraying her husband with a worthless cad.

Why? Maria must have known that this was dangerous, that proud Edward would not condone her adultery. Did she, like Sorell, Lucy Kent, David Collins and all the rest, imagine that no one would notice an affair in remote Van Diemen's Land? Or was the admiration of a man twenty years her junior so intoxicating that nothing else mattered, not Edward, not Emma, not the future – nothing but the delicious present, a delightful young man murmuring sweet nothings in her ear, praising her, flattering her, not to mention the charms of rampant sex. It must have been a powerful feeling to overcome her natural caution, displayed so steadfastly over the previous decades, and hints at the passionate woman subdued by circumstance, forced to be sensible, prudent, tactful. Surely there was an inner voice – and an outer voice of people like her brother John – saying: Charles is only doing this for what he can get from you. He's not sincere, not for a second. If so, Maria ignored it, carried away by the enchanting present.

In his memoirs, young settler George Lloyd gave two vignettes of his friend and neighbour Charles Rowcroft, who was living at Orielton. One night George galloped over to warn Charles about bushrangers. He jumped out of bed and into his clothes, and rode off like a flash of lightning, to quell miscreants with vim and vigour. On another occasion a furious barking of dogs at 2 a.m. announced to George the approach of a horseman at full speed: Charles Rowcroft. 'A friend, a friend', he called. 'Come along, my boy, quick, quick as lightning: get up, mount this horse, and ride for your life…'[9] A dashing, exciting young man, much like Edward Lord in 1805.

A suggestion of the charming scenes Maria enjoyed appears in Knopwood's diary in January 1823. 'In the eve E. Mack [his adopted daughter Betsy] and self went to the river garden; met Mrs. & Miss [Caroline] Lord, Mr. Rowcroft by the church; they went with us into the garden and eat fruit, currents, rasberrys, and apples.'[10] A warm summer evening, an attractive garden, flowers and fruit, perhaps Charles picking her a handful of luscious raspberries ... Edward Lord does not sound as if he cherished Maria much. If he was a dominant male, expecting his wife to carry out his wishes in a subordinate role, as Fawkner suggested, Maria might never have enjoyed much romance. To find at the age of 44 love, tenderness, fulfilling sex or whatever Charles Rowcroft offered must have been wonderful, wonderful enough to make Maria throw caution to the winds and indulge in her affair so openly that people noticed. She could have been far more discreet, but going to Port Dalrymple just with Charles, going to Orielton with him alone: even if it was not a passionate affair, it looked like one.

In about September 1822 someone sent word of the affair to Edward Lord in England. It could have been Robert Lathrop Murray, revenging himself on Maria's dismissing him. However, other friends of Edward's could also have told him. They, the colony's gentlemen, dropped Charles. He attended no more convivial dinners and only served as magistrate when a full bench was necessary.[11] Knopwood still socialised with him, but he never showed much discrimination in choosing his dining companions.

Maria's brother John was furious: at seeing his sister commit adultery, the insult to his patron Edward Lord, or being displaced as his sister's chief protégé?

> *Who, when the Injured Brother's Horsewhip fell*
> *Upon the Coward Back, Struck strong and well*
> *To Law then goes; his infamy to tell*
> *The Spunger*

Nothing is known of the court case, but the whole affair must have given the rest of Hobart plenty to gossip about, in this little society where, according to William Williamson, people spent their time 'every one running down the other'.[12]

Love affair or no love affair, Maria continued to operate the business, which suffered two big losses: *Caroline*'s whaling venture to the South Shetlands failed, and *Victorine* was lost. Maria tried to sell it in Sydney in July 1822 but failed, for the ship left for Hobart with its Lord-employed captain and crew. Neither ship, crew nor cargo was ever heard of again.[13]

Even worse, on 31 October 1822 terrifying news reached Hobart. Three months earlier, on 27 July, a dreadful hurricane had struck Table Bay in

Forbidding Elephant Island in the South Shetlands, where *Caroline* was sent in search of whales
(Allport Library and Museum of Fine Arts, TAHO)

South Africa, and ships there were wrecked. They included *Royal George*, with Maria's husband and two of her children on board. Maria soon heard that no lives had been lost, but the cargo was gone.[14] It was a disaster. Doubtless the cargo was insured, Edward Lord being an agent for Lloyd's, but from Maria's reaction the loss was still extremely heavy. The next *Hobart Town Gazette* carried this advertisement:

> MRS. LORD begs to call the attention of Persons standing indebted to EDWARD LORD, Esq. to the very serious Losses which he has lately sustained in his Shipping Concerns, and more particularly to the recent melancholy one of the Royal George at the Cape of Good Hope:–
>
> Even though, by the kind Dispensation of Providence, the Lives of the Passengers and Crew have been saved, yet the severe Loss which the Estate has met with, will place the Agent in that Situation as to be unable any longer to grant Time to those long outstanding Debts. Mrs. Lord begs therefore, that they will take these Circumstances into Consideration, and step forward with that Promptitude which will render legal Measures unnecessary.

She also put up for sale 'for ready Money only' – no more debts! – livestock and household items, on display at her own home: an elegant silver tea service, a handsome dinner service and sets of china 'of the most fashionable and richest patterns' – Maria's own cherished elegancies. Her landaulet, gig and carriage horses came next. In the stores, 'goods of every description' were going at reduced prices. And the final blow: her own house was for sale, though it did not sell.[15]

In December Thomas Wells, no longer Lord's agent, apparently accused Maria Lord of taking the power of attorney Lord granted him. Maria could cope with that sort of thing. A clerk made a sworn statement about the firm's books which seemed to exonerate her, and she stated that she had never seen the deed of attorney. Four magistrates concluded that no criminal offence had been committed, and that was the end of Wells. It is no surprise to read the magistrates' names: Maria's friends Humphrey, Knopwood, George Read (a fellow merchant) and Charles Rowcroft.[16]

Maria carried on the firm's usual business: organising the remaining ships, selling meat and wheat to the commissary, running the farms and dealing with problems, such as two convicts who forged her orders. The Rev. Samuel Marsden arrived from Sydney to consecrate the church and she lent him her carriage, while she and Caroline gave generous subscriptions

Maria Lord swears she never saw the deed in question, supported by those sterling magistrates, her friends Knopwood, Rowcroft, Humphrey and Read (State Library of New South Wales)

THE Treasurer of the Fund raised for the Erection of a Wesleyan Mission Chapel and Charity School, in Hobart Town, thankfully acknowledges, on Behalf of the Committee, the Receipt of the following Subscriptions, in addition to those before advertised:

	£	s.		£	s.
E. Lord, Esq. J.P.	10	0	Mr. & Mrs. J. Knox	5	0
Mrs. M. Lord	10	0	Mr. R. Bostock	3	0
Capt. Hall of the Christiana	1	0	Mr. G. Reibey, Sydney	2	2
Capt. Forbes of the Minerva	1	0	Mr. J. H. Reibey	2	2
Dr. Westbrook	2	2	Mrs. Reibey	1	1
Mr. R. Barker	2	2	Misses Iane &		

TO be SOLD, a CURRICLE & HORSES, with Harness complete, brass furniture. — Price of the Curricle and Harness, £100 Sterling; and of the Horses, £80 Sterling each. — Both Horses have been driven in single harness. — Enquire of the Groom, at Mrs. Lord's Stables, Macquarie-street.

MR. DUNN will, on Monday next, Open

Above: Maria continued to sell her possessions to raise money. In February 1823 her carriage and horses had to go (*Hobart Town Gazette*, 22 February 1823)

Left: A generous donation from Maria on behalf of herself and Edward, especially when the firm was in such difficulties (*Hobart Town Gazette*, 22 March 1823)

to an organ in the church – most respectable-sounding activities in the midst of what was surely dawn-to-dusk in the office, trying to rescue the business from disaster.[17]

There were some happy occasions. In November 1822 Maria, Charles and the Jeffreys rode to George Gunning's home at New Town 'to see the grass'. A fine crop of asparagus? A new lawn? A pleasant outing, anyway. Next month Knopwood crossed the Derwent in Maria's boat to collect a group of children from Mrs Speed's boarding school for Christmas. He drove to the school in Maria's 'chariot', and back it went to the boat bearing six excited girls including Emma Lord and Knopwood's ward Betsy.[18] Maria did not have time herself to collect Emma from school; doubtless business and dalliance kept her too busy.

Caroline, stepdaughter of wealthy Edward Lord, was a good catch as a bride. After spurning Governor Macquarie's illegitimate nephew, in 1823 aged seventeen she married 25-year-old solicitor and gentleman Frederic Dawes. This was an excellent marriage for the illegitimate daughter of a convict, even if she was not just wealthy but beautiful. The wedding sounds enjoyable. Everyone (including Charles, who was one of the two witnesses) met at church at 8.30 a.m., Betsy was bridesmaid, and the wedding breakfast was held in the Lords' home. There was a second jollification in the evening. For the wedding, Caroline made a brief appearance under her legal name of Riseley, and the announcement in the press was carefully worded: 'Miss Caroline Maria, daughter of Mrs. Lord'. Once Caroline was married, such challenges were in the past: she was safely Mrs Frederic Dawes, a proper lady. Maria celebrated with a week at Orielton with Charles and a Mr Lawrence, perhaps invited for appearance's sake.[19] If so, it was too little, too late.

MEANWHILE, EDWARD LORD'S TRIP was proving difficult. The voyage was appalling: after a long three months to Cape Town and the alarming shipwreck, he finally arrived in England in late 1822. Bad news greeted him. It is accepted in Pembroke historical circles that the Owen/Lord family was not good with money. Sir John Owen inherited an estate worth £10,000 a year, but even this was not enough. Not only was he naturally open-handed, but from 1809 he was a member of parliament, expected to hand out money as bribes to electors and officials.[20] As well, he and his glamorous wife were society leaders in London. This too was extremely expensive, with those balls, concerts, tassels of gold bullion and so on. The Owens spent lavishly. In 1819 Sir John bought an enormous London residence that had belonged to the Duc de Chartres and fitted it out 'in a style of embellishment quite unique' with pink, green and burnished gold the principal colours. There the Owens held a magnificent ball 'upon the most extensive scale': four large drawing rooms for five hundred fashionable personages, dancing in two ballrooms, eating a sumptuous supper.[21] Even £10,000 would not go far with that sort of expenditure. Two ballrooms and four drawing rooms, seldom used: common sense went out the window in the pursuit of glamour and importance.

By 1820 Sir John had pressing debts, but did not stop spending. The Owens gave a huge fancy ball in 1821, a big concert in 1822, and in 1824 another ball for five hundred fashionables.[22] Doubtless John and Edward discussed the financial situation, though with both so unrealistic about money, perhaps they decided to do nothing and hope for the best. Never one to hang back, Edward applied for more land. He had invested every shilling of his fortune in Van Diemen's Land, far more than anyone else, he wrote to his brother for forwarding to the British government; the colony had derived much benefit, but other settlers who had done far less had larger grants (untrue). He deserved more. Bathurst told the new governor in New South Wales, Brisbane, that provided no blame was attached to Lord over Moodie's charge of bribery, Lord could have another grant in proportion to the money he had to develop it – the usual custom.[23] (He gained no grant, perhaps not wishing to push his luck after his attempt to bribe Moodie.)

The British government was considering establishing a council of settlers in New South Wales to advise the governor. Edward Lord told them this would be disastrous, because these people were opposed to Van Diemen's Land. New South Wales's wealth came from British government

Big and bustling: Joseph Lycett's painting of Sydney in 1822. It was quite unrealistic of Edward Lord to claim it was about to be overtaken by Hobart (State Library of New South Wales)

spending, not its own resources, and it needed wheat from Van Diemen's Land to feed its population. In contrast, Van Diemen's Land had risen to prosperity by the actions of its settlers, and was about to outstrip New South Wales. It should have its own council.[24] Lord painted this exaggerated picture to try to increase his influence (he would obviously lead such a council), and it worked, partly due to him: in 1824 Van Diemen's Land was made independent of New South Wales with its own council. This was the one successful aspect of Edward's 1823 visit.

News of Maria's affair probably arrived in early 1823. Edward acted fast. He found an agent, Dr Samuel Hood, who had worked in Hobart as a young army surgeon and become friendly with the Lords. Lord gave him power of attorney, and in March Hood sailed for Hobart, arriving on 8 July 1823.[25] Maria Lord had had fourteen months to enjoy her affair.

Knopwood welcomed Hood but had other worries, for his much-loved daughter Betsy was lying ill in the Lords' home, cared for by Maria. The day after Hood's arrival, Knopwood went to visit Betsy and dined with Maria, Charles and three other men. Was Maria trying to brazen it out, claiming Charles was just a friend like these others? Knopwood continued to visit Betsy, but three days later Dr Scott urged him to move her from Mrs Lord's. Knopwood did, but the move was so sudden he could not find a nurse, and had himself to stay up with Betsy all night.[26] So he did not move Betsy for medical reasons. It sounds as if Scott urged him to take her away from the moral danger of living in Maria Lord's house.

Meanwhile, Hood had to take over business of which he knew nothing: running the properties and calling in Edward's debts (Edward estimated he was owed £70,000). With power of attorney Hood had full control. Maria had no legal claim to anything, despite her major role for eighteen years. However, she was the one who knew how it was run. So, Hood advertised on 10 July, it was necessary that Maria was associated with him in managing the business. They both tried hard to raise money, calling in debts and selling the shop. Several court cases, Lord v. debtors, ended in the debtors having to sell their farms. *Caroline* brought seal-elephant oil from Macquarie Island, and *Jupiter* ferried wheat and wool, then in May 1824 left to trade in Singapore.[27]

Maria Lord and Samuel Hood seem to have worked well enough together. Hood had known her before, had dined at her table; he sounds a pleasant young man, and was perhaps treating her as kindly as he could. On 9 August 1823, when she had given Hood a month's tuition, Maria Lord advertised that she intended retiring from business. A month later she advertised that she was travelling to England. Then events erupted. Two of Edward Lord's closest friends, George Gunning and Thomas Lascelles, tough ex-army officers, came to Hobart (reported Knopwood). Lascelles gave Hood some letters, and Hood, who had been staying with Knopwood, moved to Dr Garrett's. Gunning challenged Hood to a duel but it was amicably settled, and the men had dinner together – Gunning, Lascelles, Hood, Dr Scott (who sounds anti-Maria) and Dr Garrett.[28]

Maria Lord and Samuel Hood announce her retirement from business. It sounds perfectly amicable
(Hobart Town Gazette, 9 August 1823)

What happened? My reading is that Gunning and Lascelles told Hood he was being too kind to Maria Lord, who had been allowed to work with him in the business and was now gadding off to England. She should be shown to be in disgrace – and Hood should not be staying with her friend Knopwood. Hood perhaps protested, saying he was only carrying out Edward Lord's orders; Gunning and Lascelles said nonsense, and Gunning challenged Hood to a duel. Outnumbered by formidable older men, threatened with a possibly fatal ordeal by an experienced army officer, Hood gave in.

In October Hood advertised that the powers granted to Mrs Lord had been withdrawn, and Maria moved to Orielton. In theory she had no more to do with Edward's business, but she did manage Orielton, offering a reward for information about a theft. Earlier she had castigated employees for allowing goods to be stolen; now she was learning about reality. It is unlikely that Charles went to Orielton with Maria, for Gunning and Lascelles would not have accepted this. Perhaps he retired to his own property, Norwood. He was there in October 1824, when he advertised a reward for stolen sheep. He and Maria might never have met again.[29]

Maria advertises her intention to go to England
(*Hobart Town Gazette*, 6 September 1823)

Apart from being separated from Charles, there is another possible reason for Maria's seclusion at Orielton. She was only 44 and fertile, as Charles too proved; a pregnancy was not impossible. A girl named Maria Lord married in Hobart in 1842. She was described as born in the colony in 1822, though there is no record of this, and another source states she was born in England. If she was our Maria's daughter, it seems odd that no one reported such a juicy piece of gossip, but capable Maria might have managed to keep it a secret. The baby could have been born at Orielton in 1823 (the date a minor slip) and given to a respectable family to rear. Maria the younger had at least five children, one named Owen, and many descendants.[30]

In July 1824 Hood advertised again: the estate would not pay Mrs Maria Lord's debts, 'as she is provided with a proper seperate Allowance'. Hood added that debtors must pay up, but had no more success in getting debts paid than the Lords themselves. He also had to cope with recurring theft: someone (my own great-great-great-uncle) stole a bull and an ox from Lord's property at Spring Hill, other men took sheep from Orielton, two tablecloths from the Lords' Hobart inn ...[31]

That September Hood wrote to John Ingle in England, telling him that 'your mortgage on the Lawrenny Estate quite secures your whole claim on M^r. Lord'. Hood knew Lord was not satisfied with his work as agent, but:

> I cant help it – I have done my duty – I have done more than my duty – every farthing has been appropriated to M^r. Lord's benefit – and all my personal influence exerted in his behalf – I have had most difficult cards to play the most formidable opponents to combat – and let those boast who had got the better of me.

It is not clear who those opponents were (Maria Lord? Charles? other merchants? debtors?) but clearly Hood was having a hard time. He continued:

> It is true I have not been able to bring all delinquents [debtors] to book but that is not my fault – how can I compel payment where there is no civil Court – I have acted merely by moral influence. It is true I have not the talents of Wells Murray Risely & Rowcroft but I flatter myself I have common sense equal to the whole four collectively. I expect M^r. Lord hourly he has more to fear from his friends than any body else.
>
> Mrs Lord has retracted all her base assertions and by the advice of R has [turned?] them on me – he perhaps forgot his own deposition at the time.

This is mysterious: what can Maria Lord have asserted against Hood? What deposition did 'R' make, and was he Rowcroft or Riseley? Clearly there were all sorts of shenanigans going on as people jostled to do the best they could for themselves. 'Lord has immense resources in the Colony but all depends on their proper application', concluded Hood. 'No doubt his affairs will flourish when they are again conducted by <u>men of talent</u> [heavily underlined].' Hood went on to tell Ingle more exciting news: he was trying to obtain the lucrative position of treasurer, for the present incumbent had embezzled £5000.[32] Corruption went on and on.

There were two important arrivals in Hobart in 1824. May brought the new governor, upright George Arthur. Competent and decisive, an ardent evangelical Christian, happily married to the mother of his many children, Arthur intended to bring this ramshackle colony into line. So did an enthusiastic new clergyman, determined to implement the church's moral teachings. He got nowhere with Sorell, but was just the man for Arthur. They both found supporters in the wave of respectable migrants who had been pouring in since 1820: 'society is becoming very good', wrote one. It was the start of a new era. Total change was not immediate – there was still plenty of corruption, adultery and so on, and as this immigrant wrote,

Governor George Arthur, not a man to put up with corruption and skullduggery
(Allport Library and Museum of Fine Arts, TAHO)

'The merchants are trying all schemes to cheat the poor emigrant', so that had not changed – but 'it is therefore now the interest of all who would stand well with the Gov. to <u>seem</u> moral', continued the immigrant frankly. As a sign of change the church, previously almost empty, needed more pews.[33]

The second major arrival of 1824 occurred on 22 October. Edward Lord returned.

AFTER HEARING ABOUT MARIA'S ROMANCE with Charles, Edward felt no urgency to return to Hobart. He sent Hood out, but himself stayed in England for over a year, perhaps dreading appearing as that figure of fun, the husband betrayed by a younger man. However, finally he had to go and tidy up the mess.

The bad luck which dogged him on his 1822–24 journey continued to the bitter end. His return voyage took a long six months, including a terrifying storm in which lightning struck the ship's foremast. They had to limp to a port for repairs, which took five weeks. Then, right at the end, when the ship dropped anchor at Hobart, the naval officer boarded to conduct the formalities. He was new, and played by the book. Regulations stated that no communication could be made between the vessel and the shore until the cargo had been entered in the books at the naval office. When the naval officer was about to leave the ship to do this, the captain and Lord asked if they could go ashore with him, as was common practice. He said this was against the rules. Even 'very serious remonstrances' from Lord brought only an offer to ask the governor's permission. This was given, but it all meant a delay of several hours.

Fate had still not done with Edward Lord. He brought ashore a portmanteau containing a change of clothes, and when he landed a customs official insisted on inspecting it. An indignant supporter of Lord's, probably Murray, complained in the press:

this, towards a Gentleman, possessing not only the largest property in the Island, but (as is well known) as high feelings of honor and rectitude, as exist in the bosom of any man, be he whom he may! Towards him was adopted this pitiful (and here hitherto unheard of) measure of searching his portmanteau! tumbling over the linen of such a Gentleman as this, least [sic] rum or tobacco should have been there concealed![34]

It was a portent of the new regime. Under Arthur, officials had to keep to the rules. (It was not long ago that Lord had been strongly suspected of smuggling, but that was in the bad old days and no one was mentioning it publicly now.)

In Hobart, Edward Lord had one aim only: to sue Charles Rowcroft. He spent some time in Hobart, then perhaps visited Orielton.[35] He could have refused haughtily to see Maria, but it seems more likely that he did, if only to come to an agreement about the future. Edward had a hot temper but also a year to cool down. Looking at her character as it emerges from her life, Maria was probably co-operative, trying to make the best of the situation. Perhaps they made a pact: if Maria stayed in Van Diemen's Land and did not interfere in Edward's concerns, he would make her an allowance and would not alienate the children from her or divorce her, the ultimate social disgrace for a woman (but not advisable for a man, either). They seemed to remain on at least civil terms. Edward's absences, and their apparent lack of closeness before he left in 1822, might indicate that their marriage had become mundane, which would help explain Edward's lack of anger against Maria.

In early December Edward was at Lawrenny, where Knopwood and Thomas Lascelles visited him, a pleasant ride except that Lascelles' mare kicked Knopwood so hard in the leg, 'the greatest wonder it was not broke'. At Lawrenny Knopwood was in raptures, despite his aching leg: 'The house

Cattle grazing on Lawrenny's rich river flats (James Alexander)

not very good but the country the finest I have seen in V.D. Land; plains, good land for many miles, and rivers running round his 1400 acres'. In dry Van Diemen's Land, three rivers were a wonderful asset.

The next day, Knopwood and Lord rode to see John Riseley's well-kept neighbouring property. 'The mangle wirsell was more than 7 feet high one yard round – so good I never see the like', commented Knopwood. One might wonder about the usefulness of a such a huge turnip, but Riseley was clearly a keen gardener. They returned to Lawrenny, where Lord had eight gentlemen to dinner.[36] Then it was back to Hobart and the following Monday, 6 December 1824, the serious business started. In Hobart's just-established supreme court, Edward Lord charged Charles Rowcroft with criminal conversation, as adultery was termed. The case was between the two men; officially, Maria was not involved. It excited general interest, reported the newspaper: that is, everyone in Hobart was agog to hear every detail.[37]

Edward Lord was impatient to have the case finished, and there was pressure to conclude it. Lord's servant Drummond, who would have been on hand through the Maria–Charles affair, was in court from nine o'clock on Tuesday morning until 2.30 a.m. on Wednesday. Everyone had something to eat and a few hours' sleep, and it was back again in the morning, when Drummond testified from 9.30 a.m. until 2.30 on Thursday morning, with only an hour off for refreshment, as Knopwood recorded in horror. The hours must have been the same for everyone involved, from the judge down – a colossal workload, up to seventeen hours a day.[38] However, though newspapers often described court cases at length, they were silent now. Edward Lord still had plenty of power. A clerk reported that much 'nauseous detail was produced, and gossip had it that Lord wanted a divorce from 'a wife whom he is now ashamed of', while Murray wrote that Sir John Owen and Lord's other friends had set their hearts on a divorce.[39] This might have been the expected outcome, but gossip proved untrue. Edward did not divorce Maria.

The case engaged the court for an unprecedented fortnight; Hobart cases usually lasted a couple of days at most. The length of the court case is surprising. All sources assumed Rowcroft's guilt, and surely Edward Lord wanted a quick decision, without the vulgar details aired in court. Why did it take so long? Did Rowcroft put up a credible defence? If so, what? Stout denial, the traditional tactic? He was merely a family friend, and it was ridiculous to think of a lady of Maria's position lowering herself to betray

> **HOBART TOWN NEWS.**
>
> By the brig Amity we have received a series of Hobart Town Gazettes up to the 7th inst. inclusive; and also private letters of the 10th. There were no arrivals, as will be seen by our ship news, from England. The signal colours were up on the 9th, but as a high wind prevailed at the time, it is supposed that the vessel which was signalized had either been blown off the coast, or was merely passing the port. There had been twenty-four hours heavy rain, which was something new.
>
> Harvest has already commenced in many places; and excellent barley has been brought to market at 5s. per bushel.—Old wheat, which appears to be pretty plentiful, is selling for 10s. per bushel.
>
> The action for Crim. Con. in which Mr. E. Lord was plaintiff, and Mr. C. Rowcroft defendant, respecting which a general interest has been excited, was decided on the 18th ult. by a verdict for the plaintiff of £100, after engaging the Court of Van Diemen's Land for *fourteen days!*
>
> On Tuesday evening, Dec. 22, the Australian Company's ship Portland, put into port in stress of weather and to water, having lost her fore-yard, and sustained other injury, in a gale of wind off the South Cape, which lasted for 9 days. She had been 18 days from Sydney.
>
> The Aguilar, Capt. Watson, which also put into the River from contrary weather, came up to port on the 22d.

Sydney readers hear about the gripping Lord trial – but only after news of Hobart's harvest (*Australian*, 27 January 1825)

her husband with a young pauper? If so, it did not work. On 18 December, the verdict was given in favour of Edward Lord, with £100 damages. He had said that since Rowcroft was a pauper, he did not require more. Rowcroft's property passed to Lord, perhaps as payment for the £100. On 28 December, Lord held a farewell dinner for eleven people, including Knopwood and his stepdaughter Caroline. Leaving Hood in charge of the business, Edward took his four-year-old daughter Emma and sailed for England.[40]

A surprising feature of this whole affair is that Edward Lord, so vindictive in other areas, was remarkably mild towards his wife – and she had made him look a middle-aged fool. There were two occasions in Edward's life when he behaved with common sense and maturity: his ten weeks as governor in 1810, and the break-up of his marriage. Perhaps he realised their importance, and pulled out unsuspected qualities. Or possibly Edward was being practical, recognising how much he owed Maria in their business. They cooperated later: the habits of nearly two decades were not lightly broken. Perhaps, despite their well-deserved irritations with each other from time to time, some sort of love endured throughout.

THE REST OF CHARLES ROWCROFT'S STORY is as amazing as any in this book. He remained farming in Van Diemen's Land until he heard that his father, who had (astonishingly) accepted the position of English consul-general at Lima, had been shot dead while viewing a revolution with his daughter. Charles sailed for Peru. On his ship were recently widowed Jane Curling and her eight children. Ignoring his sister's situation, Charles conducted a shipboard romance, married Jane and continued to England. In London he promoted railways and ran a school and a newspaper, but was best known as an author, writing novels with social messages and several books about Van Diemen's Land. Best-known was *Tales of the Colonies*, based on his own experience, though depicting the hero as a successful patriarch.[41]

In 1852 Charles was appointed British consul in Cincinnati, where he went with his second wife and five children. Irish immigrants accused him of trying to recruit soldiers to serve in the British army, and he feared for his life. The Americans withdrew their permission for his consulship and he sailed home, but died on the way. The ship's captain thought his death mysterious, but the mystery seems solved by the way he dosed Rowcroft with opium, mercury, ipecac, quinine and then more opium and mercury.[42]

Lima in 1820, by Augustus Earle – who also painted a panorama of Hobart
(National Library of Australia nla.pic-an2822710)

Flight of Fancy:
Edward Lord visits his wife, November 1824

SCENE: *The drawing room at Orielton. As Edward rides up the drive, Maria is sitting in the pose of a devoted wife, embroidering a pair of slippers for him and planning the conversation. She has learnt from him over the years.*

Edward: Well, Maria. Here I am. What do you have to say for yourself?

Maria (*puts down slippers*): How lovely to see you, Edward! How are the children? How did Corbetta and Bill settle down?

Edward: I'm not here to talk about the children! What about this – this wretched young man of yours?

Maria: Just an innocent diversion, Edward. It was nice to have someone to chat to while you were away – such a long time – but there was nothing in it.

Edward: Nothing in it! But Murray wrote to me ...

Maria: I think he exaggerated, Edward. You know what Murray's like, such a dramatic man. My hot-headed brother John stirred him up, all through envy. He has done a good job at Orielton, though – the cattle ...

Edward: Never mind the cattle! Really, Maria, it's the outside of enough! Everyone knows you've been gallivanting about the place with a boy young enough to be your son, in a most disgraceful way, shaming my name.

Maria: It wasn't as bad as that, Edward, just gossip, and he was very helpful with business matters. But I haven't seen him for months, Edward ...

Edward: Only because Hood and Gunning stopped you.

Maria: ... and I won't see him again. It's all over. What do you want to do now?

Edward: Show him up in court for the wastrel he is!

Maria: Yes, dear, but about our family. What are your plans?

Edward: I'm going back to England, and the children and I will stay there. No more Van Diemen's Land, where people laugh at me as a cuckold.

Maria: I'm sure they don't. They admire you too much for your success in business. Now, I thought of going to England myself.

Edward: No! You stay here. I'm not having you getting up to heaven knows what where my family can see you.

Maria: Very well, I'll stay here, to please you.

Edward: My brother Sir John wants me to divorce you.

Maria: You don't really want a divorce, do you? So expensive and difficult, and not at all good for the children's reputation, or yours. And the evidence would be published in the newspapers …

Edward: H'm. Very well. You stay here, no divorce, and I suppose I'll make you an allowance.

Maria: And can I write to the children? Just little motherly letters. They'd be unhappy if they didn't hear.

Edward: I don't suppose that can do any harm.

Maria: Oh, Edward, it is good to see you again. You've been away so often and so long, I almost forget what you look like! But here you are, as handsome as ever. I'm sorry I flirted a bit, so silly of me, just like a mere woman, but it's all over now. Would you like a glass of wine? And perhaps some pie for lunch? It's your favourite, beef and leek. And you might try on these slippers and see if you like the pattern … Are you staying the night?

19. AFTER THE COURT CASE

UNEXPECTEDLY, IN THE YEARS FOLLOWING the court case, the reputations Edward and Maria Lord had built up turned round completely. Before 1824, Edward led the colony as a businessman and a citizen, outwardly at least admired and praised, while Maria was his despised ex-convict wife. After 1824, Edward lived mostly in England, and colonists criticised him as an absentee landlord stripping money from the local economy, his wild cattle a nuisance to other farmers. It was Maria who was esteemed, as a businesswoman and an upright, generous citizen. Stories about her in newspapers are respectful and admiring, as she vanquishes robbers single-handed, nurses the sick, defends her servants, gives reliable evidence in court cases and explores the country adventurously. There is no hint of criticism about her past, or her proven adultery. By her own efforts, she became one of the most successful of all female ex-convicts.

When Edward sailed away at the end of 1824, he left Maria with next to nothing, despite her having played such an important part in his business. He did give her an allowance but it sounds small, for later she thanked 'the kind friends who came forward so liberally to her assistance into business, at a time when she was suffering the greatest pecuniary distress'. But capable Maria made best use of her assets: her experience in shopkeeping, loans from these kind friends, the allowance however meagre. During the next eight months she organised her resources and opened a new shop, advertising in August 1825:

> MRS. MARIA LORD, in returning Thanks for the very kind and liberal Support which she has received, in her Endeavours to obtain a future Support for herself and her Children, begs Leave to acquaint her Friends and the Public, that she has opened her Stores, at the Corner of Elizabeth and Liverpool-streets; where she has for Sale, on Commission, British and Foreign Goods of all descriptions.

Not just a general shop, but a butcher's as well, to receive meat in payment for goods. And Mrs Lord 'trusts that the experience of the whole Colony, of her integrity and assiduity in Business, for the last sixteen years, will be sufficient guarantee for her future Exertions'.[1]

Previous pages: Hobart in 1829, by Elizabeth Prinsep. It has certainly grown since the early days, though it is still a small town. The Lords' house sits east of government house (State Library of New South Wales)

Only six months after opening her new store, Maria Lord is flourishing
(*Colonial Times*, 10 February 1826)

Mrs. Lord's Store.

MARIA LORD begs to return her grateful Thanks to her Friends and the Public, for the liberal Support she has received since she opened her Stores in Elizabeth-street, and takes the liberty of acquainting them, that in addition to her usual Assortment of Teas, Sugar, Preserves, Pickles, Spices, Butter, Cheese, Hams, and other Articles of Grocery and Provisions, she has supplied herself from the recent English arrivals, with a large and elegant Stock of coloured Prints, Muslins, Gowns of the newest fashions, Fancy Flowers and Feathers, Ladies' Shoes, Carpeting, &c. together with a great variety of other Articles in general use; Spirits and Wines, of superior flavour, in Quantities not less than 5 Gallons.—She takes this opportunity also of announcing, that she has lately added the Business of a Butcher to her Stores, and that her Friends may at all times be sure of a Supply of Meat of the very best Quality, and which she will happy to furnish them for Monthly Payments.

Naturally, this advertisement showed Maria in the best possible light. She reminded customers of her integrity and assiduity over sixteen years: the first five years, 1805–10, and the eleven since she returned in 1814. Stating that she wanted to support 'herself and her Children' was stretching reality, for Maria had only one child in the colony, Caroline, whose husband was a successful lawyer. However, it sounded good: what could be more suitable for a woman than supporting her children? That word 'integrity': was it another suggestion that she had stayed out of the widespread corruption of the time? Or a dig at Edward?

Given Maria's ability, it is not surprising that the shop was extremely successful. Six months after opening she advertised again, thanking the public for their liberal support and telling them that she had in stock 'a large and elegant Stock of coloured Prints, Muslins, Gowns of the newest fashions, Fancy Flowers and Feathers, Ladies' Shoes, Carpeting, &c'.[2] How she would have enjoyed selling her fashionable gowns, advising customers on fit and fashion, using that tact and shrewdness Fawkner praised. As well, perhaps she had some involvement with the Lord properties. She certainly did later and, with her old friend Samuel Hood managing the Lord estates, she could easily have slipped into this role now.

This might have been the most fulfilling period of Maria's life. She was running her own business in the way she wanted, and succeeding. Most of her children were in England, but possibly this was not the tragedy it would be to some. Maria does not sound particularly maternal – this was the mother who put a two-year-old in boarding school – and she was not entirely bereft, for Caroline was in Hobart and presented her with her first grandchild. Maria gave up the battle for social acceptance, but perhaps she did not mind. The push could have come from Edward, the baronet's brother, and possibly Maria was relieved to be able to stop trying. Probably more importantly to her, she was accepted by her fellows. In 1826 eight leading merchants combined to deal with forged promissory notes. Seven were men, mostly from the group of newly arrived, upright immigrants, and the eighth was Maria Lord.[3] How much more would she have valued their acceptance than snobbish young Janet Ranken's. However, after her disgrace at least one old friend dropped her. For years Knopwood did not mention her in his diary.

Occasional stories about her appeared in the press. In 1826 'John Johannes, a native of Goa' was found dead on the floor of her kitchen. 'He had been sleeping on the dresser after having eaten a very hearty supper, and fell with his legs on a person who was lying on the ground below; and who, thinking him intoxicated, merely put his legs off. In the morning he was found dead.'[4] Whether Johannes was a servant or a visitor was not mentioned, but life sounds generous (if careless) in the Lord kitchen, where the mistress allowed people to eat and drink their fill.

More evidence of a friendly household appeared in 1827. One Sunday afternoon Maria was sitting at the table after lunch. She had sent most of the servants to church (clearly they had no option), and called to the remaining one, 'William, take this dish away'. William did not answer, but Maria heard a noise in the kitchen and went to inspect – to see a stranger.

Maria Lord is accepted in the ranks of Hobart's leading merchants
(*Hobart Town Gazette*, 1 July 1826)

She ran after him, seized him by the collar and said, 'What do you here?' 'Nothing', said the man, in the time-honoured way.

Maria accused the man of robbing her, and he pulled a large shawl from his bundle and ran away. Maria followed him, caught him again and held him, despite his struggles to escape. While struggling, he pulled out a silk handkerchief and other pieces of clothing. Finally Maria saw a gentleman passing and called out, and the pair secured the man. While Maria was holding him he begged for pardon, but she refused to let him go. As she said later: 'If he had come and asked for a loaf of bread she would have given it to him, but to break open a box of apparel in the kitchen, and rob her poor servants, was not to be forgiven'. The press praised this stirring example of female heroism.[5] At almost fifty Maria was obviously strong and healthy. But she was not vindictive. The intruder did not appear in court, so she did not take the incident any further.

She did not always stay in Hobart, for she enjoyed expeditions into the bush. In 1844 a newspaper article praised the charming scenery of the River Ouse, as it ran through a stupendous mountain pass then precipitated itself over pine-clad rock to glide in peaceful repose by a lovely lake. It was a pity that the route was too difficult for ladies, continued the reporter, but two, 'more adventurous than the generality of their sex', had achieved the feat 'in the rude days of colonial intercourse' (that is, years earlier): Maria Lord

There was a reason for Maria's visits to Mrs Lord's Springs: the land is good sheep country, as these merinos show (Stuart Whitney)

Mrs Lord's Springs (left), and scenery nearby: a wild, remote spot
(Stuart Whitney)

Purple berries and a waterfall in the high country, the delight of intrepid walkers like Maria Lord
(Rebecca Aisbett)

and her friend Jane Jeffreys, a widow.[6] Charles Jeffreys died in 1826, so the expedition probably took place in the next few years, when Maria was about fifty – a testing but enjoyable walk. The scene is near a place known as Mrs Lord's Springs, a beautiful spot remote even today, in the Shannon district – just as difficult of access as the lovely lake, but providing as much enjoyable adventure for Maria.[7] How she managed to reach these remote places in the long skirts, corset and other restricting clothes fashion imposed on women is hard to imagine. She and her friend Jane were obviously indomitable.

A few years later another of Maria's abilities was praised. The Lords had been friendly with Richard and Isabella Lewis for years, godparents to their first baby. Maria kept up the friendship, as a court case in 1833 showed. Isabella Lewis broke a bone and Dr Crowther was sent for. He arrived to find Maria helping Isabella. Richard Lewis sued Crowther for defective treatment of his wife, his lawyer claiming: 'had the bones been placed in their proper position, and the case left to nature and Mrs. Lord, the patient would have been cured months before'.[8] The picture built up by these stories is of a capable, active, quick-witted, no-nonsense woman; a good friend, sympathetic to those in trouble. Now that she had no need to deal with Edward's incompetence, she could show the kinder side of her nature.

THE TRADITIONAL LORD ENTERPRISES were not nearly as successful as Maria's activities. In 1824 *Jupiter*, sent to the Pacific for a cargo, was wrecked near Tahiti. It was a total loss, though the crew survived and the ship was insured. The next year it was *Caroline*'s turn, wrecked while whaling off Macquarie Island. The crew and some of the oil were saved.[9] Two cases close together, the crew and some cargo safe: insurance fraud? But perhaps both wrecks were accidental.

In Van Diemen's Land, Samuel Hood continued to run the Lord properties, sell meat to the government and call in Lord's debts, with as little success as anyone else. Outside business, Hood was laudably involved in the establishment of the Bank of Van Diemen's Land but also acted foolishly, antagonising all-powerful Governor Arthur by making an absurd fuss about not being invited to dinner.[10] His claim to have more common sense than four other men put together sounds like an over-estimate.

Without the shop or ships and with far less profit from his estates, Edward Lord's income was drastically reduced, but this was not his only financial problem. Arriving in England in 1825, he found his brother Sir John so embarrassed that he asked Edward to repay his huge debt. Edward could

A sketch of Corbetta Lord as an unhappy teenager: her mother was on the other side of the world (Lou Smith)

not, and Sir John sued him in an undefended suit for £74,000 (though the brothers remained on good terms, so perhaps Sir John was merely trying to convince his creditors that he was attempting to repay them). Edward agreed to give his brother half his properties in Van Diemen's Land. That £74,000 raises questions. Maria was making profit in the business: how had he managed to lose so much money? Had he borrowed more than the initial £20,000 from his brother, or was the extra a colossal interest bill? Other merchants made and kept fortunes: in sharp contrast to Lord, in England, John Ingle increased his wealth by prudent speculation, built a large mansion, and died aged 91 leaving a large estate.[11]

It sounds as if Fawkner's explanation is correct: that Edward Lord wasted the money with gambling, and other 'vices' which might have included ostentatious hospitality, fine living, unwise loans and expensive trips to and from England. There are persistent rumours that Lord gambled away his money, and the Owen–Lord family in Pembroke were notorious gamblers.[12] Whatever the explanation, it is clear that by 1825 Edward's fortune had gone, though somehow he always managed to stay out of the bankruptcy court.

In England, he did have enough money to set up a new household, necessary for his children: in 1825 Emma was aged six, William eight, Corbetta ten, Edward Robert thirteen, John fifteen and Eliza nineteen. Someone had to care for them, and Edward engaged Elizabeth Storer. Born in Sydney in 1798, Elizabeth was one of five children of two convicts. In 1809 her mother left her father, a blacksmith. Poverty would have encouraged Elizabeth to find a job and in 1813, aged fifteen, she was working for the Lords. In 1817 she went to London, where she lived with 'William, a mariner'. They had two daughters, Catherine born in 1820 and Jessy in 1822.[13] William then disappeared.

After Edward Lord returned to England in 1825 (or even before), Elizabeth became his children's nurse. Perhaps she saw his name in an advertisement, perhaps the Australian grapevine in London passed round the news. In his new employee, Edward found the woman who was, from his will, the love of his life. They lived in a series of rented houses and Elizabeth started bearing children. They were known, respectably, as Lord, with Maria's children presumably told to keep silent.[14] But Edward could not make this pretence with his Lord relations. He and his new family lived mainly in Kent, about as far east from Pembroke as it is possible to go in England, well out of sight.

Keeping a mistress meant that Edward could not return to live in Van Diemen's Land, now moralistic Governor Arthur was in power. Perhaps he did not want to, though all his business activities were there. His experience in 1824, starting with a zealous customs official searching his underwear for contraband, and the threat of being charged with trying to bribe Commissary Moodie, must have shown him that Arthur was setting up a new, upright regime where opportunities for graft and corruption were fewer. England meant his new young mistress and respectable life posing as a married couple – not possible in Van Diemen's Land where everyone knew everything. Edward did not try to divorce Maria: perhaps because he did not want to hurt her and the children; perhaps because divorces required individual Acts of Parliament and were hideously expensive; perhaps because he did not want the appalling scandal (this was the man who had his convict mistress churched); or perhaps because everything was working out well with his new 'Mrs Lord', so there was no need.

An undertone of victory runs through this advertisement by Mrs Edward Lord
(*Hobart Town Gazette*, 22 September 1827)

MRS. EDWARD LORD, has the honour to acquaint her friends and the public, that circumstances have prevented her retiring from business, as she intended, and that she has removed from Elizabeth-street, to the premises lately occupied by Mr. George Lowe, in Argyle-street, where her Stores are ready to receive commission goods as usual, and where she has now on sale, a choice selection of British and Foreign Goods of all descriptions, and an assortment of hosiery, broad cloth, Irish linen, millinery, ladies' and children's boots and shoes, gloves, hats, crockeryware, china, fruit, vinegar, &c. &c. per *Medway*.

Mrs. E. Lord in returning thanks for the very kind and liberal support which she has received from her friends and the public, begs to invite their further orders, which shall be punctually executed upon reasonable terms.

Argyle-street, Sept. 17, 1827.

NEW NORFOLK.—For Sale in Elizabethtown, a desirable Residence, opposite the Church, containing eight Apartments, with three-quarters of an acre in Garden ground.

In 1827 Edward returned to Van Diemen's Land. Surely he would have needed a strong motive to leave his new household, and while it could have been the benefits of a sea voyage for his asthma, it was probably recovering those debts. He stayed for over a year. His arrival had several results. Maria advertised – unusually, as Mrs Edward Lord, emphasising the relationship with her husband – that 'measures of a private nature' compelled her to repair to England forthwith. It sounds like a threat, a weapon against Edward. She did not go; instead, in September Mrs Edward Lord advertised that she was not retiring from business as she had intended, but moving her shop to new premises.[15] So she had come to an agreement with Edward, presumably that she stayed safely in Hobart, and gained new premises.

If they were not on good terms already, they certainly were by early 1828. On 12 February Edward wrote to Governor Arthur from Morris' Inn in his usual sycophantic way:

> I trust your Excellency will excuse my intruding on Your time, but in this little community I make no doubt, inconsiderable as I am the indisposition I have been some time laboring under has reached Your Excellency's notice...

'Inconsiderable as I am', indeed! As 'a Female attendant is indispensable to an Asthmatic Patient', continued Lord, could he please keep the convict woman assigned to him, as she was honest, sober and 'unremitting in her attention and good Nursing'. It turned out that not only did everyone know he was ill, but what he and his nurse were doing so unremittingly; the principal superintendent of convicts informed Arthur that the woman was a very improper person to be returned to Lord's service. It seems she was Ann Fry, who had given birth to one illegitimate child two years previously, and was pregnant in February 1828. She was not reassigned to Lord, and he moved from the inn to his wife's house. So Edward and Maria were friendly enough for him to turn to her for care. In May, Ann Fry gave birth to a child she called Edward Fry Lord, claiming Edward Lord as the father, but he did not acknowledge the boy.[16]

Ann's claim implies that she had sexual relations with Edward Lord. What does this say about his taste in women? First, a convict pregnant with another man's child; then a servant with two illegitimate children already; now, a convict woman with one illegitimate child, described as 'on the town' and 'loose'. An elite gentleman, goodlooking enough, with a facade of wealth, Edward Lord could have chosen ladies of his own social class,

Knopwood's house Cottage Green (centre) in Battery Point (W.L. Crowther Library, TAHO)

but he preferred more earthy working-class women, perhaps the obviously sexy. Robert Murray hoped, with Sir John Owen, that Edward would divorce Maria and 'enjoy the Society of an honorable and Virtuous woman, who may know how to appreciate his value and be deserving of his affection';[17] but Edward did not seem to want this sort of woman. Perhaps virtue bored him. Or perhaps he liked powerless women he could dominate, without influential families to intervene.

If Ann was correct, Edward Lord sired a total of thirteen children: seven with Maria, two illegitimate; an eventual five with Elizabeth and one with Ann, all illegitimate – and illegitimacy was a terrible stigma, an unfair burden to place on children, even though Edward tried to hide it with his and Elizabeth's children by calling them Lord. Little is known of his relations with his children, though no one ever called him a fond father, except of his oldest son. His second son Edward Robert disliked him, but this is hardly surprising, with his father living openly with a mistress and siring another string of children, not to mention favouring Edward Robert's older brother.

As well as enjoying Ann's nursing, Edward Lord had other activities in Van Diemen's Land. He gave a splendid entertainment to his 'numerous friends', attended a public dinner on the King's birthday, and became involved in local politics, opposing Arthur by helping organise a public meeting which called for trial by jury and sent a petition to the British parliament, where Sir John Owen presented it.[18] However, Edward's main aim seems to have been to raise money, by any way possible. He put his Hobart home on the market, as well as his shares in the Bank of Van Diemen's Land and much other property, with sixty sales registered between 1827 (when the register started) and 1835.[19] It was a sign of failure. 'Lord' in Hobart's commercial circles now meant the family of James Lord, a *Calcutta* convict who made a fortune through hard work in trading, farming, smuggling and bypassing regulations.

Meanwhile, Edward Lord was pursuing his debtors as hard as he could, suing even his best friends. Knopwood owed him money, and the result of Lord v. Knopwood was that the clergyman had to sell his beloved home, Cottage Green. He was bitter, writing of 'the villainy of E. Lord and his agents'. Even worse, the agent sold Cottage Green for what Knopwood considered a low price: 'I have been truly robbed of it'. Maria Lord intervened on Knopwood's behalf, persuading the purchaser to let him stay in the house until he had organised somewhere else to live. This was kind of Maria, especially since Knopwood had dropped their friendship. Meanwhile, Edward Lord sued, among others, his old friend and supporter George Gunning.[20]

Family members were not exempt. His brother-in-law, John Riseley, lived on his own property adjoining Lawrenny. In 1827, Lord requested a new survey of the properties. It found, he claimed, that much of John's property, including the house, outbuildings and cultivated area, should be part of Lawrenny. Riseley was outraged. It shows how intensely Edward Lord wanted to retain or gain property, that he would attack his own brother-in-law, in a way that might have been justifiable legally but surely not morally. The case dragged on for decades. Lord also sued another brother-in-law, his former agent T.C. Simpson.[21]

Others sued him – notably his agent, Samuel Hood, who had resigned owing to ill-health. Hood won his case, and Lord found a new agent. 'Hood leaves this, disgusted, & no wonder', John Ingle's agent Walter Bethune reported. 'He has been labouring hard <u>& faithfully</u>, but his services have not been appreciated. I do not think M[r]. Lord knew accurately what accusation was to be brought agns[t] D[r]. Hood. In fact he was led by his legal & other advisers. However none could be substantiated'. Bethune bought land from Lord and paid him, on the understanding that the money would go towards the large debt Lord owed Ingle – but Lord was no more willing to pay his debts than his creditors were to pay him. 'I have not received <u>one sixpence</u> on your acct from Mr Lords agent', Bethune told Ingle.[22]

This visit must have been a sad contrast to Edward Lord's former life: a once-wealthy man brought low, in financial difficulties, suing his friends, led (tricked?) by others. Sycophantic Murray did his best, recalling that Lord began commercial operations and 'may therefore be truly styled the Father of the Colony', but no one else echoed this. In April 1828 Edward sailed back to England.[23] He must have known the ports between Hobart and England thoroughly by now. This was the tenth time he had made the voyage, and he had spent a total of at least 50 months, over four years, at sea: extremely expensive, and a period when he could not earn money actively himself. Perhaps he could find no other relief for his asthma.

ALTHOUGH EDWARD HAD SAID he would be absent from the colony only temporarily, he spent the next ten years in Britain. In his claims for land in Van Diemen's Land, he stated that ill-health prevented him living in the colony. Perhaps his asthma really was worse there, where it apparently started, but by now the reader knows that Lord wrote for effect rather than reporting truth. He could have disliked the colony, where gossips claimed that having squandered his fortune, he was returning to England under a cloud: 'it was said, that he gambled so much, that he was ruined'.[24] Or perhaps he just wanted to live with Elizabeth.

Cattle running from strangers on the high plains near the River Ouse (Rebecca Aisbett)

Chasing wild cattle through Central Plateau bush like this was not easy (Rebecca Aisbett)

His children with Maria were growing up. In 1829 Eliza married Thomas Mansell Esquire of Pembroke, a surgeon, nephew of the Bishop of Bristol – a most respectable alliance. Presumably the bishop was not told that his new niece was the illegitimate daughter of a convict. Edward groomed his oldest son, John Owen, to run his estates in Van Diemen's Land, and family tradition has it that John attended Oxford College, London – probably adequate, though not the best boys' school.[25] With their education complete, in 1829 Edward sent John and his younger son, Edward Robert, back to Van Diemen's Land. Edward and Sir John Owen jointly owned the properties – cattle were branded O–L – but they were managed by a series of agents, none particularly successful. Several court cases had gone against Lord, and a series of sheriff's auctions was threatened unless payment was made: up for sale were items ranging from 2000 sheep and a small farm at Sorell, to three houses in Hobart, two inns and even Orielton and Lawrenny. The partnership retained ownership of both the large properties, but it must have been difficult to find the money to avoid the auctions. The properties also suffered the problems of all primary producers, such as losing thousands of cattle in a hard winter.[26]

In these years the Black War was being fought between the Aborigines and the Europeans. It was caused by Aborigines retaliating after Europeans took their land (especially in the midlands), abducted their women and killed kangaroos, the Aborigines' basic food. Stockmen employed by the Owen–Lord partnership played their part, abducting Aboriginal women and destroying their food supply, kangaroos. In 1829 there was a report that despite an order prohibiting stockmen from keeping kangaroo dogs, 'the number of kangaroos killed lately exceeds anything before in the island', and stock-keepers employed by Edward Lord and Sir John Owen had killed 1800 animals just for their skins. The *Hobart Town Courier* thought the Aborigines could not be blamed for attacking whites, 'their real and cruel enemy'. In 1829 they robbed a hut of Edward Lord's of every movable item.[27]

In Hobart Maria Lord was living quietly. In 1828, advertising again as Mrs Maria Lord – no need to use weapons against Edward now – she gave up her shop, having presumably made enough profit to support herself in retirement. Her social life was active. Knopwood, once more her friend, recorded many dinners at Maria's with a variety of fellow guests. The most frequent was Captain Taylor who had lost *Caroline*, and was apparently staying in the house. Knopwood often reported them together: 'I dind with Mrs. Lord and Capt. Taylor, who calld on me in the morn' was a typical entry.[28] If Maria was conducting another 'criminal conversation' her husband could hardly object, with his own second family in Kent.

In August 1829 Maria received wonderful news: her two oldest sons had just sailed up the Derwent. Nineteen-year-old John kept a diary of the voyage, which reveals him as a pleasant young man. He did not enjoy daring activities – 'went up and sat on the Sky Sail mast yeard to disentangle the Vein which enterprise I am inclined to think I will not attempt again' – but did like throwing harpoons at dolphins. He killed one: 'what a glorious achievement'. His brother Edward Robert quarrelled about a monkey with another passenger, who started a fight. Edward gave him two black eyes; he sounds just as impulsive as his father. John was more of a peacemaker, noting that after the captain and three passengers drank too much and became obstreperous, 'we found it no easy matter to pacify & get them to bed'. Finally, after eleven weeks at sea, 'our anxious eyes' spied Van Diemen's Land.[29]

The Jeffreys' nephew George was staying with Maria. When she heard of the boys' arrival, he wrote, 'preparations were speedily made for their reception; and the vessel had scarcely swung to her anchor, when in walked two fine young men, most creditable specimens of native-born youth'. The elder, John, was intellectual and affable, generous and manly, 'indeed the pride of the colonists'. The boys' time with their mother was short:

A week or two passed, when the spirited young men, tired of inactive life, proceeded to obey the instructions of their father (then in England), to repair to Lawrenny immediately upon their arrival, to reside there, and to make themselves thoroughly conversant with the management of stock, and farming pursuits generally.

Under a competent overseer John made rapid progress, as George saw when he visited Lawrenny in October. It was a beautiful estate, he commented. 'No one could reasonably desire a more valuable and extensive manor than this. It comprehends everything that a man, ambitious to become a large landed proprietor, could hope or wish for.' The three young men spent a happy fortnight in visits to neighbours, entertainments and work on the property. 'We almost lived on horseback; and every hot day's ride – for it was then about Midsummer – was concluded by a glorious swim in the deep and rapid waters of the Derwent.'

Maria Lord had an agreement with the commissariat to supply thirty cattle a week, and the young men organised this, catching the cattle then sending them to Hobart. The cattle were wilder than kangaroos, wrote George, and 'riding them in' was challenging. As soon as the herd, at least

The fast-flowing Derwent at Lawrenny. John Lord was swept round this corner and drowned (James Alexander)

1500 cattle, saw a man on horseback they would gallop off, their thousands of hoofs making the earth vibrate. The horsemen chased them, up and down rocky slopes and steep hills, through forest and plain, until at last they forced them into the conical-shaped entrance of a stockyard. John enjoyed this sport and soon became one of the most skilful horsemen on the estate, excelling at using a 'long drawing-off pole' to single out a fat steer from among the enraged cattle in the stockyard. 'Wherever danger was present, there was my brave young friend to be found, at the head and front.'

On George's last day, John rode off to inspect timber for fencing. After a hot ride home he suggested the usual swim. George was cautious, as the day before he had nearly drowned in the rapid current, but John started to swim across the river. The current swept him away, and George shouted at him to come back. 'All right, all right', John replied, but at that instant the current swept him further off. He vanished round a turn in the river, and could not be found.[30]

On hearing this dreadful news Maria rushed to Lawrenny, but all she could do was order a vault built in the nearest churchyard, at New Norfolk. There was universal sympathy for the family. 'This fine young man ... had endeared himself to all the neighbourhood', reported the *Colonial Times*. It took a month to find his body, which was buried in the vault. At Maria's request, her old friend Knopwood attended the funeral, and afterwards rode home in a carriage with her and her friend Jane Jeffreys. In Hobart they had tea, then Knopwood took young Edward, George Lloyd and a friend home to seek solace in a glass of wine and a cigar.[31] But it would take more than this to compensate for the disaster – and someone had the dreadful task of writing to Edward senior, to tell him that the apple of his eye had died. It was said that he never recovered.

John Owen Lord's vault at New Norfolk (James Alexander)

20. THE FINAL DECADES

IN 1829, MARIA LORD WAS 51 AND EDWARD 48, well into middle age by the standards of the day; but both had thirty years of life ahead of them. They continued the pattern they had established in the 1820s: Maria living in Van Diemen's Land, Edward mainly in England, but never ceasing to try and make money from the colony.

In England, Edward seems to have lived unobtrusively with Elizabeth and their children. His one public activity, according to family tradition, was to attend the wedding of Queen Victoria, a major public event.[1] No guest list remains for this to be checked; if he went, did he take Elizabeth, calling her Mrs Lord? Had Queen Victoria known, she was not likely to have been amused, a mistress at her marriage.

Otherwise, Edward seemed to lead a quiet domestic life in England. He fathered more children, a total of five with Elizabeth: William Edward, Emma Eliza, Charles Owen (after another of his brothers), Mary Anne and John Henry. Unusually, Edward gave three of the children five names already used for his first family – William Edward, Emma Eliza, John – but they recalled the Owen/Lord family of which he was so proud. Parts of it, at least: he called no child after his father. The new family moved around, living in a series of probably rented houses at quite grand addresses including Down Hall, Kent (where Charles Darwin in Down House was a neighbour); Court Hill House in Wiltshire; and finally a four-storey terrace house in Bayswater, London. The only family details appear in the 1841 census. In the house that night were six-year-old Mary; Elizabeth's daughter Catherine; Elizabeth, Edward and Sir John Owen, a visitor. They had five young female servants (on whom, had I been Elizabeth, I would have kept a close eye, in view of Edward's roving one).[2] The other children, even the young ones, were presumably at boarding school, another hint that Edward was not the fondest of fathers.

Left: Braces said to have been worn by Edward Lord at Queen Victoria's wedding: he liked finery (Tasmanian Museum and Art Gallery)

Previous pages: A modern picture of Lawrenny, owned by Edward Lord until his death (Rebecca Alsbett)

As the children grew to adulthood, they married and/or established careers. Of Edward and Maria's children, John Owen and Edward Robert had gone to Van Diemen's Land; Eliza had married in Wales; Corbetta married an officer in the Indian Army; one son called William was also in the Indian Army. There is no trace of Emma as an adult, so perhaps she died. Of Edward and Elizabeth's children, Charles and possibly William became Indian Army officers, John went to Australia in the gold rush and Mary Anne died young. Both Storer girls went to Victoria with their husbands, as did Corbetta in the 1860s, too late for Maria to see her daughter again. So of Edward's eleven children and three stepchildren, only one, Emma Eliza, remained in England. Her husband, Anguish Honor Augustus Durant of Tong Castle, Shropshire, invented gadgets that cleaned chimneys, extracted castor oil, and ascertained the distance passengers travelled in railway carriages.³

12 Westbourne Terrace (centre), an impressive house for the Lord household (Google Earth)

Edward's brother Sir John Owen remained as flamboyant as ever. In 1829 his wife died, and the next year he remarried. 'The Baronet is 63 years of age, his Bride 16!' reported the *Launceston Advertiser* in disgust. (How could her parents allow it?) Having sired eight children with his first wife (three dying at birth), Sir John fathered five more with his second, the last when he was seventy.⁴ Determined to stay in parliament, in 1831 he spent tens of thousands of pounds on two elections. The first was declared void because the returning officer acted improperly, showing gross partiality towards Sir John. The bribes were worth it: he won a second election. In 1834 he was implicated in a smuggling racket and, still full of energy, at seventy he fought the last duel in Wales, badly wounding his adversary (the cause was not divulged). His money problems only worsened, and in 1841, with 'not one farthing that he can call his own', he put his Welsh Orielton on the market. He and his wife lived mostly in continental Europe where costs were lower. Despite his absence from Pembroke, Sir John remained its member of parliament, becoming the longest-serving parliamentarian of his period, the grand old man of Westminster. Despite decades of high living, he died in 1861 aged 84 – still a member of parliament, still lord lieutenant of Pembrokeshire.[5]

Sir John and his brother Edward continued to try and milk money from their Van Diemen's Land enterprises. It was uphill work. Under a series of agents the estates made no profit. Edward must have continued to owe his brother huge sums, for in 1833 their partnership was dissolved and the properties were divided, Sir John gaining the lion's share including Orielton, Edward retaining only Lawrenny and Charles Rowcroft's former property, Norwood. In 1836 a list of major landowners included Sir John with 20,000 acres. Edward was not mentioned.[6]

He was also in debt to John Ingle, his former friend, now living in England. Letters to Ingle in 1830 from his Hobart agent show the frustration of trying to squeeze repayments from Lord, whose property was mortgaged or worth little. 'With respect to getting any thing from [Lord's] cattle at present it is impossible they being mortgaged to [illegible] for two thousand Pounds'; 'I shall have great difficulty to encounter in getting any thing from Mr E Lords estate in the shape of interest should the estate be put up for sale it is very doubtful wether purchasers could be got for it'; 'you have been badly deceived in respect to the Stock and horses in Mr Lords estate they are all either sold or been mortgaged'. In 1831 Lord made his Hobart house over to Ingle for £4000, but this was only part of his debt.[7] Finally, in 1832 Sir John found a capable agent in Alexander Goldie, who cleared the estates of debt and sent the owners 'a goodly sum' each year. Occasionally newspapers expressed resentment at such absentee proprietors stripping money from the colony. In the 1840s Goldie left the brothers' employ and sued Lord for unpaid commission. He won his case, though gaining under a third of his claim.[8]

Edward Lord continued to harry anyone who might provide him with money. When his brother-in-law and former partner Thomas Simpson of Launceston died in 1832, his will referred to 'the Chancery suit with Mr Lord': Simpson felt he was in the right but, to persuade Lord to relinquish the case, he could be offered two small farms. Simpson's widow, left in poor circumstances, asked Lord to relinquish his claim. He not only refused but asked for six farms, telling her he felt sure she would accept this 'highly advantageous' offer.[9]

In Hobart William Maum, one of the rogues who had worked in the commissariat, attacked Lord. Land claims were being investigated, and

Maum warned settlers that Lord's representative had begun operations – insinuating he was claiming land unjustly. But he, Maum, 'well aware of Neddy's Integrity, took care to secure a key under his hand, to unlock the bureau, in which were deposited certain proofs of his conduct towards him and others'.[10] These obscure accusations from a scoundrel like Maum are hardly to be taken seriously – but they can have done Lord's reputation no good. 'Neddy's Integrity' sounds almost like a Hobart joke.

Edward Lord's longest-lasting battle concerned compensation for land, and his determination, underhand methods and corrupt victory were typical of the man. A former chapter described how he claimed his 1821 grants for Lawrenny had been wrongly measured, and he was owed more land. In 1832 and 1833 he tried to gain land in compensation, unsuccessfully.

In 1842 Lord tried again, applying to the secretary of state in London, who referred the matter to the Van Diemen's Land governor, who referred it to the Caveat Board. Its members decided Lord should gain compensation. Governor Denison disagreed. Lord had not been able to substantiate his claim; he should have noted the discrepancy at the time; nearly all early grants were wrongly measured anyway; Lord had already seized 459 acres of prime land illegally. Anyway, it was difficult to gain accurate information, with Goldie declining to have anything to do with Lord until his account was paid. The secretary of state refused the compensation.

In 1853 Edward and Sir John brought their big gun into action: the Duke of Newcastle, who asked the government to uphold Lord's claim. Aristocratic patronage prevailed – again. Denison wrote, surely with gritted teeth, that the long dispute would be settled, though the Duke of Newcastle in England could not possibly understand it. Finally, in 1854, 43 years after the original grants, Lord's agent received the land, though minus the 459 acres Lord had seized.[11]

EDWARD LORD SENIOR SEEMED TO HAVE little value for one commodity prized by most fathers: his eldest remaining son. Edward Robert was in Van Diemen's Land, willing to run the properties, but his father was reluctant to give him any power. Perhaps he thought his son incompetent? Edward Robert was learning his trade at Lawrenny, but even when he turned 21 his father did not let him manage it, Goldie remaining in charge. Edward Robert sometimes went to see Maria in Hobart, where they visited their old friend Knopwood, and Edward Robert enjoyed kangaroo hunts.[12] Family tradition says that he was close to his mother, and this

Either Emma or Corbetta Lord aged about twenty, looking unhappy despite her grand dress
(Tasmanian Museum and Art Gallery)

closeness surely developed in these years.

In 1838 Edward senior visited Van Diemen's Land again, bringing his and Maria's daughter Emma, nineteen, and Charlotte Lovekin, aged about 26, a companion for Emma. They travelled in the same ship as Congregational minister John West, who enjoyed hearing Edward tell stories of the island's history, 'the difficulties of those early days'. Perhaps these stories inspired the excellent history of Tasmania West published in 1852. The Lord party arrived in Hobart just before Christmas in 1838 – in time for roast beef with Maria, overjoyed to see her daughter again?[13] At one time or another she was reunited with three of the six children Edward had sent to Britain, but she never saw Eliza, Corbetta or William again. It was not necessarily Edward's decision. Perhaps they refused to make the long voyage, feeling little connection to a mother they had not seen since early childhood.

The 1838 visit was short, a bare three months, though perhaps Emma had her portrait painted by Thomas Bock. The provenance of the portrait is uncertain; it was presented to the Tasmanian Museum and Art Gallery in the 1930s by Miss Durant, a descendant of Emma Eliza, and from the clothes and age of the sitter could be either Corbetta or Emma Lord, painted in England or Hobart: the artist's name is not known.[14] The young woman looks extremely fashionable, in an elegant dress with enormous sleeves; but the grand dress only highlights her worried look, the handkerchief she clutches seeming almost ready for tears. These children could have had unhappy, neglected childhoods, torn from their mother who became a shameful secret, put in boarding school in England and seldom seeing their father, who then started living with another woman.

In March 1839 Edward senior, Emma and Charlotte left for England, taking Edward Robert and 65 bales of wool – Edward was still trying to make a profit. On the night of the 1841 census Edward Robert was visiting his sister Eliza in Wales, and the next year he married Charlotte Lovekin. They returned to Van Diemen's Land, where the first of their seven children was born at Lawrenny in 1843. Charlotte loved Lawrenny, even though the house was described as 'a mean, insignificant log-building'.¹⁵

In 1845 Edward senior arrived again, on his seventh voyage to Van Diemen's Land, over forty years since his first dashing arrival in 1804. He finally allowed his 33-year-old son to take over running the estates, and himself remained in the colony for over a year, doing his best to recoup his fortunes by, for example, applying for 30,000 acres of land near Port Davey. It has proved impossible to graze animals or grow crops in this area: whatever would he have done with it? Was it just the lure of owning land, any land? He was still exporting wool from Lawrenny, his agent William Knight organising 65 bales sent to England on his behalf.¹⁶ As well, Edward had his portrait painted, twice. He was now 65, but he was presented as a well-preserved, pleasant-looking gentleman, sharp, slightly balding but with no grey hair. A sketch by Thomas Wainewright of Edward sitting in a chair is inscribed with what he presumably considered his main claim to fame: 'Edward Lord Esq. R.M. [Royal Marines] who in 1804 erected the first house where now stands the city of Hobart Town'. Perhaps not satisfied with this, Edward also had a more traditional portrait painted by Thomas Bock. He left Van Diemen's Land for the last time in March 1847, aged 65.¹⁷

Port Davey. Even today there is no development (Peter and Kitty Courtney)

Any agreement between father and son was short-lived. By 1847 Edward Robert had left Lawrenny and was living at the smaller property of Llanstinan near Bothwell. Llanstinan was the name of an Owen property in Wales, so it was presumably part of the Owen–Lord domain in Van Diemen's Land. Edward Robert owned it, later at least. Perhaps his father felt he was not doing well enough at Lawrenny and moved him; or perhaps Edward Robert tired of working to benefit absentee landowners, and demanded his own property. He was 35, with a growing family: high time to be independent of his father. In 1854 he moved away from family properties altogether, buying Anglewood, a small but excellent property at Richmond. He was not wealthy. Charlotte told a friend in Bothwell that Edward's limited means would not allow them to send their sons to a certain school, or entertain: 'We live in so homely a style, & so very retired, that I never have courage to *invite* anyone'.[18]

ALMOST THE ONLY FAMILY MEMBER with no apparent money worries was Maria. Though retired from her shop, in the early 1830s she remained active in business, showing customers imported Saxon rams and applying for an allotment in Hobart for a stone house: 'M^r. Edward Lord has only had the indulgence of one Town Allotment – All the other houses [the Lords erected] having been built upon allotments which we have purchased'. Note the 'we': it sounds like a firm partnership still. She did not get her allotment. It is possible that she ran a boarding house in Hobart, as a later reminiscence claimed.[19] Whatever she did, it was quiet and respectable. In 1829 Henry Savery published a series of satirical sketches describing the foibles of 148 well-known residents of the small colony, including some women. He did not mention Maria Lord, once so notorious.

As in the earlier days, Maria employed stream of female convicts. One story depicted her character. During a decade in the colony, Sarah Collins committed many offences with many employers: drunk, insolent, neglecting her work, embezzling ... In 1830 she was assigned to Maria Lord. She continued to offend, serving a week's solitary confinement for being out after hours. She was returned to Mrs Lord, but six weeks later Maria charged her with insolence and wasting the provisions – an unusual

Opposite: Edward Lord by Thomas Wainewright, 1846
(Allport Library and Museum of Fine Arts, TAHO)

charge but typical of Maria, so keen on frugality. Sarah was admonished and returned again, 'Mrs Lord being willing to give her another trial'. Did she feel sorry for this woman, making such heavy weather of servitude? Sarah lasted another four months before being out after hours again. This time Maria did not take her back.[20] This is one of several hints through Maria's life that she was a kind woman, and it is not so surprising to find inscribed on her tombstone, 'Friend of the needy'. She had made enough money to be able to be generous, and perhaps enjoyed or found fulfilment in helping people who were finding life difficult – a position she had been in herself.

Edward Lord by Thomas Bock, 1846
(Tasmanian Museum and Art Gallery)

In 1833 Maria asked for her debtors to pay up, and sold many household goods in Hobart – bedsteads, chairs, plate, pictures, china, glass, even 'some fine preserves and pickles'. Perhaps she was closing her boarding-house. She could have moved to live with her daughter Caroline, who after a difficult period could offer her a home. Caroline's lawyer husband turned out to suffer from depression and alcoholism, and in about 1828 they separated, Caroline taking their two sons. She lived in Hobart, near or possibly with her mother, opening a school to support herself and her children. She was close to Maria; in 1830, for example, they travelled across the river to dine with Knopwood, 'a most delightful day', as he wrote. Thomas Giblin came to escort them home. Caroline's husband Frederic moved to Launceston, where 'from intemperance and improvidence' he was reduced to begging in the street. He died in 1832. The next year Caroline married Giblin, a rising official of the Bank of Van Diemen's Land. Upright and hard-working, a noted philanthropist, he was 'deservedly esteemed by all classes'. The Giblins had four children, including a daughter called Maria Lord Giblin. Perhaps in retirement Maria enjoyed her six grandchildren, particularly if she was living in the same house.[21]

Decades later, one of Caroline's sons with Frederic disgraced the family. Edward John Lord Dawes became a solicitor and married the daughter of a clergyman, but in 1862 embezzled £30,000 and fled to America. His wife followed with their five children, but both parents died of tuberculosis. Family tradition has it that one of the children's many aunts called Emma went to America and brought the orphans back to Hobart.[22]

By the 1830s Maria Lord was recognised as a sensible authority. She had lived in Van Diemen's Land since 1805, longer than almost anyone else, and she gave evidence in several court cases that went back to the early days. In 1834 one case concerned land ownership at Glenorchy, Maria describing who owned which land when. She had known the area since 1808, she told the court. She had owned a farm there herself (nothing about Edward's share) and frequently visited the area 'on parties of pleasure'.[23] Ah, the good old days, she must have thought. However, her life in the 1830s sounds pleasant, with Caroline, Thomas and the children, public recognition, visits from Edward Robert, and in 1838 the arrival of her husband Edward and their daughter Emma.

Devastatingly, in 1840 Caroline died, aged only 35. Of all the deaths Maria suffered, surely this was one of the saddest, for Caroline had been close to her ever since she was born, the only child Maria had been allowed to keep. Where Maria lived in the 1840s is not clear, but in 1849 she moved to Bothwell, near Edward Robert and his family. Either she, Edward Robert or both bought the Priory, an Elizabethan-style stone house of thirteen rooms with a splendid view. Maria developed it into a house and farm of 50 acres (20 hectares), the stock including Peter, a 'capital staunch cart horse';

The Priory at Bothwell, a later photograph but showing the large house on rising ground, with its splendid view (Tasmanian Archive and Heritage Office)

Jessie, a mare in foal; three cows and two heifers. A businesswoman to the last, Maria also ran a shop, and in 1857 let part of her house to the police magistrate. It was a fine large stone building, he wrote, its only drawback that 'the old lady owner' kept three rooms (which seems fair enough, since she owned it).[24]

Maria probably enjoyed life in Bothwell, a friendly, active community, where she became a respected citizen. In 1850, 46 leading residents signed an address of thanks to the retiring police magistrate, with Maria the only woman among them.[25] When Edward Robert moved his family to Richmond in 1854, she did not go with them. She was 75, and perhaps felt too old to cope with the move. Tasmania's first valuation rolls, published in 1858, showed Maria owning 50 acres at the Priory; Edward Robert with 75 acres at Anglewood and 2300 at Llanstinan; Edward senior with Lawrenny and his rival Rowcroft's property of Norwood; and Sir John Owen with Orielton, which was divided into tenant farms.[26] By this time, Edward seemed to have lost interest in what was happening in the island, but perhaps Maria had enjoyed watching the tiny convict colony develop: first into a much larger community made prosperous by wool, wheat and the convict system; then win its freedom from transportation in 1853, and three years later become the independent colony of Tasmania. She and Edward had both played their parts in the story.

IN 1857 EDWARD LORD DREW UP his final will, a complicated document with sixteen people granted annuities: in the order he gave them, his de facto wife, illegitimate children, stepchildren, wife, legitimate children and a string of other relations. Edward owned nothing in England; his only property was Lawrenny. It was mortgaged – probably, given Edward's

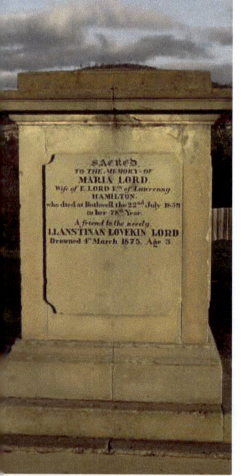

Maria Lord's tomb at New Norfolk. Llanstinan Lovekin Lord was a grandson, tragically drowned in the Derwent at Lawrenny, just like his uncle John (Rebecca Aisbett)

financial situation, to the hilt – but, unrealistic to the end, he calculated that the profits would pay off the mortgage in four or five years (although he had not paid off anything, apparently, in the last 35 years).[27]

Edward's de facto wife of over thirty years, Elizabeth Storer, was left the most generous annuity, £300 a year; but, surprisingly, Edward's adulterous wife Maria received £200 – on the condition that if she challenged his will this was forfeit, divided between the Lord/Storer children. That will stop her, one can imagine Edward thinking. The Lord/Storer children and Edward Robert, Corbetta and Eliza all received annuities, Edward Robert, the oldest remaining son, receiving the largest sum. There was nothing for Emma or William, who had possibly died.

Edward and Maria lived to good ages for the period; but their time came at last. 'News from Bothwell', Tasmanians could read one May morning in 1859. 'An old and well-known colonist Mrs. Maria Lord has been dangerously ill for some time, there are no hopes whatever of her recovery.' Maria died of 'Decay of Nature' two months later, her tombstone describing her as 'Wife of E. LORD E^{sq}. of Lawrenny'. They had lived apart for 37 years, but tombstones do not record such information. Maria also kept up the pretence of her age: it was given as 77, though she was really eighty.[28] She was buried in the New Norfolk churchyard, in the vault where her son John had been laid thirty years earlier.

Edward Lord lived almost as long. Two months after Maria's death he died in London aged 78, following an illness of a few days, with asthma if not the immediate cause at least a factor. Like Maria, he was described as he wished to be remembered. To the last he remained Edward Lord Esquire, of Lawrenny, Tasmania.[29]

21. AFTERWORD

'YOU'VE HEARD OF RAGS TO RICHES? Well, we were riches to rags.' Blue eyes sparkling, Maria and Edward Lord's 88-year-old great-granddaughter Lou told the family story – mostly from her historical research, since little of this saga was passed on to children. Maria and Edward Lord have hundreds, if not thousands, of descendants in Tasmania alone, with more in mainland Australia, New Zealand, Britain and other countries. Many stories could be told to bring the Lord saga up to date, but I have chosen to tell the story of Louisa Lord because she was Maria and Edward's only remaining great-grandchild, and because her story is a telling comparison with Maria's, a good closure for this book.

Maria and Edward's son Edward Robert, born in 1812, married Charlotte Lovekin in 1842. They lived in various Lord properties in Tasmania, ending up at Anglewood at Richmond. Charlotte died in 1861, and five years later, following the Lord tradition of age discrepancy in marriage, 54-year-old Edward Robert married Harriet Smith, aged twenty. She worked in the house, and had already borne him a child. Harriet gave birth to ten more children, the youngest, Joseph, in 1885 when Edward Robert was 73. By this time he had sired eighteen children. Years later, Harriet was kind to a daughter-in-law because, she said, she knew what it was like to be a second wife.

Joseph never told his children much about his childhood. In 1882 his father advertised for a lady, 'one of middle age preferred', to instruct children in a sound English education, so perhaps Joseph was educated at home; or perhaps he attended the local Richmond primary school.[1] There was no money for further education.

Previous page: Lou Smith as a teenager (Lou Smith)
Below: Anglewood at Richmond, where Edward Robert farmed (Lou Smith)

By this time Orielton and Lawrenny had been sold. In 1890 the Owen–Lord farming venture in Tasmania, once so huge, diminished to next to nothing, for Edward Robert let his final property and moved to the Hobart suburb of New Town. There in 1897 he died, aged 85.[2] Harriet, 51, was left with children to support and little money. Three months later she married John Pinfold, a tramway worker and family friend.

Joseph left school at a young age and went to work. When he married, in 1906 aged 21, he was a grocer. His wife was Ethel Louisa Johnstone, whose father was a baker at the Hobart gaol. She was musical, excellent at singing and playing the piano. Joseph became a woolbuyer for A.G.

Harriet Lord with her last baby, Joseph (Lou Smith)

Webster, a well-known Hobart firm, where he stayed for forty years. Ethel bore him nine children, with twins dying at birth. Louisa was the last baby, born in 1924.

When Lou was still a toddler, Ethel was diagnosed with tuberculosis, a fatal disease:

> The only memory I've got of my mother is me screaming in the hall of the house to get into Mum's bedroom because I knew something was wrong. All the aunties were there, and they wouldn't let me in, and I couldn't reach the doorknob. I carried on that much outside the door, wanting to get in, that one of my aunties picked me up, and she said, 'If you're going to be a good girl, and very quiet, and stay in my arms, I'll let you come in'. She took me in and held me, and I can see my mother now, still. After all those years, 85, 86 years, I can see Mum sitting up in bed, and she had a white lawn nightie, a pretty white nightie, and long hair that came down to here [just below her shoulders], wavy, browny coloured. It's still with you. You don't lose it. You never lose losing your mother, what you've missed.

Ethel died shortly afterwards. Three girls, Joy, Ethel and Lou, and their brother Les remained at home. Ethel's sisters wanted to take them

Joseph and Ethel in the Webster's wool store (Lou Smith)

in, 'but Dad said, "They've lost their mother, they aren't going to lose their father", and he kept us together'. Lou adored her father. 'He was a lovely man. Kindness itself.' He had a leather strop hanging up and threatened to use it if children misbehaved – but never did. He had high standards: 'it was always instilled in us to never bring shame on your family name and always tell the truth, and be honest. He drummed that into us. And our manners.'

Joseph was fond of the races, a glass of beer and a cigarette. He loved jokes and singing, with songs echoing through the house – 'Don't go down the mine, Dad', 'Two little girls in blue'. 'He used to try and make up to us kids for having a stepmother', added Lou. However, his job often took him away from home. Left with four young children, he soon married again. Lou was defensive about her stepmother, Amy. 'She was nice to me. She taught me high principles. She treated me like her own' – Amy and Joseph had three more children, Joseph keeping up the Lord tradition of large families with a total of twelve. Lou's fiery sister Joy did resent their stepmother:

> She used to give her larrydoodle. If Mum had had words with her, and that was often, nearly every day, she'd go round and she'd sing [the popular song], 'We'd be far better off in a home! We'd be far better off in a home! Far better off ...' and she'd keep it up. Mum used to hate it. Mum used to call her New Town Bull, because she'd yell and carry on. She'd say, 'The New Town Bull's out!'

Still rankling eighty years later were some of Amy's deeds. Joseph grew vegetables for the family but Amy used to sell them, and the children only had vegetables at the weekend when their father was there to see. They were not allowed butter or fresh bread, because they would eat too much.

Bread had to be yesterday's, or older. But these were usual economies, and Amy did not actively maltreat her stepchildren. Her position was difficult, bringing up seven children on a limited income – and she suffered from epilepsy. These memories hint at the possible experiences of previous children in this saga: exiled across the world from home, brought up by a step-parent, enduring family deaths.

There were more deaths for Joseph's family. When Lou was six her eldest sister died in childbirth, and a few years later her eldest brother died of tuberculosis, like their mother. But Lou's resilient character helped her. Her family could afford few books, but a friend lent her the Pollyanna books, about an orphan who coped with hard times by making up a game, always finding something to be glad about. 'I used to play the Pollyanna game, and I've done it all my life', said Lou. 'There's always somebody worse off than you are.'

No one ever mentioned Maria and Edward. Looking back, Lou was sure her father knew about them, his grandparents – but they were never mentioned. 'My brother worked with him in Websters, and they used to get wool from Lawrenny, and he never ever said once that my father owned this. He didn't say anything about his father. Convicts were no-nos. You were ashamed of them.' (When a great-great-granddaughter of Maria and Edward married in 1891, the groom's family were not at all happy at the convict connection.[3])

Joseph Lord: not unlike his grandfather Edward (Lou Smith)

The one item passed down to Joseph was a six-cylinder silver and black pistol that belonged to his grandmother, Maria Lord. Joseph kept it in a locked drawer, and the children were not allowed to touch it. 'But my brother Colin and I used to get it out and play with it – or he used to play with it. I was too scared to touch it. He knew where the key was. He was fascinated with it.'

There were a few other reminders of the past. The family visited Grandmother Harriet, a very old lady who died when Lou was five.[4] And when Joy told lies – 'she used to tell whoppers' – Aunty Nellie, Joseph's oldest sister, would say, 'There's Maria again. That's Maria coming out in her', without explaining the remark. Joy was full of life, energetic, determined. Lou remembered her practising their stepmother's signature. 'She did it! She used to wag it, and write notes why she wasn't at school. For a good while she got away with it, because she could sign it exactly right.'

Joy protected her little sister:

Lou's protector, her older sister Joy (Lou Smith)

No one would dare pick on me at school. She'd hit them in the face. Boys and all, she wouldn't worry. The New Town Bull. She was a big girl, and she'd give them one. So no one picked on me. I was too inoffensive to be picked on, anyway. I just kept out of everybody's way.

One of the children's favourite games was bowling Lou down the street outside their home. They would take an old tyre to the top of the street and tell Lou, the littlest, to curl up inside it. They would whip the tyre to gain speed,

and off I'd go. It didn't take long for the tyre to build up speed and get away from them. There was no way of stopping until I got to the bottom of Montagu Street and crossed over Ross Street to crash into our neighbour's picket fence. Just as well there weren't many cars about in those days! They used to enjoy that, and I didn't seem to mind – I'd do it again and again.

In 1934, when Lou was ten, the Duke of Gloucester visited Tasmania, and among the entertainments was a display of eurythmics by four hundred schoolgirls. A few were chosen from every school, and Lou was among those from New Town Primary. 'They did a great big map of Tasmania in white paint on the North Hobart Oval, and we had to do this dance all in our green and gold clothes, gold dresses and a little bit of green, and when the dance stopped we had to run to our given spot and sit there and make Tasmania out of kids. I was on the East Coast, near Coles Bay.' But the outfit cost six shillings:

It was a lot. I couldn't get six shillings. I said I couldn't go in it. My brother said, 'You go in it, Noonoo' – Noonoo, he used to call me – 'I'll find you the money. I'll get the money off Mr Twiddles'. Mr Twiddles was whoever of their clique had money at the time.

Mr Twiddles was good if they'd had a win on the horses. It was right up to about two days before the event, and I'm that fretful and worried about this six shillings. Anyway, he came good with it. He brought it home the day before so I could do the dance with the other girls. We loved it.

So, according to local newspapers, did the crowd of 20,000 who enthusiastically applauded 'the charming picture' made by the 'brightly clad girls'. The Duke, thought the loyal journalist, would remember it for years to come.[5] (Contemporary accounts agree exactly with Lou's memories, given 78 years later.)

Churchgoing provided Lou with love and happiness, and the kindly old minister at St John's, New Town, was like a father to her. She enjoyed Sunday School and sang in the choir at church, with two neighbours, the Misses Hickman, making her the special outfit. 'A long black skirt, a surplice, a mortar board, and a little black satin collar, and they did the lot.' They also gave her singing lessons, so she could sing solos. But despite such occasional kindnesses, much of Lou's childhood was bleak. 'I always had to battle for myself', she commented once, in a throwaway line.

School provided encouragement. A vividly intelligent girl, Lou loved her years at New Town Primary School. She passed the examination to attend Hobart High School and enjoyed two years there, but found it embarrassing to be on the free list, with government assistance for books and uniform. No one encouraged her to stay at school, and at fourteen she went to work on the china counter of a Hobart department store. She quite enjoyed it, but Cadbury's chocolate factory at Claremont offered higher wages, so at fifteen she moved there.

Her first job was decorating chocolates. Six girls stood with tubes of liquid chocolate, putting on the squiggles as the chocolates passed on a conveyor belt. It took concentration. 'You couldn't take your eyes off them. Sometimes when you'd stop, when there was a break, the floor tiles would move, with your eyes.' Rules about breaks were strict, and once when Lou was running back from the toilet, the handle on a door broke as she was pushing it open, badly injuring her right wrist and hand. She was rushed to hospital in an ambulance, the nurse worried that she would bleed to death. A complicated operation meant the hand was usable, except for three fingers. 'The doctor said to me, "You should get money for this, lassie", but no one was forthcoming with money in those days.' There was no compensation

Lou and Merv, 1940. Lou was sixteen (Lou Smith)

from Cadburys, but they did give her a job when she recovered. Lou learned to write with her left hand and worked in the planning office. Going to work in the train she met her future husband, Merv Smith, who also worked in an office at Cadburys and lived near Lou. She was thrilled when Merv asked her out to the pictures when she was sixteen.

Merv, Lou and a group from Cadburys used to climb Mount Wellington. 'We used to take chops or sausages, and we'd cook them on a pronged stick over the fire. And a billy, too.' The first time Lou made tea in the billy she put the tea in first, with the cold water – 'I didn't know you didn't make tea like that! Merv's face! He often said he didn't know why he married me after that episode.' They were happy times, recalled Lou. 'We were all young, and we used to laugh and joke and sing, and race up to the top of the Zig-Zag track to throw snowballs on the ones still coming up. Sometimes we had a tin to slide on the snow on.'

Merv's family were kind to Lou, especially his mother and his sister Clarice, who made her clothes and taught her to sew. Entertainment was often home-made. Lou sang in a local group, Peter Wiggins' band, which had six players on the saxophone, clarinet, piano and drums. They practised in Mrs Wiggins' home and sang war songs to entertain the troops, '"The White Cliffs of Dover", all those Vera Lynn songs. It was good fun.' They sang at a few dances but, said Lou, 'we were no great shakes'.

When war broke out, life changed dramatically. Merv enlisted in the navy, becoming seaman gunner on HMAS *Australia*. He and Lou were engaged, and when he knew he had leave due in 1944, they decided to get married – 'he said he couldn't leave me in the marriage market for too long'. Material was rationed, but Clarice made Lou a wedding dress out of curtain net. The kindly minister at St John's waived the wedding fee – 'Merv always said ever after that he married me because he got me cheap' – and Mrs Wiggins organised the reception, where Lou used the sheets from her glory box as tablecloths. Lou and Merv spent the first night of their honeymoon in a Hobart hotel – 'it was the thing to do in those days' – then hired a shack at Opossum Bay. It only had narrow single beds, but they managed. 'We were both skinny in those days.' But it was a brief honeymoon, for Merv had to return to war. Soon he was in action, the Battle of Leyte Gulf, where 81 men from HMAS *Australia* were killed in a week.

The ship had to return to Sydney for repairs, so Merv asked Lou to go there. She found a job making radio valves. Soon enough Merv had to return to his ship, and suffered more horrific experiences, in action at Guadacanal. 'Just a young ordinary seaman, never previously far removed from home', he was thrown into battle. 'All hell bust loose' as the Australians and Americans bombed the Japanese, and kamikaze pilots 'came straight at us, barely skimming the drink', but the Australians were saved by an American destroyer.[6] Merv was in Tokyo when peace was signed, then returned to Sydney. He and Lou went back to Hobart where Merv resumed work at Cadburys, but he was not happy, and moved to work in the office of a jam factory.

Lou and Mervyn's eldest child, Lorraine, was born in 1946. It was a difficult birth. 'I knew nothing about childbirth', said Lou. 'I had no idea what was going to happen. It was hell.' But Lorraine was a healthy baby, and Merv and Lou bought a block of land in a new suburb, Rosetta, and

Lou and Merv's wedding, 1944. From left: Clarice Moore, Merv's sister, with her daughter Valerie and husband Les; Merv; Lou in her dress Clarice made of curtain net; her father Joseph; Lou's half-sister Amy, told not to smile because she had had her teeth out; Merv's brother Doug (Lou Smith)

Above: The Smith family: Kevin, Lorraine, Roger, Merv, Veronica, Lou and Dawson (Lou Smith)

Left: Lou with her baby son Dawson at Rosetta (Lou Smith)

started to build a house. They had to wait two years for roofing iron from Japan – 'The Japs got even with us!' – but they built a happy family home. Five more children were born: Rodney who sadly died at birth, Veronica, Dawson, Roger and Kevin. Lou's sister Joy married a member of a strict religious sect and was immersed in domesticity, bearing, raising, feeding and clothing nine children.

Lou enjoyed life at Rosetta. The neighbours were friendly, and they all used to go for picnics, or get up impromptu square dances at home. Lou became involved in community activities, and found she was a natural leader. She helped build a preschool, was president of Parents and Friends groups at her children's schools, and was busy with church activities. For some years Merv's mother lived with them. She was an excellent cook, said Lou appreciatively – 'she knew how to make a meal out of practically nothing'. Merv moved to work as state secretary of the Returned Services League, a job at which he excelled. He was awarded the OAM for his services. But life was not always easy. The war had changed Merv, as it did so many people. Before it he was a gentle man who could not kill even an unwanted kitten, but after the horrors of war his nerves were bad. With five children, money was tight, and every penny counted. Because of a misunderstanding, Merv resigned from the RSL and after a period of unemployment – 'horrendous' – took another job where he was not happy.

Lou and Merv had always loved South Arm, at the entrance to the Derwent. Lou first went there when she was about ten, when her sister took her on a Cadburys' employees' picnic. 'We never had much, and it was a magic day.' After the honeymoon at nearby Opossum Bay, Lou and Merv thought they would like to retire there. In the late 1960s the bank manager advised them to buy, since land values were about to rise, so they bought a block close to the beach with a magnificent view across the river to Hobart and Mount Wellington. They worked at 'the Tote' (betting agency) to raise the money, built a house, and moved there in 1971.

Everyone loved Opossum Bay, with its beautiful views and its close and friendly community. Lou became a leader there, too. She was determined to restore the old hall, which was in a terrible state, so infested with vermin that badminton players had to stamp their feet to scare off rats and mice before they could start. Lou led moves to raise money for renovations, including a highly successful nude calendar by the community's older ladies – though Lou did not pose herself. Merv retired, and the children married and produced grandchildren, three of them loving Opossum Bay so much that they live there themselves. Merv died in 2005, but Lou still lives in her beloved house, supported by her five children, twelve grandchildren and nine great-grandchildren. At 90 she attended meetings of the local community group, her garden group, Probus, church, dancing and creative writing. She served up a delicious home-made lunch, with peas from her garden and stewed apricots from her tree, which she froze in bulk for use during the year. Lou liked the idea of a projected development, a golf course with a walking path and cycleway round the coast. When she

Lou and Merv enjoying a joke (Lou Smith)

Lou outside the church in Pembroke where her great-grandfather Edward was baptised (Lou Smith)

heard protesters claiming that 90 per cent of the small community opposed it, she went into action. She circulated a petition in favour of the development, gained 400 signatures, and presented it to the local council. The development went ahead. Maria Riseley would be proud of her great-granddaughter, still dynamic at ninety.

IN MIDDLE AGE Lou developed another interest. Once when she and Merv were going to a function at government house, her father said, 'You might see a painting of your great-grandfather there, because he was acting governor'. Merv said, 'Rubbish', recalled Lou. 'That's the wealthy Lords from Sandy Bay. You're nothing to do with them.' But Lou was curious, and joined a family history group. 'I thought, I'll find out what's behind it.' And she did, with the whole Lord and Riseley story appearing. The family was fascinated, and she and Merv visited England and Wales, where they were shown over Orielton. However, it was Maria with whom Lou felt the strongest bond, and she felt Maria's example gave her strength. 'I thought, if Maria could put up with what she had to put up with, I can do this.'

Lou's children also became fascinated with the family history, and continue the research. Once Lou's son Kevin said to her, 'I saw the old girl's home on the internet' – meaning Maria and The Priory, which had been turned into accommodation. Lou and her son, daughter-in-law and grandsons went to stay. There were stories that a ghost of a woman haunted the house. Marjorie Brennan, who lived at The Priory in the 1970s, once saw a ghostly old lady sitting on a chair in the drawing room. She felt the presence so strongly she wanted to throw out the chair.[7] In the house, Lou was sure her great-grandmother Maria was near her. 'I felt she was a friendly presence, a spirit rather than a ghost.' Kevin too was sure he saw

Maria's ghost, and managed to capture it in a photograph. It showed, said Lou, 'a shadow image of Maria's face in profile on the side of the mirror, holding an old candlestick with a lit candle. The sleeve of her dress was lace and she was reaching out towards me. Although we could sense her presence at the time we were unable to see her'.

THERE ARE OBVIOUS SIMILARITIES between Maria Riseley and her great-granddaughter Lou Smith. Both were intelligent, capable and determined. Both had limited formal education, and a fairly tough childhood in a large family. Both overcame hardships and succeeded. But life provided them with different opportunities. Lou's upbringing with family and church emphasising high principles meant she stayed on the right side of the law and of society's expectations, and she also had a much happier marriage. Maria's husband offered her the chance to succeed in business, but his attitude and removal of her children meant she was denied much of the warm, supportive family life Lou cherished. In old age their stories came back in parallel, however; both pillars of their communities, assisting others, living long and – certainly in Lou's case, possibly in Maria's – contented lives.

Lou's ninetieth birthday was celebrated in 2014 at the South Arm hall. The 150 guests included all her 44 descendants, some not yet born. Lou was determined that her great-grandmother Maria Lord would be part of the celebrations, and her granddaughter played two songs written for Maria by Alexander Laing in the mid-nineteenth century: a fitting commemoration and continuation of the saga of the Riseley–Lord family in Australia.

Sadly, Lou died shortly afterwards, but her indomitable spirit lives on in her large family.

Louisa Smith nee Lord, great-granddaughter of Maria and Edward, at her home at Opossum Bay
(Alison Alexander)

APPENDIX 1:
ITEMS MARIA RISELEY WAS FOUND GUILTY OF STEALING

ITEM/S	VALUE
2 gowns	£2/5/–
1 petticoat	8/–
3 yards muslin	5/–
1 pair stays	2/–
1 bonnet	1/–
1 apron	2/–
1 pair stockings	1/–
2 caps	1/–
3 pairs sleeves	3/–
11 handkerchiefs	£1/2/–
9 yards lace	9/–
1 lid of a box	1/–
16 yards calico	£1/14/–
1 shift	5/–
2 pairs sleeves	2/–
1 yard quilting	1/–
2 yards dowlas (coarse sheeting)	1/–
1 yard linen	2/–
5 linen doyleys	2/6
1 pair gloves	1/–
24 yards ribbon	6/–
30 yards galloon (trimming)	2/6
1 knife	2/–
1 box	6d
1 glass	6d
2 watch strings	2/–
3 earrings	1/6
3 bottles	3/–
3 tablecloths	15/–
5 napkins	10/–
1 pair breeches	2/–
1 pair window curtains	£2/–/–
2 tassells	2/–
3 yards linen	13/–
3 linen doyleys	1/–

(a yard is roughly a metre; twenty shillings or 20/– make a pound, £1)

APPENDIX 2:
THE LORDS' MAIN PROPERTIES

EDWARD LORD owned, leased, bought, sold and exchanged dozens pieces of land. His first grant of 100 acres was beside the Hobart Rivulet in today's South Hobart. He exchanged this for land in Sandy Bay. Macquarie granted Lord 500 acres bounded north and east by the Derwent, perhaps on the later Domain.[1] What happened to these pieces of land is not clear; there was no register of transactions.

Ingle Hall's land was granted to John Ingle, but Edward Lord either lived or had his shop there before he left Hobart in 1811.[2] Ingle planned to leave Hobart by 1816 at the latest and it is unlikely that he built a large house. The house later known as Ingle Hall was first mentioned by contemporaries in 1816, as the Lords'. It seems most likely that Edward Lord built this grand house on his return in 1814. The Lords lived there until 1823. From 1824 businessman Richard Lewis rented it, in 1828 holding the licence for a pub, The Leek, probably in the house.[3] In 1831 Edward Lord passed the house to John Ingle as part of his debt, and in 1884 the Ingle estate sold the house to businessman J.C.E. Knight. Tenants included Lewis until 1846, the Hutchins School (1846–49) and many landladies, one naming it Ingle Hall in 1872. It was mostly used as a superior boarding-house or coffee palace, but was also an Anglican youth club and a commercial school. For sale in 1934, it was leased by lawyers and insurance agents. In 1949 the government bought it, planning to demolish it and erect an office block, but this fell through and it was used for offices and the Lady Clark children's library. In 1962 the *Mercury*, next door, bought the house, later establishing its Print Museum there. When the *Mercury* moved in 2014, Detached Cultural Organisation bought both buildings to form an arts centre.[4]

Edward Lord established **Orielton Park** near Sorell in 1814. It was excellent country for sheep and wheat, though its water supply was unsure. In 1833 Edward passed it to his brother John in part payment of his debt. Owen's agent Goldie probably built a two-storey sandstone house there in the 1830s. Heavily mortgaged, Orielton was let to tenant farmers. In 1881 the mortgagees sold it to Alfred Parker, who sold it to Launceston businessman A. Hart. In 1907 fire destroyed the top storey of the homestead, but the lower storey was repaired. The house had a succession of owners, and in 2014 it had little land.[5]

In 1821 Edward Lord established his 14,000-acre property **Lawrenny** on the River Derwent at Ouse. After his death in 1859 it was run by trustees, who in 1882 sold it to Joseph Clarke, a Melbourne butcher. In 1896 Henry Brock bought 'the finest agricultural and pastoral estate in the colony', and the family made it famous throughout the world for wool, according to the *Examiner* (which shows what the Lords could have done). Presumably it was the Brocks who built its magnificent two-storey mansion. After the Second World War, the government acquired the land for soldier settlement. Since then a series of private individuals has owned the house. The most recent owners restored the house and established a superb garden.[6]

APPENDIX 3:
FAMILY TREE FOR EDWARD LORD AND MARIA RISELEY

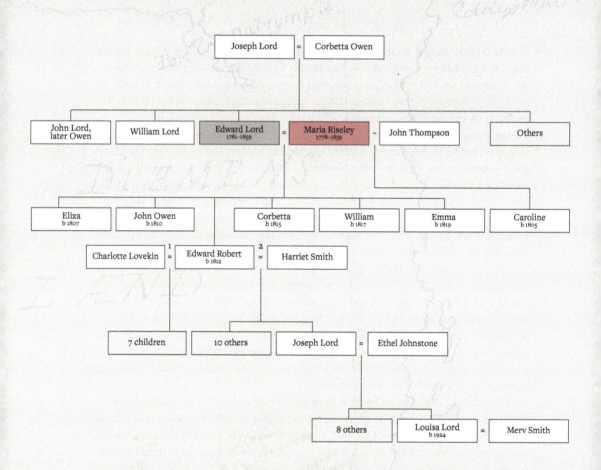

ENDNOTES

Abbreviations

ADB	*Australian Dictionary of Biography*
CC	*Cornwall Chronicle*
HRA	*Historical Records of Australia*
HTC	*Hobart Town Courier*
LA	*Launceston Advertiser*
MP	*Morning Post*
NLA	National Library of Australia
SG	*Sydney Gazette*
SLV	State Library of Victoria
SLNSW	State Library of New South Wales
TAHO	Tasmanian Archive and Heritage Office

Introduction

1. J.P. Fawkner, *Reminiscences of early Hobart Town*, Malvern, 2007, pp. 47–8.
2. John West, *The History of Tasmania*, London, 1852, reprinted Sydney, 1971, p. 32.
3. West, p. 69; ML, Wentworth Papers, W. Wentworth to D. Wentworth, 9 April 1816.

1. Edward Lord goes to Australia

1. http://www.historyofparliament online.org/volume/1790-1820/ member/owen-sir-hugh-1782-1809, 26 June 2013; Dillwyn Miles, 'Lord of Orielton, 1781–1859', *The journal of the Pembrokeshire Historical Society*, no. 14, 2005, p. 21; *Berrow's Worcester Journal*, 31 Mar 1831.
2. *Oracle*, 3 June 1794; R.L. Howell, 'The Pembroke Yeomanry', *The Pembroke Historian*, no. 2, 1966, pp. 75–7.
3. NLA MS 9789, Rienits, 'Edward Lord: the first tycoon of Van Diemen's Land', ch. 1, p. 18; *MP*, 11 Feb 1861; information from Eton archivist Eleanor Cracknell.
4. John Currey (ed.), *Records of the Port Phillip Expedition*, vol. 2, Melbourne, 1990, p. 16.
5. Marjorie Tipping, *Convicts unbound*, Melbourne, 1988, p. 49; *HRA* 3, 1, pp. 24, 26, 230.
6. Barbara Hamilton-Arnold (ed.), *Letters and Papers of G.P. Harris*, Sorrento, 1994, pp. 26–7, 21–2.
7. Hamilton-Arnold, pp. 20–2, 27; information from Pam Titherley; A.W.H. Humphrey, *A voyage to Port Phillip and Van Diemen's Land*, Malvern, 2008, pp. 25–31, 35–41.
8. Hamilton-Arnold, pp. 22, 30–1, 81; Humphrey, pp. 37–8.
9. Hamilton-Arnold, pp. 45–6.
10. Humphrey, pp. 35, 40–1; Hamilton-Arnold, p. 46.
11. N.L. Pateshall, *A Short Account of a Voyage Round the Globe*, Melbourne, 1980, p. 24; Humphrey, p. 47; *Age*, 7 June 1862.
12. Hamilton-Arnold, p. 47.
13. Humphrey, p. 54; Robert Knopwood (ed. Mary Nicholls), *The diary of the Reverend Robert Knopwood*, Hobart, 1977, pp. 26–31; Hamilton-Arnold, pp. 49–50.
14. J.H. Tuckey, *A voyage to establish a colony at Port Philip*, London, 1805, p. 13; SLV, 3661.1B, p. 12, 3661.2, pp. 4–5, 54; SLV, MS 8695, Fawkner, 'Reminiscences', p. 5, 42–3; Hamilton-Arnold, p. 25; Knopwood, p. 34; Currey, *Records...*, vol. 3, pp. 38, 120.
15. Knopwood, p. 38; Hamilton-Arnold, p. 50.
16. Hamilton-Arnold, p. 64; *HRA* 3, 1, pp. 38–40, 53; Tuckey, p. 190; Pateshall, p. 32.

2. Founding Hobart Town

1. Knopwood, pp. 40–2; Humphrey, p. 5; Hamilton-Arnold, pp. 58–9.
2. Humphrey, pp. 65–7.
3. *HRA* 3, 1, pp. 221–7; Harris, p. 61.
4. *HRA* 3, 5, pp. 134–54.
5. NLA 1887951, Report from the Select Committee on Transportation 1812, Appendix, p. 77.
6. Hamilton-Arnold, p. 60.
7. Fawkner, *Reminiscences*, p. 20; Fawkner, 'Reminiscences', p. 17; *HRA* 1, 3, pp. 258–9.
8. Knopwood, pp. 44, 48, 51.
9. Knopwood, pp. 63, 64, 69.
10. A.G.L. Shaw, 'Some officials of early Van Diemen's Land', *THRAPP* 14/4, 1967, p. 133; Benjamin Bensley, *Lost and found*, London, 1859, p. 149.
11. Peter Benson Walker, *All that we inherit*, Hobart, 1968, p. 139; Fawkner, *Reminiscences*, pp. 72–3.
12. TAHO NS395 [Thomas Keston], 'Secret memoirs', p. 116.
13. West, p. 36; Humphrey, pp. 82, 87–8; Knopwood, p. 54.
14. *Ipswich Journal*, 18 Aug 1804; Humphrey, pp. 82, 91.
15. Hamilton-Arnold, p. 65.
16. Humphrey pp. 91–2.
17. Humphrey, p. 92; *HRA* 3, 1, p. 250.
18. Hamilton-Arnold, p. 66; Humphrey, p. 92.
19. Knopwood, pp. 54, 77–8, 63.
20. Knopwood, pp. 59, 62.
21. Knopwood, p. 688.
22. Knopwood, p. 73; Fawkner, *Reminiscences*, p. 49.
23. Knopwood, pp. 74–7.
24. *HRA* 3, 1, pp. 322–3; Fawkner, *Reminiscences*, p. 46.
25. MS9789, fn 36, ch. 3, no page number. Rienits notes Edward Lord's death certificate was endorsed 'Asthma, 50 years'.
26. Anne-Maree Whitaker, *Joseph Foveaux*, Sydney, 2000, p. 75.
27. Knopwood, p. 78; *SG*, 21 April 1805; Fawkner, *Reminiscences*, p. 49.

3. Obscure beginnings

1. Bedfordshire county records, http://www.bedfordshire.gov. uk/CommunityAndLiving/ ArchivesAndRecordOffice/ SearchOurCatalogues.aspx, 26 June 2014: many mentions, e.g. AD904, GK56/5, L22/17, P100/6/22–23, OR1276, HSA1668/W/13.
2. Huntingdon County Archives, Spaldwick Baptisms Register, Hannah Maria Risely, 20 Dec 1778; Spaldwick, Molesworth and Catworth baptism registers 1779–1795.
3. Jessie Wagner, *John and Sophia Riseley*, Claremont, ND, p. 12.
4. Huntingdon County Archives, Churchwarden's Account Book for Spaldwick Church, 1743–1896, HP79/5/1, payments to Mr R. Riseley, April 1777–Mar 1796.
5. Huntingdonshire marriage index: Charlotte Risely 1801, Nancy Risely 1804, Sarah Riseley 1808.
6. *London Gazette*, 17 July 1892.
7. National Archives, Kew, ASSI 31/10.
8. Information from Louisa Smith.
9. *MP*, 12, 13 Aug 1802.
10. National Archives, Kew, ASSI 94/1537 no 45; ASSI 31/10, Surrey Summer Assizes 1802.

331

11 The Committee, *The Third Report of the Committee for the Society for the Improvement of Prison Discipline*, London, 1821, pp. 60–1; information from Justine Pearson, Surrey History Centre.
12 E. Guilford, 'Morgan, Molly', *ADB* vol. 2, p. 259.
13 *Hampshire Telegraph*, 7, 14 Nov 1803; *Bury and Norwich Post*, 9 Nov 1803; *MP*, 15 Nov 1803.
14 http://www.jenwilletts.com/convict_ship_experiment_1804.htm, 12 Sep 2014.
15 C. Bateson, *The Convict Ships*, Sydney, 1983, p. 169.
16 *Hampshire Telegraph*, 12, 19 Dec 1803; *MP*, 16 Dec 1803, 4 Jan 1804; *Bury and Norwich Post*, 21 Dec 1803; *Ipswich Journal*, 31 Dec 1803.
17 Bateson, p. 169; *SG*, 24 June, 1, 22 July 1804.
18 NLA 1887951, p. 109.
19 Ibid, pp. 32–3, 52–3, 55.
20 *SG*, 19 June 1803, 1 April 1804, 9 Dec 1805; SLNSW, V1805/1505/1A Thompson Carolina.
21 Fawkner, *Reminiscences*, pp. 47–8.
22 SLNSW, V1805/1505/1A Thompson Carolina.
23 ML A2015, p. 502, King to Collins, 26 Sep 1805.
24 Fawkner, *Reminiscences*, pp. 47–8.
25 ML A2015, p. 515, King to Collins, 24 Dec 1805.
26 *SG*, 29 Sep, 6 Oct, 1 Dec 1805; Knopwood, p. 96.

4. **Famine Years**
1 Fawkner, *Reminiscences*, p. 50.
2 Hamilton-Arnold, pp. 72–3, 81–2.
3 SLV, 3661.2, vol. 2, p. 44.
4 *HRA* 3, 1, pp. 324–30; Fawkner, *Reminiscences*, pp. 67, 31–2, 55; Knopwood, p. 94.
5 Knopwood, pp. 88, 117; Hamilton-Arnold, p. 85, 95.
6 NLA 1887951, p. 80.
7 TAHO, PRO CO201/65.
8 L. Robson, *A history of Tasmania*, vol. 1, Melbourne, 1983, p. 58; Knopwood, pp. 110, 112.
9 Utas Royal Society Collection, RS90/1, 1b, 5(1), James Belbin's pocket book 1808–1810, list of ships 1809, 4, 20 Feb; Knopwood, p. 114; Hamilton-Arnold, p. 65.
10 Fawkner, *Reminiscences*, p. 47.
11 Whitaker, p. 43.
12 Fawkner, *Reminiscences*, pp. 47–8.
13 TAHO AF394/1/10; TAHO LSD355/1/8, p. 14.
14 Fawkner, *Reminiscences*, pp. 50–2.
15 *SG*, 30 Mar 1806; Fawkner, *Reminiscences*, pp. 52, 48.
16 Fawkner, *Reminiscences*, p. 56.
17 *HRA* 1, 7, p. 443.
18 Fawkner, *Reminiscences*, p. 48.
19 Knopwood, pp. 128–9.
20 Fawkner, *Reminiscences*, pp. 68–9.
21 Knopwood, pp. 147–8, 130, 143.
22 Knopwood, p. 256.
22 *HRA* 3, 1, pp. 386–9; Knopwood, p. 130.
23 John Currey, *David Collins*, Melbourne, 2000, p. 260; John Earnshaw (ed.), 'Select Letters of Janes Grove', *THRAPP* 8/2, 1959, p. 38.
24 Hamilton-Arnold, p. 86.
25 Walker, *All that we inherit*, p. 146; James Backhouse, *A narrative of a visit to the Australian colonies*, London, 1843, pp. 212–3.
26 NLA 1887951, p. 79.
27 Anonymous, 'Account of the Game in Van Diemen's Land', *The Sporting Magazine* ..., vol. 31, London, 1808, pp. 105–8 (thanks to David Woodward).
28 Fawkner, *Reminiscences*, p. 64; Knopwood, pp. 152–3.
29 Knopwood, p. 140; Irene Schaffer, *Land musters, stock returns and lists*, Hobart, 1991, p. 243.
30 Knopwood, pp. 136–7.
31 Fawkner, *Reminiscences*, p. 41.
32 Knopwood, p. 79; ML MSS 700, D. Collins to his mother, 2 Sep 1807.
33 Knopwood, pp. 126, 145; Hamilton-Arnold, p. 98; NLA 1887951, pp. 78–9.
34 *HRA*, 3, 1, pp. 346–7, 370, 500–1.
35 Fawkner, *Reminiscences*, pp. 72, 75; Knopwood, p. 139.

5. **Marriage**
1 *HRA* 3, 1, pp. 245–6, 394, 562, 564, 577, 399, 403–4, 420.
2 Fawkner, *Reminiscences*, p. 84; SLV, 3661.2, p. 42; NS395, pp. 123–4.
3 SLV, MS 6501, Maum letter, 22 Jan 1808.
4 NS395, p. 108.
5 NS395, pp. 108–115.
6 Fawkner, *Reminiscences*, pp. 82, 96; SLV, 3661.6, p. 2; NSW Colonial Secretary's Papers, image 801; PRO CO201/65, f 233.
7 ML, CY reel 178, Safe 1/51, images 925–7.
8 Anne Salmon, *Bligh: William Bligh in the South Seas*, Auckland, 2011, p. 460; John Ritchie, *Lachlan Macquarie*, Melbourne, 1986, pp. 102–4.
9 Knopwood, pp. 155–6.
10 Hamilton-Arnold, p. 97; Currey, *Collins*, p. 259.
11 *HRA*, 3, 1, pp. 396–8; *HRA* 1, 6, pp. 565–7; Knopwood, p. 158; *SG*, 22 May 1808.
12 Whitaker, pp. 2, 5–6; *SG*, 25 Sep 1808; *HRA* 1, 7, pp. 128–9.
13 Whitaker, p. 2; *SG*, 25 Sep 1808; *HRA* 1, 7, pp. 128–9.
14 TAHO, RGD36/1/1, no. 24, 8 Oct 1808.

6. **Strife in 1809**
1 *HRA* 3, 1, pp. 422–3; *HRA* 1, 7, pp. 129, 329.
2 'Collins, David', *ADB* vol. 1, pp. 236–40.
3 Rex and Thea Rienits, 'Bligh at the Derwent', *THRAPP* 11/3, 1963, p. 115.
4 Hamilton-Arnold, p. 111.
5 Hamilton-Arnold, p. 111; TAHO CON40/1/7, p. 5.
6 Currey, *Collins*, p. 270; Hamilton-Arnold, pp. 112–3.
7 Hamilton-Arnold, pp. 109, 129.
8 Hamilton-Arnold, pp. 48, 67, 108, 113–4, 127–8.
9 Hamilton-Arnold, pp. 110, 114–5; *HRA* 3, 1, p. 416.
10 Hamilton-Arnold, pp. 111, 127–31; *HRA* 3, 1, p. 444.
11 ML, MS 62, pp. 19–35.
12 Utas, Belbin pocket book, 28 Sep, 3, 26 Oct 1809.
13 NS395, pp.123–5.
14 Fawkner, *Reminiscences*, pp. 89–90.

15 *HRA* 1, 7, p. 125; Fawkner, *Reminiscences*, pp. 85–86; Hamilton-Arnold, p. 125; Belbin pocket book, 29 Mar 1809.
16 *HRA* 1, 7, pp. 125, 129.
17 *HRA* 1, 7, pp. 125–6, 128–9.
18 Currey, *Collins*, p. 288.
19 *HRA* 1, 7, pp. 126, 130; Hamilton-Arnold, p. 125; Rienits, 'Bligh', p. 114.
20 NS395, p. 105.
21 *HRA* 1, 7, pp. 126, 128, 130, 158; Belbin, pp. 3–4.
22 Hamilton-Arnold, pp. 125, 127; Rienits, 'Bligh', p. 117; *HRA* 1, 7, pp. 127, 153–4.
23 *HRA* 1, 7, pp. 127, 155–6, 159–60, 164, 171, 175.
24 NS395, p. 106.
25 *HRA* 1, 7, pp. 161, 172, 175; NS395, pp. 105–6; Rienits, 'Bligh', pp. 119–20.
26 Rienits, 'Bligh', pp. 120–4.
27 Currey, *Collins*, p. 295.

7. Dramatic times for the Lord family

1 http://www.historyofparliament online.org/volume/1790-1820/ member/owen-sir-hugh-1782-1809, 12 June 2014, biography of Hugh Owen MP; Nannette Pearce, 'Your Life in the county', April 1996, http://www.cenquest.co.uk/Bas%20 Gaz/O(FP).htm, 12 June 2014; *Morning Chronicle*, 14 Aug 1809; *MP*, 19 Aug 1809, 10 May 1810.
2 TAHO NS32/1/1, April 1810 (baptism).
3 *HRA* 1, 7, pp. 33, 77, 169, 221; *HRA* 1, 6, p. 643.
4 *HRA* 1, 7, p. 253; Fawkner, *Reminiscences*, pp. 95–6; Currey, *Collins*, p. 300.
5 *HRA* 1, 7, p. 288; *SG*, 21 April 1810.
6 House of Commons Select Committee of Transportation, 1812, p. 78; SLV, 3661.2, vol. 1, p. 6.
7 *HRA* 1, 7, p. 288; NS395, p. 118.
8 SLNSW, NRS 936, 4/3490A, p. 70.
9 Currey, *Collins*, p. 358.
10 *HRA*, 1, 7, pp. 288–91.
11 *HRA* 1, 7, pp. 289–91, 346; *HRA* 3, 1, pp. 451–2.
12 *HRA*, 3, 1, p. 451; Currey, *Collins*, pp. 305–6, 310, 318.
13 Fawkner, *Reminiscences*, p. 95.
14 *HRA* 3, 1, pp. 439–41, 452.
15 NS395, pp. 119–20; *Mercury*, 19 Jan 1911.
16 NS395, pp. 123–4.
17 *HRA* 3, 4, pp. 721–4, 746; *CT*, 16 Nov 1831.
18 ML, DLADD 282/6, M. Bowden to E. Lord, 5 June 1811.
19 *HRA* 3, 1, p. 452; *HRA* pp. 1, 7, 358.
20 *HRA* 3, 1, p. 454; *HRA* 1, 7, p. 358; SLNSW NRS 936, 4/3490A p. 107.
21 *HRA* 1, 7, p. 261, 346, 358–9; *HRA* 3, 1, p. 455; NSW NRS 936, 4/3491 pp. 3–4.
22 Utas, 'Report on the Historical Manuscripts of Tasmania', no. 6. 1967, p. 36.
23 NLA 1887951, p. 80; DLADD 282/6.
24 'Ship News' in *SG*, 1 Mar–1 Oct 1811 for scarcity of ships; *SG*, 11 May, 29 June 1811; ML A772, p. 32, Gov. Macquarie's memorandum, 16 June 1811.
25 DLADD 282/6.
26 *HRA* 1, 7, pp. 390, 442–5.
27 SLNSW NRS 935, 4/3490D, p.143; NRS 897, 4/1724, pp. 30–1; NRS 935, 4/3491, p. 8.
28 *SG*, 17 Aug 1811; ML A752, p. 95. ML dates this document as 1812, but Lord was not in Sydney then.
29 *HRA* 1, 7, p. 357; *SG*, 28 Sep 1811; *The Times*, 5, 11 May 1812; *Caledonian Mercury*, 7 May 1812; *Morning Chronicle*, 1 May 1812; *York Herald*, 9 May 1812.
30 Whitaker, p. 79.
31 PRO CO201/155, f. 486; *Hampshire Telegraph*, 25 Sep 1809; *MP*, 10 May 1810; *Caledonian Mercury*, 7, 12 Nov 1812.
32 *HRA* 1, 8, pp. 160, 318, 644–5; *HRA* 1, 11, p. 236; T. Rienits, 'Lord, Edward', *ADB* vol. 2, pp. 127–8.
33 NLA Rienits, 'Edward Lord', ch. 1, p. 9; PRO CO201/155 f 485.
34 Select Committee on Transportation 1812, pp. 78–81.
35 http://www.oldbaileyonline. org/browse.jsp?id=t18120916-84-defend673&div=t18120916-84#highlight 23 Dec 2014.
36 *HRA* 1, 11, p. 237.
37 PRO CO201/102, f. 116; *SG*, 3 April 1813.
38 PRO CO201/102 f. 116 ff; *SG*, 9 Jan 1813, reporting the only arrival of a ship from England between 31 Oct and 6 Feb, when Davey sailed for Hobart.
39 SLV MS 10913, pp. 29–31.
40 MS 10913, p. 97.
41 *SG*, 4 Jan, 8 Feb, 17 Oct 1812; SLNSW NRS 897, 4/1727, pp. 94–5.
42 *SG*, 3 April, 28 Aug 1813.
43 *SG*, 10 April 1813.
44 *SG*, 10 April, 5 June 1813, 1 Jan 1814; SLNSW NRS 935, 4/3491, pp. 434–5.
45 *HRA* 1, 7, pp. 725–6; *HRA*, 1, 8, pp. 160, 318, 644–5.
46 *SG*, 27 Sep 1822, 10 July, 4 Sep 1813, 29 Jan, 5 Feb 1814; SLNSW NRS 937, 4/3493, pp. 41, 46, 96–8.

8. Interlude: scandal in government house

1 ML, DLADD 282/6.
2 Journal of Alexander Huey, *The Garrison Gazette*, Summer 2009–10, http://73rdregiment.tripod.com/ sitebuildercontent/sitebuilderfiles/ ggsummer0910.pdf 26 Dec 2014.
3 *HRA*, 1, 7, pp. 261, 328, 358, 710; *HRA* 3, 1, pp. 443–8.
4 *SG*, 1 Sep 1810; Hamilton-Arnold, pp. 137–8.
5 SLNSW NRS 4/3490A, pp. 107–9; 4/3492 pp. 130–1.
6 ML, DLADD 282/6; SLV MS 10913, page number illegible but after p. 54, 8 Feb 1811; SLNSW NRS 936, reel 6003, pp. 139–41, 178–80; NRS 935, reel 6002, pp. 10, 27, 56, 64, 76, 119, 125, 132, 134, 138, 140, 142.
7 SLNSW NRS 4/3491, pp. 146–8.
8 NS395, pp. 129–30.
9 ML DLADD 282/6.
10 SLNSW NRS 4/3492, p. 95; NS395, p. 137.
11 NS395, pp. 130, 134; *HRA* 3, 1, p. 484.
12 Henry Melville, *The history of Van Diemen's Land*, Sydney, 1965, pp. 14–5.
13 NS395 pp. 133–4; ML DLADD 282/6.
14 NS395, pp. 145–6; *SG*, 10 Aug 1811; SLNSW NRS 936, 4/3492, p. 30.
15 Charles James, *A collection of the charges, opinions, and sentences of general courts*, London, 1820, p. 583.

16 *HRA*, 3, 1, p. 370; ML DLADD 282/6.
17 Lachlan Macquarie, *Journals of his tours ...*, Sydney, 1979, pp. 56–61, 78; *HRA* 3, 1, pp. 465, 478.
18 *HRA*, 3, 1, p. 475.
19 Knopwood, pp. 180; *HRA* 3, 2, pp. 114, 579; Fawkner, 'Reminiscences', p. 51. SLNSW NRS 898, 4/433, p. 26; ML A314, p. 69.
20 Knopwood, p. 218; *HRA* 3, 2, p. 24; ML NRS 898 special bundles 1794–1825, image 813, no 32; image 814, no 33; 'Kent, Thomas', *ADB*, vol. 2, pp. 44–6.
21 *CT*, 1 June 1827, 6 Nov 1829.
22 *SG*, 25 Sep 1830; *Sydney Monitor*, 9 Oct 1830, 31 Mar 1832.
23 SLNSW 4/1729, pp. 353–6; *SG*, 6 July 1811, 15 Feb 1812.
24 J.W. Beattie, *Glimpses of ... the early Tasmanian governors*, Hobart, 1904, pp. 20–1; *HRA* 3, 1, p. 480.
25 *HRA* 3, 1, pp. 475–7; Beattie, pp. 20–1; *SG*, 27 July 1816; *HTG*, 3 May 1817, 19 May 1821, 24 May 1823; SLV MS 10913, p. 97.
26 *HRA* 3, 2, pp. 1–2, 52–4; *HRA* 1, 8, pp. 243, 460.
27 SLNSW NRS 4/1729, pp. 109–49, 161–88; *HRA* 1, 8, p. 460.
28 Knopwood, pp. 175–6; *SG*, 10 Feb 1816; http://www.arnistonalive.org.za/uploads/downloads/Info/The%20Shipwreck%20of%20the%20Arniston.pdf 26 Dec 2014.
29 *HTG*, 8 June 1816; *Gentleman's Magazine*, 24 Oct 1815, p. 636; *HRA* 1, 8, p. 460.
30 *Caledonian Mercury*, 29 Nov 1852.

9. Yet another inadequate governor

1 Fawkner, 'Reminicesnces', p. 47; Beattie, p. 22; *HRA* 1, 8, p. 556.
2 P. Eldershaw, 'Davey, Thomas', *ADB* vol. 1, pp. 288–9; TAHO, Thomas Davey correspondence file.
3 Eldershaw, 'Davey'; TAHO CSO1/1/334/7619, M. Davey to Bathurst; Beattie, pp. 22–3.
4 CSO1/1/334/7619; Beattie, p. 22; http://www.nationalarchives.gov.uk/trafalgarancestors/results.asp, 14 April 2013; http://www.historyofparliamentonline.org/volume/1790-1820/member/ryder-hon-dudley-1762-1847, 14 April 2013.
5 TAHO, Thomas Davey correspondence file; CSO1/1/334/7619; PRO CO201/65/126; Beattie, p. 22; *Lancaster Gazette*, 29 Feb 1812; *HRA* 1, 8, p. 598.
6 Beattie, pp. 22–3; *HRA* 1, 7, pp. 789–90; *HRA* 3, 2, xii; Shaw, p. 133; PRO CO210/65, pp.191, 215–56; West, p. 47.
7 West, p. 47; *HRA* 1, 8, pp. 458–9.
8 *HRA* 1, 8, p. 242; *HRA* 3, 2, pp. 13–24.
9 *SG*, 13 Feb 1813; Beattie, p. 23.
10 *SG*, 10 April 1813.
11 NS395, pp. 147–8; Beattie, pp. 23–4.
12 [Edward Abbott], *Cookery for the many*, London, 1864, reprinted Hobart, 2014, pp. 280–1.
13 *HRA* 1, 8, p. 458.
14 West, p. 357.
15 John Hayes, 'Reminiscences of Early Tasmanian Life' in the author's possession; *HTG*, 24 Aug 1816.
16 West, p. 47; *HRA* 3, 2, pp. 622–3, 648–51; Eldershaw, 'Davey'.
17 *HRA* 3, 3, pp. 115, 126, 151–3, 167; *HRA* 1, 8, p. 459; Beattie, p. 24.
18 SLV, 3661.2 vol. 2, p. 85; West, pp. 47–48.
19 Fawkner, 'Reminiscences', p. 60–1; *Critic*, 3 Sep 1920; West, p. 48.
20 Knopwood, pp. 168, 179, 185, 188–9, 238, 240, 249–50.
21 *HRA* 3, 2, pp. 33–52, 609; ML A752 p. 230.
22 *HRA* 1, 8, pp. 242, 458–60; *HRA* 3, 2, pp. 141, 146–9, 633–4; Beattie p. 25; TAHO, Thomas Davey correspondence file.

10. The Lords become established

1 *HRA* 1, 11, p. 237.
2 *SG*, 16 April, 7 May, 25 June 1814, 20 May 1815, 4 May 1816.
3 Knopwood, p. 210.
4 *HTG*, 1 Mar 1817.
5 *HTG*, 22 June 1816, 18 Jan, 10 May 1817; *HRA* 3, 3, p. 582; *HRA* 3, 2, pp. 75–6; SLV MS10913, p. 116.
6 Anne McKay (ed.), *Journals of the Land Commissioners*, Hobart, 1962, p. 2; *HTG*, 15 June, 28 Sep, 5 Oct 1816.
7 *HTG*, 5 April 1817.
8 *SG*, 4 Mar 1814; Knopwood, p. 167; SLNSW NRS 937, 4/3493, pp. 96–8.
9 Knopwood, p. 181; *HRA* 1, 8, pp. 588–9; *SG*, 4 June 1814, 6 May, 2 Sep 1815.
10 Knopwood, pp. 235–7; *HTG*, 20 July 1816.
11 Knopwood, pp. 171, 174, 191.
12 ML A256 Piper Papers, p. 599.
13 TAHO NS1332/1/12, The Alexander Laing Story, p. 2.
14 SLV MS 10913, pp. 105, 13, 115, [112].
15 NS1332/1/12, p. 12.
16 *HRA* 3, 2, pp. 110, 114, 126, 152–3; *HRA* 1, 8, p. 556; ML A752 pp. 229–31.
17 ML A752 pp. 229–31; *HRA* 3, 3, p. 492; SLV MS 10913, pp. 13, 110–11.
18 *HRA* 3, 2, pp. 177–8; ML A752 p. 231.
19 *HRA* 1, 8, p. 458; *HRA* 3, 2, pp. 61–2.
20 ML A256, vol. 3, p. 31.
21 *CT*, 19 Oct 1831; *HTG*, 6 Oct 1821.
22 TAHO LSD355/1/8, p. 11; Knopwood, p. 234; Appendix 2.
23 Knopwood, pp. 175, 188, 196; *HTG*, 25 Jan 1817.
24 Knopwood, p. 231; *HTG*, 11 May 1816.
25 Knopwood, pp. 177–8.
26 Knopwood, pp. 175–6, 197–8, 239.
27 Knopwood, p. 207.
28 Knopwood, p. 229.
29 Whitaker, pp. 65, 78, 104; John Ritchie, *The Wentworths*, Melbourne 1997, p. 93
30 Knopwood, pp. 165–270 passim, especially pp. 244–5, 210, 226, 174–9.
31 Knopwood, p. 218; CON31/1/1, p. 31; *HTG*, 21 Dec 1816.
32 LMSS12/7/318.
33 Knopwood, pp. 224–5; ML A314, Lord to Broughton, 10 Feb 1816.
34 *Courier*, 20 Feb 1850; Knopwood, p. 239.
35 Schaffer, pp. 86–94.

11. Skullduggery at the Commissariat

1 Ritchie, *Macquarie*, p. 106.

2 PRO CO201/89, f. 87.
3 *HRA* 1, 6, p. 700.
4 *HRA* 3, 1, p. 17.
5 *HRA* 1, 7, pp. 468–74; Knopwood, p. 158.
6 *HRA* 3, 1, pp. 390–2, 824, 443, 452; *SG*, 9, 16 June 1810; *HRA* 1, 7, p. 389.
7 NS395, pp. 142–3; *HRA* 3, 1, p. 508.
8 *HRA* 3, 1, pp. 455–6; SLNSW NRS 936, 4/3490D pp. 139–41; NRS 936, 4/3490A, pp. 178–80; NRS 935, 4/3491, p. 27.
9 ML DLADD 282/6.
10 NS395, p. 150.
11 *HRA* pp. 3, 1, 478; *HRA* 3, 2, pp. 23–4; SLNSW NRS 936, 4/3492, pp. 56–7.
12 SLNSW NRS 897, 4/1729, pp. 181–5, 214–5; *HRA* 3, 2, p. 552.
13 *HRA* 1, 7, pp. 466–70, 608; SLNSW NRS 897, 4/1729, pp. 29–32.
14 *HRA* 3, 5, p. 99; *HRA* 3, 2, pp. 552–6; *SG*, 23 Sep 1815.
15 *HRA* 3, 2, pp. 557–8; SLNSW NRA 4/1730, pp. 402–3; *SG*, 17 Sep 1814; *Hampshire Advertiser*, 2 April 1842.
16 *HRA* 3, 2, pp. 41, 115; *HRA* 3, 3, p. 226; *HRA* 1, 9, p. 249.
17 *HRA* 3, 3, pp. 603–8; *HRA* 3, 2, pp. 115, 638–9.
18 *HRA* 1, 9, pp. 715, 762; *HRA* 3, 2, pp. 598, 625.
19 *HRA* 3, 3, p. 474.
20 *HRA*, 3, 3, pp. 474, 608–9; *HRA* 3, 2, pp. 592, 150.
21 *HRA* 3, 2, pp. 154, 156, 160, 169, 604; *SG*, 27 July 1816; *HTG*, 28 Sep 1816.
22 *HRA* 1, 9, pp. 715, 762; *HRA* 3, 2, p. 154; V. Parsons, 'Broughton, William', *ADB*, vol. 1, pp. 157–8.
23 *HRA* 3, 2, pp. 591–5, 169.
24 ML A752, pp. 229–31.
25 *HRA* 3, 2, pp. 197, 612, 627; *HRA* 3, 3, pp. 479–80.
26 Charles James, *A collection of the charges, opinions, and sentences of General Courts Martial*, London, 1820, pp. 811–3; *HRA* 3, 3, pp. 226–7, 618–9; *HTG*, 18 Jan 1817; R. Wettenhall, 'Hogan, Patrick, *ADB* vol. 1, p. 548–9; *HRA* 3, 4, pp. 693–5.
27 ML A314, CT1178; SLV MS10913, p. 106; LMSS12/7/318; Rex and Thea Rienits, 'The Broughton Case', *THRAPP* vol. 15, 1967, p. 34.

28 *HRA* 1, 9, pp. 762–4, 768–70.
29 *HRA* 3, 2, p. 592; *HRA* 1, 9, p. 770.
30 *HRA* 1, 9, pp. 762–3, 768–70; *HRA* 3, 3, p. 313.
31 *HRA* 1, 9, p. 769; *HRA* 3, 3, p. 614.
32 *HRA* 3, 3, pp. 613–5.
33 PRO CO201/89, ff 87–91.
34 *HRA* 3, 2, p. 614.
35 *HRA* 3, 2, pp. 614–5, 243, 264.
36 *HRA* 1, 9, pp. 768–72.
37 *HRA* 1, 9, pp. 764, 766–7; *HRA* 3, 2, pp. 293, 298, 304, 316, 659.
38 Knopwood, pp. 274, 276; *HRA* 3, 3, p. 353.
39 ML A314, pp. 49–50.

12. The Lords' involvement with bushrangers

1 *HRA* 3, 2, p. 195.
2 James Boyce, *Van Diemen's Land*, Melbourne, 2008, p. 77.
3 *HRA* 3, 2, p. 55.
4 *HRA* 3, 2, p. 55; *HRA* 1, 8, pp. 264–5.
5 *HRA* 3, 2, pp. 75–8.
6 NS1332/1/12, The Alexander Laing Story, p. 4.
7 *HRA* 3, 2, pp. 110, 568–70.
8 *HRA* 1, 8, pp. 567–8; *HRA* 3, 2, pp. 131; Knopwood, pp. 199–206.
9 *HRA* 3, 2, pp. 110, 113, 133–4, 136.
10 *HRA* 3, 2, p. 163.
11 *HRA* 3, 2, pp. 590, 603–4; NS1332/1/12, p. 6.
12 *HRA* 3, 2, p. 594.
13 *HTG*, 11 Jan 1817; *HRA* 3, 2, p. 644.
14 *HTG*, 5, 12 April 1817.
15 *HRA* 3, 2, pp. 194–5, 238, 257, 262–3, 276; Knopwood, pp. 257–8, 261–2.
16 *HRA* 3, 2, pp. 234, 245–6, 248–9.
17 *HRA* 3, 2, pp. 253–4; Knopwood, p. 266; NS395 p. 166.
18 *HRA* 3, 2, p. 265; Knopwood, p. 257; *HTG*, 5 July 1817.
19 NS1332/1/12, p. 5; John Hayes, 'Reminiscences'.
20 *HRA* 3, 1, pp. 555, 564; SLV, 3661.6, J. Fawkner, 'Some account of the marriage and subsequent fate of George Watts', p. 1.
21 Fawkner, 'Watts', p. 2.
22 Fawkner, 'Watts', p. 2.

23 *SG*, 4 Dec 1813; *HTG*, 17 Aug 1816, 18 Jan, 21 June 1817, 5 Oct 1816, 3 Oct 1818.
24 Knopwood, pp. 222–3.
25 *HTG*, 6 Sep, 11, 18 Oct, 13 Dec 1817; *HRA* 3, 2, p. 278; Fawkner, 'Watts', pp. 5–7.
26 *HRA* 3, 2, p. 363; NS1332/1/12, p. 11.

13. Interlude: appalling activities in the Naval Office

1 Shaw, pp. 129–41; *HRA* 1, 7, pp. 584–5; West, p. 56–7.
2 *HRA* 3, 2, pp. 173, 344, 351, 360; Shaw, p. 135.
3 Shaw, pp. 136–7; TAHO, MM128, Diary of Dr John Hudspeth, 13 Oct 1821.
4 *HRA*, 3, 2, pp. 611, 151–2, 109, 168, 178, 281–2, 613.
5 *HRA* 3, 2, pp. 23–4, 611.
6 *HTG*, 30 Aug 1817.
7 R. Wettenhall, 'Drummond, John', *ADB* vol. 1, p. 327; M. Austin, 'MacKellar, Neil', *ADB* vol. 2, p. 170; *SG*, 29 Jan, 16 Dec 1804, 5 Dec 1812.
8 *HRA* 3, 2, pp. 116, 572; *SG*, 4, 11 Feb 1815; *HRA* 1, 8, pp. 469–70.
9 Knopwood, pp. 216, 239, 266; *HTG*, 6 July 1816.
10 *HRA* 3, 2, pp. 271–2; *HTG*, 30 Aug 1817.
11 *HRA* 3, 2, pp. 272, 293–4, 630–1, *HTG*, 20 Sep 1817; SLNSW, Colonial Secretary's Papers p. 109, Campbell to Drummond, 25 Oct 1817.
12 *HTG*, 3, 24 Oct 1818, 12 June, 4 Dec 1819; Wettenhall, 'Drummond'; *SG*, 12 Feb 1820.
13 *HTG*, 24 June 1820; *Mercury*, 13 June 1862, 10 Sep 1885, 28 Dec 1896.

14. Governor Sorell

1 Beattie, p. 26.
2 *HRA* 1, 9, p. 347.
3 NS395 pp. 152–3.
4 R.M. Garvie, 'Sorell, William', *ADB*, vol. 2, p. 449; Jane Sorell, *Governor, William and Julia Sorell*, Bellerive, 1986, p. 88.
5 *Caledonian Mercury*, 4 May 1807; Garvie, 'Sorell'; *HRA* 3, 2, p. 338.

6 *London Chronicle*, 11 Dec 1788, 25 June 1767; *MP*, 7 July 1817.
7 *MP*, 7 July 1817.
8 *MP*, 7 July 1817; *Caledonian Mercury*, 23 Nov 1812.
9 Sorell, p. 88.
10 *HRA* 3, 4, p. 847; *SG*, 15 Mar 1817; *HTG*, 12 April 1817.
11 *HTG*, 26 April 1817; *HRA* 3, 2, p. 196; Knopwood never shows Lord and Davey together.
12 *HRA* 3, 2, pp. 611, 243, 304.
13 *HRA* 3, 2, p. 631; *HRA* 3, 3, p. 223.
14 Knopwood, pp. 187–8, 191; *HRA* 3, 2, pp.175, 272; *HRA* 1, 9, pp. 359, 398.
15 *HRA* 1, 9, pp. 397–8, 418; *HRA* 3, 2, pp. 199, 201; NRS 897, 4/1727, pp. 94–5; *SG*, 10 April 1813.
16 *HRA* 3, 2, pp. 205–6, 237, 629.
17 *HRA* 3, 2, pp. 206–7, 212, 214, 216–21, 629–31.
18 *HRA* 3, 2, pp. 207–8, 221–2, 237; *HTG*, 16 May 1818.
19 *HRA* 3, 2, pp. 279, 325, 329; *HRA* 3, 4, p. 746.
20 ML DLADD 292; Knopwood, p. 276.
21 ML A1399, M. Lord to W. Walker, 30 Oct 1819; *HTG*, 19 Sep 1818; *HRA* 3, 3, p. 522.
22 ML A256 vol. 3, pp. 403–5.
23 Charles Jeffreys, *Van Diemen's Land*, London, 1820; G.W. Evans, *A … description of Van Diemen's Land*, London, 1822, pp. v–ix.
24 Wilfred Hudspeth, *Profile of a Pioneer*, Hobart, ND, pp, 95–6, 99, 101.
25 Ritchie, *Macquarie*, passim and pp. 93–7.
26 NS395, pp. 153–4, 170.
27 *SG*, 21 July 1821.
28 Beattie, p. 28.
29 *HRA* 3, 2, pp. 337–9, 376–7; ML, BT 11, pp. 4742, 4740.
30 *HRA* 3, 3, pp. 220–1; *HRA* 3, 4, pp. 681–5; Knopwood, pp. 266, 299, 335, 339.
31 *HRA* 3, 4, pp. 681–5.
32 Sorell, pp. 88–90; *CT*, 21 Mar 1832, *Morning Chronicle*, 18 Mar 1837; *MP*, 8 June 1848; *Mercury*, 12 April 1864.

15: Edward Lord, entrepreneur
1 PRO CO201/146 f. 743; E.R. Henry, 'Edward Lord', THRAPP, 20/2, 1973, p. 99; Clarke and Spender, *Life lines*, Sydney, 1996, p. 152.
2 Schaffer, p. 140; Rand, p. 12.
3 LSD 406/1, Edward Lord, 12 June 1821, 7000, 3000 acres; *HRA* 3, 4, p. 338; *HRA* 3, 5, p. 571.
4 *HTG*, 6, 27 Mar 1819, 3 June 1820; Rand, p. 10; ML B425, 13 Feb 1823.
5 ML A586, p. 93; Beattie, illustration before p. 27 (no source given).
6 *HTC*, 19 July 1833; *HTG*, 3 Feb 1821, 11 Nov 1826; *CT*, 27 Jan 1835; H. Widowson, *Van Diemen's Land*, London, 1829, pp. 94–5, 105, 108.
7 Rosalie Hare, *The voyage of the Caroline*, London, 1927, pp. 130, 136.
8 *HTG*, 29 Jan, 11 Mar 1820; *CT*, 12 Jan 1827; West, p. 59; Shaffer, p. 140.
9 *HRA*, 3, 3, p. 684.
10 Rand, pp. 10, 12.
11 Widowson, pp. 94–5; *Colonial Magazine*, vol. 1, 1830, p. 184.
12 ML B425, 12 June, 2 Aug 1821, 13 Feb 1823; TAHO NS473/1/8, pp. 35–6.
13 James Ross, *The settler in Van Diemen's Land*, Melbourne, 1975, pp. 56, 61–9, 81–3.
14 *HTC*, 11 Nov 1826, 5 July 1828; West, p. 104.
15 TAHO NG14/1/1, p. 4; *HTG*, 14 Nov 1818.
16 *HTG*, 11 July 1818, 23 Mar 1822; information from Mary Ramsay.
17 Rand, p. 2; *HTG*, 22 July 1820, 16 Jan 1824; *HTC*, 17 July 1835.
18 Brian Plomley and Kristen Anne Henley, 'The sealers of Bass Strait and the Cape Barren Island Community', THRAPP, 37/2, 1990, p. 62; *HTG*, 14 Feb 1818; Naomi Parry, 'Musquito', ADB supplementary volume, 2005.
19 Nicholas Clements, *The Black War*, Brisbane, 2014, p. 69.
20 *HTG*, 23 Aug 1823.
21 Rand, p. 12.
22 *CT*, 27 Nov 1838; ML A1193, CY reel 519, p. 321; *HRA* 1, 10, pp. 661–2.
23 PRO CO201/146 f. 707 ff.
24 ML A594, CY reel 884, frame 455; SLV MS 10913, p. 144.
25 *HTG*, 18 Aug 1821, 19 Jan 1822; *SG*, 8, 29 Sep, 29 Dec 1821; *CT*, 6 April 1827.
26 ML A586, p. 99; A1351, p. 284.
27 SLV MS 10913 pp. 102, 147.
28 *HTG*, 1 Aug 1818.
29 *HRA*, 3, 3, pp. 338, 340–1.
30 LMSS322, Peter Harrisson's journal, pp. 18–29.
31 *HRA* 3, 3, p. 312.
32 *HTG*, 9 Sep 1820.
33 *HTG*, 24, 31 May 1817.
34 *HTG*, 6 July 1816, 3 May 1817, 24 Jan 1818.
35 *HTG*, 29 Mar, 26 April 1817, 2 Dec 1820, 12 May 1821; Knopwood, p. 291.
36 *HTG*, 1817–22 passim; 26 Jan 1822; *HRA* 3, 2, p. 273; Knopwood, pp. 303–4.
37 SLV MS 10913, p. 112; *HTG* 1817–22 passim, e.g. 3 April 1819.
38 *HTG*, 28 July 1821, 23 Aug 1817; *SG*, 9 Aug 1817.
39 *HTG*, 28 Feb, 11, 25 April, 16 May 1818.
40 ML A1399, E. Lord to Robinson, 22 Feb 1821; *SG*, 22 Sep 1825; *HTG*, 4, 28 April, 9 June 1821.
41 *HTG*, 13 Jan, 16, 30 June, 1 Sep, 17 Nov 1821.
42 *HTG* 14 Feb, 7 Mar 1818; Knopwood, pp. 276–7.
43 *HRA* 3, 2, pp. 310–1; *HTG* 21 Mar, 16 May 1818, 13 May 1820; SLV MS 10913, pp. 121, 124.
44 *HTG*, 12 June, 9 Oct 1819, 13 Jan, 10 Feb 1821; ML A1399, M. Lord to Eyre Lord, 1 July 1820.
45 NG14/1/1, p. 8.
46 *HTG*, 2, 23, 30 Mar, 27 April, 4 May 1822; NS473/1/8, p. 23.

16: Maria Lord, businesswoman
1 Shaffer, p. 140; Fawkner, *Reminiscences*, p.47; NG14/1/1, p. 5.
2 *HRA* 3, 3, p. 679.
3 ML A1399, M. Lord to unknown, 28 Aug 1819; to Risk, 28 Aug 1819; to Ker, 7 May [1820]; to Duncan, 14 Oct 1820.
4 ML A1399, M. Lord to Thrupp, 6 Feb 1820.
5 ML A1399, M. Lord to Jones & Riley, and W. Baker, 28 Aug 1819.

6 ML A1399, M. Lord to Sorell, ND [p. 14].
7 ML A1399, M. Lord to Baker, 20 Nov, 11 Sep 1820.
8 ML A1399, M. Lord to Walker, 14 Aug 1820; Janette Holcomb, *Early Merchant families of Sydney*, Melbourne, 2013, ch. 8.
9 ML A1399, M. Lord to Walker, 30 Oct 1819, 27 May 1820.
10 ML A1399, M. Lord to Duncan, 22 June, 1 July, 14 Oct 1820.
11 ML A1399, M. Lord to Walker, 30 Oct 1819; to Ker, 7 May 1819; *HTG*, 18 June 1824.
12 ML A1399, M. Lord to Walker, 30 Oct 1819; to Baker, 11 Sep, 20 Nov 1820.
13 ML A1399, M. Lord to Jones & Riley, 28 Aug [1819]; to Baker, 28 Aug 1819; to Walker, 30 Oct 1819; to 'Sir', 15 Jan 1820.
14 ML A1399, M. Lord to Eyre Lord, 1 July 1820.
15 ML A1399, M. Lord to Duncan, 22 June [1820]; to Hull, 10 Oct 1819; to Walker, 11 Aug 1820.
16 SLV MS 10913, p. 128.
17 P. Eldershaw, 'Wells, Thomas', *ADB* vol. 2, p. 576; C. Murray, 'Murray, Robert Lathrop', *ADB* vol. 2, p. 272; R. Barker and A. Stenning (eds), *The record of Old Westminsters*, London, 1928, vol. II, p. 678; John Alger, *Napoleon's British Visitors and Captives 1801–1815*, Westminster, 1904, p. 104.
18 The colony's only Charles Robinsons were convicts, CON41/1/34 pp. 284, 310; NS473/1/8, p. 67.
19 *HTG*, 10, 17 Feb 1821; LMSS12/1/447, E. Lord to Simpson, 29 Oct 1821.
20 *SG*, 27 Sep 1822; NS473/1/8, pp. 35, 26, 56, 66, 29, 14–15, 72, 11, 23.
21 NS473/1/8, pp. 24–5, 2–4, 38–9, 34, 33, 40, 46.
22 NS473/1/8, pp. 9, 36, 63, 66, 70, 75.
23 NS473/1/8, p. 60.
24 NS473/1/8, pp. 35–6.
25 NS473/1/8, pp. 64–5, 67, 81–2; *HTG*, 27 July 1822.
26 NS473/1/8, p. 42.
27 Rand, p. 12; SLV MS 10913 p. 10; Knopwood, pp. 313–4; *HRA* 3, 3, pp. 679–81.
28 *HRA* 3, 3, pp. 295, 680–1, 695.
29 *HRA* 3, 3, pp. 679–80; *HRA* 3, 4, pp. 5–6.
30 ML A1399, M. Lord to Hull, 13 Mar 1820; *HRA* 3, 3, pp. 669–70.
31 Lucille Andel, *Clerk of the House*, Melbourne, 1984, p. 5.
32 *HTG*, 9 Jan, 7 Aug, 4 Dec 1819, 22 Jan, 23 Sep, 11 Nov 1820, 4 May, 6 Oct 1821.
33 Clarke and Spender, p. 151; ML B293, B 294 passim e.g. 24 Oct 1815.
34 SLV MS 10913, pp. 133, 125, 103, 115, 101.
35 SLV MS 10913, p. 30.
36 *HTG*, 13 June 1818, 22 July 1820.
37 West, p. 560.
38 Information from Barry Riseley.
39 G. Walsh, 'Reibey, Mary', *ADB* vol. 2, p. 373; TAHO MS248/173–4, J. Franklin to Simpkinson, 22 Feb 1838.

17. Life outside business

1 *CT*, 30 Dec 1834; *CC*, 10 April 1844.
2 *HRA* 3, 3, p. 681; *HTG*, 25, 28 April 1821; Macquarie, *Journals*, passim.
3 *HTG*, 8, 15, 22 Dec 1821, 5 Jan 1822, 15 May 1819, 2 Feb 1822, 1 Nov, 13 Dec 1823; TAHO NS37/1/50, Bank of VDL, Register of shareholders.
4 *HRA* 3, 4, pp. 724, 735; Knopwood, p. 299.
5 ML A314, p. 49.
6 Knopwood, p. 300.
7 *HTG*, 12 June 1819; A256, Lord to Piper, 6 Dec 1819.
8 Information from Louisa Smith; *MP*, 4 Jan 1820, 17 May 1816, 25 June 1814; *Lancaster Gazette*, 10 June 1815.
9 *MP*, 11, 22 May, 17 July 1820.
10 ML AD 288/36, Lord to Treasury, 18 April 1820; Goulburn to Lord, 22 April 1820; PRO CO324/121, f. 81; http://www.historyofparliamentonline.org/volume/1820-1832/member/owen-sir-john-1776-1861, 6 June 2014.
11 *HTG*, 17 Mar 1821; TAHO, Edward Lord correspondence file; PRO CO201/111, reel 100, pp. 644–7; CO201/102 f. 116.
12 PRO CO201/102 f. 330; CO201/142, f. 118; CO201/102 f. 334; *HRA* 3, 3, pp. 30, 73.
13 ML A256, Lord to Piper, 5 Dec 1820.
14 NG14/1/1, p. 1; PRO CO210/102, f. 330.
15 ML A1399, M. Lord to Eyre Lord, [Jan 1820].
16 Clarke & Spender, p. 152.
17 NG14/1/1, p. 5; D.C. Shelton (ed.), *The Parramore Letters*, Hobart, 1993, p. 61.
18 NG14/1/1, p. 5.
19 Clarke & Spender, p. 152.
20 Knopwood, pp. 298, 301, 308, 334, 340.
21 *CT*, 20 Mar 1838.
22 CSO1/780/16657, pp. 387–8; Knopwood, 1822 passim.
23 NS473/1/8, pp. 28, 41.
24 CON40/1/7, image 241.
25 CON40/1/5, image 285.
26 CON40/1/3, image 216; CON40/1/9, image 238; CON40/1/1, image 259; CON40/1/13, image 113.
27 CON31/1/15, image 15; CON31/1/9 image 29; CON31/1/29 image 23.
28 *HTG*, 19 July 1817, 2 Oct 1819; Knopwood, p. 173; information from Louisa Smith.
29 *HRA* 3, 2, p. 237; ML, A1677/3, pp. 1119–21; Knopwood, pp. 376, 537.
30 *MP*, 24 Dec 1822.
31 ML, A1677/3, pp. 1119–21, 1139–41.
32 ML, A1339, p. 31.
33 http://www.library.mq.edu.au/digital/under/research/officers73rd.html#t, 5 June 2014; NG14/1/1, p. 1; Knopwood, p. 344.
34 Knopwood, pp. 303, 317, 342; SLV MS 10913, p. 118; Wagner, *Riseley*, p. 12.
35 *HTG* 15 May 1819, 1 Jan 1820, 28 April, 12 May 1821, 6 July, 9 Nov 1822, 16 Jan 1824.
36 TAHO, John Riseley correspondence file.
37 Fawkner, *Reminiscences*, p. 47; Knopwood, pp. 256, 255.

18. Enter Charles Rowcroft

1 Charles Rowcroft, *Confessions of an Etonian*, London, 1852, vol. 1, p. 144; C. Hadgraft & J. Horner, 'Rowcroft, Charles', *ADB* vol. 2, p. 402; information from Eton College archivist, Eleanor Cracknell.

2   HRA, 3, 4, p. 1; C. Rowcroft, *Tales of the Colonies*, London, 1843.
3   NG14/1/1, p. 1–2; HRA 3, 4, pp. 144, 413; HTG, 15 Dec 1821.
4   ML A166, CY 9280.
5   HRA 3, 4, pp. 471–3.
6   Knopwood, pp. 356–9; HTG, 27 April 1822.
7   Knopwood, 1822 passim; birthday p. 362.
8   Knopwood, pp. 364, 367.
9   G.T. Lloyd, *Thirty-three years in Tasmania and Victoria*, London, 1862, pp. 17–19.
10 Knopwood, p. 382.
11 HTG, 12 Nov 1825; Knopwood, pp. 388, 398.
12 NG14/1/1, p. 4.
13 SG, 28 June, 12 July, 30 Aug, 8 Nov 1822.
14 *The Times*, 15 Oct 1822; HTG, 2 Nov 1822.
15 HTG, 2 Nov 1822.
16 ML, DLADD288/6, 15; Knopwood, p. 373.
17 Knopwood, p. 384; HTG, 11 Jan, 31 May 1823.
18 Knopwood, pp. 372, 374.
19 Ritchie, *Macquarie*, p. 182; HTG, 24 May 1823; Knopwood, pp. 390–1.
20 http://www.historyofparliamentonline.org/volume/1820-1832/member/owen-sir-john-1776-1861, biography of Sir John Owen, 15 Feb 2014; J. R. Phillips, *Memoirs of the Ancient Family of Owen of 'Orielton', Co. Pembroke*, London, 1886; Henry Owen, *Old Pembroke Families in the ancient County Palatine of Pembroke*, London, 1902.
21 MP, 23 June 1819.
22 http://www.historyofparliamentonline.org/volume/1820-1832/member/owen-sir-john-1776-1861, 15 Feb 2014; MP, 5 May 1821, 1 July 1824; *Morning Chronicle*, 7 June 1822.
23 HRA 1, 10, pp. 235–7; HRA 1, 11, p. 235.
24 PRO CO201/146 f. 743.
25 Knopwood, pp. 210–84 passim; HTG, 3, 17 Aug 1816, 17 Jan, 27 June 1818.
26 HTG, 26 July 1823; Knopwood, pp. 393–4.
27 Rienits, 'Lord, Edward'; HTG, 26 July, 13, 20, 27 Dec 1823, 30 Jan, 29 Feb, 12 Mar 1824.
28 HTG, 9 Aug, 6 Sep 1823; Knopwood, pp. 393–6.
29 Knopwood, p. 399; HTG, 11 Oct, 8 Nov 1823, 2 Jan, 16 April, 11 June 1824, 30 July, 12 Nov 1824.
30 Thanks to Nicole Becker, one of these descendants, for sharing her research.
31 HTG 25 June, 2, 30 July, 12 Nov, 3 Dec 1824.
32 Jack Richards, *Fifteen Tasmanian Letters 1824–1852*, ND, letter 12.
33 Shelton, pp. 23, 53, 58. The clergyman was William Bedford.
34 HTG, 29 Oct 1824, 21 Jan, 4 Feb 1825; *Australian*, 27 Jan 1825.
35 HTG, 5 Nov 1824; Knopwood, p. 433.
36 Knopwood, pp. 435–6.
37 HTG, 24 Dec 1824.
38 Shelton, p. 61; HTG, 17 Dec 1824.
39 HTG, 10, 17 Dec 1825; Knopwood, pp. 436–7; Shelton, p. 61; ML A754, p. 267.
40 HTG, 24, 31 Dec 1824; Rand, p. 41; ML A754, pp. 226, 228; Knopwood, pp. 437–8.
41 HTG, 9 Sep 1825, 20 May 1826; HTC, 18 Mar 1836, 19 April 1845; *Australian*, 23 April 1844; Hadgraft and Horner.
42 Hadgraft and Horner; *The Times*, 11 Oct 1856, *Hampshire Telegraph*, 18 Oct 1856.

19. After the court case

1   HTG, 3 Mar 1827, 13 Aug 1825.
2   CT, 10 Feb 1826.
3   HTG, 1 July 1826.
4   HTC, 7 Jan 1826.
5   HTC, 5, 19 Jan 1828.
6   CC, 10 April 1844; information from Michael Ball. It is probably the Devil's Den, between the Julian Lakes and Lake Augusta. It would have been accessible on horseback in the 1820s, though 'a bit of a trek'.
7   Mrs Lord's Springs mentioned CC, 7 Dec 1839, and on modern maps.
8   CT, 16 July 1833.
9   HTG, 25 Feb 1825; CT, 9 Sep, 7 Oct 1825.
10 HTG, 2 July 1825; 7, 21 Jan, 22 April 1826; CT, 28 April, 12 May 1826, 18 May 1827.
11 Henry, 'Edward Lord', p. 100; K. Green, 'Ingle, John', ADB vol. 2, p. 3.
12 Walker, p. 143; when I visited Orielton in 2013, the gambling was well-known folklore.
13 SG, 17 Sep 1809, 4 Sep 1813, 28 June 1817; Ancestry.com: 'England, Select Births and Christenings, 1538–1975', vol. 3, p. 154.
14 1841 census, England: Class: HO107; Piece: 482; Book: 6; Civil Parish: *Down*; County: *Kent*; Enumeration District: 13; Folio: 4; Page: 3; Line: 1; GSU roll: 306875.
15 HTG, 16 Feb, 3 Mar, 22 Sep 1827.
16 Knopwood, p. 514; CSO1/241/5841; CSO1/288/6893; CON40/1/3, image 157, Ann Fry; Eustace FitzSymonds, *A looking-glass for Tasmania*, Adelaide, 1980, pp. 131–2; RGD32/1/1 no 2602; SWD24, pp. 302, 28.
17 ML A754, p. 267.
18 CT, 9 Mar 1827, 18 April 1828, 9, 16, 23 Mar 1827; HRA 3, 5, p. 653.
19 Henry, p. 103; TAHO NS37/1/51, Bank of VDL, register of shareholders, pp. 310–29.
20 HTG, 14 Jan, 30 July 1825, 13 Jan 1827; CT, 9, 23 Sep 1825, 5 Jan, 23 Feb 1827, 3 Jan 1829; Knopwood, pp. 527–31; Henry, p. 102.
21 HRA 3, 5, p. 565; Wedge, p. 35; Eustace FitzSymonds, *Mortmain*, Hobart, 1977, p. 22; LMSS122, will of T.C. Simpson.
22 HTC, 13, 20 Dec 1828, 23 May 1829; HTC, 10 May 1828; PRO CO280/9 f. 346; Richards, Bethune to Ingle, 2 July 1828.
23 CT, 22 May 1829; HTC, 26 April 1828.
24 HTG, 17 Mar 1827; HTC, 10 May 1828; PRO CO280/227 f. 487; Webb, p. 29; Benson Walker, p. 143.
25 *Standard*, 13 April 1829; TAHO, Edward Lord correspondence file.
26 Richards, Hood to Ingle, 12 Feb 1825, 20 April 1830; HTC, 4 Dec 1830, 6 Dec 1828, 3 Jan, 23, 30 May 1829; CT, 26 June, 21 Aug 1829.

27 *HTC*, 31 Jan, 23 May 1829.
28 *HTC*, 20 Sep 1828; Knopwood, p. 527.
29 TAHO, NS301/1/2.
30 Lloyd, pp. 290–4.
31 Knopwood, 8 Aug, 10, 14 Dec 1829; *HTC*, 7 Nov 1829; *CT*, 13 Nov, 18 Dec 1829.

20. The final decades

1 TMAG owns a pair of braces said to have been worn by Edward at the ceremony.
2 Ancestry.com: Class HO107; Piece 482; Book 6; Civil Parish, Down; Country, Kent; Enumeration district 13; Folio 4, p. 3; GSU roll 306875.
3 *London Gazette*, 18 July 1862; Jessie Wagner, *Edward Lord*, passim.
4 *LA*, 18 April 1831; *MP*, 11 Jan 1815, 28 Nov 1816, 5 May 1818, 30 Sep 1831, 11 Feb 1861.
5 *Bristol Mercury*, 21 June 1831; *Standard*, 16, 17 Sep 1831; *Hampshire Advertiser*, 19 July 1834; John May, *A Chronicle of Welsh Events*, Swansea, 1994, p. 67; *Bury and Norwich Post*, 14 July 1841; *MP*, 8 Mar 1841, 11 Feb 1861.
6 *CC*, 9 April 1836; *Mercury*, 11 May 1889; Henry, p. 100.
7 Richards, Read to Ingle 21 Jan, 8 Mar, 13 April, 20 April 1830; Henry, p. 102.
8 *Mercury*, 11 May 1889; *HTC*, 25 Feb 1832, 21 Feb 1834; *Courier*, 24 Sep 1841; *CT*, 25 Feb 1834, 21 Mar 1848; *HTC*, 22 June 1832, 6 Sep 1833; *Observer*, 19 Dec 1845; *Courier*, 29 Mar 1888.
9 LMSS122/1/1–2.
10 *CT*, 12 Nov 1839.
11 PRO CO280/60 f 328; /58 f. 303; 227 ff. 434–501; /319 f. 29; /314 f. 382; /272 f. 459; CO408/32, f 47.
12 *CT*, 21 Mar 1848; Knopwood, pp. 592, 651.
13 West, p. 560; *CT*, 25 Dec 1838.
14 Information from Jane Stewart, TMAG.
15 *CT*, 26 Feb 1839; *HTC*, 29 Mar 1839; *CC*, 31 Jan 1844; Ancestry. co 1841 census: Class HO107; Piece 1451, Book 1, Civil parish St Mary; County Pembrokeshire; Enumeration district 15; Folio 20, p. 5; GSU roll 464346.
16 M.D. McRae, 'Port Davey and the South-West', *THRAPP* 1959, 8/49; *Observer*, 19 Dec 1845; *CT*, 21 Mar 1848; invoice held by TMAG.
17 *CT*, 19 Mar 1847.
18 *Courier*, 4 Sep 1847, 25 Feb 1854; *Mercury*, 1 Feb 1875; *Examiner*, 10 April 1856; FitzSymonds, *Mortmain*, pp. 239–40.
19 *CT*, 6 Nov 182; TAHO CSO1/83, p. 181; *Mercury*, 12 Sep 1903.
20 CON40/1/1, p. 34, image 239.
21 *CT*, 13 Jan 1826; *HTC*, 4 Oct 1828, 3 Jan 1829, 3 May 1833; *LA*, 10 July 1832; *CC*, 23 Aug 1880; *Mercury*, 23 Aug 1880; Knopwood, p. 567.
22 *Courier*, 17 Jan 1852; *CC*, 4 Jan 1862; *Examiner*, 11 Mar 1862, 18 April 1867, 3 Nov 1868; *Argus*, 6 Mar 1862; *Mercury*, 17 April 1867.
23 *CT*, 30 Dec 1834.
24 Trudy Cowley, *1858 valuation rolls for central and eastern Tasmania*, New Town, 2005, p. 64; *Mercury*, 23 Aug 1859; Andel, p. 34.
25 Mary Ramsay, 'Clifton Priory, Bothwell Tasmania', 2008, pp. 3–4; *CT*, 2 July 1850.
26 Cowley, pp. 64, 78–9.
27 TAHO, Edward Lord correspondence file.
28 *Mercury*, 16 May, 26 July 1859; TAHO RGD 1859, no. 1775; Maria Lord's tombstone, New Norfolk.
29 *Launceston Examiner*, 24 Nov 1859; Rienits notes Lord's death certificate was endorsed 'Asthma, 50 years' (NLA, MS 9789, ch. 3, fn 36).

21. Afterword

Unless otherwise stated, all information provided by Louisa Smith.
1 *Mercury*, 17 Jan 1882.
2 *Mercury*, 8 Sep 1897, 14 Mar 1890; Tasmanian Post Office Directory 1892, p. 330.
3 Information from Alison Shoobridge.
4 *Mercury*, 24 April 1929.
5 *Mercury*, *Examiner*, 15 Nov 1934.
6 'World War II by Able Seaman Lawrence Mervyn Banks Smith', in the possession of Louisa Smith.
7 Mary Ramsay, 'Clifton Priory, Bothwell', 2008.

Appendix 1

National Archives, Kew, ASSI 31/10.

Appendix 2

1 Henry, p. 101.
2 TAHO, LSD355/1/8, Meehan survey, 1811, p. 11.
3 Knopwood, p. 234; *HTG*, 10 Dec 1824, 28 June, 27 Sep 1828; *HTC*, 3 Oct 1829; *Critic*, 8 June 1923; *Mercury*, 19 Jan 1935.
4 Henry, passim; *Courier*, 1 Aug 1846; *Mercury*, 28 July 1910; Valuation rolls, *HTG* 1858 p. 280; 1865 p. 33; 1874 p. 31; 1885 p. 41.
5 Henry pp. 103–4; *Mercury*, 2 Aug 1881, 30 July 1907.
6 Henry, pp. 103–4; *Daily Telegraph*, 28 Jan 1896; *Examiner*, 7 Nov 1940.

SELECT BIBLIOGRAPHY

BOOKS AND ARTICLES

Australian Dictionary of Biography, vols 1 and 2

Charles Bateson, *The Convict Ships*, Sydney, 1983

J.W. Beattie, *Glimpses of the lives and times of the early Tasmanian governors*, Hobart, 1904

James Boyce, *Van Diemen's Land*, Melbourne, 2008

Patricia Clarke and Dale Spender, *Life lines*, Sydney, 1996

Nicholas Clements, *The Black War: fear, sex and resistance in Tasmania*, Brisbane, 2014

Trudy Cowley, *1858 valuation rolls for central and eastern Tasmania*, New Town, 2005.

John Currey (ed.), *Records of the Port Phillip Expedition*, vols 2, 3, Melbourne, 1990

John Currey, *David Collins: a colonial life*, Melbourne, 2000

Historical Records of Australia, series 1 and 3.

John Earnshaw (ed.), 'Select Letters of James Grove', *THRAPP* 8/2, 1959

J.P. Fawkner, *Reminiscences of early Hobart Town*, Malvern, 2007

Eustace Fitz-Symons, *A looking-glass for Tasmania*, Adelaide, 1980

– *Mortmain*, Hobart, 1977.

E.R. Henry, 'Edward Lord', *THRAPP*, 20/2, 1973

A.W.H. Humphrey (ed. John Currey), *A voyage to Port Phillip and Van Diemen's Land with Governor Collins*, Malvern, Victoria, 2008

Barbara Hamilton-Arnold (ed.), *Letters and Papers of G.P. Harris 1803–1812*, Sorrento, 1994

Robert Knopwood (ed. Mary Nicholls), *The diary of the Reverend Robert Knopwood, 1803–1838: first chaplain of Van Diemen's Land*, Hobart, 1977

George Thomas Lloyd, *Thirty-three years in Tasmania and Victoria*, London, 1862

Lachlan Macquarie, *Journals of his tours in New South Wales and Van Diemen's Land 1810–1822*, Sydney, 1979

N.L. Pateshall (ed. Marjorie Tipping), *A Short Account of a Voyage Round the Globe*, Melbourne, 1980

Mary Ramsay, 'Clifton Priory, Bothwell Tasmania', 2008, unpublished paper in possession of author

Anne Rand (ed.), *Journals of the Land Commissioners for Van Diemen's Land 1826–28*, Hobart, 1962

Jack Richards, 'Fifteen Tasmanian Letters 1824–1852', ND (Tasmanian Archive & Heritage Office)

Rex and Thea Rienits, 'Bligh at the Derwent', *THRAPP* 11/3, 1963

John Ritchie, *Lachlan Macquarie: a biography*, Melbourne, 1986

James Ross, *The settler in Van Diemen's Land*, Melbourne, 1975

C. Rowcroft, *Tales of the Colonies: or the adventures of an emigrant*, London, 1843

Irene Schaffer, *Land musters, stock returns and lists, Van Diemen's Land 1803–1822*, Hobart, 1991

A.G.L. Shaw, 'Some officials of early Van Diemen's Land', *THRAPP* 14/4, 1967

D.C. Shelton (ed.), *The Parramore Letters*, Hobart, 1993

Jane Sorell, *Governor, William and Julia Sorell, three generations in Van Diemen's Land*, Bellerive, 1986

Marjorie Tipping, *Convicts unbound: the story of the Calcutta convicts and their settlement in Australia*, Melbourne, 1988

J.H. Tuckey, *A voyage to establish a colony at Port Philip in Bass's Strait*, London, 1805

Jessie Wagner, *John and Sophia Riseley and their family*, Claremont, ND

Jessie Wagner, *My great great grandfather Lt. Edward Lord, Royal Marines*, Claremont, 2005.

Peter Benson Walker, *All that we inherit*, Hobart, 1968

Gwenda Webb, *Bothwell the gateway to the highlands*, Launceston, ND

Thomas Wells, *Michael Howe*, Hobart, 1818

John West, *The History of Tasmania*, London, 1852, reprinted Sydney, 1971

Anne-Maree Whitaker, *Joseph Foveaux*, Sydney, 2000

ARCHIVES

Tasmanian Archive and Heritage Office

AF394, Hobart maps

CON40, CON31, convict indents

Correspondence files for Edward Lord, Thomas Davey, John Riseley

CSO1, Colonial Secretary Office correspondence

LSD355/1/8, Meehan survey 1811.

NG14/1/1, letter from William Williamson, 1820

NS301/1/2, Journal of John Owen Lord, 1829

NS473/1/8, Maria Lord letterbook

NS395 [Thomas Keston], 'Secret memoirs'

NS1332/1/12, The Alexander Laing Story

PRO CO, correspondence from the Public Record Office, London

RGD, records of births, marriages and deaths

Launceston Community History Room

LMSS122/1/1–2 will of T.C. Simpson

LMSS12/7/318 letter, G.W. Evans to E. Lord

LMSS322 Peter Harrisson's journal

LMSS12/1/447 E. Lord to T. Simpson

University of Tasmania Special & Rare Collections

RS90/1, 1b, 5(1), James Belbin's pocket book 1808–1810

RS.12, Diary of the Rev. Robert Knopwood, 1805–1808

University of Tasmania, Department of History, 'Report on the Historical Manuscripts of Tasmania', no. 6, 1967

Mitchell Library, State Library of New South Wales

A166 'The Spunger' by Robert Lathrop Murray

A256 Piper Papers

A314 Broughton Papers

A495, A596, A685 Calder Papers

A586 Sorell Papers

A767, A752, A754 Wentworth Papers

A772 Governor Macquarie's Memoranda

A2015 Governor King's Letter Book

A1193 NSW Governors' Despatches 1813–79

A1399 letterbook, James Lord and Maria Lord

A1677 Hassall Papers

BT Bonwick Transcripts

B293, B294 Knopwood papers

B425, letters of Robert and George Dixon

DLADD 282 documents relating to early Sydney and Hobart

MS 62 Belbin family reminiscences

MSS 700, David Collins to his mother

SLNSW NRS 935, papers from SLNSW available on Ancestry

State Library of Victoria

MS 3661 Fawkner Papers

MS 8695 Fawkner 'Reminiscences'

MS 10913, MS 6501 Calder Papers

National Library of Australia

MS 9789, Rienits, 'Edward Lord: the first tycoon of Van Diemen's Land'

1887951, Report from the Select Committee on Transportation 1812

Huntingdon County Archives, Churchwarden's Account Book for Spaldwick Church, 1743–1896; births, deaths and marriage indexs

National Archives, Kew, ASSI 94/1537 no 45; ASSI 31/10, Surrey Summer Assizes 1802

NEWSPAPERS

Britain: *Berrow's Worcester Journal; Bury and Norwich Post; Caledonian Mercury, Gentleman's Magazine, Hampshire Telegraph; Ipswich Journal; Lancaster Gazette, London Gazette; Morning Chronicle, Morning Post; Oracle, The Times, York Herald*

Australia: *Age, Colonial Magazine, Colonial Times, Cornwall Chronicle, Courier, Launceston Advertiser, Launceston Examiner, Hobart Town Courier, Hobart Town Gazette, Mercury Sydney Gazette, Sydney Monitor*

WEBSITES

http://www.historyofparliament online.org/volume/1790-1820/member/owen-sir-hugh-1782-1809

http://www.bedfordshire.gov.uk/CommunityAndLiving/ArchivesAndRecordOffice/SearchOurCatalogues.aspx

http://www.historyofparliament online.org/volume/1790-1820/member/owen-sir-hugh-1782-1809, 12 June 2014, biography of Hugh Owen

http://www.cenquest.co.uk/Bas%20Gaz/O(FP).htm, 12 June 2014

http://www.oldbaileyonline.org/

http://www.library.mq.edu.au/digital/under/research/officers73rd.html#t, 26 June 2013, list of officers of 73rd regiment.

http://73rdregiment.tripod.com/sitebuildercontent/sitebuilderfiles/ggsummer0910.pdf

INFORMATION FROM INDIVIDUALS

Michael and Nicola Ball, Nicole Becker, Eleanor Cracknell (Eton archivist), Jo Huxley, Justine Pearson (Surrey History Centre), Mary Ramsay, Barry Riseley, Alison Shoobridge, Louisa Smith, Jane Stewart, Ian Terry, Pam Titherley, David Woodward

ACKNOWLEDGEMENTS

MANY PEOPLE have assisted me in writing, illustrating and producing this book. Louisa Smith, great-granddaughter of Edward and Maria Lord, has been a wonderful source of information, photographs and inspiration, not to mention hospitality. I really enjoyed using her story to link Edward and Maria to the present. Thanks as well to her family, and to Barry Riseley, Doug Chipman and Alison Shoobridge, also Lord relatives; and to Nicole Becker, possibly a relative.

I would also like to thank: Chris Millican of Orielton Field Studies Centre in Wales; staff of the Huntingdonshire Country Record Office; Caroline Kesseler, Hunts Family History Society, who found the record of Maria Riseley's birth; staff of the Bodleian Library and National Archives, Kew; Eleanor Cracknell, archivist at Eton College; Tessa Adams in Cornwall for information about the Riseley family; Justine Pearson of the Surrey History Centre; staff of the Mitchell Library, State Library of Victoria, Launceston Community History Room and, as ever, the Tasmanian Archive & Heritage Office (everyone) and the Tasmanian Museum and Art Gallery (Jane Stewart, Jo Huxley and Ian Terry); Brendan Lennard, for advice about architectural history; Hamish Maxwell-Stewart, for modelling the uniform of the 73rd Regiment; Bernard Lloyd on the history of drinking; David Woodward for a helpful sporting article; Colette McAlpine for finding convicts assigned to the Lords; John Short for information about early Hobart; and Pam Titherley, a descendant of Edward Lord's servant. For helpful discussion I would like to thank Kim Boyer, Patsy Hollis and Karen Gunning.

As usual, I have given talks about the Lords to many groups, especially my U3A class (thanks to Leone Scrivener for organising it). Audience comments and feedback has been invaluable. So many people with far more varied backgrounds and experience than I can hope to have, provided valuable insight into the Lords' story, widening the scope of the book.

I would like to thank the present owners of the Lords' houses and/or property, for allowing visits: Penny Clive of Ingle Hall; Irene Glover of Mrs Lord's Springs which she bought in 1979 (and Stuart Whitney for his company); John and Mardy Grosvenor of Orielton (and Pat Mavromatis for arranging it); and Ross Mace of Lawrenny. I would also like to thank Mary Ramsay, and Nicola and Michael Ball, for information about the Lawrenny district and agricultural matters.

Gathering the images was an absorbing task, as I tried to find areas of Tasmania still largely as they were in the Lords' day. I would like to thank photographers Rebecca Aisbett, James Alexander, Peter and Kitty Courtney, Alwyn Friedersdorff and Pru Bonham, Stuart Whitney and Paul Yonna for entering into this quest with great enthusiasm and skill. For permission to reproduce images I would like to thank Mark Heath of Spaldwick, England; Roy Precious of Antiques and Fine Art, Wiltshire; staff of Haverfordwest Library, Wales; and in Australia Lewis Woolley, John Short, the Tasmanian Museum and Art Gallery, the Tasmanian Archive and Heritage office (particularly Jacek Piotrowski), the National Library of Australia, the State Library of Victoria, the State Library of New South Wales, the University of Tasmania Library, Sydney Living Museums, and the Diocese of Tasmania.

A number of people read the text and gave excellent advice for which I am extremely grateful: Chris Goodacre, Sue Johnson, Marian May, Leonie Mickleborough, Michael Roe and Christine Wilson, as well as family members. Naturally, the responsibility for mistakes remains mine. Henry Reynolds very kindly read the text and provided the quotation for the back cover.

The book would not exist without the designer, Julie Hawkins of In Graphic Detail. She has done a marvellous piece of artistic work, with every page beautifully considered and balanced. Julie entered into the spirit of the project with huge enthusiasm, and became not only the designer, but also proof-reader and general advisor, discussing every aspect of the book with me. I could not have wished for a more skilled designer.

I extend my grateful thanks to John and Leigh Spiers of Edward Everett Root Publishers for giving this book a second life.

As ever, my family has been very supportive. Thanks to my dear children Ted, Cathy and Jude for their help in commenting on the text, and their general enthusiasm. Specifically, I would like to thank Jude for her beautiful paintings on pp. 297 and 313; Cathy for her PR advice; and Ted for his financial assistance. Also wonderful have been my sister Jo for her helpful comments, especially on the Introduction; and my niece Rebecca for her excellent photography and for braving Bronte Park and its dead snake. Most of all, thanks to my husband James, who has lived with the Lords for the last few years. He has accompanied me on information-gathering and photography excursions, answered many questions, read the text and been generally supportive throughout, even if he still refuses to read *Persuasion* to find out the social position of a baronet at the time.

Alison Alexander

Edward Lord's travelling writing desk
(Tasmanian Museum and Art Gallery)

INDEX

EL   Edward Lord
ML   Maria Lord
E&ML   Edward and Maria Lord
VDL   Van Diemen's Land

A

Abbott, Major Edward 126, 140, 145, 182, 200, 202
Aborigines, Tasmanian 3, 22–3, 173, 184, 191, 211–3, 296–7
Adultery 16–17, 29–30, 57–8, 82, 152, 186, 192, 194, 197, 200, 202–3, 248, 250, 265, 275
Agricultural Society 211, 244, 258
Aisbett, Rebecca 150, 206, 212, 256–7, 288, 295–6, 302, 312
Alcohol/ism 12, 16, 27, 49, 53–4, 101, 112, 114, 122, 124–8, 154–5, 196–7, 220, 310
    Lords sell 133, 215–6, 238, 258
Alexander, James 9–10, 20, 22, 35–7, 115, 134, 150, 276, 298–9
Allan, David 155
Allport, Mary Morton 85, 195
Anglewood 308, 312, 316
Ankers, Fanny and Daniel 152–4
Archer, Thomas 144, 162, 245
Arthur, Lt.-Gov. George 3, 241, 274–6, 289, 291–3
Austen, Jane 5, 8, 90, 133, 193, 250

B

Balls (entertainment) 119, 128, 141, 143–6, 248, 264
Bank of VDL 244–5, 289, 294, 310
Bate, Samuel 112, 115, 182
Bathurst, Lord 100–2, 104–5, 190, 194, 202–3, 214, 247, 270
Belbin family 79–80, 83, 136
Bethune, Walter 294
Bigge, Commissioner 203, 216, 237
Birch, Thomas 97, 162, 245, 251–2
Black War 3, 211, 296–7
Blaxcell, Garnham 102, 104, 112, 196–7
Bligh, Gov. William 42, 50, 66–8, 76, 80–5, 90–2, 101, 197
Blow-my-skull 125–6, 147
Bock, Thomas 306–7, 310
Boothman, John 151–3, 183
Bothwell 308, 311–13

Bowden, Dr Matthew 92, 96–8, 103, 110, 112–5, 118, 124, 152–3, 183
Bowen, Lieut. John 20
Brisbane, Gov. Thomas 213–4, 270
Brock family 329
Broughton, William 144, 156–62, 172, 195, 198, 240, 247, 252
Brumby, James 238
Bushrangers 67, 122, 136, 168–79, 182, 191, 198, 212, 254, 265, 289
The Bushranger's Lover 169

C

Calcutta 11–13, 16–17
Cape Town 112, 192–3, 213, 221, 264, 267, 270
Caroline 218, 220, 248, 256, 266, 272, 289
Castlereagh, Lord 100
Cattle, Lords' 59, 103, 134, 169, 207–8, 210–11, 220–1, 224, 231, 235, 284, 295–6, 298–9, 304
Catworth 34, 36–7, 257–8
Cazzar (Caesar?) 138
Ceylon, *see* Sri Lanka
Coal River Valley 132–3
Cockerell, William 238
Cockerill, Mary 173
Coleman, Richard 137
Collins, David 10–11, 13–14, 16–17, 44–5
    Lt.-Gov. 20–2, 24–31, 48, 53, 55, 57–9, 62–4, 66, 68–9, 71, 76–85, 96–8, 110, 114, 140, 152
    death 90–3, 95
Collins, George 84
Collins, William 11, 44, 50, 52, 69, 76, 80, 82, 112, 143, 146, 152, 182–3, 220
Commissariat 26, 56, 81, 101, 134–5, 150–65, 168, 176, 206, 209, 213, 233, 235, 268, 298, 304
Convict stain 5, 38, 70, 129, 144, 146, 187, 241, 250, 284, 319
Convicts 11, 17, 23–4, 29, 31, 34, 40–5, 51–2, 54–5, 57–8, 63, 69–70, 76–7, 83, 95, 101, 118, 122, 127, 144, 151, 168, 171, 173, 175, 183–4, 186, 191, 196, 199–200, 218–9, 221, 247, 262
    as workers 14, 20, 25–6, 28, 67, 202
    assigned to Lords 104, 146, 170, 209, 211, 253, 308, 310
    ex-convicts 4, 24, 51–2, 70, 83, 91, 136, 144, 154, 191, 232, 249, 252, 298

344

Corruption 3, 5, 27, 55, 62–3, 80, 82, 98, 105, 110, 113–4, 118–9, 126–7, 129, 140, 150–65, 182–3, 198, 213–4, 216, 232, 239–40, 274–5, 291, 303
Cottage Green 293–4
Court system, VDL 114, 119, 147, 161, 198, 245, 251, 274, 266, 272, 274, 277, 287
Courtney, Kitty and Peter 307
Cox, Louisa, *see* Kent, Louisa
Craig, W.H. 122 and book cover
Cremorne 20, 22
Crime in VDL 24, 63, 83, 132, 156, 186, 209, 211, 239, 273
Currency 27, 53, 159–60, 215, 228–9, 286

D

Davey, Lucy 122–3, 129, 137
Davey, Margaret 122–4, 129, 144
Davey, Lt.-Gov. Thomas 102, 122–9, 132–3, 136–7, 139–41, 143–4, 146–7, 153, 155–61, 169–72, 183–4, 190–1, 195–6, 200, 215, 249
Dawes, Edward John Lord 310
Dawes, Frederic 269, 310
Denison, Lt.-Gov. William 305
Derwent, River 20, 81, 84–5, 140, 146, 187, 195, 197, 206, 244, 298–9, 312
Derwent Star (newspaper) 91
Detached Cultural Organisation 329
Dhotman, Margaret 237, 252
Dickson, John 232–3
Dillon, Peter 214
Dixon, George and Robert 209
Domestic violence 79–80, 117, 119
Drummond, John and Elizabeth 146, 183–7, 196–7
Dry, Richard 252–3
Duels 115, 184, 246, 272, 303
Duncan, John 227
Durant family 303, 306

E

Earle, Augustus 279
Eddington, Peggy 64, 175–6
Elliott, Nathan 186–7
Endeavour, replica 34, 41
Evans, George 20, 146, 182, 198–9, 228
Evans, Mary 185

Experiment 34, 40–1, 77
Exports 3, 132, 135–6, 160–1, 206, 213, 220–1, 239, 307

F

Famine in Hobart 48–54, 57, 59, 80, 175
Farming 48, 59, 63, 80, 101, 110, 118, 128, 136, 198, 208–9, 210, 215–6
Fawkner, John Pascoe 17, 26, 58–9, 177, 239
  quoted 2–3, 30–1, 43–5, 48, 51–4, 62, 64, 79–80, 91, 93, 99, 122, 128, 175–7, 224, 259, 266, 285, 290
Female Factory, Parramatta 2–3, 42–4
Flights of Fancy 5, 71–72, 86, 106, 163–5, 178, 280
Folley, John 63
Fosbrook, Leonard 11–12, 57, 118–9, 124, 151–4, 182–3
Foveaux, Joseph 51, 68–9, 78, 82, 90, 100, 122, 151
Franklin, Jane 241
Frederick 220
French activity 9, 11, 17, 23
Fry, Ann and Edward 292–3

G

Gambling 99–101, 114, 192, 203, 215, 290, 295
Geils, Lt.-Gov. Andrew 116–9, 153
George IV (Prince Regent) 192, 194, 200, 203
Germain, Hugh 55
Giblin, Thomas 310–11
Gibson, David 211, 238
Glenorchy 244, 311
Goldie, Alexander 304–5
Gordon, James 126, 182–3
Granger, Mary 76–7
Grove, James 55, 58
Gunning, George 245, 258, 269, 272–3, 294

H

Harris, George 11–12, 14, 16–17, 20–1, 22, 24–5, 27–30, 44–5, 48–51, 53, 55–8, 68, 77–80, 91, 93, 95, 110, 112, 182
Harrisson, Peter 216, 233
Harrowby, Lord 122–3, 129
Hassall, Thomas 196, 254–5
Hayes, John 127

Hobart 2, 4–5, 20, 22, 24–5, 28, 48, 50–3, 59, 81–2, 94–5, 110, 115, 118, 122, 190, 200, 252, 255, 271, 284

Hogan, Patrick 144, 154–9

Hood, Samuel 146, 271–5, 278, 285, 289, 294

Horse racing 99, 114–5, 134

Howe, Mike 169–75, 177, 212

Hudson, Martha 77–9

Hull, George 224, 235–6

Humphrey, A.W.H. 11–12, 14, 16, 20–2, 25–31, 43, 45, 56, 59, 124, 146, 183, 268

Hunting 16, 25–8, 48–9, 55–6, 168, 202, 305

Huon pine 132, 141, 185, 197, 206, 218–9

I

I'Anson, William 56, 78

Immigrants from Britain 3, 70, 198–9, 203, 209, 221, 249, 263, 274–5, 286

Ingle Hall 94, 141, 143, 267, 284, 294, 304, 329

Ingle, John 11, 44, 50, 52–3, 85, 93–4, 132, 136, 141, 155–6, 175, 183, 207, 218, 273–4, 290, 294, 304, 329

J

James Hay 101–2, 104–5, 133, 139

Jeffreys, Charles 141, 184, 186, 195–7, 199, 252, 254, 264, 269, 289

Jeffreys, Jane 252, 254, 264, 269, 289, 299

Jericho 56, 168–9, 216

Johnson, Lieut. James 16, 54

Johnston, Major George 67–8, 145

Jones, Captain 196

Jones & Riley (& Walker) 226–7

Jupiter 185, 195–6, 218–9, 227, 229, 272, 289

K

Kandy 116–7

Kangaroo 141, 195–6, 264

Kangaroo Island 135, 218–9

Kearley, George and Mary 12, 22

Kemp, Anthony Fenn 102, 157–8, 197, 203, 236

Kent, Louisa 192–4, 200, 202–3

Kent, Thomas 117, 124, 183, 186

Kent, William 192–4, 199, 202–3

Keston, Thomas 63, 80, 83–4, 91, 95–6, 112–4, 124–5, 152–3, 199–200, 203

Kimbolton Park 258, 277, 294

King, Gov. Philip 11, 16–17, 28, 31, 45, 48, 68, 156

Kingston (Brown's River) 63

Knopwood, Rev. Robert 17, 25–6, 29–31, 48–9, 54–9, 83, 91–3, 95, 115, 124, 128, 136, 141, 143–6, 173–6, 182–3, 235, 237, 246, 251, 257, 266, 268–9, 271–2, 276–7, 278, 286, 293–4, 297, 299, 305, 310

   diary entries 132, 171, 195, 197, 248, 252, 258–9, 264–5

L

Lady Nelson 62, 64, 66

Laing, Alexander 136, 139, 170–1, 177, 327

Land commissioners 208, 211, 213

Lascelles, Thomas 126, 146, 170, 176, 184, 233, 272–3, 276

Launceston 197, 214, 218, 227, 232–3, 239, 252–3, 257–8, 310 *and see* Port Dalrymple

Lawrenny (VDL) 206–12, 224, 258, 273, 276–7, 296, 298–9, 302, 304–5, 307–8, 312–13, 317, 319, 329

Laycock, Lieut. 58

Lewis, Neil Elliott 187

Lewis, Richard and Isabella 137, 184, 217, 289, 329

Lima 279

Llanstinan 308, 312

Lloyd, George 265, 297–9

Lloyd's insurance company 247, 267

Loane, Roland 96, 98, 114–5, 186, 197, 214, 237, 245–6, 252

Lord, Amy 318–9

Lord, Caroline (*later* Dawes, Giblin) 43–5, 57, 103, 132, 105, 145, 246, 248, 250, 252–3, 256, 258–9, 264–5, 268–9, 278, 285, 310–11

Lord, Corbetta (E&ML's daughter) 145, 253–5, 258, 264, 267, 290, 303, 306, 313

Lord, Corbetta (EL's mother) 9–10, 145, 255

Lord, Edward 111–2, 151–2

   asthma 31, 68, 146, 218, 246, 292, 295, 313

   autocratic 76–80, 83, 95–6, 150

   Bligh and 81–4

   Broughton and 158–62

   bushrangers and 168–79

   business activity 26–8, 45, 50–6, 76, 82, 96–7, 101–2, 104–05, 135–7, 139, 155, 158–62, 197, 206–21, 231–2, 239–40, 289–91, 304, 306–7

   character 2, 5, 20–1, 29, 64–6, 76–80, 84, 98, 100, 197–8, 220, 224, 245, 249, 252, 278–9, 294

childhood 8–10
children 45, 56, 90, 103, 145, 253–6, 293, 296, 299, 302–3, 305–8, 313
chooses ML 3, 43–4
civic leader 147, 171, 244, 271, 293, 295
Collins David and 20, 26, 29–31, 59, 68, 76, 78, 82
corruption 62–3, 93, 105, 139, 150, 10–54–8, 162, 213–6
Davey and 132–3, 136, 139, 144, 159, 171, 195
death 313
divorce 276–7, 291, 293
employees 75, 104, 145–6, 169–70, 209–12, 218, 224–5, 257, 277, 296–7, 302
exports 135, 220–1
extramarital affairs 290–2
financial problems 146, 158, 190, 267, 270, 289–90, 295
friends 11–12, 16, 20, 25, 29–30, 51, 56, 64–6, 78, 85, 92, 96, 100, 102, 110, 112, 128, 133, 136, 141, 145–7, 151, 161–2, 170, 184, 196–8, 215, 218, 220, 233, 246, 272, 274, 293, 304
gambling 99–100, 290, 295
governor, acting 91–3, 95–7, 247, 326
hospitality 25, 57, 96, 113, 128, 134, 141, 143–4, 146, 150, 197, 240, 252
houses 26–8, 52, 57, 141, 228, 237, 302–4, 307
integrity 240, 304–5
land 26, 45, 48, 52, 59, 63, 68, 76, 94–5, 100, 104–5, 117, 133–4, 207–11, 224, 247, 276–7, 270, 294, 305, 307, 312
loans/debts 76, 100, 133, 156, 159, 190, 197, 207, 216–8, 239, 264, 272, 292, 304
Macquarie and 92–3, 95–8, 100, 102, 104–5, 161–2, 199, 247
magistrate 68–9, 83, 247
marines, career in 9, 11–12, 16–17, 25, 59, 62, 67–8, 76–8, 81, 84, 100, 307
marriage 69–70
method of gaining own way 64–6, 150, 158–62, 168, 177, 195, 213–4
portraits 307–10
profit 132–3, 190, 206, 239, 250, 289–90, 294, 302, 304, 306–7, 312–13
relationship with ML 44, 58, 69–70, 221, 251, 259, 265–6, 276, 278–9, 292, 313
reputation 284, 305
retires to England 290–1, 295–302, 312–3
Rowcroft and 263–4, 266, 271, 275–8
smuggling 54–5, 140, 196
social position 4–5, 28, 70, 240, 292, 302
Sorell and 195–8, 207, 215, 240, 244, 246
sport 55, 99, 134
sued by others 98, 245, 290, 294, 296, 304
sues others 276–8, 294, 304
weaknesses 172, 231, 258
Van Diemen's Land and 101, 206–7, 220, 247
visits VDL after 1824, 292, 306–7, 311
will 312–13
Lord, Edward and Maria
  agents 97–8, 103, 136, 152, 224, 226–7, 231–4, 239, 247, 268, 271, 273–4, 289, 294, 296, 304–5, 307
Lord, Edward Robert (E&ML's son) 103, 105, 132, 197, 253–5, 290, 293, 296–9, 303, 305–8, 311–13, 316–7
Lord, Eliza (E&ML's daughter) 57, 103, 105, 132, 145, 197, 253–5, 290, 296, 303, 313
Lord, Emma (E&ML's daughter) 253, 264–5, 269, 278, 290, 302–3, 306, 311, 313
Lord, Emma Eliza 302–3
Lord, Eyre (EL's brother) 231, 256
Lord, Harriet 316–7, 319
Lord, James (no relation) 50, 52, 294
Lord, John (EL's brother) 8–10, 28, 59, 90 *and see* Owen, Sir John
Lord, John Owen (E&ML's son) 90, 103, 105, 132, 145, 253–5, 290, 296–9, 303, 312–13
Lord, Joseph (EL's father) 9–10, 255, 302
Lord, Joseph and Ethel 316–9, 323, 326
Lord, Joy 317–20, 324
Lord, Louisa 316–22 *and see* Smith, Louisa
Lord, Maria *and see* Riseley, Maria
  bushrangers and 169
  business ability 3, 51–2, 132, 224–5
  business activities 93, 101, 103, 132, 139, 206, 208, 213, 215, 217, 224–40, 245, 266–9, 272–4, 284, 298, 308, 311–12 *and see* shops
  bushwalking 244, 287–9
  character 79, 224–6, 233–4, 240, 249–52, 259, 265, 276, 286, 287, 289, 294, 310, 319, 326
  Charles Rowcroft 264–6, 268–9, 273, 277–8

charity 103, 231, 251, 268–9, 284, 310
children 90, 97, 103, 132, 145, 253–6, 273, 285, 297, 299, 303, 305–6, 311
convict past 77, 129, 144, 169, 226, 240–1, 249–51, 259, 284, 319
death 313
debts, calls in 217, 229, 233, 238, 310
domestic activity 143–5, 253
employees 177, 209, 211, 225–7, 232, 234, 253, 286, 308, 310
friends 184, 237, 251–3, 286, 289, 294, 297
frugality 144, 209, 224, 310
ghost 326–7
governor's lady 91–2
health 146, 232, 313
integrity 239–40, 251, 259, 284–5
literacy 230, 232, 249–50
nurses 271, 289
relationship with EL 2–3, 196–7, 220–1, 231, 239, 256, 259, 265–6, 276, 278–9, 292, 308, 313
reputation 284, 286, 313, 319
retirement 272–3, 292, 297, 308, 310–1
Riseley family and 101, 103, 145, 233–4, 248, 256–9
shops 136–8, 206, 214, 231, 237–9, 258, 284–5, 292, 297, 312
social activities 143–4, 244, 269, 297, 311
social position 57, 69, 144, 240, 248–9, 251–2, 255, 285
son Edward Robert and 305–6
sons' return 297–8
Sydney, visits 97–8, 102–3, 105, 118
vanquishes robber 286–7
Lord, Maria, younger 273
Lord, William (EL's brother) 9–10
Lord, William (E&ML's son) 224, 253–4, 258, 264, 267, 290, 303, 306, 313
Lord. William (EL & ES' son) 302–3
Lord/Storer children 291, 302–3, 312–3
Lovekin, Charlotte 306–8, 316
Luttrell, Dr 182–3, 231
Lycett, Joseph 4, 59, 65, 88–9, 108–10, 135, 162, 168, 187, 190, 227, 252, 271
Lyttleton, Lieut. William 116

M

McCarty, Denis 62–3, 96, 153
Mack, Betsy 145, 265, 269, 271–2
Mackellar, Lilias and family 183–7
McLachlan, Mary 186
Macquarie, Elizabeth 248–50
Macquarie, Gov. Lachlan 52, 90–1, 110, 113–9, 122–9, 135, 139–40, 144, 152–62, 169, 171–3, 182–7, 190–1, 195–200, 215, 220, 226, 241, 248–50
    dealings with EL 92–3, 95–8, 100, 102, 104–5, 161–2, 199, 247
    visits VDL 115, 203–4
Macquarie Point (Hobart) 154, 207
Marsden, Rev. Samuel 268
Maum, William 153–6, 158–9, 164, 304–5
Mauritius 212, 220
Maxwell-Stewart, Hamish 115
Mears, Mary 40
Meehan, James 52, 94
Molesworth 34–6
Moodie, Affleck 213–4, 270, 291
Morgan, William 138
Mountgarrett, Dr James 182–3
Mrs Lord's Springs 287–9
Murray, Lt.-Gov. John 96–8, 110, 112–7, 119, 139, 152–3, 175
Murray, Lucy 110, 113–7, 144, 186
Murray, Robert Lathrop 232, 234, 263–4, 266, 274–5, 277, 293, 295
Musquito 177, 211–2

N

New Norfolk 65, 76, 132, 208, 299, 312–3
New South Wales Corps 11, 67, 80, 110
New Town 262, 269, 317–8, 320–1
Norfolk Island 45, 62, 64–5, 211
Norfolk Islanders 62–5, 82–5, 95–6, 110, 136
Norwood (property) 273, 278, 304, 312

O

Oatlands 134
Ocean 11–14, 16, 22
Ogilvie, Robert 231

Opossum Bay 323–5, 327
Orielton (Wales) 8–10, 14, 43, 134, 141, 303, 326
Orielton Park (NSW) 105, 136, 233
Orielton Park (VDL) 134–5, 139, 150, 169, 173–4, 176, 208–9, 211, 213, 233, 235, 256–8, 265, 269, 273, 276, 296, 304, 312, 317, 329
Owen, Lady Charlotte 103, 246, 270
Owen family 8–9, 28, 34, 90, 150, 207, 253, 270, 302
Owen, Sir Hugh 9, 14, 28, 76, 90
Owen, Sir John 90, 100–4, 132, 150, 210, 240, 246–8, 270, 277, 289–90, 293, 297, 302–5, 312, 329

P

Palmer & Co. 140
Parramatta 2, 102–3, 110
Parramore, William 249, 274–5, 277
Paterson, Col. 76, 78, 83–4
Patronage 5, 10, 25, 34, 76, 90, 100, 122, 127, 154, 192, 194, 199, 203, 305
Pearling 100, 104–5
Pembroke 8–10, 17, 270, 291, 303, 326
Pembrokeshire 8–9, 304
Piguenit, W.C. 210
Piper, Capt John 64–6, 126, 184, 198, 248
Pistol, ML's 254, 319
Porpoise, HMS 54, 80–1, 84–5
Port Dalrymple 58, 64, 135–6, 169, 218, 225–6, 238, 264
Port Davey 307
Port Phillip 11, 14–17, 25
Power, Matthew and Hannah 17, 29–30, 55, 57–9, 64
Prinsep, Elizabeth 284
The Priory, Bothwell 311–12, 326–7
Promissory notes 159–60, 215, 228–9, 237, 286
Pubs, Hobart 59, 132, 176

R

Ranken, Janet 250–1, 286
Rayner, William 238
Read, George 268
Reardon family 95
Reibey, Mary 240–1

Religion, influence of 25–6, 57, 76, 110, 182, 244, 274–5, 321, 325, 327
Richmond (Tas) 308, 312, 316
Rio de Janeiro 12, 14, 17, 53, 110
Risdon 20–3
Riseley, Caroline 2, 43–5, 269 *and see* Lord, Caroline
Riseley, Catherine (*later* Taylor, Simpson) 101, 103, 145, 232, 250, 256–8
Riseley, John 34, 233–4, 240, 256–8, 263–6, 274, 277, 294
Riseley, Maria *and see* Lord, Maria
    business activities 45, 50–4
    character 5, 35–6, 43, 45, 51
    childhood 34–5
    children 2, 42–5, 57
    convict, as a 39–45, 51–2, 57–8, 68, 70
    crime and trial 36–9, 328
    domestic activities 35, 41, 57
    education 35, 69
    and EL 203, 42–4, 58
    marriage 69, 71–3
    social position 57–8, 70
Riseley, Robert and Mary 34–6, 103, 246, 258
Riseley, Sophia 256, 258
Robinson, Charles 232
Rose, David 238
Ross (township) 208
Ross, James 209–10
Rowcroft, Charles 262–6, 268–9, 271, 273–4, 276–9, 304, 312
Royal Forest Club 146–7
Royal George 258, 264, 267

S

Sainson, Louis de 262
St David's church 244–5, 268–9, 275
Salvage 214
Sandy Bay 57, 63, 81, 92, 326, 329
Scott, Dr James 271–2
Scott, Thomas 208, 211, 224, 244, 254
Sealing 22, 132, 135, 218, 220, 272
Sexuality 39, 41–3, 70, 169, 265–6

Shannon, River 177, 210, 289
Sheep 59, 134, 150, 176, 211–2, 224–5, 256, 258, 273, 287
Shipman, Francis 101, 151–3
Ships, Lords', *see Caroline, Jupiter, Spring, Victorine*
Shop, Lords' 45, 50–4, 58, 63, 79, 82, 93, 136, 155, 206, 214–5, 237, 239, 272
Simpson, Thomas 232–3, 257, 294, 304
Smith, Dawson 324
Smith, Kevin 324, 326–7
Smith, Lorraine 323–4
Smith, Louisa 322–6
Smith, Merv 321–7
Smith, Roger 324
Smith, Veronica 324
Smuggling 54–5, 80, 95, 110, 112, 127, 139–40, 184, 195, 276, 294
Social class 4–5, 24, 34, 43–4, 57, 76
Sorell, Harriet 192, 202–3
Sorell, Lt.-Gov. William 161, 168, 173–5, 177, 183, 185, 191–203, 207, 212, 215, 232, 236, 244, 246–8, 250, 257–8, 262, 274
South Hobart 63, 329
South Shetlands 220, 266–7
Spaldwick 34, 36
Spring 105, 135–6, 195, 218
Sri Lanka 116–7, 119, 145, 257
Stanfield, Daniel 136–7
Stewart, Major 197
Storer, Catherine and Jessy 290, 302–3, 313
Storer, Elizabeth 105, 290–1, 293, 295, 313
Sydney 2–4, 11, 27, 31, 41–2, 50, 52, 55, 67–8, 78, 80–2, 96–9, 102–5, 112, 117–9, 123, 135–6, 152–3, 155–6, 161, 185, 218, 225–7, 232, 240–1, 271

T

Taylor, Captain 297
Taylor, Lieut. James 103, 145, 257
Thompson, John 42, 44
Thylacine 78, 134–5
Tin Dish Holes 134, 169
Trading 26–7, 45, 50–1, 54–5, 58, 82, 96–7, 101–2, 133, 195, 214, 237
Tremby family 211

Troy, Richard 238
Tuckey, Lieut. James 15–17

U

Union 112

V

Van Diemen, Charles Frederick 211
Van Diemen's Land, development 3–5, 22–4, 101, 132, 147, 198–9, 206–7, 247, 270–1, 312
Verandah Stores/House 236–7
Victoria, Queen, wedding 302
Victorine 218, 266
Voyages Britain–Australia 11–14, 40–1, 100–1, 246, 248, 256, 267, 270, 275, 295, 306–7

W

Wainewright, Thomas 307–9
Wales 8–10, 23, 90, 143, 210, 303
Walker, William 227
Waterloo Club 146–7, 184
Watts, George 175–7, 185
Webster, A.G. 317–9
Wells, Thomas 232–5, 268, 274
Wentworth, D'Arcy 99, 101, 145
Wentworth, W.C. 4
West, Rev. John 3–4, 123, 127–8, 210, 240, 306
Whaling 50, 59, 102, 128, 132, 220–1, 266–7, 289
Wheat 3, 27, 49, 59, 63, 132–3, 135, 139, 152–62, 208, 210, 213–4, 218–9, 221, 235–6, 239, 264, 268, 270, 272, 329
Whitfield, Joseph 138
Whitney, Stuart 287–8, inside back cover
Williamson, William 248–51, 259, 266
Women's position 11, 50, 54, 132–3, 224
Wool, growth/export 208, 221, 239, 264, 272, 306–07
Wright, Lieut. 112, 114–5

Y

Yapp, Sarah and William 36–9
Yonna, Paul 143
York Plains 169, 244
Younge, Dr Henry 182